Principles of Police Patrol

N. F. IANNONE, M.S.

Inspector of Police (Ret.)
Los Angeles Police Department
Chairman, Police Science Department
Fullerton College

McGraw-Hill Book Company

New York	London	São Paulo
St. Louis	Mexico	Singapore
San Francisco	Montreal	Sydney
Düsseldorf	New Delhi	Tokyo
Johannesburg	Panama	Toronto
Kuala Lumpur	Paris	

About the author   N. F. Iannone is Chairman of the Police Science Department of Fullerton College, Fullerton, California. He is a retired Inspector of Police of the Los Angeles Police Department. His law enforcement experience, spanning twenty-four years, includes service in all ranks, through Captain of Police, in the Patrol Bureau. Additionally, he served as Commander of the Training Division for an extended period of time, as an Area Commander of the Detective Bureau, and in many staff positions. His teaching experience covers thirty-six years starting at the Los Angeles Police Academy. He taught police courses for many years at the California State University, Los Angeles, and Fullerton College. He has been active as past president of the California Association of Administration of Justice Educators and has served on many state committees, such as the Attorney General's Committee on Police-Minority Relations and the Advisory Committee of the Commission on Peace Officer Standards and Training, and on numerous educational advisory committees. He has assisted in the preparation of instructional programs such as *Assigning Patrol Personnel I—Distribution, Assigning Patrol Personnel II—Deployment, Administration of Criminal Justice*, and has authored the textbook, *Supervision of Police Personnel.*

Library of Congress Cataloging in Publication Data
Iannone, N F
    Principles of police patrol

    1. Police patrol.   I. Title.
HV8080.P212   363.2'32   74-9617
ISBN 0-07-031667-8

Principles of Police Patrol

1234567890 KPKP 7987654

The editors for this book were *Ardelle Cleverdon* and
Myrna W. Breskin, the designer was *Tracy A. Glasner,*
and its production was supervised by *Valerie A. Klima.*
It was set in Metrolite by Monotype Composition Co., Inc.
It was printed and bound by Kingsport Press, Inc.

Contents

To Elizabeth Harrington

Preface

The problems facing law enforcement officers in contemporary society are of great complexity. A rapidly expanding crime rate—far outstripping the growth in population—has placed an extraordinarily heavy burden upon the police in general and the patrol force in particular. Against a background of civil disorder and antisocial behavior, patrol officers must bear the brunt of the responsibility for maintaining order and suppressing crime; yet, rarely are sufficient patrol personnel available to perform all the complex tasks traditionally required of them. As a consequence, individual patrol officers often find themselves in the middle of a dilemma. Patrol officers can give superficial attention to all the police incidents brought to their attention—sometimes with the net result that they treat few of them well. Or, the types of police incidents to which they respond can be reduced as a matter of policy so that the officers can concentrate only upon those incidents which can be dealt with effectively. In either event service to the public is reduced—sometimes to an unacceptable level.

Society can ill afford to wait for the realization of other alternatives such as increased personnel or the development and application of sophisticated gadgetry. There is, however, one alternative which may help solve the dilemma. Officers may be taught methods that will enable them to accomplish their tasks more efficiently, safely, and effectively. They will then be able to render a much higher level of service with the same effort. It is with this objective in mind that *Principles of Police Patrol* was prepared.

Principles of Police Patrol is organized to include the problems most frequently encountered by patrol officers, some general principles for the solution of these problems, and finally, some specific practices and techniques that have proved effective in perplexing or hazardous patrol incidents. The number of routine tasks at which the patrol officer must be adept is infinite. However, since most of them can be accomplished adequately by the application of basic principles of patrol and common sense, no attempt is made in this text to treat all of them in detail. Instead, fundamental guidelines are included to alert the practitioner and the pre-police student, who will eventually serve in the patrol force, to the common mistakes which so often plague law enforcement officers. It is hoped that they will be able to avoid these pitfalls once they are aware of them. Major emphasis is placed upon the more complex patrol activities. The techniques that successful officers have found to be most effective in performing their duties are treated in depth.

An overview of the background, functions, and objectives of the patrol force is provided to delineate the scope of the individual officer's patrol function and the legal restraints placed on him. Techniques of patrolling a beat are discussed to acquaint beginning officers with the tenets of patrol and to give experienced officers an opportunity to reassess their practices. Methods of observing, recording, and reporting police incidents are treated to enable patrol officers to communicate their findings more effectively. A discussion of preliminary investigation functions is included so that costly errors which often result in prosecution failures can be avoided. Methods of making field contacts with pedestrians and handling police incidents involving vehicles are suggested to help officers carry out their responsibilities more effectively and safely.

In addition, a variety of nonemergency calls for service and tactics which have proved useful to officers in handling major crimes in progress are described in depth. A discussion of incidents involving hostages and survival techniques against attacks from ambush, firebombs, booby traps, and infernal devices is included to help officers avert tragic errors which might place their lives or the lives of others in jeopardy. Unusual occurrences and some special problems of patrol are treated in detail so that patrol officers can improve their proficiency.

Finally, review questions and practical problems which students can solve by applying the principles and techniques they have learned are provided to enrich their learning experiences.

Although patrol officers are the core of successful police operations, training to make them more skillful and productive has too often been neglected. *Principles of Police Patrol* will thus be of value in filling this void.

The author wishes to express his most grateful appreciation to Deputy Chief of Police Marvin D. Iannone, Los Angeles Police Department, for his many suggestions which were of material benefit to this book; to Lieutenant Robert M. Smitson, Officer in Charge, Special Weapons and Tactics Unit (SWAT), Los Angeles Police Department, for his thoughtful suggestions and expertise in patrol operations; and to the many other persons who have been so helpful in providing materials for the text.

The author is also grateful to Mr. Robert A. Stettler, Criminalist, Orange County, California, Sheriff's Department Crime Laboratory, for his most constructive assistance in the development of those parts of the book relating to the patrol officer's preliminary investigation activities and to Mrs. Rosemary Barnett for her diligence in preparing the manuscript.

Nathan Iannone

1

Introduction to Police Patrol

The responsibility for maintaining public order and for the prevention and detection of crime is entrusted to the executive civil force of a state, the police. In a perfect system of government, the police should curb individual liberties only when such liberties are abused. That ideal state has never been achieved, nor is it likely to be, yet an effective police system can be instrumental in maintaining some semblance of public order and preventing anarchy.

The level of antisocial behavior fluctuates with the moral and legal restraints society imposes on its members. As these restraints weaken in a community, lawlessness increases. The public then inevitably turns to the police and demands that they exert greater efforts to control crime. The job of maintaining an appropriate, acceptable level of law enforcement sufficient to keep crime and disorder within reasonable limits is a burden police officers must assume. Their actions must be characterized by restraint even when harsh action seems reasonable.

The major share of this burden falls upon patrol officers, not only because they are members of the largest unit in a police agency but because they are, by the very nature of their position, most adaptable and responsive to the constantly changing needs for police services in the community.

Evolution of Police Patrol

Since the beginning of recorded history, people have found it necessary to protect themselves, their families, and their property from marauders and intruders. Primitive people banded together in families, then in villages, for mutual protection. As villages grew into tribes and societies with common interests, it became necessary for them to select certain people to form patrols which would protect the entire group.

Since patrol is fundamental to police operations, it has played a dominant role in the rise and fall of organized police forces throughout the ages. If it functions efficiently and if its power is not harshly invoked, the essential tranquility of the state may be maintained. If it acts arbitrarily and unjustly, rebellion is bound to follow. This sequence of events has been recorded all too frequently in the pages of history.

The Greeks, Egyptians, and Romans found patrols to be an effective means of controlling the populace, but the powers of the police were not always used for worthy purposes. During the reign of Augustus, the police became a stabilizing institution in Rome. Under his successors, they were used as instruments of tyranny. Under barbarian rule after the fall of Rome, all traces of an organized police force disappeared.

It was not until 785 A.D. under the rule of Charlemagne that a police service was revived. His capitularies contained a large number of regulations governing weights and measures; tolls; markets; sales of food, grain, and cattle; burial of the dead; and measures to be taken to control famine and pestilence. These capitularies were much like modern ordinances.

After Charlemagne's death, the capitularies were destroyed, and a state of anarchy again plagued the people. As the Normans settled in France, they established a highly repressive police system. Regular patrols were established to restore public safety at the expense of public liberty. The system adopted by the Normans formed the basis for the police code introduced into England by William the Conqueror.

Before the Normans came, the many tribes that inhabited England enforced their own laws. Each tribe was responsible for the crimes of its individual members. Each organized its own police and conducted its own system of patrol. Every tribal member was, in effect, a police officer. The leader of the tribal police, selected each year by the members, was responsible for apprehending lawbreakers, bringing them to justice, and punishing them. He had the authority under the *posse comitatus* (the power of the county) to summon others of the tribe to assist him in keeping the peace and arresting offenders. If the offender escaped, the community was required to indemnify the victim for damages. Funds for this purpose were raised through a per capita tax. Standards were established by code for compensating victims according to the damages they suffered at the hands of the criminal. Tribal philosophy held that redress for wrongs could be satisfied by the payment of a fine. For this philosophy, an elaborate system of fines emerged. Offenders lost their liberty and became slaves if they failed or refused to pay an imposed fine. Thus slavery grew in England as a direct result of the police problem.

In Anglo-Saxon England, the administration of justice was purely a local affair and the system was basically democratic. This was changed by William the Conqueror, who placed a leader of his own selection in charge of each shire (similar to a county in America). This system created the position of sheriff, which is still in existence today. The sheriff became responsible for keeping the peace in his jurisdiction. As a result, local responsibility disappeared.

Law enforcement efforts in the early nineteenth century did not meet with popular acceptance. Robbery, forgery, counterfeiting, and violence rose to a deplorable level in London and the provinces. Both watchmen and innkeepers contributed to the crime rate. It was estimated that one out of every twenty-two persons in the population was a criminal. Property was not safe from thieves, and the highways were menaced by bandits.

Law-abiding citizens formed vigilante patrols to combat crime. A strict penal code was adopted by Parliament making 160 crimes punishable by death. In some months, an average of forty persons were hanged each day in London alone. These severe punishments failed to slow the crime wave and only served to turn the public against such harsh enforcement of the law.

In 1829, Sir Robert Peel, home secretary, made his first efforts to establish the London police, which later became the foundation for the London metropolitan police system. He met with bitter opposition from a suspicious populace, which accused him of trying to enslave the people of England by arbitrary and tyrannical methods. Even the major newspapers of London openly urged the people to revolt. Armed secret societies were formed to combat the police. In spite of the opposition, Sir Robert was able to prove to those who doubted his motives that efficient police methods could control crime. He advanced the principle, "Let the punishment fit the crime." By his efforts, over one hundred capital offenses were repealed. Within ten years, crime, which had nearly destroyed London, was no longer a major problem.

The police system Sir Robert organized was subsequently extended throughout Great Britain. In 1839 and 1840, statutes were enacted that permitted the formation of paid police within the shires. These police were appointed by magistrates of the counties.

Many of the principles upon which early English and European police systems were based still apply to law enforcement in America. Local rule still exists almost everywhere. Home rule has traditionally been preferred to the formation of a national police. In some areas of the country, victims of crime are compensated or provisions for this have been made by the various legislative bodies. This trend appears to be spreading under the theory that a society which tolerates crime has some responsibility to the victims of that crime. Police administrators have learned from history that law enforcement which is not popularly accepted will not survive long, nor will any system which is based on harsh, arbitrary punishment.

Organized police forces serving local government were first established in this country during colonial times. Boston formed a night patrol as early as 1636. The police force in New York was founded in 1658. It was called the "rattle watch" because patrol officers were expected to rattle and shake doors to determine if they were locked. Philadelphia had its own night watch in 1700, but its patrol officers were feared by the populace because of their power and bad reputation. In New Haven, these patrol officers were called night watchmen. They enjoyed no better reputation there than in Philadelphia because of their harsh, arbitrary methods.

The night watchmen in colonial times received no pay for their work. They were either citizens who had volunteered their services to protect their communities or persons who had been found guilty of some offense and were allowed to perform patrol duties in place of jail sentences, hard labor, or fines.

Policing soon fell into general disrepute because of the type of persons performing the service. When not enough reputable volunteers could be recruited, it became necessary to pay night watchmen. They were called "leatherheads" because the public believed no intelligent or honest person would take such a job. It was generally believed that when they did, their purpose was to establish an illicit income.

Police patrol in America was limited to the hours of darkness until the early nineteenth century, but little by little it was expanded to all hours of the day. In the colonial American cities, these police services were ridden with corruption. Boston, determined to overcome the bad reputation of its night watch, established a day police force in 1838. In 1833, Philadelphia had established a daytime police operation for much the same reason. It had been joined to the night force under the command of a captain of police. The organization formed the pattern for modern American municipal police forces.

The Patrol Function

Wilson[1] considers policing to be essentially a patrol service which is the nucleus of a department, with specialized activities developed around it as aids. The International Association of Chiefs of Police[2] has described the general function of the patrol force as the most fundamental of all police operations. It provides the basic services for which any department was established.

Its main functions are the prevention and repression of crime, the apprehension of criminals, the maintenance of the peace, and the protection of life and property. In any community the primary responsibility for these functions falls on the patrol officers.

Officers assigned to field patrol duties perform a wide variety of tasks. They are responsible for taking appropriate action when they observe or are informed of matters requiring police attention. They must make all types of criminal and noncriminal investigations; take crime reports; and handle stolen, lost, or abandoned property. They

[1] O. W. Wilson, *Police Administration*, 2d ed., McGraw-Hill Book Company, New York, 1963, p. 231.
[2] International Association of Chiefs of Police, *Manpower Allocation and Distribution*, Case no. 3., Washington, D.C., 1966, p. 2.

must provide aid to those in need—the lost, the destitute, and the injured. They are obliged to assist other agencies at the scenes of unusual incidents, such as fires, and render services in many other situations. When they are not occupied with these functions, officers should engage in preventive patrol designed to reduce the incidence of crime.

The investigation of traffic accidents and the enforcement of driving regulations require a great deal of police time if the appalling cost in human lives and the immense economic losses on our highways are to be reduced. This can only be achieved by an effective level of selective enforcement, with the enforcement effort proportional to traffic accidents with respect to time, place, and type of violations causing the accidents.[3] When special units are not available for these traffic activities, primary responsibility for them falls upon the patrol officer.

Crime Prevention   Crime prevention is inherent in the patrol officer's position. The mere presence of a patrol officer on the streets tends to restrain criminal activity. Crime prevention simply defined refers to activities directed toward keeping violations from happening. This is one of the more important roles of the patrol force.

Crime is the result of both a desire on the part of an individual to commit an offense and an opportunity—real or imagined—to commit it. Desire can be repressed by patrol only by making the risk of apprehension so great that the criminal will seek victims in an area where there is more freedom to operate. The opportunity to commit crime, however, can be reduced, if not eliminated, by skillful and diligent patrol. One method that can be used, for example, is to have frequent but irregular inspections of establishments which are likely to be victimized by criminals. If they do not know when to expect the officer, criminals ordinarily become apprehensive and therefore have less tendency to engage in criminal activity.

Response to Calls   The patrol officer equipped with communicating equipment is usually the first representative of the police to respond to calls from the public. These involve every conceivable type of incident. Some result directly or indirectly from crimes. Others relate to emergencies resulting from accidents or catastrophies as earthquakes; fires; floods; plane, bus, or train crashes; and the like.

---

[3] International City Managers' Association, *Municipal Police Administration*, 6th ed., Chicago, 1969, p. 115.

Frequently the police help to locate lost persons, assist distressed or injured individuals, or settle noncriminal disputes.

In departments where specialized traffic accident investigators are available, the patrol officer is not ordinarily dispatched to the scene of a traffic accident; however, in even the largest jurisdictions with specialized traffic units, the patrol officer must investigate collisions when all available traffic personnel are occupied. The officer must therefore be familiar with the essentials of accident investigation in order to carry out such assignments quickly and efficiently. The officer should also appreciate the economic impact of traffic accidents on the public—the property damage involved, the loss of time which results from the traffic congestion caused by accidents on the highways—in addition to the tremendous loss of life from these occurrences.

Providing Services for Public Convenience   Often officers are called upon to render services for public convenience. They are expected to take action to expedite the movement of persons at special events and at other places by providing relief from congestion and conflict.

Control of Unusual Incidents   The patrol officer is responsible for taking appropriate action in virtually every incident that occurs on the beat. Appropriate inspections at strike scenes and other gatherings, even if they do not involve disorderly conduct, are necessary. Field intelligence must be provided to superiors to be used as a basis for plans to cope with such situations should they develop into large-scale public disorders.

Arrests of Offenders   The arrest of persons who commit crimes is ordinarily a discretionary function. Except when otherwise specified by departmental policy or by court directive, the decision to arrest or not to arrest is left to the judgment of the officer. Usually common sense will dictate the most desirable course of action an officer should take.

In making a decision, an officer should consider the nature of the offense; its seriousness; whether a warning or another course of action would better serve the interests of the law, the police department, society, and the offender; whether the act will be repeated, etc. The answer will be obvious in felony cases, which are serious offenses punishable by prison sentences, and in serious misdemeanor cases. The answer may not be as apparent in other cases. Officers will usually develop some personal standards to help them determine their course of action in the so-called "gray" areas involving minor offenses. However, they must adhere to the law and the organizational objectives and policies in every case, irrespective of personal convictions, or risk the consequences of any deviations. No officer should ever depart from the principle that the law must be enforced fairly.

Officers must constantly be aware of how their own attitudes and convictions affect their decisions. They must avoid allowing their attitudes to be shaped by the unpleasant and sordid aspects of their job. An old adage expresses how a person's attitudes toward crime and criminals may be subconsciously affected by personal experiences. First he abhors, then he condones, then he embraces. While this may not accurately describe the reactions of a vast majority of persons, certain changes in social attitudes toward crime have undeniably contributed to the rapid increase in criminality in recent times.

Investigation of Crime and Case Preparation   The patrol officer is usually responsible for initiating the investigation when a crime has been committed on his beat. Officers must be guided by the regulations of their department which specify the extent of such inquiries. In conducting the preliminary investigation, they should locate pertinent evidence, protect it from contamination or destruction, and collect and preserve it for examination and eventual use in prosecuting the criminal. Patrol officers must interview witnesses and victims and interrogate suspects. They should record their findings in their personal notebooks and in official reports. These will constitute the department's memory of the incident and will establish a basis for initiating criminal action against the perpetrator.

Presentation of Case in Court   The last direct contact an officer has with an arrestee occurs when the officer appears as a witness against the defendant in a court of law. This process has become more time-consuming than it has ever been in the past and demands expert ability from an officer who is preparing to present a criminal case in court. Instead of the one primary issue of whether the defendant is innocent or guilty, there are now many procedural issues which must be resolved before the question of innocence or guilt is determined. As a consequence, the officer is exposed to many frustrating experiences in bringing criminals to justice. It is important to be familiar with current case law in order to comply with the many procedural safeguards provided for the defendant.

By raising an infinite number of procedural challenges and by using other delaying tactics, the defendant can postpone the trial for months. Witnesses, including officers, are often required under subpoena to return to court time and again. The lay person subjected to this inconvenience often becomes a hostile witness, usually to the advantage of the defendant.

One-Man versus Two-Man Patrol

There are those who believe the one-man patrol car is superior in many ways to two-man units. Others object to this claim. There are advantages and disadvantages to both types of patrol. An officer who is assigned to one type should concentrate upon strengthening its favorable aspects and eliminating its inherent weaknesses.

Two-Man Units   Proponents of two-man units contend that they are safer because one officer can give support to the other. They contend that driving is a full-time operation and that the lone officer is incapable of observing well and driving safely at the same time. Further, the high-speed driving that emergencies and pursuits often involve is dangerous and requires the driver's full attention. The driver cannot safely use the radio or firearms under these conditions.

There are those who maintain that the patrol officer working alone is likely to overlook suspicious persons and conditions because of the danger involved. Opponents of this assertion are quick to counter by showing that very few law enforcement officers lack physical courage. The argument that dangerous calls require the response of two or more one-man units and therefore this type of operation is uneconomical is not well founded. It is just as expensive to dispatch a two-man unit—except for the equipment involved—as two one-man units. It is almost as expensive to keep two officers in one unit off the air for reports, meals, etc., as two officers in one-man units.

One-Man Units   Those who support one-man patrols claim that it is more economical because it provides equal if not better service for less money. More units can be fielded with the same number of officers. Since salaries constitute the major part of any police budget, the one-man unit is cheaper. In addition, more patrol units are available to give the public a greater feeling of security.

Fewer distracting personal chores and conversations occur in the one-man operation because each officer is subject to radio calls at any time. The lone officer is therefore often reluctant to leave the vehicle and radio unattended to take care of personal business. Personality clashes are minimized in one-man unit operations because officers have fewer intimate contacts with each other.

If it is conceded that two officers working together are safer than an officer working alone, the single officer can compensate for this by being more alert and by avoiding unnecessary and pointless risks. Assistance can easily be summoned when it is needed, and even though this may cause some delay, usually it is not critical.

Initiative and self-reliance are necessarily developed when an officer has no one else to rely on, and this can produce a better officer. The officer working alone knows that he or she alone must make most of the decisions faced each day. Such responsibility increases confidence and competency. Each officer knows that he or she will receive credit for good work and will be held accountable for any failures, since he or she alone is responsible for what occurs on the beat.

Unquestionably, there are situations in which two-man units are justified because of the unusual nature of the population served, the area, the time, and the hazards constantly present; but a mass of data have supported the effectiveness of a one-man patrol for ordinary operations.

If officers are properly trained to avoid needless risks while alone by calling for assistance when needed, if they are trained in patrol techniques, and if they are given effective communications and safety equipment, the major unfavorable aspect of a one-man unit operation—safety—can largely be overcome.

Types of Patrol

While there are numerous types of police patrol available in modern police work, selection of the types most suitable for a particular locality is usually an administrative decision. Some characteristic advantages and limitations of each type are mentioned here to suggest how an officer might use them more productively in carrying out his patrol function.

Foot Patrol   The oldest type of patrol is that conducted on foot. It is still a highly effective way of combating such crimes as burglaries, robberies, thefts, purse snatchings, and street muggings in highly congested areas. Undeniably, aggressive foot patrol is a very useful type of patrol which places the officer in direct, intimate contact with the public and gives him a source of field intelligence not otherwise readily available. While he is accessible to the public and is able to inspect property carefully and investigate pedestrian suspects on his beat, his ability to engage in repressive patrol is limited by his lack of mobility. Foot patrol is therefore relatively expensive.

An officer on foot can easily be kept under observation by persons intent on committing a crime, and if they are mobile, they can easily escape apprehension. This same lack of mobility makes it impossible for him to take action against persons using vehicles to commit crimes except under the most unusual circumstances.

A lack of effective communications equipment will further hamper his operations. Even though he has modern portable radio equipment available, it often has limited range and usually does not provide a completely adequate means of communicating with headquarters.

Because of these inherent disadvantages, foot patrol is not utilized as much as it formerly was. Yet it can be used with excellent results in conjunction with motorized or bicycle patrol if effective portable communications equipment is provided. An officer can patrol a much wider area more safely when there is a means of conveying information to headquarters. The techniques of patrol on foot are discussed in detail in Chapter 3.

Motorized Patrol   Motorized patrol is the most economical type of patrol. It provides the greatest mobility and flexibility of operations. Wider coverage is therefore possible, and considerably more incidents can be handled. Motorized patrol officers should look upon their vehicles primarily as a means of communication and transportation. They can best use them to move from place to place, but should not rely upon them exclusively in performing their duties of observation while on patrol. If they leave their vehicles and patrol on foot in those places most exposed to crime, they can cover a much broader area and with greater effectiveness than foot patrol officers. In addition, high-performance vehicles permit them to contend with the criminal and traffic law violator on an equal basis. Vehicles can only be pursued effectively by other vehicles.

Special equipment needed routinely by the patrol officer can be carried conveniently in a police car. The foot patrol officer must operate without it. High-powered radio receivers and transmitters are an integral part of the modern radio car. These are immediately available to the radio car officer. With this equipment, he can transmit information concerning his activities to headquarters. He can also respond quickly to calls for service. It is thus apparent that the effectiveness of vehicular patrol combined with foot patrol far exceeds patrol conducted *exclusively* on foot or in a vehicle.

The radio car officer can compensate for his inability to observe well from a moving vehicle by learning to drive more defensively, by patrolling more slowly, and by leaving his vehicle frequently to observe on foot. He can also improve his contacts with the public by increased foot patrol if he uses discrimination in selecting those areas where this can be employed productively.

Mounted Patrol   Mounted police patrols were used as early as 1655 in England under Oliver Cromwell in an organized effort to quell the civil disorders that followed the wars with Spain. Officers patrolling on horseback have remained a part of the patrol force in many modern law enforcement agencies, although their use is not as widespread as it was in the past. The New York Police Department has had a large mounted division ever since it was formed in 1871. This division is still being used effectively for a wide variety of tasks, although it is gradually being replaced by small motor scooters used on beaches and in parks.[4]

In thinly populated and recreational areas, the mounted officer can cover terrain which cannot be covered by motor vehicles. Searches for lost or injured persons or crime victims in these areas cannot always be best accomplished by aircraft because of limitations of visibility. Often, when a detailed search is necessary, it can only be made by persons on the ground operating on foot or mounted on horses.

Horses can also be used to good advantage in patrolling bridle trails and parks. They are effective in crowd and traffic control and in civil disorders under special circumstances because of their mobility and size. However, they can easily panic if dissidents use darts, pepper, or prods of various types. The value of horses for certain patrol duties is unquestioned, although the dangers to their riders on urban streets and the limited situations in which they can be used effectively have tended to discourage police departments from including them in the patrol force.

[4] Rich Sassone, "New York's Mounted Police," *Law and Order*, vol. 20, no. 11, November 1972, pp. 38–44.

Aircraft Patrol   Helicopters and small aircraft have gradually found their way into modern police use. In rugged territory where widespread searches are often necessary for lost or injured persons or wrecked planes, helicopters and small planes have been used with good results. They have been found to be an economical way to transport executives to professional conferences, etc., when time-saving must be considered. Plane transportation over long distances for prisoners being extradited or delivered to prisons is much safer and perhaps cheaper than transportation by automobile or train.

Patrol officers in helicopters can provide intelligence for traffic, crowd, fire, and unusual occurrence control (such as riots, ambushes, and the like) in congested areas. They are also useful in deploying surface units to cordon off areas in all types of incidents. If tear gas is dispersed from helicopters against an unruly crowd, however, helicopter operations must be limited because of the effect they have on wind currents and the distribution of chemical agents.

In open areas, they have proved valuable in traffic law enforcement where cars moving at high speeds can be observed. When communications with surface vehicles are provided, helicopters are useful in reducing the number of dangerous pursuits. They are a relatively new means of criminal surveillance from the air and are used in conjunction with vehicles on the ground.

Helicopter patrol has had varying degrees of success. Some claim that its impact on crime is dramatic. Others contend that it merely drives burglars from one area to another but does not reduce the overall burglary rate. The public often complains that helicopter patrol is a costly, noisy, prying arm of law enforcement. Undoubtedly, it can be effectively used in a number of ways to support ground personnel. Whether its cost is justified cannot easily be assessed without a long-term evaluation.

Bicycle Patrol   Enterprising officers have often used bicycles to good effect in specialized operations designed to prevent crimes that occur on streets, in alleys, and in public areas where autos cannot patrol and where silent operations are desirable. They can be used effectively to patrol large areas such as parks and beaches, and have much the same effect as foot patrol.

Their main disadvantage is that they are not equipped with long-range communications equipment. With the vast improvements in modern electronics, however, this disadvantage will gradually disappear.

Motor Scooters and Motorized Bicycles   This type of equipment enables the officer to patrol beaches, parks, and other public recreation areas with much the same efficiency and with many of the same disadvantages as bicycle patrol.

Modification of Principles and Techniques

The techniques used by officers in carrying out their patrol functions may vary substantially from case to case depending on the circumstances. No hard-and-fast rules can be provided for every incident officers encounter. They must therefore occasionally modify the basic principles and techniques they have learned to meet the needs of a situation. In this way they will be able to carry out their duties reasonably safely and, at the same time, comply with the regulations of their organization and rules of law.

Summary

When antisocial behavior increases to an unacceptable level in a community, it is inevitable that the public will turn to the police and demand that they take action to relieve the problem. This burden eventually is passed down to the individual patrol officer, who is most responsive to community needs.

Since the beginning of history people have found it necessary to protect themselves, their families, and their possessions from others. A form of patrol designed to provide this protection gradually evolved as society grew. At first it was a nighttime service, but it gradually was extended to include patrol at all hours of the day. The patrol force established in Philadelphia in 1833 formed the basic pattern for modern municipal police organizations.

The effectiveness of a police organization is directly related to the effectiveness of its patrol force. Since patrol units are available to provide services to the public at all times, they are the nucleus of any police operation.

The functions of the patrol officer include crime repression and prevention, the response to calls, the provision of all types of services for the public convenience, the control of unusual incidents, the arrest of offenders, the investigation of crime and the preparation of cases for prosecution, and the presentation of the investigation in court.

The patrol officers perform their duties by motorized patrol or by patrolling on foot, on a horse, on a bicycle, or on a motor scooter. Each type of patrol can be adapted to serve a particular purpose.

Motorized patrol should be combined with patrol on foot to best accomplish its objectives.

Small aircraft have limited use for observation or rescue work. Helicopters are one of the newest additions to the patrol force, but their effectiveness has not yet been clearly established.

Patrol officers will find that they must improvise techniques for performing some of their many duties. They must also modify the basic principles and techniques of police patrol to meet the needs of unusual situations. Those techniques found to be most effective should be studied and practiced. Those found to have weaknesses should be modified so that they may be applied safely and in accordance with department regulations and rules of law.

Review

Questions

1. What is the meaning of crime prevention?
2. What is likely to happen in a society if the repressive activities of the police become overly harsh?
3. Who advanced the principle, "Let the punishment fit the crime"?
4. What is meant by home rule?
5. Why were daytime patrols first established in Boston and Philadelphia?
6. Why were early colonial night watchmen called leatherheads?
7. What is selective patrol?
8. Why is the patrol force considered the nucleus of a department?
9. What services is a patrol officer often expected to render for the public convenience?
10. Describe how the officer can overcome the disadvantages of one- and two-man units?

Exercises

1. Describe the cycle which occurs when moral and legal standards deteriorate in a community and how this affects the police.
2. Explain why police efforts must meet with public approval or fail.
3. Describe several early English and European principles that still apply to modern police.
4. Enumerate and discuss the *major* functions of the patrol officer.
5. Describe generally how radio car patrol officers can best carry out their preventive patrol functions.
6. Explain how an officer's attitude might affect the arrests he or she makes.

7. Discuss the arguments for and against one-man patrol units.
8. Compare one-man patrol unit operations with those of two-man units. Which do you favor and why?
9. Name five types of police patrol and describe the advantages and disadvantages of each.
10. Describe some of the major services the patrol force provides the community which do not involve crime.

2

Observation, Perception, and Recollection

The ability to observe people, happenings, and things with discrimination and translate these observations into necessary action probably contributes more to the patrol officer's effectiveness than any other factor. Officers are not born with the ability to observe efficiently. They can learn to do so, however, by training themselves to observe with all their senses and to organize their attention so that their minds become aware of what is happening.

The Processes of Observation, Perception, and Recollection

Observation always precedes perception. In a technical sense, it involves the gathering of stimuli by the sensory organs. These are the eyes, ears, nose, taste organs, touch organs, and kinesthetic cells which provide the sensations of motion, balance, etc. When such stimuli are transmitted to the brain and the brain becomes aware of

17

them and recognizes or understands them, such stimuli become the basis for conscious actions. This is perception. Dewey and Humber[1] describe it as an experience that has acquired meaning. The nature of the action taken or to be taken then becomes a matter of conscious decision based on these perceptions. Secondary reflexes which result from training and conditioning and do not involve conscious thought are not a factor in perception.

The processes of observing, perceiving, and recollecting are essential to effective police work. The powers to really "see" through the senses, to understand or become mentally aware of what was seen, and to remember what was observed are underdeveloped in the average person. Because of this the average person is poorly equipped to relate accurately what happened. Simple perceptions can usually be translated into perfectly acceptable reports purely from memory, without any written notes; but as time passes, the ability to remember details of the observation diminishes, and inaccuracies begin to creep in. Generally, forgetting is swiftest soon after learning. It then proceeds more slowly.[2] Consequently, the sooner information is recorded after it is acquired, the more accurate it is likely to be.

Factors Affecting Observation

When observations are faulty, the decisions based on them are more apt to be wrong. The capacity to observe accurately is dependent on many factors, both physical and environmental.

Sight   The eye is one of the most important of the sensory organs and the one that is most often mistreated. Even a slight impairment of vision can detract greatly from an individual's capacity to observe accurately. An inability to judge distances accurately; a deficiency in depth perception or peripheral or side vision; or an inability to distinguish colors—most commonly the reds and greens—may be enough to disqualify an officer as a witness in court or may contribute to his becoming so accident prone that he cannot perform his duties adequately. Many of these conditions can be corrected easily if they are caught in time. If they are not, they may become progressively worse.

---

[1] Richard Dewey and W. J. Humber, *An Introduction to Social Psychology*, The Macmillan Company, New York, 1966, pp. 161–62.
[2] David Krech and Richard S. Crutchfield, *Elements of Psychology*, Alfred A. Knopf, Inc., New York, 1958, p. 419.

The size of an object, its distance, and the light conditions under which it is observed may materially influence the accuracy of an observation. Because the eyes accommodate to light mechanically, a person leaving a lighted area and going into a dark one will be unable to see until his eyes adjust to the darkness. An officer would therefore be at a disadvantage if he were to leave a lighted area and go into a dark room where a suspect was hiding. Some of the disadvantage could be removed, however, if he closed one eye before going in to allow it to adjust. It would be better to enter swiftly, take cover, and wait for the eyes to adjust to the darkness before taking further action.

Objects directly in front of the eyes can be seen more clearly than those off to the sides. These can be observed with considerable accuracy through side or peripheral vision, however, if they are not too far back and especially if they are moving. The expert driver learns to rely upon his side vision to warn him of hazards on his right or left.

Actual size, distance, and light may appear distorted due to optical illusions. The simple Müller-Lyer illusion in Figure 2-1 demonstrates how size may appear different although the lines are identical in length.

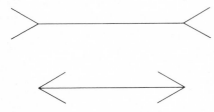

Figure 2-1. MÜLLER-LYER ILLUSION. The equal lines appear unequal because of the arrowheads.

This demonstrates simply how perceived size, shape, color, texture, movement, change, etc., are influenced by their surroundings. Most police officers have had victims of robberies describe the weapon used in the holdup as "big as a cannon." These victims often exaggerate the weapon size because of their expectations, because of the nearness of the weapon, and perhaps because of their ego. In the same way the victim of an assault often describes the assailant as being much larger than he really turns out to be.

Objects are not perceived as single items isolated from each other. They are perceived in relation to each other, and therefore are influenced by their environment. Frequently, a person's perceptions do not correspond with the actual physical dimensions and properties of the object.[3]

[3] Krech and Crutchfield, *Elements of Psychology*, pp. 17–29.

Even a person's emotional involvement will affect perception and may cause him or her to remember an object in a distorted way. Early tests by Siepola[4] indicated that individuals, without realizing it, tend to distort the meaning of things they experience through their senses according to what they expect. When the persons tested were told that certain words to which they would be quickly exposed had to do with animals, they generally distorted certain nonsense words to coincide with a form meaningful to them. The word chack was interpreted as chick, wharl as whale, dack as duck, etc. Persons told that these nonsense words related to travel or transportation interpreted them in a high percentage of the responses as check, wharf, deck, etc., respectively. This distortion might take place in the mind when the stimuli percieved are fairly close to what the person expects them to be.[5] The more a person is trained to focus his attenton on what he observes, the less chances there are that he will make errors in his obsevation or distort its meaning. Proofreaders train themselves to focus their attention on the structure of the copy they are proofing; but even so, they overlook errors because they often see what they expect to see. For example, there are three printing errors in this paragraph. These may not have been noticed becuase the reader failed to fully focus his attention on what he actually saw. This is the classical "proofreader's illusion" and merely exemplifies the fact that people see without really seeing. Officers must therefore try to verify by some other means, if possible, what they believe they saw. Photographs of a scene might reveal the proper perspective of details that appeared distorted when observed directly. However, the camera can also be used to cause distortion. Everyone has seen a picture of a distorted foot brought about by camera position alone. Therefore, a photographer must ensure against distortion in photographs so that they give a fair representation of the scene. Physical measurements might be required to establish distances accurately for the purpose of reinforcing visual observations and photographic evidence.

Dim light may cause distortions in observation. Experience shows that persons firing sidearms under dim, artificial light tend to shoot low. It is common for persons who drive at dusk to misjudge distances. Details of objects are indistinct, and errors in describing people are common when observations are made under such conditions. The

[4] E. M. Siepola, "A Study of Some Effects of Preparatory Set," *Psychology Monograph*, n.d., vol. 46, no. 210, p. 102.
[5] Krech and Crutchfield, *Elements of Psychology*, p. 102.

features of a person under a typical street light at night usually cannot be observed with a high degree of accuracy from 15 yards. During the daytime, even persons with excellent vision often cannot describe persons accurately from 50 yards away, except for general characteristics such as height, weight, and the like. Usually these are not enough for identification.

Objects near the ground may not be seen readily unless the observer is conscious of what to look for or where to look for it. He should direct his attention to those areas where he might miss seeing an object because it blends into the background.

The inability of most persons to observe, remember, and recite the details of incidents is well known to police officers. Most have experienced cases in which several untrained persons witnessed an event, yet no two of them were able to give the same account of what happened. There probably were many reasons for their errors, but most of them probably happened because the observers had not trained themselves to observe details carefully. Either they were not trained to discriminate between essential and nonessential matters, so that their attention was dispersed over the whole incident rather than concentrated on specifics; or illusions, bias, or physical impairment distorted their observations.

If six reasonably alert persons who observed a traffic accident at an intersection were separated and asked about what they saw, they probably would give six different versions of exactly what happened. Even though each one told the truth and tried to relate exactly what he saw, their accounts would vary so much that a person reading their descriptions and not knowing the real facts would not realize that all six were describing the same accident. The estimated speeds in the accounts usually vary widely—probably from 25 to 55 miles per hour, with other estimates somewhere between those extremes. It is not impossible that one witness would say that both cars were going in the same direction. Another might insist they were driving at right angles to each other, and the third might contend that they were going in opposite directions. One might say that one car was going north and the other west. Another might claim the cars were proceeding south and east. Some may identify the cars as 4-door sedans. Others may say they were 2-door coupes. It would not be surprising if one witness insisted that a pickup truck was involved. Probably not one of the witnesses would be able to fix the time of the accident accurately, nor would any of them be able to give the real colors of both cars. Most of them probably could not tell what state license plates were on the cars, and some of them would not even be able to state with certainty whether the drivers were men or women.

All these inaccurate descriptions result from a lack of ability to observe, perceive, and remember. If any of these processes fail, the account of what actually happened will be inaccurate. The witnesses may have seen the accident, but they did not get a true mental picture of what happened because they had not trained themselves to observe.

Hearing   The source of sounds coming from the right or left can ordinarily be easily distinguished. Errors can easily occur, however, in areas congested by buildings, trees, hills, etc. Even on a crowded parking lot, sometimes it is exceedingly difficult to determine the source of the sound when a car horn starts blaring. Loud sounds tend to be heard as coming from close objects, soft sounds as coming from more distant ones. When distances of sounds are judged by intensity, they will often be wrong unless the observer has trained himself to recognize the sounds and associate them with his experiences. Any hunter has experienced the illusion that the sound of a gun fired at a considerable distance seems to come from nearby or vice versa, depending on the temperature, wind, and other factors in the environment. He can soon learn, however, to judge these distances more accurately by directing his attention to them.

He usually will also find that almost imperceptible head movements tend to help identify the exact location of the sound source. Tilting the head from side to side will enable him to tell a sound directly above from one below. Rotating the head from right to left will help him recognize that a sound source is directly in front or directly in back. As the head turns to the left, the sound from the front arrives sooner at the right ear than at the left, and thus the brain can establish its source.

Touch   The sense of touch is not well developed in most people. The blind train themselves remarkably well to compensate for the loss of sight by developing their other sensory organs. The senses of touch and hearing are usually relied upon to provide this compensation. Fortunately, the patrol officer's sense of touch is not one of his critical needs. But it can be developed by practice. He can learn to perform tasks such as field stripping a weapon or loading it in the dark when the occasion arises.

Training the Powers of Observation, Perception, and Recollection

Patrol officers must train themselves not only to observe with all their senses, but to become mentally aware of what they have seen. Persons, places, objects, and incidents must be given their attention. They must train themselves to become aware of detail as distinguished from generalities if they are to become effective observers. They must be conscious of time relationships so that they can gauge accurately the amount of time which has elapsed between two incidents. The ability to calculate or judge time is well developed in the animal kingdom. Certain animals, such as migratory birds, do so by physiological mechanisms that produce glandular changes. Not so with humans. Most of their judgments of time are based on conditioning and association. People estimate the time involved in an incident or between incidents largely upon the basis of the events which occurred during the period in question. If you train yourself to recollect precisely what events took place between two incidents or while one incident was happening, you will be able to estimate the time involved with a high degree of accuracy.

Officers must also train themselves to gauge speed and distance and to recognize the distinction between colors and the varying degrees of light. They can make their observations effective through practice and experience and by looking at objects and events as if they were preparing themselves to testify in court with the opposing party subjecting them to searching cross-examination.

Officers should train themselves by constantly observing situations, recording what they have seen, then checking to see if they have accurately described their observations. This should be done as a matter of everyday practice—not only while the officers are on duty, but also when they are off duty—until they have disciplined themselves to a point where they can make effective observations and meaningful descriptions. An officer should walk through a room making observations of as many objects as possible. He should then test his powers of observation and recollection by describing what objects he saw in the room and their positions. He should write down these descriptions, then go back and check them for accuracy. Nothing will more quickly develop his powers of observation than this kind of practice.

Memory Training   Any system of memory training helps remembering indirectly by teaching people to learn more efficiently. It has value only when it increases this capacity. The process of learning *efficiently* is the very core of memory training.[6]

An intention to learn what is heard, read, or observed must be present, or memory will be poor. If something is not remembered, the reason is not that the memory itself is poor but that there was a failure to learn in the first place. Attention must be present if learning is to take place. If there is an intention to learn, attention will probably be present. This involves concentration during the learning process so that understanding will take place. Understanding is usually achieved through attention to stimuli, and this results in little forgetting.

The use of *imagery* is important to learning and remembering. A photographic image in the mind's eye of the thing, person, or event observed helps recollection greatly. Things to be learned should be associated with other familiar things. William James[7] classically described the process of remembering by association when he said, "In mental terms, the more other facts a fact is associated with in the mind, the better possession of it our memory retains." *Rehearsing* and *reciting* while learning helps retention. Repetition strengthens responses. Observation of persons or things should be started with a view of the *total image* followed by attention to details isolated from the whole.

Studies reported by Krech and Crutchfield[8] generally supported the conclusion that the more firmly information is acquired, the better it is retained. Evidence indicates that the more attention is focused on particular items rather than on groupings of items, the greater is retention. The more efficient the methods of acquiring information are, the greater is the ability to recollect.

Describing Observations   Once the officer has observed, he must be able to describe what he saw. His observations, no matter how accurate and complete, are of no use to anyone else if he is not able to remember details and describe what he has seen in a manner that will give others an accurate picture of the thing, person, or situation observed.

Memories may change radically with the passing of time and become more and more inaccurate. This is especially true in those

[6] Norman L. Munn, *Psychology*, Houghton Mifflin Company, Boston, 1956, pp. 278–80.
[7] William James, *Principles of Psychology*, Holt Publishing Company, New York, 1908, p. 294.
[8] Krech and Crutchfield, *Elements of Psychology*, pp. 420–425.

cases where new facts are constantly being assimilated or where emotions or prejudices are involved. Therefore, notes made at or near the time of the observation literally become an officer's memory. He cannot be expected to remember all the details of the many incidents he experiences, and so he must reinforce his powers of recollection by written records. These should contain the specific details showing the *who, what, where, when, why,* and *how* of the matter. A detailed discussion of these descriptive factors is contained in Chapter 4.

The ability to remember detail is invaluable to officers, but they need not tax their memory unnecessarily by trying to remember everything. There will be enough incidents in their work which they will have to remember without adding to the burden by failing to record what should be recorded.

Systematic Observation   Officers who make the most effective observations develop some sort of system. They learn what to look for, they learn how to tell the important from the nonessential, and they learn the value of systematic observation. Haphazard observations—jumping from top to bottom, side to side, then to the middle—of a person, situation, or thing will cause the viewer to miss many important details.

Observation of Places and Events   The following system of observation is useful for observing places and events. Look at the whole object, person, or event. Focus your attention on details. Then select a starting point from which you can observe all the details of the place by progressing methodically from point to point in a straight line or in a circle. This procedure and the written or oral description resulting from it are logical and easily absorbed by the mind.

If you must observe a room in detail, select a starting point as you enter the room. Continue looking around the walls back to the starting point, then look at the floor and ceiling. Give important points or objects special attention. This logical pattern should be followed in your description so that you will give the most accurate picture.

Observation of Persons   Before patrol officers can become truly effective, they must develop the ability to observe and describe people so completely and accurately that others—even those who are untrained—can recognize the person described if that person is seen.

Likewise, the ability to develop concrete images or mental pictures of persons described to officers is an essential part of their stock-in-trade.

To observe persons, begin at the head and move logically down to the feet. During the preliminary observation, take into account sex, color, height, and weight. Then proceed with an inventory of the physical characteristics of the person. Attention should be directed to unusual characteristics. It is necessary to select peculiarities, mannerisms, or characteristics which particularly help identify that individual. Without them, a description becomes common, ordinary, and nonidentifying.

Personal descriptions usually start with the name, if it is known, race, and national derivation, if the latter is descriptive. The age, height, weight, build, color of eyes, color of hair, and complexion follow. These characteristics, however, only generally describe a person. Several persons in a group of one hundred people picked at random would probably fit any general description. If some unusual characteristics are not included, even an experienced police officer might have trouble picking the right person from a crowd.

If a description does not identify the person sought, then it has not served any useful purpose. On the contrary, it may cause a lot of time to be wasted as officers look for a vaguely described individual. A full list of descriptive characteristics is included in Chapter 4.

Describing Persons   The ability to describe the observed person accurately can be easily developed if officers know what to look for and how to describe what they have seen. Most persons have some common features which are not good points for recognition except as they complement other characteristics which distinguish one person from another. Distinctive traits or characteristics, peculiarities, mannerisms, or unusual features obviously are the best means of recognition if they are described in words that enable another person to visualize the individual described.

Summary

Observation involves the process of gathering images through the sensory organs of sight, sound, touch, taste, smell, and motion. When sensations from observations are transmitted to and registered by the brain, the person has perceived. Perception becomes the basis for conscious reactions or decisions. The ability to observe, perceive, and recollect is underdeveloped in the average person. The accuracy of his statement of what he believes he observed must therefore be viewed with some suspicion. If either observation or perception is faulty, the recollections based on them will likewise be erroneous.

An impairment of the sensory organs, such as color blindness, partial deafness, etc., or illusions of perceived size, shape, color, and movement may cause substantial distortions in the recollection of matters observed. This is exemplified by the Müller-Lyer illusion, the "proofreader's illusion," and the experiences most police officers have had with the distortions that often occur in witnesses' testimony.

The so-called "memory systems" do nothing to change the capacity for remembering. These systems stress methods of making learning more efficient and meaningful. No one can remember what has not been learned in the first place. Learning becomes more efficient when there is an intent to learn, when there is attention, when imagery is strong, when the things to be learned are associated with other familiar things, when there is repetition of the things learned, and when there is whole-part observation followed by isolation of details with attention fixed on them.

Studies have revealed that information is acquired more firmly when more attention is directed to isolated items rather than groupings of items; and the more efficient the learning process, the better the recollection of that which has been learned. These principles apply directly to the process of learning through observations which all officers must master before they can become truly effective.

Those officers who make the most effective observations and retain what they have learned have developed some sort of system. They observe places and happenings systematically by viewing the whole, then focusing their attention on important details. They learn what items are important and which are nonessential, and conserve their learning time by their discriminating observations.

Observations of persons involve the same techniques that generally apply to observation of places and events. Persons should be viewed systematically, from the head to the feet. The physical peculiarities and unusual characteristics that distinguish one person from all others must then be noted.

Review

Questions

1. What does the term observe mean?
2. What is the difference between observation and perception?
3. What is meant by the expression "to see through the senses"?
4. When is forgetting swiftest?
5. What colors are most often involved in color blindness?

6. What is peripheral vision?
7. How does peripheral vision affect observations?
8. How might you compensate for distortions in vision?
9. What is a "proofreader's illusion"?
10. What are the most distinctive parts of a description of a person?

Exercises

1. Explain how perceptions become the basis for conscious action.
2. Explain how physical impairments or deficiencies affect observations.
3. Explain the effects of dim light on visual acuity. Give an example of a distortion it might cause.
4. Give an example of an illusion caused by the environment around an object.
5. Describe how emotions may cause distortions and inaccuracies in observations.
6. Explain how a patrol officer can improve his ability to make accurate observations.
7. Explain how the so-called "memory systems" help a person remember things.
8. Describe the technique that should be followed in observing and describing a place (room); an individual; an incident.
9. Give an example of a distortion of sound and explain how it happens.

3

Beat Patrol

In every law enforcement jurisdiction engaging in patrol, officers are ordinarily assigned to specified areas or patrol beats so that the work of the patrol force may be apportioned somewhat equally among them. Officers are responsible for accomplishment of the patrol mission on their assigned beats. They must be alert to prevent criminal activity; to maintain the peace and good order; and to protect persons, their property, and their welfare. The absence or presence of disorders, breaches of the peace, accidents, and crime indicates how effective police activity has been. Patrol officers are primarily accountable for these incidents if they exist and are entitled to much of the credit if they are absent.

Preparation for Duty

In order that the patrol officers may best accomplish their mission, they must become thoroughly familiar with the geographical profile of the community, the existence and nature of places or conditions that are hazards or give rise to crime, and the public services available to members of the community.

Reporting for Duty Report for duty a few minutes before the scheduled roll call time so that you may check your mail for subpoenas or inquiries from other officers that may need a response, and attend to any other matters that may require your attention.

Equipment Check You should make certain that your sidearm, shotgun, flashlight, and handcuffs are in proper working order. Ammunition should be of current issue free from dents or crimps that may prevent proper loading. Shotgun cartridges can easily be damaged so that they will not properly feed into the chamber if they are dropped or otherwise handled carelessly. Examine all clothing and equipment so it is ready for inspection and use. If equipment such as a helmet, unbreakable goggles for special duty in civil disorders, brush fires, etc., and mace dispensers are provided, you should inspect them for serviceability before you leave the station.

If you are furnished with a first aid or investigation kit, you should inspect it to ensure that it is properly filled and serviceable. You should also make sure your flare supply is adequate for a complete tour of duty.

Obtaining Current Information If pin maps are maintained, check them at the beginning of each watch to acquaint yourself with the current crime picture on your beat. Daily occurrence recaps should also be reviewed if such data are not given at the briefing session. If, for example, auto thefts or thefts from autos are increasing on your beat, you might plan how to concentrate your efforts in those areas where the statistical data show such crimes are occurring. You should analyze those crimes which show a pattern to determine the best method of coping with them. Places where vehicles are stolen or recovered on your beat may provide clues to the possible routes over which they were driven into or out of your patrol area.

You can acquaint yourself with incidents that have happened on your beat by discussing with officers on other watches the problems they have encountered. You will also gain much valuable intelligence from these discussions regarding problem areas, potential hazards, and suspects that will affect your own patrol activities.

Wanted Persons and Probationers   If photographs of wanted suspects are posted in the briefing room or elsewhere, you should study these each day for additions. You should also familiarize yourself with the names and pictures, if possible, of persons in the community who have been granted probation for serious offenses upon the condition that they voluntarily submit to a search when requested to do so by any peace officer.

Prepatrol Vehicle Inspection   An officer ordinarily is not expected to make those inspections of a vehicle which can only be made reasonably well by trained mechanics in normal fleet maintenance operations. You can, however, increase the safety factor by making the following simple checks before taking an automobile onto the streets for operation under the demanding conditions of police patrol:

Damage Inspection: Many police departments require supervisory inspection of vehicles and drivers at the end of each shift before the relieving officers assume responsibility for that unit. At this time, new damage, if any, is recorded on a control sheet kept for each car. The drivers concerned are required to make appropriate reports of damage if it has not been previously reported. Vehicle malfunctions are also noted. A relieving officer accepting a vehicle without checking it for fresh damage may be held responsible for it later when the damage is discovered.

Safety checks: After the initial inspection for damage is completed, the driver should examine tires for any observable weaknesses and evidence of cuts, bulges, overinflation, underinflation, excessive wear, or any other dangerous condition. Corrective action should be taken as indicated.

The officer should then close and lock doors and adjust the seat for best control of the brake pedal and steering wheel. A soft, spongy brake pedal indicates that a defective hydraulic brake system or faulty brake adjustment is a possibility. This condition may lead to a serious malfunction and should be corrected by a competent mechanic.

Rearview and sideview mirrors should be adjusted to give proper view to the side and rear. High- and low-beam lights, red or colored lights and warning lights, and the siren should be checked for proper operating condition.

The seat belt and shoulder straps should be fastened and adjusted for proper tension before the vehicle is moved. Many agencies require their personnel to use such safety devices at all times while driving.

Experience has shown that a substantial reduction in serious traffic accident injuries has resulted from their use.

Other Inspections: Because of faulty searching procedures, officers occasionally will fail to find contraband or weapons hidden on an arrestee at the time of the arrest. Arrestees, consequently, at times will hide contraband such as a narcotic, dangerous drug, stolen property, or a weapon behind or under seats of the police vehicle to keep it from being discovered on them when they are searched at the station. Therefore, before you take a vehicle on patrol, you should examine under and behind seats and other places where prisoners might conceal these materials. You should exercise extreme care in searching behind seat cushions to avoid being cut by razor blades, sharp knives, or other objects.

If your car is equipped with a fire extinguisher, it should be checked for serviceability. Dry chemical extinguishers require little service, but those containing carbon dioxide should be regularly inspected.

Becoming Familiar with a Beat

If they are to provide an appropriate level of service, patrol officers must have a thorough knowledge of the characteristics of their beats. They must become familiar with public transportation routes, locations of streets and highways, the general patterns of population distribution throughout the area, the cultural characteristics of the district, the locations of public service buildings, industrial facilities, etc. More essential—and more directly related to the performance of their assigned duties—they should have a thorough knowledge of the locations, layout, and numbering systems of streets, the locations of police call boxes, fire alarms, night telephones, schools, parks, playgrounds, major buildings, hospitals, and the like.

Ideally, officers should know the people who customarily frequent their beat and these people's habits and occupations, so that they may notice strangers whose actions or presence should be scrutinized. By becoming acquainted with the persons who live or work in the area, they may develop valuable sources of information. Barbers, bartenders, small business merchants, operators of newsstands, liquor stores, apartment houses, taverns, pool rooms, etc., are in an ideal position to observe incidents and receive information which will be passed to an officer who has earned their confidence. If it is properly assessed and utilized, this intelligence may help the officer keep the beat free of the undesirables who are often associated with criminal activity.

Preventive Patrol

Preventive patrol is most effective when it is irregular. When beat coverage is regular and routinized, officers provide an opportunity for crime because their activities can be anticipated by the law-breaker, who can plan a crime accordingly, knowing that it will not be interrupted by the officers.

Prevention of crime is not solely the responsibility of the patrol officer. When you aggressively patrol your beat; investigate suspicious persons, things, and incidents; check the security of property; minimize by repressive patrol activities the opportunities for criminals to break the law; and inform others how to reduce their exposure to crime, you have done about all that you can to prevent crime through patrol. Your efforts can be reinforced if the householder, the property owner, and the merchant can be convinced to take steps to keep from becoming victims of the criminal.

Crime Repression and Prevention   Much of the time patrol officers spend in the field without specific assignments should be spent visibly patrolling areas most exposed to crime. You should use your free time to become better acquainted with the geographical arrangement of your beats and the persons residing and doing business there. You should become familiar with the conditions that contribute to criminal activity and take whatever action you can to eliminate them. While you can do little to keep people from wanting to commit crime, you can, by active, visible patrol, create the impression that you are always present at the times and in the locations where criminal activity is greatest. This is the essence of selective patrol. Its objective is to reduce the criminal's opportunity to commit crime.

The patrol officer's activities will not significantly affect the incidence of crimes of passion; but, since most criminals are opportunists, they will commit their illegal acts when and where they believe the risks of arrest are slightest. Officers can make these risks seem unattractive by aggressive, selective patrol. Your patrol efforts can have a substantial effect in curbing the activities of some criminals, such as addicts who will often take unusual risks in stealing to support their habit.

Patrol officers can carry out their repressive patrol activities by frequent inspections of persons, places, and objects exposed to crime. You should watch for elderly persons in dark areas who might become the victims of street muggers, purse snatchers, or assailants. You should especially check children in unusual places at unusual hours to determine if you must take action to protect the juveniles from harmful influences.

Patrol officers should make security checks of business and industrial premises in exposed locations. In residential areas, you should be alert for burglars and thieves. You should patrol frequently in areas where automobiles and other property are exposed to attack.

Effective repressive patrol requires asking persons observed under suspicious circumstances to explain the reasons for their presence. Gatherings that are a potential source of unlawful activity should be given appropriate attention so that action may be taken in time to prevent public disorder.

Patrol officers should use every means at their disposal to encourage people in the community to help the police prevent crime. You should impress upon members of the community that the efforts of the police to prevent crime will be of little value without public cooperation. Proprietors of businesses should be urged to make their premises secure against criminals by installing and using proper locks, lights, and alarms. Storekeepers should be encouraged to arrange their displays so that the displays cannot be used as a shield by customers who steal money from the cash register or merchandise from the shelves. Merchants should be persuaded to remove firearms, expensive jewelry, furs, or other merchandise from places where they can be stolen by window smashers or shoplifters. Business people should be discouraged from accumulating large sums of money, which increase their exposure to robberies.

Every opportunity should be taken to encourage residents to keep garages closed if they contain bicycles, tools, or objects that can be easily carried away. Officers should describe to residents, whenever possible, some of the simple but effective locking devices which keep opportunistic thieves and burglars from entering buildings. Most citizens do not realize that criminals are not likely to enter a reasonably secure building if they can find one which is an open invitation to the thief. Louvered windows not protected with grillwork are a burglar's delight. Horizontally or vertically sliding doors and windows can be easily secured with inexpensive devices which will prevent easy entry, but it should be impressed on residents that these precautions are useless if the doors are left open or are not secured with a reasonably effective lock.

Burglars and thieves will also enter a building more readily if they believe it to be unoccupied. Therefore, lights and radios should be left on when residents leave, papers and deliveries should be discontinued, and neighbors should be alerted when premises are left unoccupied for extended periods.

Correcting Physical Hazards While a large share of your time is devoted to the observation, investigation, or assistance of persons, you should also be aware of physical conditions on your beat that may require attention. You should correct any condition which endangers the public health, safety, or welfare, or notify the appropriate agency promptly if you are unable to take corrective action yourself.

When obstructions, defects, nuisances, or other conditions dangerous to the public are left uncorrected in areas over which a governmental agency has responsibility, and injury or property damage result, considerable liability exists to such an agency. Therefore, it is imperative that the agency be notified promptly so that the necessary corrective action may be taken and the possibility of liability eliminated. Likewise, it is essential that you promptly make the necessary notifications when you observe out-of-order traffic control lights, damaged or obstructed traffic signs, unprotected excavations, broken street lights, or other conditions which are hazardous. This is part of your preventive patrol function.

Patrol Demeanor

The manner in which the patrol officers conduct themselves should at all times be businesslike, courteous, and alert. The police cars you drive are a means of transportation and should be used for police business only. Any appearance of inattentiveness to duty in public view will directly affect the confidence the public has in you as a police officer.

The individual patrol officer is perhaps the most important member of the police department in maintaining good public relations. You have the most frequent personal contacts with individual citizens and you most often establish an image of the police in the public's mind.

You must be especially careful when you are uniformed and are patrolling your beat in distinctively marked cars. If you appear slovenly, are discourteous to those with whom you come in contact, are indifferent to people's problems, and conduct yourself unprofessionally, you will give the entire department an unsavory reputation. You will tend to confirm many citizens' stereotyped low opinions of all police officers. The dedicated, hard-working, considerate officer is tarred by the same brush. The average person has limited opportunity to assess the law enforcement personnel in the community except through observations of the patrol officer's general appearance while performing routine duties.

The first impressions the public gets of its police officers are usually the most important. These impressions are most directly related to the officers' attire, bearing, and demeanor. If the officers are neat and well-groomed, and have a businesslike demeanor, the first impression is apt to be favorable. It will be supported or reversed by subsequent, more intimate contacts the officers have with the public in the course of any official duties. One inconsiderate or discourteous act by an officer might create hostility in a citizen toward the police which may never be overcome.

While firmness is necessary at times in contacts with the public, it should never be practiced as a substitute for courtesy. An officious attitude should be meticulously avoided. Rude, discourteous, or arbitrary conduct can never be permitted if a high state of professionalism is to be maintained in the police service.

Patrol Techniques

Every officer should be aware that different problems are encountered on a beat during daylight hours than during hours of darkness. The methods of patrol should therefore be modified depending upon the time of day, the type of beat, and the conditions under which the patrol takes place.

Beat Patrol—General Procedures   After clearing by radio for patrol, the patrol officer's first activity at the beginning of a tour of duty should ordinarily be a quick inspection of the conditions on the beat. This will give the officer a general picture of any unusual matter that may demand immediate attention.

Once this initial inspection has been made, you should direct your efforts toward more careful observation of those areas where the crime hazards are greatest. You should patrol your beats irregularly, often backtracking in a manner which cannot be predicted by the criminal. Your speed should not be so fast that you have little opportunity to observe, and not so slow as to obstruct traffic. Speeds of 15 to 25 miles per hour are recommended under normal conditions.

A substantial part of the time should be devoted to foot patrol in areas where inspections can best be made on foot. Officers should remain within hearing distance of their radios whenever possible if they leave their cars; however, if you have access to a portable radio and can utilize your mobile receivers and transmitters as relays, you can maintain communications with their dispatchers although you may be a considerable distance from your unit.

Inspections of Exposed Places—General Patrol officers should concentrate their repressive patrol efforts upon those places which have experienced the highest incidence of crime. Car lots are especially vulnerable to thefts and should be inspected frequently. Places which contain large numbers of undesirables, including criminals, prostitutes, gamblers, bookmakers, narcotic users or peddlers, potential street muggers, and purse snatchers, should receive special attention. Bars, pool halls, cheap eating places, etc., often attract such persons. Areas which have a high concentration of businesses that are exposed to criminal attack, such as liquor stores, small markets, service stations, and other small businesses, should be inspected regularly.

Considerable time should be spent in areas where bus depots or major transfer points for travelers are located. Stores keeping valuable merchandise in display cases exposed to window smashers, shoplifters, and other thieves should receive a good deal of the officer's attention. The mere presence of an officer in the vicinity has a deterrent effect upon potential criminals.

Action should be taken immediately when criminal acts are observed in such places, unless the circumstances are such that different tactics are indicated. Sometimes it is better if uniformed officers give the impression that they did not notice a particular act which may indicate that prostitution, bookmaking, or some other vices are taking place. Plainclothes investigators are often better able to make the investigation. In such cases where an immediate arrest is considered inadvisable, the evidence obtained and the observations made should be brought to the attention of the concerned investigators.

Inspection of Closed Business Premises In an attempt to suppress criminal activity, every patrol officer should make it a part of the daily patrol routine to inspect the business establishments on the beat. Learn where safes and cash registers are located so that if they are not in their usual location at any given time, you may be alerted to possible criminal activity.

If you are assigned to night duty, you should become familiar with the location of night lights so that you can investigate if the lights are turned off. You should acquaint yourself with the alarm system used in large businesses and the area it serves so that you may be alerted to possible criminal activity in a particular part of the establishment should the alarm sound. You should know the locations of entrances, exits, windows, gratings, and skylights, and the means of securing these against intruders.

You should become familiar with the habits of employees in arriving and leaving their places of business. You should know when businesses open and close so that you can assess any unusual activities around them at other times. You should learn what type of operations the businesses are engaged in so that you will be able to recognize possible illegal practices carried on in connection with ordinary operations. Bookmaking, gambling, numbers rackets, etc., are often carried on in connection with normal business in bars, barber shops, industrial plants, and the like.

During hours of darkness especially, and during hours when businesses are closed, you should exercise great vigilance in inspecting these establishments to prevent burglaries, thefts, and other crimes. To do this, doors, windows, and other accessible areas where illegal entries may be made should be examined. Use your spotlight extensively for this purpose. Suspicious conditions should be investigated carefully to determine if the premises are being or have been attacked. Assistance should be summoned if signs of forced entry or other circumstances indicate the presence of a criminal. A supervisor should also be notified promptly if a search appears necessary. Until assistance arrives, station yourself in a strategic location where you can make an arrest if the criminal tries to leave.

When enough assistance arrives to secure the outside of the building and to make the necessary search of the interior, this should be done in a systematic, methodical manner. When appropriate, notify the proprietor. Open doors or windows should be closed and secured, if possible, and a note should be left in a conspicuous place to tell the proprietor of the action taken if immediate notification is not necessary. A detailed discussion of building searches is contained in Chapter 10.

Inspections of Places Open for Business   It is difficult to stop the criminal who attacks a victim on the spur of the moment when the opportunity presents itself. The criminal who goes to great lengths to case an establishment and make meticulous plans for attacking it can frequently be thwarted by the patrol officer inspecting the premises.

Liquor stores, large markets, and the like usually are lucrative targets for robbers during business hours. The patrol officer assigned to a beat which includes such businesses particularly exposed to criminal attack should contact the persons in charge to advise them of the inspections that will be made from time to time. They should be asked to notify the police if suspicious persons are observed loitering around the store or in the parking lot, and should be asked to record descriptions of any suspicious persons and license numbers and descriptions of their cars. These should be turned over to the police. Many burglaries and robberies have been solved and much property recovered as the result of such leads.

Officers making inspections during regular business hours should assume that if they walk carelessly into the premises during a holdup, they are in an extremely dangerous situation. Almost invariably, robbers have dangerous weapons, and they are usually willing to use them to avoid apprehension. The officer should therefore always take precautions to avoid becoming the victim of a robber.

Upon arriving at an establishment, the patrol officer should park nearby but out of sight of the office or entrance. Notify your dispatcher of the inspection before leaving the police unit so that if you are not heard from in a short time, a backup unit can be dispatched. Remove the ignition key from the car when you leave it.

Observe the parking lots and streets immediately adjacent to the premises for any suspicious vehicles. You should be especially alert for a single person in a car parked where there are easy exits to a street, or parked on the street in a position where other vehicles cannot block it. The front and rear license plates should be compared, and the number recorded. License plates difficult to read because of mud, plates that have numbers changed with tape, rear plates that are bent to make reading difficult, loose plates, those attached with wire for ease in detaching, a bug-splattered plate on the rear, or a rear plate without a current registration tab should be viewed with great suspicion. Such conditions may indicate that the car or plates are stolen.

If you are in a one-man unit, when you find such suspicious conditions, check the license number to find out if it is stolen. You should then request assistance before investigating the interior of the building further. You should be alert for suspicious persons who may be lookouts for a robbery or who may be casing the store. If observed, they should be kept under surveillance, if possible, until assistance arrives.

Every business inspection of this type should be made with caution. The officer should not be lulled into complacency by the routine nature of this activity. Officers often tend to become careless especially when nothing suspicious has been observed on the outside of the building. When this happens, you place yourself in a position where you might be cut down by a bandit's bullets before you can protect yourself.

The precautionary measures that officers take will depend in large part on what they have observed outside the building. Obviously, if your suspicions have not been aroused there, your approach and entry will be somewhat different than when something has been observed that leads them to believe the establishment is being held up. Detailed procedures for deploying at the scene of a robbery in progress are described in Chapter 10.

If there is reasonable cause to believe a crime is taking place, officers should take a vantage point from which they can cover the exits and observe the interior of the premises without being observed. From this position, you should carefully inspect the interior to determine if everything appears normal. If so, two officers should enter, leaving at least one outside to observe in the event that the other officers are taken hostage by the bandits. You should keep separate, with weapons ready.

The actions of all persons inside should be looked upon with suspicion until it is determined otherwise. A known employee may be forced by a bandit to signify that all is well. If there is the least suspicion that this is the case, the officer should ask the employee to step over to talk. In this way you can ascertain whether or not anything is wrong. An employee may say nothing to the officer to indicate that he or she is being held up, but the employee's actions may reveal that he or she is. In such cases you should not indicate that you have seen anything out of order but should leave the premises, arm yourselves with your shotguns, take positions of advantage, and wait for the suspects to leave. When they do, you can apprehend them at a place where gunfire will not jeopardize the safety of innocent customers.

Investigations of Persons   Persons loitering around bus stations, stores, banks, or other places where business is transacted should be investigated if their conduct or presence appears suspicious. Persons who loiter around schools or playgrounds where children play, without apparent business, should receive special attention. Potential molesters should always be the object of the patrol officer's attention.

Persons observed under suspicious circumstances in unusual places at unusual times, such as in alleyways, on dark streets, or in residential areas, should be asked to explain the reason for their presence. Prowlers who are potential burglars, muggers, or peeping toms are frequently apprehended by such inquiries. Each time patrol officers investigate persons who have come to their attention under suspicious circumstances, they should be aware that the people may be committing a crime, have just committed one, or be wanted for one.

Persons peddling merchandise or soliciting subscriptions or alms or otherwise engaged in canvassing in business establishments or residential areas should be checked to determine the legality of their activities. Any necessary action should be taken to keep such persons from engaging in schemes to bilk the public.

When patrol officers observe large crowds, they should determine the reason for the gathering. If it is illegal or if conditions suggest that a civil disorder is likely, you should notify your superiors promptly and summon assistance to preserve order and prevent the commission of crimes. Groups should be discouraged from gathering unlawfully or loitering on the streets. Whatever enforcement action is needed to prevent illegal activities or those which lead to delinquency should be taken.

Lost children or adults and mentally deficient persons unable to care for themselves should be taken to the police station. Stranded or destitute persons or those in need of special aid should be referred to appropriate public or private agencies for assistance.

Observation of Vehicles   One of the commonest serious crimes is the theft of vehicles. Often stolen vehicles are used in connection with other crimes. Vehicles should therefore receive special attention from the patrol officer. Those which contain persons or materials which arouse your suspicions should be investigated, as should those parked near banks, small stores, or markets or in any unusual location with the motors running or under suspicious circumstances. A registration check should be made when time permits to determine if the license plates attached to the vehicle are registered to it.

Patrol on Foot   The basic techniques of patrol are much the same whether it is done on foot or in a vehicle; however, a much more detailed inspection is possible on foot than from a car. Observations between buildings or in narrow passageways ordinarily cannot be made satisfactorily from a vehicle. Therefore, the radio car officer should spend a good deal of time patrolling on foot in those areas where crimes are most prevalent and where detailed, close observations are suggested. Officers can often use the spotlight of their car to good advantage in lighting these areas while they are making inspections.

During the daytime, the officers on foot should make themselves conspicuous, unless for some reason they have to patrol covertly. Visible patrol, whether on foot or in a vehicle, is preventive since it makes the public aware of the constant presence of the police. This has a tendency to deter criminal activity.

Ordinarily the officer patrolling on foot should walk near the curb of the sidewalk. This position gives the officer a better view of both sides of the street. Walking near the buildings along the sidewalk may at times be indicated, for example if a suspect is placed under surveillance. Ordinarily this is rather difficult during the daytime when the officer is in uniform, but at night, officers can observe persons quite effectively if they walk on the inside portions of the sidewalk where they can quickly step into a doorway or shadow to avoid being seen.

Most of the tenets of beat patrol are applicable to foot patrol at any time of day, but it is especially important that officers practice them when they are on foot at night. You should vary your coverage of an area so that your movements cannot be predicted by a criminal. At times, you should backtrack and patrol irregularly, just as you would in a vehicle. Often you should just stand quietly and inconspicuously in shadows to listen and observe.

You should check doors of business establishments by firmly and quietly turning the doorknobs and pushing to determine if they are securely locked. The noise caused by shaking the door may alert burglars inside a building and allow them to conceal themselves until the officer moves on. The glass in doors and windows should also be examined to see if panes have been removed by an intruder.

The officer should watch for any evidence that a burglar has gained entrance to a building by a fire escape, through the roof, or by way of a ground ladder that may have been pulled down by a rope, pole, or wire. Ladders leaning against buildings, boxes or materials piled against walls, or ropes hanging from roofs may have been used by a burglar to get into the building through the roof or skylight.

The officer should also be alert for evidence that boxes or materials piled against a building may conceal a hole in the wall. Jewelry, liquor, and fur stores are often entered by tunnel jobs. Tunnels may start from an outside wall or come up through the floor from an adjoining building. The officer should therefore not only carefully observe the outside of establishments which deal in expensive merchandise, but peer through the windows for any indications that an entry has been gained by tunneling. Misplaced furniture, showcases, or boxes placed against walls may indicate that a burglary is in progress or has occurred. When lights which are ordinarily left on are out, the officer should become suspicious and should try to determine the reasons.

When a crime of this nature is discovered while it is in progress, the officer should not try to enter the building alone and apprehend the perpetrator. Even though there is good reason to believe that a victim's life is in immediate danger, an officer may create a bigger problem by entering alone. Rather, officers should summon assistance by radio, if available, or by telephone and wait in a strategic location where they can observe until assistance arrives. They can then deploy the assisting officers at exits such as fire escapes, windows, etc., before an attempt is made to apprehend the suspect inside (see Chapter 10).

Patrol Hazards

Patrol officers on foot should always be alert for an attack. You should stand quietly and listen before turning a blind corner or entering an alley. You should be especially vigilant at night in alleys, behind buildings, in parking lots, or in other dark places where you may find it necessary to patrol. Sometimes an attempt will be made to lure them into such isolated areas so that you may be attacked by criminals waiting there in ambush.

By walking toward oncoming traffic, you will be better able to protect yourself from injuries which might be inflicted upon you —intentionally or unintentionally—by approaching vehicles or by persons in them. Officers on foot have been injured and killed by intoxicated motorists. They have also been injured by objects thrown at them from passing vehicles.

Patrolling officers should avoid silhouetting themselves against a lighted background when they approach a suspect or a potentially hazardous location to make an investigation. An attacker who is using firearms or thrown missiles against an officer is much less likely to succeed if the officer blends with the background instead of being silhouetted against it. Officers should take advantage of shadows, doorways, bushes, or other hiding places when they wish to observe without being seen.

An officer in a one-man motorized unit should not leave his or her vehicle to make investigations, issue citations, or handle other police incidents without first notifying the dispatcher of the location and the type of activity to be performed. If officers are out of service for longer than approximately ten minutes, they should communicate again with their dispatcher. This procedure is a safety precaution so that assistance may be dispatched if officers are off the air for an extended period and do not respond to the dispatcher's coded signal inquiring about their safety. When they return to their vehicle after disposing of a particular matter, they should promptly notify the dispatcher that they are back in service and again available for call.

Defensive Driving

Officers driving automobiles have much to occupy them. Under ordinary conditions, the operation of a motor vehicle requires full, undivided attention; however, the very nature of the patrol officer's duties makes it necessary not only to drive but to observe people, things, and incidents at the same time. Consequently, officers are exposed to many hazards under conditions which increase the probability of their becoming involved in traffic accidents. They must compensate for these added hazards by driving defensively.

They must make allowances for the lack of driving skill of other motorists. They must try to anticipate driving mistakes of others so that they may avoid becoming traffic accident statistics. Defensive drivers train themselves to notice those conditions that may affect them and to recognize accident-producing situations far enough in advance to take necessary preventive action to avoid a collision.

Driving a vehicle is not just steering it. Drivers must constantly observe persons and things around them that are potential hazards. They must decide what they must do to prevent a driving conflict if they are to drive efficiently and safely. This consciousness of things and occurrences around you and an awareness of how they affect you is the process of perception described in Chapter 2. As was noted there, the ability to perceive efficiently vitally affects almost everything an officer does. It plays a particularly significant role in the way the officer operates a motor vehicle.

Mechanics of Driving Perception   It might be well to briefly review the process of perception. The brain interprets the images and stimuli transmitted to it by the eyes and other senses. Such interpretations will not result in meaningful responses unless the observer is paying attention to these images. They may be meaningless when the brain is preoccupied with other things. Because of this, a driver might see dangerous objects, but the brain might not interpret them as such. A driver may therefore not respond quickly enough to avoid an accident.

Perception does not only involve the mechanical processes of seeing, hearing, smelling, tasting, touching, or movement. It includes mental awareness and possibly some degree of understanding of the observations made. Consequently, drivers who allow their attention to be distracted by matters not related to their driving will soon become involved in a collision.

Most driving perception is based upon observations which start with the central vision. This is the narrow central cone of vision which enables a person to identify the details of things observed. Fringe or peripheral vision involves the upper, lower, or side visions. It precedes central vision. When you see an object or event out of the corner of your eye, you can focus your central vision on it to identify detail. The image then can be interpreted by the brain.

Training in Driving Perception   Drivers can train themselves to perceive efficiently by constantly being alert for and observing those things that affect them on the road. They should develop their powers of observation through fringe vision by moving their eyes frequently. They can learn to see potentially dangerous objects and happenings from the sides or above without having to focus attention on specific objects too often. Although it is necessary to fix central vision on objects for detailed identification, drivers should avoid focusing their whole attention on one object for an extended time. If they do, they will find themselves staring. This is called fixation of vision. It will result in fatigue and inattention, and will often be accompanied by daydreaming and preoccupation.

Fixation of vision may start in as little as two seconds. Almost every motorist has experienced the tranquilizing effect of watching the white lines on streets or the hood emblem for extended periods of time. You soon become almost hypnotized, with the result that your attention becomes distracted from your driving. You then become a candidate for a dangerous collision since your mind is no longer interpreting the images transmitted by the senses.

Expert drivers avoid staring. Instead, they train themselves to glance quickly at objects, to focus their visual attention on detail for only short periods of time, and to avoid staring at objects around them. They learn what to look for. They train themselves to look at the total traffic picture rather than to focus their attention on only fragments of it. They concentrate their observations on matters directly related to their driving. These procedures of effective perception require discrimination. Drivers must be selective in their observations since the mind cannot be aware of everything. Drivers must concentrate on objects only in proportion to their relative importance or they will eventually be in a traffic accident.

Accident-Producing Hazards The main physical accident-producing hazards are pedestrians, objects, and other vehicles. Pedestrians are especially vulnerable to injury or death if they are struck by or run into moving vehicles. Even a slight, low-speed bump may cause serious injury if the pedestrian's head strikes the pavement. The officer must watch out for persons—especially children—stepping into the roadway from behind parked vehicles, bushes, or other obstructions. Persons leaving parked vehicles often open the doors of their vehicles without realizing the hazards they cause. If animals dart into the roadway, a driver may react unconsciously and swerve into a head-on collision with fatal results. At high speed on narrow roadways, drivers should steel themselves to strike a small animal rather than to swerve off the road or into oncoming traffic. Even a collision with an animal as large as a deer is less dangerous than a head-on accident with another vehicle. Many of these are fatal.

Fixed objects such as high curbs, low pipes which cannot easily be seen, chains across driveways or entrances to alleys or parking lots, drainage dips, and other barriers may cause considerable damage to vehicles if they are struck at even low speeds. Front-end alignment and tires can be easily damaged by impact with curbs, standpipes, or other fixed objects. The officer should be constantly alert for these hazards especially during periods of low visibility in or around parking lots and alleys at night. The extensive damage to vehicles caused by even low-speed impacts with such objects may mean taking the car out of service for expensive repairs for many days.

Other moving vehicles are the most frequent cause of traffic accidents involving patrol officers. They must watch for sudden or unexpected movements of vehicles ahead, behind, approaching from the opposite direction, approaching from an angle, passing, or being passed. Bicycle riders are particularly dangerous. Although damage to a patrol car which collides with a bicycle is usually slight, the rider is often seriously injured. Children are especially vulnerable to injury when they ride their bicycles in the street. Their actions are often most unpredictable. Patrol officers therefore must be on the alert for the unexpected when they patrol in an area frequented by bicyclists.

Hazard Factors in Defensive Driving   Four major factors must be considered by a defensive driver. The first of these is self-induced. It involves driving with a physical impairment—drowsiness. The other three are the position of the other vehicle, the movement of other drivers which might cause an accident, and the defensive action that can be taken to avoid a collision.

When drowsiness sets in and drivers continue to operate their vehicles, they are foolhardy. It usually is only a matter of time until they become traffic accident statistics. The extreme danger of this condition must be recognized, and simple remedial action taken. Usually the symptoms are treated by opening the windows, stopping the car and walking around it several times, or drinking a stimulant such as coffee. When drowsiness results from physical fatigue, the cause should be treated rather than the symptoms. Usually the condition will not occur if the officer gets enough rest and sleep before reporting for duty.

When another vehicle is ahead—either standing or moving—it becomes a potential cause of a traffic accident if it suddenly starts, slows, stops, backs, or changes lanes to the right or left. If it is standing, it may be a hazard to the officer who is preoccupied with other things, is inattentive, or miscalculates distances.

Tailgaiting, or following too closely, is a frequent cause of accidents. The officer would thus be well advised to avoid following other vehicles very closely. A rule of thumb that provides a reasonable safety margin to a driver following another car is to allow *at least* one car length between your car and the one being followed for each 10 miles per hour you are traveling on dry pavement. On wet pavement, this distance should be *at least* doubled.

You should watch traffic well ahead for conditions which might cause a driver in front of you to stop suddenly. Rear-end collisions at speeds as low as 5 miles per hour can cause damage costing several hundred dollars to repair and give rise to costly lawsuits if whiplash or other injuries result. Drivers of vehicles striking others from the rear are almost invariably responsible for the collision.

An officer operating a patrol unit is not often troubled by other vehicles following too closely, although inattentive, intoxicated, or careless drivers approaching from the rear have caused many serious collisions with stopped police units. Officers can usually avoid being struck from the rear when they are moving by glancing into the rearview mirror frequently and noting the positions of vehicles behind. Signals indicating slowing or stopping should be given well in advance. Gently pump the foot brake to cause the brake lights to flash. This will often attract the attention of an inattentive motorist behind. Every attempt should be made to give such drivers a reasonable opportunity to respond as necessary. Slow, gradual stops indicate attentive driving. If a stop in traffic is necessary, be sure that the vehicle does not roll backward and cause a hazard to other traffic.

Oncoming vehicles are perhaps the greatest of all traffic hazards because of the extremely high incidence of traffic fatalities resulting from head-on collisions. *Almost any defensive action to prevent such a collision is warranted.*

Vehicles approaching from the opposite direction and straddling the center line or making turns in violation of another driver's right-of-way are responsible for a high percentage of the fatal and injury traffic accidents. Right-of-way is generally interpreted to mean the right to the immediate use of the highway. Failure of oncoming drivers to lower their headlight beams also is a factor contributing to many accidents.

To avoid these hazards, the officer should keep to the extreme right-hand side of the roadway to maintain clearance and stop if necessary. The mere fact that a driver has a right under the law to the immediate use of the road does not mean that that driver should insist upon that right at the cost of a traffic accident. The defensive driver should not rely upon turn signals given by other motorists. Turning blinkers are often left in operation unknowingly. Their operation does not necessarily signify what the driver intends to do.

High beams should not ordinarily be used in heavily traveled or well-lighted areas, although many motorists carelessly drive with them in operation. Drivers approaching such a vehicle should lower their beams as a signal for the approaching motorist to do likewise. They should also direct their vision away from the center of the oncoming lights and to the right side of the road to avoid the glare and retain full vision. They should reduce their speed if they are troubled by "light blindness."

When other vehicles approaching from an angle turn into or cut across the patrol officer's course, or back from a parking area or alleyway in front of him, the officer should be prepared to yield the right-of-way—especially at intersections, alleys and driveways—to prevent an accident even when the law favors the officer. Prudence should dictate that patrol officers look both ways twice before entering an intersection where traffic conflicts may occur. Often, the first glance does not reveal a hazard which is observed upon the second look.

When other vehicles which are attempting to pass cut in front of police units too fast, officers should reduce their speed or move to the right if necessary to avoid a collision. Police vehicles moving slower than the normal flow of traffic should be driven in the right-hand portion of the road so that the hazards arising from other vehicles passing on the right may be reduced. The statement that drivers who are being passed repeatedly on the right are driving in the wrong lane should be kept in mind. Furthermore, when a police vehicle is patrolling slower than the normal flow of traffic, other vehicles tend to pile up behind. The result—congestion and irritation to other motorists.

When other motorists increase their speed to prevent being passed or turn or change lanes so that they conflict with the passing police vehicle, and enforcement action is not indicated, officers should reduce their speed and allow the other drivers to move ahead. Appropriate signals should be given by the patrol officer who is preparing to pass to notify other drivers of the impending movement. You should pass only after it appears that the other vehicle will not turn in front of you and become a hazard. You should glance at the left or right front tire of the car being passed, depending upon which side you are passing, to determine if its angle indicates that the car is starting to turn.

In passing parked cars, the officer on patrol should watch for signs that they are about to start moving—possibly into a traffic lane. Persons sitting in the driver's seat, front wheels turned out toward traffic lanes, vehicles with lights on or motors running as indicated by the exhaust, should alert the officer to a potential hazard.

Nothing can be more disconcerting than to have a car door suddenly open directly in the path of the patrol vehicle. This can be avoided if officers maintain the proper distance between their vehicles and those stopped at or near the curb. When this cannot be done because of the condition of traffic or narrow streets, reduced speed will usually be indicated.

Defensive Driving Rules

The foregoing discussion of defensive driving practices would suggest several rules which will make the patrol officer's driving not only more pleasant but vastly safer.

Looking Ahead   Drivers should look as far ahead as possible in their lane of travel so that they may notice conditions which may require a reaction on their part. Likewise, when turning, look as far ahead, around a corner or up a side street, as possible.

The road should be scanned at least a full block ahead in normal city driving and up to one-half mile ahead on the open road so that the driver may be aware of hazards, such as accidents, excavations, rocks, traffic delays, animals, and the like, in time to avoid becoming involved in a collision. Scan the roadway from side to side. Keep your eyes moving—about every two seconds—to avoid a hypnotizing effect. A particular object should not be watched for a period much longer than that. Observations not related to driving should be made by quick glances when necessary.

As has been previously indicated, the driver should avoid looking directly into approaching headlights but should look to the side of the roadway to avoid being blinded by glare. Drivers should not "overdrive" their headlights; i.e., they should not drive so fast at night that they could not stop or take evasive action safely *within their range of visibility* if the need suddenly arose.

Driving in One Lane   Drivers should drive in the center of the lane. They should avoid hugging either side. On roads with two or more driving lanes on each side of the center strip, they should drive in the right lane when it is safe to do so. Veering sharply to avoid objects is extremely dangerous. The danger can be avoided, or at least reduced, if the driver looks ahead and is prepared for emergencies.

The vehicle should be driven at a constant speed if possible when lane changes are made. Passing or changing lanes should be avoided at intersections, hillcrests, and curves.

Planning Turns   When making a turn, the driver should look as far ahead as possible in the direction of the turn to see if the turn will interfere with other motorists. Turns to the right should be made from as near the right-hand curb or edge of the roadway as practicable. The turn should be made into the right-hand lane of the street onto which the turn is made. Left turns likewise should be made from the left-hand lane into a left-hand lane. They should be made from a turning lane if one is provided or as near as practicable to the center of the roadway if there is only one opposing lane in each direction. When the intersection is free of cars or pedestrians which might become a hazard, the turn may be made safely and smoothly from the center of the intersection after yielding to all approaching traffic, which constitutes an immediate hazard. Be aware of the speed and distance of oncoming traffic. It is better to err by waiting for approaching motorists and allowing sufficient time and clearance before starting the turn than by attempting to make it in front of a potential hazard. The front wheels should be kept pointed straight ahead until the turn is actually started. If they are turned to the left while you are waiting for oncoming traffic to pass and your vehicle is struck from behind, it will be forced into the path of the oncoming traffic.

Intersection Hazards   Look at the left side, the right side, the left, and again the right before entering an intersection. The second look often reveals things not seen at first. Keep looking to the left, right, and front while continuing through intersections. Blind intersections—those which do not afford clear vision for at least 100 feet to the left and right from 100 feet back—constitute dangers to which the patrol officer should be especially alert. Proceed slowly as you observe around and beyond buildings, bushes, parked cars, and other obstructions.

At signal-controlled intersections, you should proceed only when the light in your direction has changed to green and then only after other cars waiting alongside proceed if they block your view to the left or right. In all cases you should be alert for pedestrians who may be crossing the street in front of other cars which may be blocking your view.

The mere existence of traffic-control lights or signals at an intersection is no guarantee of safety to a motorist entering the intersection even though the motorist does so lawfully. Neither can it be safely assumed that other drivers will stop before entering a roadway from an alley or driveway.

Use of the Hands   The fingertips of the left hand should be used to move the turning blinker lever. The left arm may occasionally be used to supplement the turning blinkers. If you doubt that the automatic blinkers are operating properly or that they are visible to other drivers, arm signals should be used.

The steering wheel should be gripped with the left thumb when the fingers of the left hand are used to actuate the turning blinker lever. The hands should usually grip the wheel at the two and ten o'clock positions so that they balance each other and provide the best control. Sharp turns should be made by turning the steering wheel in a hand-over-hand fashion for maximum control.

Starting and Backing   Most vehicles equipped with automatic transmissions will not start with the shifting lever in the drive or reverse positions. Occasionally, because of maladjustment of the shifting mechanism, they will start and lurch forward or backward dangerously when the shifting mechanism is in a neutral position. They should therefore be started with the shifting lever in the park position and the emergency brake fully engaged. When the motor starts, all gauges should be checked for proper oil pressure, fuel, etc. When shifting into gear, the driver should firmly depress the brake pedal, shift, then release the parking brake before moving.

In backing the vehicle directly to the rear, you should look to the rear over your right shoulder. When backing to the left, you should look over your left shoulder and in other directions for hazards.

Braking and Accelerating   When stopping the vehicle, the driver should center the ball of the right foot on the brake pedal and press firmly but smoothly. Ease the pressure slightly just before the vehicle stops, then reapply it for smoothest performance. When the vehicle is stopped or parked, the emergency brake should be applied fully. The shifting lever should be put into the park position. This will keep the car from moving if the brakes release as they cool. As an added precaution against a runaway police car, the front wheels should be turned sharply inward to the curb if the vehicle is parked facing downhill. If it is parked facing uphill, the front wheels should be cramped sharply outward so that they back into the curb.

When you are manipulating the accelerator, rest the heel of the foot on the floor beside the accelerator, depending upon its location in a particular vehicle. Soft eggshell pressure should be applied for smoothest and most economical operation.

Emergency Vehicle Operation

Every year, several thousand serious traffic accidents occur between motorists and patrol officers driving vehicles under emergency conditions. The motorists do not heed the red or other colored emergency light and siren or do not see or hear them. The patrol officer driving under emergency conditions with a colored light properly displayed and a siren in operation often believes that the siren is clearly audible to others. This is not the case. While some motorists respond by stopping or yielding to the emergency vehicle when they hear the siren, many others do not. Either they do not hear the sound or they stop in traffic and become a hazard to the emergency vehicle and to other motorists. The material presented in this chapter is limited to problems of driving in response to emergency calls. The techniques of pursuit driving are treated in Chapter 8.

Siren Audibility   Tests have revealed that siren audibility—especially to oncoming motorists and to those around a corner from the emergency vehicle—is extremely limited. The sound does not bend around curves or corners. Buildings and other solid objects deflect the waves so that they don't always warn motorists approaching from side streets or around curves. Bushes, trees, hills, etc., tend to absorb the sound and muffle it so that around-the-corner audibility is sometimes poor.

Traffic conditions may make it impossible for other motorists to drive to the right-hand side of the roadway to yield to the emergency vehicle even if they see the red light and hear the siren. Traffic noises, radios, rolled up windows, normal conversations, and motor and other sounds distract and blunt the alertness of the average motorist to approaching emergency vehicles. Flashing neon signs and advertisements of all kinds compete with the red light of the police car for the motorist's attention. With all this, one assumes that the average motorist has normal perception. Many, however, do not. Operator's licenses may be secured—even under the most restrictive laws—by persons whose sight and hearing are exceedingly poor.

Tests made by the Los Angeles Police Department, the California Highway Patrol, and other agencies[1] revealed that the siren of the emergency vehicle could not be heard at times until the emergency vehicle's front bumper was even with the rear bumper of the car ahead. Even when drivers are alert for siren sounds and concentrate on hearing them, they usually can't until the car approaching from the rear is within six car lengths. These conditions are seldom duplicated on the highways when other motorists are not necessarily concentrating on the conditions under which they are driving in the way they were in the tests.

Patrol officers on emergency calls often make the dangerous assumption that other motorists will comply with the law and yield to the emergency vehicle. Sometimes, however, even though the red

---

[1] Los Angeles Police Department, "How to Operate a Motor Vehicle under Emergency Conditions," *Daily Training Bulletin*, vol. 1, no. 54, 1949, pp. 105–12; Paul Ditzel, "The Risks of Rescue," *Westways Magazine of the Southern California Automobile Club*, March 1969, p. 7.

light is clearly visible to them and they are easily able to hear the siren, motorists do not respond because they sometimes believe that officers are prone to use their emergency equipment when there is no valid justification for doing so. They have been heard to say about a passing police car with red light and siren in operation, "Just another police officer going to lunch." They may intentionally refuse to yield the right-of-way because they have been led to believe that most emergency calls are not really urgent. Such attitudes can have fatal effects if they cause the motorist to be indecisive for even a split second.

The foregoing suggests that patrol officers refrain from driving with their red light and siren activated whenever possible. They should never rely upon it to protect them from other drivers and should not use it unless they have notified their dispatcher of the necessity for doing so in an emergency situation. The dispatcher can then alert other police, fire, rescue, or ambulance units in the area of the existence of such emergency and can exercise some control over the number of vehicles utilizing their emergency equipment at the same time in the same area. Officers can be of no value in a real emergency if they are involved in a traffic accident along the way.

Legal Aspects of Emergency Driving   The laws of most states clearly impose a responsibility upon the drivers of emergency vehicles to drive with due regard for the safety of others using the highways. Even though they are on an assigned emergency call and may be, under the law, privileged to violate the rules of the road, they are civilly and possibly criminally responsible if they cause injury to others through arbitrary exercise of that privilege. This is the law regardless of the officer's good motives. What is considered an arbitrary exercise of the privilege to violate the rules of the road under emergency conditions depends upon the facts of each incident.

It is thus apparent that officers should seriously consider how reasonable a jury might later think their actions were under the circumstances. They should govern their driving habits accordingly with common sense and reasonableness. There is no formula for determining reasonableness. Each case must be decided on its own merit.[2] Officers not only have a legal responsibility to other motorists, but also have a responsibility to their organization to avoid any action which will tend to reflect adversely upon it.

[2] *Go-Bart v. United States,* 282 U.S. 344, 75 L. Ed. 374 (1931).

Driving Conflicts   Many emergency call collisions occur at intersections. This suggests that exceptional caution should be exercised by the driver of an emergency vehicle on approaching them. Even with the green light in your favor, you cannot allow yourself to rely upon your red light and siren for protection. When you enter against the red light, you are exposed to exceptional hazards and should reduce your speed accordingly. Some cities have installed traffic signals which can be automatically regulated by emergency vehicles. These have not been perfected to a point where they can give any assurance of safety to the patrol officer. In fact, the contrary is probably true—they tend to give a false sense of security.

Between intersections and in open areas, the police car should be driven near the center of the road so that oncoming drivers will see the emergency lights approaching. Officers should avoid passing other cars on the right except when no other course is open to them and then only after they have turned off their siren. You should proceed with extreme caution even when you are reasonably certain that the car being passed will not turn to the right in your path. The only safe assumption that the driver of a vehicle should make— especially when it is being operated under emergency conditions— is that other motorists do not see the vehicle or the red light or hear the siren, and that if it is possible for them to do the unexpected, they'll do it!

Use of Siren   When use of the siren is justified, it should be operated so the sound fluctuates from a low to a high pitch throughout its tone scale. If kept at a high, wailing pitch, the constant intensity will become inaudible to many drivers or will be confused with radio or other high sounds. In either case the result is the same— the motorist will fail to heed its warning and may cause a disastrous collision. Where traffic conflict might occur, the siren should be activated early enough to give drivers and pedestrians a reasonable opportunity to yield the right-of-way to the emergency vehicle.

Officers should avoid sounding a siren suddenly when they are right behind another vehicle or immediately before they enter an intersection. Even under ideal conditions, motorists often cannot immediately determine the direction of travel or the position of the emergency vehicle and therefore have a tendency to react slowly. When they suddenly hear a siren close to them, they may be so startled by it that they will swerve to the right or left, or stop suddenly in the emergency vehicle's path.

Summary

The patrol officer is responsible for the maintenance of good order on a beat, the protection of persons, their property, and welfare, and the prevention of crime. In order for officers to best accomplish this mission, they must acquaint themselves with those hazards that spawn crime and attempt to rid the community of them. Officers are also responsible for rendering a high level of service to the public. To do so, they must familiarize themselves with available services in the community where a person in need of assistance may be referred when they cannot provide the service themselves.

Before officers begin a tour of duty, they should review the current information about incidents that have occurred on their beats during preceding watches. Pin maps, crime summaries, and discussions with other officers will provide them with such intelligence.

They should completely examine their vehicle before taking it onto the streets. This inspection will enable them to determine if new damage on it has been properly reported, if the car is in safe operating order, and if it contains evidence or property concealed by arrestees.

When they arrive at their beat, they should quickly make a general inspection to see if there are problems that require immediate attention. Such problems should be resolved so that the officers may then direct their efforts to other duties. Repressive patrol measures should be directed primarily toward those areas where the greatest crime and accident hazards exist. The patrol officer should patrol these areas irregularly—often backtracking and always avoiding activities that would tend to make their patrol routine and predictable to the criminal.

They should closely observe persons whose activities are unusual and should take action to investigate suspicious conduct. Locations where undesirables congregate should be inspected frequently and enforcement action taken promptly when criminal activities are observed.

Vehicles demand much of their attention because they are often used in the commission of crimes. When patrol officers observe cars parked under suspicious circumstances near markets, liquor stores, or other businesses exposed to crime, they should try to determine if an offense is in progress. If assistance is needed, it should be summoned. When it arrives, a closer investigation should be made to determine what action is indicated. If a robbery or other major crime is taking place, they should arm themselves with their shotguns, take positions of advantage, and apprehend the criminals as they leave the premises.

Persons observed under suspicious circumstances at unusual times and places should be investigated to determine the reasons for their presence. The officer should be aware of the possibility that such persons are committing a crime, have just committed one, or are wanted for one.

Much of your patrol is conducted on foot. The vehicle enables you to move from place to place and cover a wide area, but you should leave it frequently to make inspections in congested areas on foot. The techniques of foot patrol are much like those of mobile patrol. The techniques used in the daytime will vary somewhat from those used at night, but the objectives are much the same. Officers should inspect establishments on their beat to determine if they have been attacked, to apprehend criminals committing offenses, to secure property when necessary, to provide service to persons who require it, and to repress crime.

Always be alert for attack, especially when you patrol alone on foot at night. When you leave your vehicle to make an investigation, you should notify your dispatcher of the reason and the location so that assistance may be sent if you do not clear within a reasonable period.

The duties of radio car patrol officers are such that they must drive their vehicles and, at the same time, observe people, things, and incidents around them. They must therefore adopt those tenets of defensive driving that will enable them to perform their duties and, at the same time, drive safely.

When you operate your vehicle under emergency conditions, you must recognize the limitations of your equipment. If you are to avoid the dangers of driving under such conditions, you must learn to compensate for the driving deficiencies of other motorists. You must learn to anticipate motorists reactions when they see your red light and hear your siren. You must constantly be aware of your liability if you arbitrarily exercise your right to violate the rules of the road when you drive under emergency conditions.

Review

Questions

1. What safety checks of a vehicle should be made before it is taken on patrol?
2. What is preventive patrol?
3. How can preventive patrol best be accomplished?
4. What are some of the physical hazards a beat officer should recognize and report?
5. What evidence would you look for outside a building at night that might indicate a burglary is being or has been committed?
6. What is defensive driving?

7. What are some of the most common types of incidents that cause car damage during routine patrol?
8. What is meant by the term selective patrol?
9. What brings about fixation of vision?
10. How can fixation of vision be prevented?
11. What is the most dangerous assumption commonly made by officers driving their cars under emergency conditions?

Exercises

1. Explain what information patrol officers should familiarize themselves with in preparing for patrol.
2. Explain how an inspection of a vehicle should be made before it is taken on patrol.
3. Describe what patrol officers should know about their beats.
4. Describe what you would do if you observed a person whom you suspect is a "lookout" seated in a car near a large market. The vehicle is in a position giving easy access to the street. The motor is running. You are alone in your radio car.
5. Describe what you would do if you observed a ladder leaning against the wall of a market. It is 2:00 a.m. There are neither cars nor people on the market parking lot. You are alone in your radio car.
6. Describe the hazards officers face when they patrol a beat on foot at night; during the day.
7. How should an officer patrol a beat on foot at night?
8. Describe the techniques of defensive driving.
9. Explain the laws relating to the liability of officers when they drive under emergency conditions.

4

Field Notetaking

A description of much of the work performed by peace officers each day eventually finds its way into a written report. The quality of their performance is not often directly observed by superiors. However, the official reports officers prepare are invariably reviewed, and it is largely from these that their efficiency is formally or informally measured.

If the reports are complete and accurate, it soon becomes apparent to superiors that the officer has developed an effective method of recording the many details of the incidents which he or she is exposed to each day. Usually this is the officer who has made good use of one of the most important tools—the field notebook. It is an officer's unofficial memory.

Notebook

Few officers have cultivated the ability to recall from memory the details of a complex investigation or other police incidents several hours, days, or months later when it becomes necessary to prepare a report, testify in court, or otherwise describe them. You need not record every minute detail about a case in your notebook, but you should record enough data about a particular event to refresh your memory of related facts. You will soon develop a form of shorthand that will mean as much to you as court reporters' notes mean to them. In addition, the mere fact that you are making written notes at the time of an occurrence will tend to impress the details of the incident upon your mind. You will soon learn the type and amount of key information you should record in your notes to give you full recollection. At first, you should record too much detail rather than too little. As your system of notetaking improves with experience, you will tend to record less general information because your ability to discriminate between the important and the nonessential will increase.

Often a police agency will regulate the type of notebook officers must carry. No attempt will be made here to support the bound notebook used by some departments or the loose-leaf type used by others. There are advantages and disadvantages to each. Where an option is given as to the type to be carried, several factors should be considered in making a choice.

Bound Notebook   Bound notebooks prevent loss of pages and are easy to mark and file permanently for future reference. They have the disadvantage of being the subject of scrutiny by a defense counsel if an officer uses them to refresh his memory on the witness stand. Generally the law permits witnesses to use written matter to refresh their memory when they testify, but if such material is used, it must be produced for inspection by the adverse party who may cross-examine the witness upon it and may read it to the jury.

Opponents to the bound notebook maintain that this cross-examination may extend to other matters written in the book. These notes may be a source of embarrassment to officers if they have not been discreet about what they have recorded. However, if prosecutors are alert and protect witnesses as they should, they can object to the reference to such alien written matter on the basis that it is not relevant or material to the issues. The objection will usually be sustained under the rules of relevancy and materiality.[1] Officers should be admonished, however, to use their notebooks only for job-related information to forestall attempts by a defense counsel to use the book to impeach or discredit them when they testify.

Officers can further protect themselves from possible embarrassment by refreshing their memory from their notes before going on the witness stand and not using them while testifying. This is not practicable in some complex cases which do not come to trial until months or years after the notes were made. However, before testifying, officers should carefully review the details of each case written by them when the matter was fresh in their memory. This is the *minimum* testimonial preparation you should make in any case.

Loose-leaf Notebook Proponents of loose-leaf notebooks argue that they are more desirable than bound notebooks as notes can be more easily organized and reorganized if they are loose. It is further argued that the loose-leaf book enables the officer-witness to take to the witness stand only those notes he must use in testifying in that particular case. Confidential information and other data can be removed so the adverse party cannot read it. This sometimes gives a jury an erroneous impression, however, since defense counsel may suggest that the notes have been edited to eliminate those which could have been favorable to the defendant.

Whatever type of notebook is chosen, it should be carried at all times when an officer is on duty. It should therefore be small enough to carry in a shirt or coat pocket. A notebook of the thickness of a deck of playing cards and about 3 by 5 inches will conveniently fit the usual shirt pockets of uniformed officers without detracting from their appearance. If the corners are rounded slightly, they will not as readily wear holes in the pockets.

Notetaking—General Requirements

An officer's notes must be clear, concise, and accurate. They must be written legibly so that the officer and others may read them if necessary. They should be concise but complete enough to cover all the pertinent facts that are necessary to prove a case. Accepted

---

[1] *Relevancy* is that quality of evidence which makes it properly applicable in determining the truth or falsity of the matter at issue before the court. *Materiality* is that characteristic of evidence that gives it a legitimate and effective influence or bearing on the decision of a case.

abbreviations should be used, but a shorthand system not readable by anyone but the writer should be avoided. Fragmentary sentences which may be difficult to recall later without subjective interpretation of the missing parts should likewise be avoided. When witnesses testify from notes made months or years earlier, jurors will often question the accuracy of their testimony if the notes contain only bits of information. The jury will reason that if the witness cannot recall that portion of a case for which he needs his notes to refresh his memory, how can he remember enough to fill in the blank parts by memory alone. This may be false reasoning, but the officer will find it exists in all too many cases.

Who—What—Where—When—Why—How

Notes kept should record accurately the *who, what, where, when, why,* and sometimes the *how* of an incident about which the officer may be required to testify later. This can best be done by the use of short sentences or phrases. The time and date of the event, the correct names and addresses of all persons present or otherwise involved, including officers, suspects, victims, and witnesses, should be recorded. Both residence and business addresses and telephone numbers should be obtained and recorded in most cases.

An exact description of the scene where a crime has occurred and an accurate description of property and vehicles involved are usually necessary for reports and courtroom testimony. These data should include information regarding the condition of a vehicle when it was found, if such condition is pertinent, such as a hot or cold radiator, a clean or dirty windshield, the license, motor or serial number, etc. Booking and report number should be recorded for future reference if an arrest and/or crime report is made.

Personal opinions and conclusions should be left out of the notebook except in those cases where the officer can properly testify to opinion evidence, such as in a case involving a condition of sobriety, intoxication resulting from drugs or alcohol, sounds, speed, etc., or when he is permitted to draw a conclusion from the evidence, such as in cases involving speed determinations from skidmarks, etc.

Who Was Involved A list of suggested descriptive data is included as a guide to describing a person who may be a victim, suspect, witness, or arrestee. Detailed physical descriptions of victims and witnesses often need not be included in reports, as this would serve no useful purpose in the ordinary incident; however, the description of a murder victim might be essential. Some items obviously will be excluded from time to time because they are unnecessary, while others may be added as the need arises. For example, a person may be described as having a deep cleft in the chin, an amputated left hand, and a stiff right leg which causes a pronounced limp. Such a person need not be described in as much detail as a person who is average in most respects and has no unusual characteristics which are attention-getters.

Name: Record in full. Initials should not be used. A wrong name may result in the loss of a case because a witness necessary to the prosecution could not be located. Is the exact name Joan or Joanne, Frank or Francis, etc.? Is the name spelled correctly, i.e., Morisson or Morrison, Myer, Meyer, or Maier? If complete physical identifications are not essential, at least the full names, addresses, and telephone numbers should be obtained from everyone involved in the incident whenever possible. Include victims, persons reporting the incident, those who may provide additional information, police officers at the scene, owner of the property, etc., in this list.

Alias: All known nicknames, monikers, and other assumed names of suspects with their spellings should be included. Suspects can often be identified through the moniker file even though their true names are unknown.

Address: The present and all known past addresses, with approximate dates of residency, of perpetrators of crimes should be recorded. These addresses will help to locate them, should it be necessary, in the future. Business addresses and telephone numbers should be noted, as should the residence telephone numbers of witnesses, victims, and, at times, suspects.

Sex: Record whether the persons involved are male or female. If other than normal, sex characteristics should be indicated, i.e., effeminate, baby face, etc.

Race: Although the races of mankind have never been precisely classified, the common descriptive terms are: Caucasian, Black, Red (American Indian), Oriental, Brown (Indian, Filipino, etc.). Appropriate abbreviations may be used.

National origin: German-American, Russian, Italian-American, Mexican-American, etc.

Place of birth: Address and city if known.

Citizenship: If needed. Original or acquired.

Age: Exact age and date of birth should be given if known. If unknown, an estimate should be given in multiples of five years.

Height: Exact height if known. If estimated, height should be compared with officer's own height. *Small* stature would be 5'0" to 5'3". Medium would be 5'3" to 5'8". Large would be 5'8" and up.

Build: Slender, medium, stout, fat.

Eyes: Color: blue, gray, yellow, hazel, brown, dark brown, black, green. Size: small, large, slanted. Other descriptive characteristics: protruding or sunken, mismatched, bloodshot, sacks.

Hair: Color; straight, wavy, kinky, curly. How combed; thick or thin. Baldness: frontal, occipital, complete, total. Other characteristics: widow's peak, etc.

Complexion: Florid, sallow, pale, fair, dark, pimpled, blotched, freckled.

Visible scars or marks: Those in sight when person is dressed should be described.

Occupation: Means of livelihood, past or present, if pertinent.

Marital status: Married, single, divorced, separated, annulled, widowed, if pertinent.

Head: Large or small; inclined forward, backward, or sideways.

Forehead: High, low, or medium; sloping, bulging, straight; receding hairline.

Eyebrows: Bushy or meeting, slanting—up or down, straight or arched, penciled.

Nose: Small, large; pug, hooked, straight, flat, turned up; nostrils flared or narrow; twisted to right or left.

Mustache: Color, size, shape.

Mouth: Large or small; straight or arched—up or down.

Lips: Thick or thin; puffy; pale, protruding; hair.

Teeth: Large or small; even or uneven; projecting; fillings; missing.

Ears: Small, large; close to head or projecting.

Chin: Small, large; square, full; cleft, dimpled; double.

Face: Long, round, square, full, fat, thin; sunken cheeks; high cheek bones; pockmarked.

Neck: Short or long; thick or thin; adam's apple; puffed; folds in back.

Shoulders: Broad or narrow; erect or stooped; round or square.

Stomach: Flat or bulging; firm or trembling.

Hands: Large or small; fingers short or long; missing.

Posture: Erect or slumping; stooped; hunchback.

Walk: Erect or stooped; slow or fast; long or short stride.

Dress: Hat and shoes: color, style. Suit: color, style; neat, slovenly; conservative, loud. Type of clothing customarily worn: work, sport. Dress: cheap, expensive.

Speech: Slow, rapid; clear, mumbling; impediment. Accent: type, i.e., French, Spanish, Bostonian, etc.

Habits: Clean, dirty; chews, smokes; addicted; any unusual habits.

Diseases: Unusual diseases which would indicate special treatment needs such as deafness, T.B., etc.

Relatives-associates: If known, names and addresses should be recorded to give possible place where person may be located.

Characteristics: Describe any individual traits not covered in above items such as clicks teeth; boisterous and loud, or quiet; talks from side of mouth, etc.

In describing a wanted suspect, those traits or characteristics which distinguish that person from any other and which might serve to identify him or her in a crowd should be stressed. The description should be restricted to actual characteristics. The absence of certain characteristics need not be noted. Attention should be focused on distinctive items which best serve as identification.

What *Happened*   Notes should concern what took place, the sequence of events, the type of property attacked, stolen, lost, etc., the offense or offenses involved, vehicles used, and evidence found. For example, a description of the building attacked should include enough detail to enable the officer to describe it to the satisfaction of a jury as needed. An accurate description of property stolen, lost, or found or otherwise pertinent should be included for later reference. Vehicles or modes of transportation used should be described. Notes about the type of evidence found and its description are essential for later reference.

Where *Did the Incident Occur*   The exact geographical location where the incident happened should be determined and noted. The position in which evidence was found may be vital to show precisely what happened. For example, the pocket in which narcotics were found or the place in the car or room where they were found may be essential in a case involving possession of narcotics in which the arrestee's dominion and control over the evidence is vital to a prosecution. It may be imperative to prove the exact location in which a weapon was found in order to show that a homicide resulted from a criminal act rather than a suicide or accident. It may be essential to show precisely where a crime took place in order to prove jurisdiction and to show which agency is responsible for the prosecution. In burglary cases, it may be necessary to prove the point of entry and departure as circumstantial evidence that the perpetrator entered a building with the necessary burglarious intent. In a traffic accident case, the precise location of a witness who claims to have observed the parties involved before the collision may be of value in assessing the credibility of such a person as a witness. Sometimes his position at the time he alleges he observed an incident or the parties to it would prove that he could not have witnessed what he claims to have seen.

Where the general geographical location of an incident must be established, the street address and the city should be used. Post office box numbers or rural route numbers should not be used for this purpose. In rural areas, this may not be possible, and so the officer should record distances from fixed objects or positions, such as intersections, highway mileage posts, telephone or power pole numbers, or the like. These are unlikely to change frequently and can therefore be considered stable references. Addresses should include apartment numbers if an apartment house is involved, or room numbers if the event occurred in a hotel or motel. Precise locations may be required if a search warrant is to be secured to search premises. The Fourth Amendment to the United States Constitution prescribes that the area to be searched under authority of a warrant must be described with particularity. This requirement is being adhered to regularly by courts.

Sometimes locations and positions are extremely difficult to describe in words. A sketch, diagram, or photograph may be useful in these cases. Their preparation and use are described later in this chapter.

When *Did the Incident Occur* The date and time at which the incident occurred are important in almost all police incidents. The time the officer received the call or assignment, the time of arrival at the scene, and the time necessary notifications were made may all prove to be important and should be recorded for later reference.

The importance of accurate time records becomes clearly apparent when a suspect's alibi must be challenged. The exact time a death occurred may be vital to prove the order in which a husband and wife died, for inheritance purposes. Occasionally in fatal traffic accident cases, a husband and wife will both perish. In states which have community property laws, usually the property of the deceased is inherited by the survivor. Thus it is imperative that the sequence of death be accurately recorded to assist the courts in settling the estate of the victims. Time of death may also play an important part in the settlement of some insurance cases, pensions, workmen's compensation, etc.

Times should be noted exactly and should follow prescribed policy in using the twenty-four—hour or the a.m.-p.m. system, i.e., 20:01 or 8:01 p.m. Special care should be exercised during the several hours following a change in time from Standard to Daylight Saving to indicate whether the incident occurred during Standard or Daylight Saving time. This might be of considerable importance in liquor or gambling law violations where the law imposes time restrictions upon liquor-dispensing or gambling establishments.

The time should be followed by the month, year, and day. If the time of occurrence is unknown, estimate the occurrence within a certain period according to the evidence available. Often, for example, a burglary occurs sometime between 6:00 p.m. Friday, when a family leaves for a weekend outing, and 6:00 p.m. Sunday, when they arrive home and discover the crime.

Some crimes become more serious if committed during the nighttime. Nighttime is usually defined as the period between sunset and sunrise. These times are precisely determined; therefore, it becomes imperative to definitely ascertain and record the exact time for an offense such as burglary in order to establish whether it was committed during the daytime or during the night.

How *the Incident Was Accomplished*   The way a crime was committed or the circumstances leading to an incident may be important to establish the intent of the parties. Evidence should be noted showing how the property or victim was attacked, i.e., cut screen, pried back door, pretended to have or simulated a gun, sprang on victim from bushes, snatched purse on bus, etc. The officer should also try to learn precisely how the incident was accomplished—the method of accomplishment or the *method of operation* of the criminal. This modus operandi or M.O. represents the criminal's unique procedures. It may sometimes point to the identity of the perpetrator just as surely as fingerprints would. The modus operandi is virtually a trademark of the criminal's method which may be exceedingly valuable. Particular expressions or words spoken before, during, or after the main act, such as, "Give me a bottle of V.O.," may be a part of the suspect's M.O.

Evidence showing how the burglar deactivated the alarm system, how he entered the building, how the fire was started, how the rapist approached the victim, how the bunco criminal swindled his victim, etc., may also be part of the criminal's M.O. These acts may be uniquely different from the methods of other criminals committing the same type of crime. A series of burglary cases may involve an entry into the premises by way of an open back window, but such methods are so common that they cannot be considered M.O. However, if the burglar entered a building by an open back door, raided the icebox, drank soft drinks, wrote on the wall, and committed other acts which were unique, these methods could properly be considered an identifiable M.O.

Why *the Act Occurred* The reason for the occurrence—the motivation for it—is never essential to the proof of a criminal act but is valuable evidence which might lead to the identification of the perpetrator. Did the criminal commit the act out of revenge, fear, anger, or passion? Why was the victim attacked? Was the property destroyed, or was the victim killed for insurance? Was the business operating at a loss? The proprietor may therefore have a motive to burn the premises or steal the merchandise for insurance and attempt to give the appearance that the fire was accidental or the theft was the result of a burglary.

While answers to "why" questions may or may not be readily determinable, they often provide valuable clues leading to the person responsible for the act. Thus, the officer should approach the investigation with a questioning mind concerning any possible motive that might explain why the incident occurred. Initially, don't jump to conclusions until you are reasonably certain that a particular motive may be involved, nor should your manner or actions show that you are suspicious. Rather, concentrate on securing whatever evidence is available to determine the facts. For example, a complaint of rape may or may not support a serious criminal charge. The officer must approach such inquiries judiciously with an open mind. Be alert for circumstances which may reveal a particular reason for the victim to rationalize conduct which led to the offense.

Checklists and Stamped Guides Many agencies provide field officers blank forms of the most commonly used police reports in three-ring binders. These may be used to make the original handwritten reports of crime or complaints and will guide the officer in obtaining the data required; however, in some investigations much detail is gathered which is not reflected in the formal report. Officers should not neglect to record such information in their notebooks since it will not be included in the crime report. It may be valuable for future reference either in a criminal prosecution or in a civil proceeding which may take place several years later.

If a list of information is not provided, officers may prepare their own lists for the various types of reports. Such a list can be modified as you gain experience in the various aspects of report taking.

Some agencies provide rubber stamp lists of the data which must be obtained for reports in connection with an investigation. These can be stamped in your notebook to guide you in your report-writing function. For example, you will frequently be called upon to conduct a traffic accident investigation. You may be at a loss as to how to proceed because you handle this type of activity infrequently. You may not be thoroughly familiar with the basic data required for the complex, standard traffic accident report form, but by following the stamped guide placed in your notebook as shown in Figure 4-1, you will be able to obtain all the information you need to complete the necessary reports.

DR. NO. ....

Date ....Time ....

Acc. Occ. On ....

....

Name ....

Add. ....

Res. Ph. ....Bus. Ph. ....

Employer ....

Add. ....

How Inv. ....

Going ....

Sex ....Descent ....Age ....

D. L. No. ....

No. D. L. Date of Birth ....

Veh. Yr. .... Make .... Style ....

Veh. Lic. Yr. .... State .... No. ....

Pres. Own. ....

Add. ....

Occ. of Pty. ....

Prts of Veh Dam .... Amt. ....

Other Prop Dam ....

....

Figure 4-1.   TRAFFIC ACCIDENT INVESTIGATION STAMP. *(Courtesy of the Los Angeles Police Department.)*

Description of Property

If stolen or lost property is to be returned to its rightful owner when it is found or recovered, there must be some means of establishing ownership. If this is not possible, then ordinarily the presumption exists that the person who has possession of the property has title to it. It would be fruitless to try to prosecute a thief if the property found in his possession cannot be identified as belonging to someone else. It is therefore important that an officer taking a report on stolen or lost property record its description accurately and in some standard manner. This will make it possible to index the information in the various police files so that the owner of the property recovered from thieves, pawnshops, or others can be identified and the property returned to him.

Stolen Property Files   Stolen property files are maintained by states, most large cities and counties, and the Department of Justice. When stolen property is recovered and described on a police report with sufficient detail, the identity of the owner can usually be established but only if the initial report of its theft or loss contained enough detail to make indexing possible.

Describing Stolen or Lost Property   When a report is taken on lost or stolen property, at least the following information should be obtained for the description.[2]

Quantity

Kind   of article or merchandise, or *type* with details indicating the specific type such as: man's watch, wrist; revolver; radio, portable; dress; etc.

Trade name,   commercial or manufacturer's name, or name under which sold such as: Typewriter, portable, *Underwood*; watch, man's pocket, open faced, *Waltham*; etc.

Identifying features   such as serial or parts numbers (used with care on firearms to differentiate between parts and serial numbers), case or movement numbers (on watches or clocks), names, initials, inscriptions, identifying marks (made by manufacturer or owner), repair identification marks, etc.

[2] California State Department of Education, *Police Report Writing*, California State Peace Officers Training Series—74, Sacramento: 1964, pp. 57–68.

Physical description, exact model, style, size, shape, thickness, etc. Added descriptions: firearms—model, caliber, barrel length, type of sights, and any other identifying feature should be described; watches or clocks—size, shape, descriptive features not otherwise listed; jewelry—mounting, setting, design, etc.; utensils—number in set, dimensions, design, etc.; cameras—size of case and film, design, etc.; radios, televisions—size of set, tubes or transistor, dials, control bands, accessories, speakers (sizes and kinds), type of turntable or tape deck, stereo, cartridge type in tone arm, etc.

Material, i.e. blue steel, sterling silver, walnut, etc.

Color or finish.

Condition, including date of purchase if pertinent in determining value, usability, state of repair, appearance, etc.

Value, market or depreciated value. Estimated from initial cost, age, normal life, and salvage. Value estimated if market value not known.

Sketching

Mere word descriptions often do not portray the exact relative positions of articles found at the scene of a crime; neither can a photograph present accurate dimensions in their true perspective. For this reason, a sketch of the scene might be needed to show accurately to the jury and in reports the exact positions of objects and evidence in relation to other objects.

Photographic representation may be affected by the angle of the picture or cluttered with nonessential objects which tend to confuse jurors. For these reasons, photographs should be supplemented by sketches where both are indicated in the more serious incidents. The photographs provide the many details of the scene including essential as well as nonessential objects, while the sketch can be used to present only matters pertinent to the case. It will also provide a permanent record of the physical facts in the case. Both are used extensively to portray traffic accident, homicide, and major crime scenes.

Samen[3] divides sketches into three general categories: rough sketches, finished sketches, and scaled drawings. The *rough sketch*

[3] Charles C. Samen, "Major Crime Scene Investigation," *Law and Order,* vol. 19, no. 10, October 1971, pp. 73–76.

made after the scene has been photographed need not be drawn to scale but should show actual measurements and relationships between evidence and objects. It provides the basis for scaled drawings, often made by a cartographer in cases of major importance. *Finished sketches* are exact duplications of rough sketches but drawn to scale by using layout templates and true measurements from the rough sketch. *Scaled drawings* are final drawings made primarily for court testimony with all locations of rooms, furnishings, etc. Clear plastic overlay material can be placed over the drawing so that the witness may mark with wax marking pencils the exact location of evidence or place movable cutouts of evidence on the drawing to show its position to the jury.

Rough Sketch Sketches made by the average patrol officer can be very effective and useful when used as a basis for reports or to supplement testimony in court. Each sketch or series of sketches should be planned to show that part of the crime or accident scene which will provide a fair representation of matters relevant to the case. One sketch may incorporate all the details needed about the surrounding area and the immediate scene. In other cases, several sketches should be made to provide this representation if a wide area needs to be portrayed.

Photographs, if they are needed, should be taken before sketches are made so that the scene in its unaltered state may be recorded on film. If a Polaroid camera is available to the officer, he may examine the developed film before starting his drawings to see if the photograph contains what is needed.

The patrol officer needs no particular ability as an artist to make an adequate rough sketch of a crime scene. He needs only a notebook, a small plastic straightedge or traffic accident template with cutouts for drawing vehicles to scale, a pencil, a metal measuring tape, and an ability to discriminate between relevant evidence and articles, materials, or relationships which have no value to the inquiry. If he remembers to include any item and its relationship to other matters which may later prove significant in determining what happened and how, he will probably prepare perfectly acceptable sketches. If he is to err, it is better to include too much data than too little.

The nature of the incident will dictate how sophisticated and detailed the sketch should be; however, each should be planned systematically. If the officer develops a system and a logical manner in his sketches, they will become easier to make and be more useful to him, to the court, and to a jury which must base its findings upon the evidence made available to it.

Rough sketches should be kept as simple as possible. They are nothing more than "floor plans" of the scene showing directions, distances, and sizes, and related portions of relevant evidence and objects. If unnecessary detail is included, the sketch will be crowded

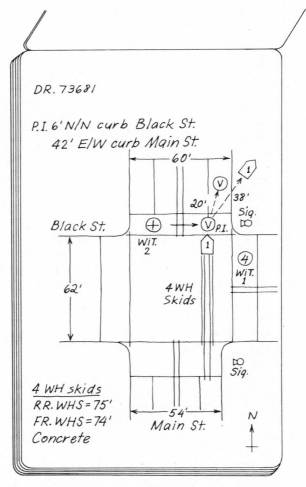

Figure 4-2. ROUGH SKETCH. This type of sketch should be used in connection with the information shown in Figure 4-1, if it is used to depict a traffic accident scene.

and will confuse the viewer. Essential items might be hidden or obscured by nonessential detail. They need not be drawn precisely to scale, but all measurements must be included so that a scaled finished drawing can be made from them if needed. Articles of evidence shown in the sketch, furniture, etc., should be kept in the same proportions on the drawing as possible.

Before preparing the sketch or series of sketches, the officer must decide what he is going to include. He should then constantly check such items against the actual scene to ensure that everything that may be needed later is in the sketch. When interior sketches are made of a room, walls should be drawn first with open spaces for doors to and from the room. By systematically placing windows and furniture in the drawing in a clockwise order starting at the door, all necessary objects will be included. Evidence can then be positioned by drawing it in its proper perspective, identifying it with a letter or number, and cross-referencing it in the descriptive legend. If furniture has been moved after the incident but before the time the drawing is made, it should be replaced to its exact position at the time of the incident and shown there on the sketch. Witnesses familiar with the surroundings may help to reconstruct the scene so that the sketch will be a true portrayal of it.

Sometimes a rough sketch of the scene of a crime is very valuable if it is available before witnesses and victims are interviewed, because their respective positions may better be explained by referring to it. Pertinent information should be placed on the sketch when it is being prepared at the scene and not entered from memory later as this may destroy its credibility in court.

The officer should adopt a uniform method of identifying articles of evidence or reference points and adhere to that system so that he will not forget which were used when he refers to his drawing many months later in court. Only abbreviations which are *common* and conventional symbols or symbols which are cross-referenced to a legend should be used. In this way, he will be able to give the jury an accurate portrayal of the scene long after it has been changed.

Every rough sketch should be oriented. Ordinarily, north should be at the top. Positions of evidence should be placed accurately on the sketch in relation to reference points that are unlikely to be changed, such as permanent curbs at an intersection, bearing walls, fire hydrants, light standards, windows, doors, etc.

Measurements After walls and other fixed reference points, furniture, and other movable objects have been drawn on the sketch and evidence has been shown in its relative position, accurate measurements must be made. Walls and other fixed items to be shown should be measured first. Positions of objects or evidence then should be measured. Points of entry, the body of the victim, weapons, evidence, skid marks, etc., should be included whenever they may be pertinent to the investigation, as should directions in which doors and windows open, the exact position of the body in a homicide case, whether the body was lying face down, up, or on either side, whether furniture was overturned, if lights were on or off, if the telephone was off the hook, and the like. When precise measurements are essential, a steel or metallic tape which stretches very little should be used. Measurements should all be taken by application of a consistent standard; i.e., some measurements should not be taped, while others are paced.

When two officers are involved in taking measurements, both should verify them by exchanging places so that both may testify to distances from the sketch. Two measurements should be taken of the position of a body when the position is important, as in a criminal homicide. One measurement should be taken from the head and one from the feet, with both measurements related to fixed reference points.

Ordinarily, large areas or long distances can be specified with sufficient accuracy in yards or tenths of a mile. Small areas or short distances may require measurements accurate to one-eighth of an inch.[4] Pry mark dimensions, bite marks, bullet holes, etc., may require precise measurements.

The simplest and easiest way to position evidence and objects on the sketch is by the coordinate method. Inside rooms or at intersections, an object can be placed on the sketch in its exact position by measuring the right angle distance from two points of reference, i.e., 3 feet, 10 inches from the south wall and 6 feet from the east wall, or 24 feet south of the north curb and 16 feet west of the east curb. In out-of-doors areas where reference points are not as easily available as at intersections or in rooms, measurements are made from fixed reference points.

The position from which photographs are taken should be indicated so that the jurors may place themselves in the same relative position as the photographer. The notebook should also be used to record information that might later be needed to qualify or explain in court any unusual aspects of photographs presented as evidence. Notes

---

[4] Samen, "Major Crime Scene Investigation," p. 74.

should be used to supplement the sketch with detailed descriptions of each item cross-referenced to the sketch. This avoids placing too much detailed data in the sketch itself.

Skid marks in traffic cases are often critical to prove speed when other evidence is not available. These should be measured with a tape or measuring wheel and recorded on the sketch showing the pattern of the marks, their length, where they started, and where they ended. This will help establish the identity of the vehicle which left them.

All pertinent data regarding date, time, case number, address or location of the scene represented by the sketch, light conditions, names of persons who can testify that the sketch is a fair representation of the scene, the type of offense, and any other data that may later be pertinent should be noted.

Types of Sketches Soderman and O'Connell[5] classify the different types of sketches as the *locality sketch*, which gives a broad picture of the incident and the surroundings including the location of buildings, roads, and the like; the *sketch of grounds*, which portrays the immediate scene and its nearest surroundings, such as the floor plan of a house and its surrounding patio; and the *detailed sketch*, which shows the details of the scene itself. When it is necessary to portray some evidence located in or on walls or ceilings, such as bloodstains, bullet holes, etc., such details are often best shown in a sketch known as a cross projection. In this type of sketch, walls and ceilings are shown on the same plane as the floor.

Summary

The reports prepared by officers reflect their efficiency and are a basis for measuring their capabilities. Most of these are based upon the notations they make in their notebooks in connection with incidents they are called upon to handle. This notebook is one of the most important tools. It is the official memory of what they have done. With experience, they will tend to develop a form of notetaking which will give them full recollection of what happened; however, their notes should not become so abbreviated that they are unable to use them to refresh their memory months or years later when they are called upon to testify to the facts of a case.

[5] Harry Soderman and John J. O'Connell, *Modern Criminal Investigation*, 5th ed., Funk and Wagnalls Company, New York, 1962, pp. 80–84.

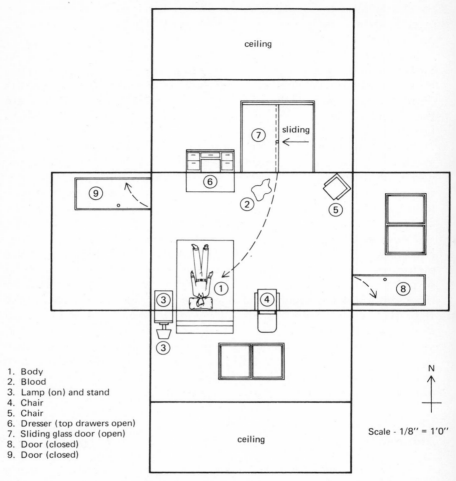

1. Body
2. Blood
3. Lamp (on) and stand
4. Chair
5. Chair
6. Dresser (top drawers open)
7. Sliding glass door (open)
8. Door (closed)
9. Door (closed)

Scale - 1/8" = 1'0"

Figure 4-3. CROSS-PROJECTION SKETCH. Evidence and other details can be placed in true perspective in relation to other objects in the room.

The type of notebook they use will probably be determined by their department's rules. There are advantages and disadvantages to both the bound and the loose-leaf notebooks which they should weigh in making a selection when they have the option. The size, general usefulness, and adequacy for court reference should be considered.

Officers should take more notes than they may need rather than too few. They can always disregard those which are of no value, but they cannot usually add the notes they need later in court.

Notes should be clear, concise, and accurate. They should incorporate the who, what, where, when, how, and sometimes the why of the incidents they handle. Sometimes, it is well for officers to use a stamped impression of a particular report to guide them when making notes for such a report until they become thoroughly familiar with the information needed. They may find it helpful to make a checklist they can refer to when collecting information or recording data for police reports to be made later.

In more serious incidents, they should make a sketch of the scene to supplement their notes and the photographs taken. If they make their sketches in a systematic manner and include items and their relationship to other items which may later prove to be significant in explaining what happened and how, they probably will make perfectly acceptable sketches. They should choose a uniform method of identifying evidence or reference points and stick to it. Common abbreviations and symbols only should be used. They should be cross-referenced to a legend so that they will be clear to them months later. Measurements should be accurately made and recorded on the sketch to show the position of evidence in relationships to fixed points and the distances involved. Positions from which photographs have been taken should also be indicated on the sketch to show the perspective of the photographs to the jurors.

A sketch of the immediate area and the perimeter around the crime scene should be prepared to show a broad view of the incident scene and surrounding area. Often, in addition to the detailed sketch of the scene, it is desirable to show its relationship to the immediate surroundings. This will show positions or locations of evidence and items that portray what happened and where.

Review

Questions

1. What should be the size of your notebook? Discuss your reasons.
2. Define the terms relevancy and materiality.
3. Enumerate some of the *basic* requirements of field notes.
4. What is a "moniker"? How can it be used to identify a person?
5. Why is it sometimes desirable to determine the motive for a crime?
6. Why are photographs of a crime scene sometimes not as valuable as a sketch to show what happened?
7. What are the three categories of sketches?
8. Why is a Polaroid camera valuable at the scene of a crime?
9. Why should a person be consistent in how he takes measurements?

10. How should items of evidence be shown on a sketch?
11. How should long distances—i.e., 2 miles—be specified on a sketch?
12. Describe the coordinate method of showing evidence on a sketch.
13. Why should the position from which photographs were taken be shown on a sketch?
14. Define a locality sketch, a sketch of grounds, and a detailed sketch, and give an example of each.

Exercises

1. Discuss the advantages and disadvantages of a loose-leaf type notebook; a bound notebook.
2. Why are good field notes necessary?
3. What is some of the key information that you would be likely to record in your notebook if you were assigned to a robbery call? A burglary call? A wife-beating call?
4. Discuss the court rules or statutory provisions which would govern if you were to refresh your memory on the witness stand from your notes.
5. Draw a rough sketch of a classroom to show the typical details that should be included in most sketches.
6. Explain how you would plan to make a sketch of a crime scene.
7. Describe the system you would generally follow in making such a sketch.

5

Communicating and Reporting

The word *communicate* means to make known, to inform, to convey knowledge or information. To report is to make a record of, to relate, or to tell. People communicate with each other through many media such as oral statements, written reports, radio, teletype, and the like. When they do, they use word symbols to express thoughts. Often the symbols chosen to express ideas or convey information are not very exact or definite. When they are vague and abstract, the readers or listeners tend to be confused. The result is that they do not arrive at the conclusion that the person sending the message intends.

Regardless of the efficiency and sophistication of the mechanical means used to transmit information, if the information is not clearly expressed in the first place, its clarity will not be improved in transmission. Likewise when a clear message is communicated through equipment used improperly, the message will probably be garbled or distorted and of little use. Therefore, officers must pay attention not only to the structure of their messages but to how they use their equipment to transmit them.

No attempt will be made in this chapter to discuss in depth the many police reports an officer must use. That is the subject of a complete text. Rather, some techniques of using specific communications equipment and some fundamentals of clear writing will be emphasized.

Police Radio Equipment

The development and refinement of the radio has revolutionized police communications. It has enabled the patrol officer to be in constant touch with headquarters and has given the officer's superiors a means of supervising and controlling operations.

Information can be transmitted swiftly to help in the proper and efficient performance of the job. When a call for service is received by the complaint center at police headquarters, it can be recorded and almost immediately relayed to the radio car officers in the field. Their response is then delayed only by the time it takes to travel from the place they received a call to the scene, unless there has been a delay in transmitting the message because of an overload on their radio channel. This is often brought about by improper use of the radio.

Police Radio Frequencies   Radios used on police mobile equipment operate on frequencies assigned by the Federal Communications Commission. Each department or group of departments is assigned certain frequencies. The number of frequencies available to the police is not unlimited, so each department must make the best use of those assigned. Ordinarily, one channel will service about thirty-seven police units without serious overloading.[1]

Use of Radio

A police radio system can be only as efficient as the people using it. If they consider its limitations and use it prudently, it will seldom fail to meet the demands placed upon it.

[1] International City Managers' Association, *Municipal Police Administration*, 5th ed., Chicago, 1969, p. 360.

Mechanics of Operation   The basic components of the radio equipment in a police car are the microphone, the transmitter, and the receiver. When a radio transmission is to be made, the officer should remove the microphone from its cradle, place it about one inch from and about forty-five degrees to the side of his mouth, engage the switch, pause briefly, then start his message. The switch activates the transmitter and should be fully engaged in the *on* position so that the transmitter motor reaches full speed before the message is started.

Broadcasting Procedures   Unnecessary repetition of messages results in loss of air time. Much of this can be eliminated if the officer avoids broadcasting with a pencil, gum, or some object in his mouth, speaking too fast, slurring words, or transmitting when there is excessive interference from passing planes, trains, trucks, sirens, and the like.

If it becomes necessary to broadcast when the police siren is being sounded, the officer should do so during the low tones if practicable. If not, the microphone should be held against the larynx—in the throat just below the jaw—to block out as much outside noise as possible and to cause the voice vibrations to enter directly into the instrument. The principles and techniques of pursuit broadcasts are described in detail in Chapter 8.

When information is requested from the dispatcher, it should be framed as a question that can be answered with a "yes" or "no" whenever possible. The officer should talk slowly, clearly, and deliberately when he communicates using established codes whenever they apply.

Difficult or unusual names should be spelled, but common ones need not be. Telephone, house, social security, operator's, motor, serial, or other lengthy numbers should be repeated. Simple ones should not be.

Whenever practicable, the sequence of information that is used in form reports for a particular crime should be followed in describing suspects to simplify the dispatcher's task in recording the data. If information is needed about several suspects or vehicles, the dispatcher should be asked for a clear frequency. One vehicle or person should be described at a time. Juveniles under eighteen years should be identified as such if their records are kept separate from those of adults. When the dispatcher is asked to pass on information to some other person, the officer can help him by giving him a general reason. When service is needed from street maintenance crews, the coroner, or public utilities agencies, or when an ambulance or fire equipment is necessary, the reason for the service should be specified so that appropriate equipment may be sent. When a backup unit, a supervisor, or an investigator is needed at the scene of an incident, the reason should be given in sufficiently specific terms so that they may assess the urgency of the call. Requests for service should be canceled when the need no longer exists.

Calls for *help* should not be made unless help is urgently needed. Calls for help are Mayday calls which should be reserved for those situations where an officer is in immediate danger. Units responding often "throw caution to the wind." Calls of this nature should not therefore be lightly made. A call for assistance, conversely, does not imply the same degree of urgency as a call for help.

Faulty broadcasting procedures by individual units may cause a radio transmission system which is normally adequate to become cluttered with poorly planned, nonessential, or conflicting broadcasts. This reduces its operational efficiency considerably. When two or more units on the same frequency try to use it at the same time, the dispatcher usually cannot understand either and must waste air time asking that the messages be repeated. Therefore, each officer using his radio can conserve air time by listening for a few seconds before transmitting to make sure the frequency is not in use and by planning the messages he wishes to broadcast. He can do this by outlining in his notebook the essence of what might take a long time before trying to broadcast. If the matter requires much conversation and is not urgent, he should use a land line telephone. He will then gain maximum use from his equipment.

In the standard two-way systems, only one officer at a time can communicate with the same dispatcher on a single frequency. Any unnecessary transmissions may thus deprive other officers of air time they might urgently need. The adverse effects brought about by the misuse of the radio by one unit may not, in themselves, be critical, but should all units on that frequency fail to exercise restraint, the entire system might become ineffective.

The problem is even more critical with three-way systems in which radio units can communicate with each other without supervision by the dispatcher unless he intervenes. This is important when he has an emergency message and the patrol officers are conversing about less important matters. All mobile units on such frequencies may monitor radio transmissions of all other units. Much closer supervision over the use of this car-to-car equipment is therefore needed than is the case with the two-way systems in which the dispatcher can exercise some control over field units. Unnecessary communications between units use air time that might be needed by other units and may interfere with other broadcasts from the central transmitter. It is therefore imperative that officers refrain from using their radios for any nonessential purpose.

When no broadcasts are heard for an unusual period, the officer sometimes is tempted to make a check over the air. The transmitter may be in working order, but if the receiver is dead, the officer usually cannot receive broadcasts. Repeated calls to the dispatcher will only cause interference with other units on the same frequency. The problem is sometimes due to a blown fuse on the receiver, a defective vibrator, or foreign objects such as metal paper clips. These often stick to the speaker magnet when they are jammed into the speaker grill and cause a malfunction.

Squelch Control Radio reception is sometimes garbled or distorted by noise. This may result from improper adjustment of the audio controls much as in a standard radio or television. On radios equipped with a squelch control which works in harmony with the volume control, this can usually be easily corrected. This is done by turning the volume fairly high, then—when the station is off the air—turning the squelch control clockwise to a position where noise is heard, and finally reversing the squelch control counterclockwise just to a point where the noise disappears.

Mechanical Failures Transmitter failures may be caused by a blown fuse or relay or an improperly connected battery which causes reverse polarity. The transmitter motor will not turn in the proper direction and broadcasting will be impossible. These minor problems can easily be corrected by a mechanic or radio technician.

Open Microphone There may be a great deal of interference and some embarrassment to the officer if he carelessly places his microphone in its holder or jams it into his glove compartment in such a way that the switch remains open. With some equipment, the receiver is shut off when the microphone switch is on. One officer's inability to receive a call might cost another his life when he needs help. The officer cannot be informed of his open microphone by the dispatcher when the mike switch is engaged. Other units on three-way systems and the dispatcher on two-way systems can hear conversations and noises from within the police car but have no practical way of informing the officer involved.

Stakeout Broadcast   Officers going out of service on a stakeout should promptly notify the dispatcher of the location so that other units may be alerted and avoid "burning" the operation should they drive by. Once the stakeout is over, the unit should promptly notify the dispatcher, who will relay the message to other units.

Engineering Problems

Technical problems of design sometimes add to the interference which results from improper use of the equipment. These engineering problems have been reduced considerably over the years, but some still remain. For example, radio car broadcasts in one part of the country sometimes interfere with those in another area because of a phenomenon called a skip effect. Interference with other systems may extend far beyond the immediate area in which the transmission is clear enough to be useful, but these are matters for the engineer to correct.[2] The officer cannot do much to eliminate them. He can reduce the man-made interferences for which he is responsible, however.

The radio car officer may be troubled at times by his inability to transmit or receive clear messages because of a "dead spot," a condition caused by large buildings, power lines or devices, hills, and the like. While modern equipment has largely eliminated this problem, the officer can easily correct it when it occurs merely by moving his vehicle.

Dictating Equipment

Some agencies use tape recorders so that the officer may dictate his reports of police incidents promptly after they occur. At this time, the details are fresh in his mind, and the information can be placed on tape for later transcription. The officer may be able to call reports to headquarters by telephone connected to recorders, or the tape can be dictated in the field into a pocket recorder.

Efficiency in dictating can be developed by practice. Improper techniques result in loss of time in transcription, waste of materials used in transcribing reports, and waste of the officer's time in doing over what could have been done right in the first place. He should go

[2] International City Managers' Association, *Municipal Police Administration*, p. 359.

over his dictated reports carefully and learn from them what his dictating weaknesses are.

Garbled words resulting from improper or careless diction or too rapid speech result in many transcription problems and undoubtedly result in many needless report errors. Poor organization or a lack of continuity or clarity in a report result from the same errors that cause confusion in broadcasting and report writing as discussed elsewhere in this chapter. Most errors can be eliminated if the officer making his or her report will organize the material in some logical sequence before dictating, then speak clearly and slowly using simple expressions and short sentences. A few written notes prepared beforehand will help organize the report so that it will provide a complete, clear picture of what happened.

Portable Radios

The use of portable broadcasting equipment by the police has increased considerably during recent years. The limited range of walkie-talkies small enough to carry conveniently and the problem of dead spots have limited their value in the past; however, these problems have largely been eliminated in more sophisticated and efficient equipment such as the inexpensive mobile relay repeater. With this equipment, a police car transmitter can easily be converted from a standard radio unit to a repeater which relays broadcasts from a portable radio through the car transmitter to the dispatcher. Such a system lets the officer leave his mobile unit to patrol or perform other police work on foot some distance from it and still communicate as if he were in his unit. The flexibility of this equipment is limited only by the number of cross-connection facilities installed at the central control. Officers can use this equipment to communicate with each other as in the standard three-way system either directly or through the dispatcher. These systems work very effectively if the area between the officer and his relay transmitter contains no dead spots. As with standard car broadcasting equipment, this can ordinarily be overcome by moving to another place to transmit over the portable set. Such equipment is extremely valuable in stakeouts where officers must keep in constant contact with each other, in civil disturbances where officers can transmit intelligence from within the crowd itself, and in major disasters where communications are imperative between rescue services. It is equally useful in searches conducted in open, wooded, or brushy areas to keep searchers in touch with each other, and for many other tactical situations where portable radio communications are needed. It is a must for officers deployed at sites of barricaded suspects.

Telephone

One of the most important of all communication systems that we have is the telephone network, which places the police virtually within arm's length of almost any citizen. The telephone is one of the most useful pieces of equipment available and perhaps one of the most misused. In person-to-person contacts, the overtones in communicating—friendly gestures, pleasant facial expressions, a smile, a handshake, or other physical movements—may affect or compensate for a disagreeable encounter and make it less distasteful to the citizen. When he calls the police by telephone, however, perhaps for his first direct contact with police, his impressions of them are formed by what he hears over a mechanical device. If the voice he hears is discourteous, sarcastic, abrupt, or otherwise unpleasant, his opinion of the whole department usually is lowered. If he is or has been a supporter of the police, he may withdraw his support. If he has been somewhat neutral in his opinion, one unpleasant telephone contact will usually sway him against law enforcement. If he has been an antagonist of the police, a disagreeable contact will only confirm his opinion and reinforce his antagonism. In any event, the police image is not improved by poor telephone manners. Every telephone contact between an officer or other representative of the police and other persons, inside or outside the organization, should reflect an unmistakable willingness to be of service.

Telephone Demeanor   As in any contact with the public, courtesy should be practiced at all times. It is especially important when the contact is by telephone because so many contacts are made through this medium. Nowhere is the old adage "courtesy begets courtesy" more applicable. Courtesy costs nothing but a little effort and pays huge dividends. A thank you is a must in almost every telephone conversation.

Telephone conversations should be conducted in moderate tones. A voice that is too low or too loud either will not be heard or will have an unpleasant and distracting effect upon the listener and will distract others working nearby. A well-modulated voice spoken directly into the mouthpiece held within one inch of the mouth will produce the best results.

Noise   Outside noises in the vicinity of the speaker sometimes enter the mouthpiece and cause "feedback" so that the speaker cannot hear the other party. This can be reduced by placing the palm of the hand tightly over the mouthpiece rather than over the free ear when listening.

Receiving and Transferring Calls   An officer should ordinarily answer telephone calls by giving his department, his rank, and his last name. He should handle as many calls as he can without transferring them unless the caller requests to talk with a particular person or the information requested can best be obtained from some other source. If there is to be a delay in the transfer, the caller should be told so that he may wait or call back. Ordinarily, unless other instructions have been received, the person taking the initial call should not ask the caller to identify himself. Informants seldom wish to reveal their names to persons other than their contact. Furthermore, although it may be appropriate to screen calls for administrators, many callers draw the conclusion that the person they are calling will talk with only certain persons. Generally, operating personnel should talk with any caller unless there is a particular reason for not doing so.

A pad and pencil should be available when a call is first answered so that messages can be taken without delaying the caller by searching for writing materials. Messages should be taken for others cheerfully if it appears that this is what should be done. When they are taken, they should not be so brief or sketchy that they are meaningless. Enough care should be taken in writing them to ensure the recipient understands what is meant.

Planning Conversations   Considerable time and expense can be saved if the officer will plan his conversation ahead of time when he must make a lengthy call, especially if it is long distance. A few notes will serve as a guide so that he may cover everything he wishes to discuss in one call.

Fundamentals of Clear Writing

Any report an officer makes to describe what he or others said, did, or learned should let the reader know exactly what the writer wants him to know. Poorly written reports will create confusion and misunderstanding in the mind of the reader just as ambiguous, inaccurate testimony will adversely affect a juror.

Ideally, a written report is the department's memory. A report should be so complete, so clear, and so easy to read that a superior, another police officer, a complaint officer in the district attorney's office, a judge, a juror, or any other person reviewing it can completely understand the matter described without having any previous knowledge of it. Every statement must not only be capable of being understood, but be incapable of being misunderstood.[3] This quality in reports can best be achieved if the writer follows some simple rules for clarity, simplicity, accuracy, and validity.

Clarity   The first, and perhaps the major, problem in writing is the difficulty of achieving clarity. The clarity of a report depends not only upon how clear each word and each sentence is, but upon how clear the whole report is. Writing is really an exercise in logic wherein the writer is trying to justify a conclusion. Each of several sentences in a paragraph may be accurate and understandable by itself, but if because of their illogical arrangement the reader draws an incorrect conclusion, the report does not meet the test of clarity or of validity. Validity of a report requires that the evidence support the conclusion that should be drawn from it.

Clarity in written communications is all important. When an oral report is made to a superior, he can ask questions if the meaning is not clear. He usually does not have an opportunity to do this, however, when he receives an unclear written report. He may waste a lot of time guessing what was meant and may often make costly mistakes in doing so.[4] Readers want a report that is carefully organized with facts to help them picture ideas. Words that don't say what they mean, those that say nothing concrete or are put into a report to make it impressive are not favored by readers. Abbreviations may be used but only when they are authorized and are clearly understandable. If the meaning of an abbreviation is questionable, it should never be used. Abbreviations may be used freely when they are customary and will not confuse the reader.[5] For example, the abbreviation sup. ct. may be interpreted as superior court or supreme court. Abbreviations of this type should therefore not be used. When an abbreviation might be misunderstood, the word should be spelled out.

Sometimes, because of the limited space available on a police

[3] Madeline Warnock, "Editing for Better Understanding," in Herman M. Weisman (ed.), *Proceedings of the 1962 Institute in Technical and Industrial Communications,* Fort Collins, Colorado, 1962, p. 20.
[4] N. F. Iannone, *Supervision of Police Personnel,* Prentice-Hall, Inc., Englewood Cliffs, N.J., 1970, p. 67.
[5] Rudolph Flesch, *The ABC of Style: A Guide to Plain English,* Harper and Row, Publishers, Inc., New York, 1964, p. 3.

form such as a traffic citation, the officer has a tendency to use too many abbreviations. Superior officers, the violator, court personnel, the complaint officer, records personnel, and others review these. If they do not understand what has been included by the officer, his image—if not his case—suffers.

Simplicity Short sentences properly punctuated and simple but precise words correctly spelled will add a great deal to the clarity of a report. Long, complex sentences tend to confuse. A long word may not be inappropriate, but if a short one will do just as well, it should be used. A policeman merely has to read some of the statutes he uses daily to conclude that they almost defy interpretation because of their length and ambiguity. Short words are not necessarily more precise than long ones, but usually they can be more readily understood by the average reader. Words should be used to express rather than impress. The most important consideration is that the words used accurately reflect what is meant. Because of the multiple meanings of so many words in the English language, clarity is sometimes difficult to achieve. The five hundred most-used words in our language have an average of twenty-eight meanings per word.[6]

A report should be brief without sacrificing clarity. No more words should be used than necessary and no fewer than needed. Trivia and nonessential wordage should be avoided. These only waste the time of the writer and the reader and add nothing constructive to the report.

Completeness In the interest of completeness—especially in criminal proceedings—all information should be reported when it is useful or necessary to determine the truth of the matter. This is the basic requirement of the principle of relevancy and materiality. The *who, what, where, when, why,* and *how* of an event and the manner of describing persons, property, and things are described in Chapter 4.

Negative aspects of an incident should be reported as well as those which are positive to give all sides of the case. This is especially true in criminal matters so that the prosecutor will not be caught by surprise by evidence he should have known but did not until the trial started. For example, it can be embarrassing if information known to the investigator is first learned by the prosecutor when his own witness reveals it on cross-examination by the defense counsel. Often the harm done to the case cannot be repaired.

---

[6] William R. Van Dersal, *The Successful Supervisor in Government and Business,* Harper and Row, Publishers, Inc., New York, 1962, pp. 107–108.

Accuracy   All information put into a police report must be accurate. The officer must meticulously avoid giving the impression that a statement he makes is true when he merely guessed that it was. If there is not enough evidence to reach a sound or meaningful conclusion, one should not be made. To do so would only mislead others. On the witness stand, a person testifying to a matter as a fact when he does not know it to be a fact might be guilty of giving false testimony.

Opinions and Conclusions   When an opinion or conclusion is expressed, it should be clearly labeled as such. Supporting evidence should be reported so that a person receiving it can evaluate the soundness of the conclusion. A prosecutor, for example, must know if an arrest, a search and seizure of evidence, or a warrant have been based on adequate probable cause. Whether or not a case can be successfully prosecuted might be dependent upon the existence of probable cause. Often, the facts establishing it are somewhat vague, but sooner or later the issue must arise. Therefore, the officer should report the facts that support his actions so that time and money need not be wasted on a prosecution that cannot succeed.

Objective Language   Objective words should be used rather than subjective ones. Statements such as "the suspect exposed himself indecently" or "Jones used vulgar language in the presence of children" are subjective since the officer is drawing a conclusion that is usually the prerogative of the court or jury. Exactly what the suspect did that was indecent should be described objectively without the subjective opinion. The exact language which was vulgar should be reported without the opinion. Likewise, the identity of the children present and their ages would be more concrete than referring to them only as children. This identity is sometimes placed in a list of witnesses, then cross-referenced by name or number in the narration. The person reviewing the report will then not find it necessary to assume something which is not in evidence.

Reporting Style—General

Every officer must adapt his particular style of writing to the needs of his organization. In some departments, reports are highly specialized with a report form for almost every type of crime or incident. Space is provided for particular information needed for one purpose or another. These forms usually are developed to standardize reports, to save the time of officers and clerical help, to make report analysis easier, and to provide a format from which information can easily be extracted for the various specialized files for the Department of Justice or as required by law. Some of the special files are the modus operandi file, which often is kept to show the method of operation or trademark of a criminal who committed a particular crime, the nickname or moniker file from which a suspect might be identified from a nickname, a stolen property file used for the identification of stolen and recovered property other than automobiles, an auto theft file, etc.

In the smaller departments, report forms are ordinarily a combination of the fill-in and narrative type. Filling out those portions of reports in which boxes are provided for specific information is usually simple. The completion of the narrative account of what happened is considerably harder because of the difficulty some officers have in describing an incident with total clarity.

Standard rules of grammar and punctuation should be followed in all reports. The simpler the style, the less need there is for punctuation. When a report requires a considerable amount of punctuation, clarity usually suffers because of punctuation errors. A good stenographer's guide and a standard college dictionary are invaluable aids and should be referred to by an officer when he is doubtful about a rule of grammar, spelling, or punctuation. These should be readily available in places where officers prepare reports. Spelling, punctuation, and composition errors can be reduced considerably if officers learn how to use the guides and use them when they are needed.

Report Format The heading of a report indicates the type of incident and the details of time, place, persons involved, and case number. It should contain all the information necessary to let a reviewer identify it without reading the details.

The first paragraph tells generally what occurred. This is the topic paragraph. It is sometimes labeled the summary of investigation, synopsis, or summary. It lets a person learn the essentials of the subject matter quickly.

The first or topic sentence of each of the following paragraphs describes the essence of that paragraph. Succeeding paragraphs elaborate upon those preceding until everything that has been learned about the case is detailed.[7] A conclusion should be included if the

[7] N. F. Iannone, *Supervision of Police Personnel*, p. 68.

nature of the case makes one necessary, but it should be clearly identified.

Narrative Reports   When a report is prepared in narrative form, the information should follow a logical, systematic pattern. It should describe the course of events from the beginning to the end of the officer's involvement in the case. It should relate all pertinent facts learned by the officer and should describe what the suspect, victim, and witnesses said or did that is relevant to the matter. The so-called "newspaper style" of writing a narrative account of an occurrence usually simplifies expression and provides the clearest description of what happened. The narrative style of report writing can be adapted to any type of case. It will provide a complete, understandable description of events if the material is carefully organized. If it is not, it will cause confusion and misunderstanding.

Chronological Reports   Chronological reports are those in which a sequence of events is described in the order in which such events occurred. While this type of report is simple and easy to organize, it sometimes results in incomplete reports because it restricts the writer to a particular pattern. When several events occur at the same time, it sometimes becomes difficult to show each in its proper relationship to the case.

Evidence of Corpus Delicti

Every report, be it a traffic citation or a complicated crime or arrest report for a robbery, should contain sufficient evidence to establish a prima facie violation. *Prima facie* proof of a crime is that amount of evidence which, on its face, is sufficient to prove the corpus delicti (the elements of a crime) until overcome by other evidence. Sometimes a defendant will submit his case to a judge solely on the written report made by an arresting officer. Should the prosecutor permit such a procedure, the court is obliged to determine innocence or guilt *solely* on the basis of the evidence submitted. If a prima facie violation is not established in the report, the court must acquit the defendant no matter what the judge has learned about the case from other sources.

This information is also needed by the complaint attorney in the prosecutor's office who assesses the case at the time an application is made for a criminal complaint against a suspect. If evidence is not available to prove all elements of the crime, the complaint is invariably denied. The same amount of evidence is required before a grand jury indictment can be issued. Without a complaint or accusation by the grand jury, the police are powerless to proceed further in a prosecution. The only recourse then is to secure sufficient evidence to prove the elements of the crime.

Writing Deficiencies

Reports frequently fail to serve the purpose intended for several reasons. The writer does not provide the evidence to support his conclusion; he fails to use simple, specific, and objective words and expressions to make his meaning clear; or he fails to discriminate between essential and nonessential data and includes trivia and complicates the report with irrelevant information.

If, from an officer's testimony in court, the court or jury draws a conclusion different from that suggested by his reports, he is discredited as a witness. He must therefore be very careful that his reports meet the basic tests of clarity, accuracy, completeness, and validity. It is on the basis of these that his credibility may eventually be tested when he is required to testify in court under oath.

Testifying in Court

The criminal investigation activities of the police have as their ultimate purpose the identification, apprehension, and prosecution of those who violate the law. The latter process is the last phase in the administration of justice in which the officer plays a prominent role. His testimony in court reflects how effectively he has prepared his case. This will depend directly upon how carefully he has recorded what he learned during his investigation.

Case Preparation   Everything the officer has done in connection with a criminal investigation may have a vital bearing upon the outcome of the case in court. He may have meticulously recorded every detail of his inquiry in his notebook and official reports, but if he fails on the witness stand to present clearly the evidence to the jury and court, the criminal may escape punishment.

There are those who tell officers that admitting on the stand that they have discussed the case with others will weaken their testimony in the eyes of the jury. Nothing could be further from the truth. As standard procedure before going on the witness stand, every officer should review his case with others who have participated in the investigation. This does not suggest that stories are invented, but rather suggests that pretrial preparation of a case is a professional and perfectly acceptable procedure. Every part of the case to which the officer can properly testify should be thoroughly reviewed before he goes on the witness stand.

Because of the extremely heavy case loads most prosecutors have, they frequently have little time to review cases with the investigating officer before the trial. For this reason, the officer should take every opportunity he may have to discuss the case with the prosecutor before the court proceedings start.

The investigating officer is ordinarily permitted to sit at the counsel table during the trial or hearing and can be extremely helpful in acquainting the prosecutor with unusual aspects of the case. Most investigating officers carry a note pad for this purpose. They jot down brief pertinent notes and pass them to the prosecutor as the case progresses to avoid interfering with his concentration by talking with him. Conversation and notes should be pertinent to the case. The officer should take great pains, however, to avoid giving jurors the impression that he is out to "hang" the defendant.

Personal Appearance of Witness   The personal appearance of the officer on the witness stand unquestionably has a considerable psychological impact on the jurors. They often judge his credibility by his appearance. This suggests that he pay close attention to his manner of dress. If he is dressed in civilian clothes, he should wear a conservative business suit with a shirt and tie rather than flashy sports clothes. He should be carefully groomed and should exhibit the same pride in his appearance that he does in his profession whether he is in civilian clothes or in uniform. Either is acceptable attire in court although, psychologically, the uniform probably gives an authoritarian impression and might bias a juror against him.

Courtroom Demeanor   An officer sitting in the courtroom either before or after testifying should refrain from any such expressions as shaking his head when he disagrees with testimony, nodding when he agrees, or grimacing with disapproval, contempt, or disgust. To do so may tend to discredit him in the eyes of the jurors as his acts may be interpreted as an indication that he has an emotional rather than an impersonal involvement in the case. He should sit attentively with a stoic expression—not seeming disinterested or overinterested in what is taking place on the witness stand.

Testifying—General Procedures The officer is often the first witness to testify. His testimony ordinarily is the most important part of the state's case. If he is the investigator, he is expected to know more about the case than anyone else. Sometimes his testimony is the only evidence that is available to the prosecution. In any case, his testimony is usually vital to a conviction.

When he is called to testify, he should approach the witness stand briskly and seat himself erectly but not stiffly after taking the oath. Preliminary questions are asked to show his name and occupation for the record and to establish his relationship to the case. This is the first opportunity the jurors have to formulate an opinion of his credibility. The prosecutor then asks him a series of questions to bring out the facts of the case. Much of the initial testimony he gives will ordinarily be a narrative account of what evidence he obtained in the investigation. At this time, the value of proper pretrial preparation will become most apparent. This account should be given in a matter-of-fact manner in conversational tones loud enough for counsel, the court, and the jurors to hear comfortably. Gestures and other bodily movements should be controlled to avoid distracting the jurors.

Responses to Questions When the officer concludes his initial account of what happened, the prosecutor will ask him questions devised to bring out more detail about the incident and to clarify those parts of the testimony that were not clear. The defense counsel will then be given the opportunity to question him. When asked a question by either counsel, the officer should consider the answer carefully, then reply deliberately, courteously, and forthrightly. This will give a reasonable opportunity for a timely objection before the answer is given. Should he not understand the question, he should ask that it be repeated. His responses should be directed to the jurors or, in a court trial, to the counsel asking the question.

Should either the prosecutor or defense counsel make an objection to a question or to a response, the officer should stop his testimony until the court rules on the objection. The blurting out of an answer *after* the objection has been made is highly improper and should be avoided, as it might constitute grounds for a mistrial.

The officer's answers should be responsive, i.e., they should answer the questions asked. Some questions cannot be properly answered without qualification, but the witness should not elaborate unless he obtains the permission of the court. Usually he will be allowed to qualify his response when necessary.

Information volunteered is often considered nonresponsive, especially when it does not relate directly to the question asked. As a result, it is excluded if it is likely to prejudice the jury. Volunteered testimony may also provide a basis for admonishment by the court and may cause the jury to disbelieve the testimony.

The prosecutor is responsible for asking the questions needed to establish the state's case. Should additional evidence be required from the witness after he has left the stand, he may be recalled with the court's permission.

The response "I don't know" rarely discredits an officer's testimony unless it indicates to the jurors that the case was poorly prepared and therefore is weak. A witness is not permitted to arrive at an answer by speculating or guessing. Such a procedure is tantamount to testifying to a fact which the witness does not know to be a fact. This may constitute a serious offense.

A witness is permitted to give his opinion and to draw conclusions based on the evidence he had collected in certain cases, such as intoxication, speed, etc. He is not permitted to do so in matters in which he does not have the special training or experience required of an expert witness. It is better for the officer to avoid subjective conclusions unless he is asked for them. Rather, he should use objective terms in describing what he learned so that the jurors can draw their own conclusions. These will coincide with his own if he has properly described the evidence to them.

Cross-Examination   The second stage of the testimony is the cross-examination in which the defense counsel has the right to question the witness about any evidence he produced during direct examination. The primary objective of most defense counsels in the cross-examination is to discredit the evidence, the prosecution witness, or both. A defendant is entitled to an acquittal if a reasonable doubt is raised that he committed the offense charged. Toward that end defense attorneys will direct most of their efforts. They will try to rattle the witness to make him appear to be inaccurate in his testimony. He must therefore expect courtroom tactics directed at discrediting him.

He will soon learn how well he has prepared his case. If he remains alert and calm, testifies forthrightly, and refuses to allow his testimony to be distorted, the jurors will accept it at face value.

There is no place on the witness stand for discourtesy, sarcasm, or an obvious show of disrespect—either toward the defense attorney or toward the judge who makes a decision the officer doesn't particularly like.

Summary

Thoughts, ideas, and information are expressed orally or in writing by the use of word symbols. These symbols are often so complex, abstract, or imprecise that they do not convey the meaning intended. Sometimes the manner in which sentences are arranged may cause a wrong conclusion to be drawn from a report and destroy its validity.

Radios, recorders, and telephones are, aside from written reports, the primary mechanical means for communicating. What might otherwise be good information may be distorted or garbled by improper use of such equipment.

Radio frequencies assigned to police agencies are limited. Therefore the best possible use must be made of them. They are like party lines on a telephone system. When many radio units must use a single frequency, they must conserve air time so that the most urgent messages will receive priority. This can be achieved if officers avoid nonessential conversations with their dispatchers and between themselves in their car-to-car system, if they communicate in such a manner that their messages will not have to be repeated, and if they plan their transmissions ahead to make the best possible use of air time.

Engineering problems involving dead spots and skip effects have been largely eliminated, but mechanical malfunctions often result from improperly connected batteries, improper adjustment of the squelch control, blown fuses, or defective vibrators. Metal objects which fall or are jammed into the grill of the speaker sometimes stick to its magnet, causing it to malfunction.

When recording equipment is available for the dictation of reports, officers can make the best use of it by applying a few basic techniques. They can improve their dictating ability by reading transcribed reports critically to determine where their weaknesses are, organizing their material before dictating it, and using simple, clear language.

The principles of dictation apply equally to the use of the telephone, but some additional factors must be considered by the officer when he uses the telephone to communicate with others. The telephone is the only medium through which many people come in direct contact with the police. The voice they hear over it represents the department to them. Courtesy and an attitude that reflects a sincere desire to be of service are essential if the best possible police image is to be established with the public.

Reports are a never-ending cause of misunderstanding between people. Usually, by applying some simple rules of expression, much of this problem can be eliminated. Clear writing requires clear thinking. Clarity can be achieved by using simple, precise, and objective words joined in short sentences. Many writing weaknesses result from the writer's inability to place the right word at the right place and to organize his thoughts by putting sentences together so that the reader will draw the intended conclusion from the evidence.

Some written reports are highly structured so that basic data can be placed in boxes. Even these generally require additional information about what happened because of the great variety of police incidents that require reports. The additional information may be reported in chronological order or in pure narrative form without following a strict time sequence; but whatever pattern is followed in describing the subject matter and organizing the report, it should meet the requirements of clarity, accuracy, and completeness.

Review

Questions

1. What agency assigns radio frequencies to police departments?
2. How many mobile units may ordinarily be serviced by one radio frequency without seriously overloading that frequency?
3. What is the difference between a call for help and a call for assistance?
4. What are the main limitations on portable radio equipment?
5. What are overtones in communicating?
6. Why are overtones so important in telephone conversations?
7. How can feedback caused by noise be prevented or reduced during a telephone conversation?
8. Why should lengthy long distance telephone calls be planned ahead?
9. What is an objective expression? Give an example.
10. What is a subjective expression? Give an example.
11. What is a chronological report?
12. What is a narrative report?
13. Define prima facie; corpus delicti.
14. Why should a crime or arrest report contain evidence of at least a prima facie corpus delicti?
15. What is the usual objective of a defense counsel in the cross-examination of a witness?

Exercises

1. Describe the steps which should be followed in making a short radio transmission.
2. How should the procedure be modified if the transmission is long?
3. Explain how a two-way radio system differs from a three-way system.
4. Describe how the squelch control should be adjusted.
5. What are some of the technical problems that occasionally

interfere with good radio transmission? What can the officer do to overcome them?

6. Describe the more common man-made problems that interfere with mobile radio communications.
7. Describe two common causes of transmitter failure.
8. Describe three common causes of vibrator failure.
9. Explain how an open switch on the microphone might affect a radio communications system.
10. What are some of the most common faults in dictating police reports on tape? How can these be eliminated or reduced?
11. Enumerate and describe the fundamentals of clear writing.
12–13. Rewrite the information given in items 12 and 13 in the proper form for the narrative part of a crime report. Use whatever style is considered best for this report. Assume additional details if they are needed for a complete report. Underline the information you add. Refer to previous chapters if necessary in describing property.
12. Vict. stated that he put his jewelry on this morning about 8:00 a.m. before taking his wife to church. Vict. stated that when he returned home, he took his jewelry off and put it in a Boulava watch case that he uses to put his jewelry in. Vict. stated that he placed the jewelry case on top of the dresser in the bedroom. Later on he went to pick up his wife at church, and he could not locate her. He then came back home and went back after her later on and still could not locate her. Vict. stated that he returned home and went to the garage. According to him, his wife came home shortly thereafter. He heard her talking to someone in the kitchen, but when he went in the house, she was alone. He and his wife started to argue. She denied anyone was with her. He stated that he went out to the garage again to keep from arguing. When he returned to the house, he discovered that the jewelry was gone. Vict.'s wife stated that she was in the house and did not notice that the jewelry was missing. Vict. stated that when he left home each time, all the doors and windows were locked. When he returned home, the doors and windows were still locked. There was no evidence of forcible entry. Ofcs. checked the house for any entry. They found the back door could not be locked because of a broken latch. Property missing was:

1 stick pin—white metal w/white stone cluster—no. of stones unk.—	$ 250.00
1 ring (mans)—yellow metal w/one lge. white stone in center—	$ 650.00
1 watch (mans wrist) yellow metal, 12 white stones on face—brand name unk. & serial # unk.	–$ 275.00
Total	$1,175.00

13. P/R stated that she let susp. A visit her at her home on two occasions. She then told him not to come back any more. He came to her home on Jan. 3 (this year), cut the screen on the front door, and tried to enter. P/R refused to let him in. He then called her on the phone and threatened to throw lye in her face. On Jan. 20 at 11:40 p.m. above susp. appeared again & commenced to beat on the door. P/R, using a chrome plated, 2″ barrel, 22 cal. 9-shot revolver with brown plastic handles, ser.# P 28965, Barrel # H & R 821, fired one shot through the door facing and into the edge of the door. The bullet fell out and could not be found. Notifications made. No want on gun. Registered to victim.

6

Field Interrogations, Identifications, and Arrests

The police activity of inquiring into a person's identity and the reason for his or her presence at an unusual time and place or under suspicious circumstances plays an important role in the prevention of crime and the apprehension of criminals. Such contacts have been variously referred to as field shakes, field interrogations, field inquiries, and field contacts. Their quality and the frequency with which they are conducted will contribute materially to the success of the patrol force in repressing crime.

Legal versus Practical Implications in Field Detentions

While there are some legal limitations to an officer's right to stop and question individuals—even without arresting them—the courts have consistently held that such activities are legitimate whenever they are reasonably necessary to protect the public safety. Every officer will sooner or later find he has to choose between imagined or real legal restraints and practical safety considerations when he stops and questions a person whom he does not have sufficient cause to arrest. If he acts in good faith and if there are reasonable grounds for stopping the person, a thorough pat-down or frisk for concealed weapons would be justified. If found, the weapons could be used as evidence. There are no hard-and-fast rules which hold under all circumstances, but if doubt exists, the officer should use whatever means are reasonably necessary to determine if the suspect is armed.

Legal Considerations   In two landmark decisions, the Terry and Sibron cases,[1] the United States Supreme Court pointed out a number of guidelines for officers to follow in stop-and-frisk cases:

1. A *seizure* under the Fourth Amendment is involved whenever an officer restrains another person and prevents him from walking away by physical force or a show of authority; not every contact between an officer and a citizen involves a seizure.
2. If a seizure is involved, a pat-down of the outer clothes of the person in an attempt to find a weapon is a *search* which must be based on reasonable grounds if any weapon or evidence seized is to be admissible against the person under the Fourth Amendment.
3. An officer may stop and detain a person under appropriate circumstances to make an investigation for possible criminal acts even though there may not be sufficient cause to make an arrest; and, based upon his experience, if he has reasonable cause to believe the person may be armed and presently dangerous, he may properly conduct a *limited* search of the outer clothing in an attempt to discover weapons which might endanger him. If he finds such evidence, it may be used against the person.
4. The search would be justified even in the absence of reasonable cause to make an arrest if the facts available at the time would satisfy the reasonable-man test, i.e., would the facts warrant a man of reasonable caution and prudence believing that his safety or that of others was in danger. An officer is not entitled to seize and search every person on the street or every person of whom he makes inquiries, without reasonable grounds for doing so.
5. A search incident to an arrest must be based on probable cause.

[1] *Terry v. Ohio*, 392 U.S. 1, 88 S. Ct. 1868, 20 L. Ed. 2d 889 (1968); *Sibron v. New York*, 88 S. Ct. 1889, 20 L. Ed. 2d 917 (1968); see also *Peters v. New York*, 36 LW 4589 (1968).

It may be justified not only by the need to protect the arresting officer from an assault with a concealed weapon but by the need to explore for evidence or contraband. It may properly involve an extensive search of the person.

A search for weapons made without reasonable cause to arrest must be limited by the circumstances which make its need apparent. It must be restricted to those measures necessary to discover weapons that could harm the officer or others nearby. It is something less than a full search. Nevertheless, when officers have reason to believe that they are dealing with an armed and dangerous individual, they have a right to make a reasonable search for hidden weapons *regardless of whether they have probable cause to arrest the person for a crime.*

Basis for Stopping, Detaining, and Searching   Pedestrians or motorists on the street may be stopped and detained for questioning when the circumstances under which they are observed are such as would convince a reasonable person that an inquiry should be made in the interests of public safety. The detention must be based upon the objective perceptions of the officer rather than upon vague suspicions or subjective feelings. If the grounds for the detention are not based on reasonable cause, any evidence seized will not be admissible in court if charges are brought against the suspect based on the incident. This reasonable cause may not be enough to justify an arrest but may still justify a temporary detention. It may be established by the unusual or suspicious circumstances under which the suspect is observed, the time, the location, the conduct of the person, and his connection with some activity related to crime. Officers may require a motorist to step from his vehicle and may make a cursory search of his person if there are reasonable grounds for believing that the driver is armed.

Grounds for search may be established by the nature of the crime of which the individual is suspected, whether it involved a weapon, the time of day, the place of the stop, the officer's knowledge of the reputation or record of the suspect, the number of officers making the stop, the number of suspects, their demeanor, evidence of weapons present, furtive or evasive actions, and the like. One factor may not be sufficient by itself to justify a search, but a combination may provide ample basis to detain and search. The right to detain does not automatically give the right to make a cursory search for weapons, but the officer does have the right to protect himself from unexpected attack by searching for and by relieving the suspect of any weapons when the circumstances are such that there are reasonable grounds to believe that he is armed. The search for weapons, however, cannot be used as a general exploratory search for contraband or evidence.[2]

Once the suspect is detained, he or she may be held as long as is reasonably necessary to accomplish the inquiry. Detention of a suspect for a period beyond what is reasonable under the circumstances becomes unlawful, and any evidence taken during the period of unlawful detention would not be admissible against him under the McNabb-Mallory rule;[3] however, new facts developed during the inquiry which suggest additional inquiry may justify further detention and investigation.

Practical Aspects of Field Interrogations

Field interrogations should not be made indiscriminately for the purpose of "blackening the book," or showing a large quantity of work on the officer's log. Every officer should realize the true worth of selective field contacts. Reports of such contacts are a source of valuable information to investigators and frequently provide clues about suspects that might not be available from any other source.

Attempts to mislead superiors by field contact reports that have been prepared from old citation books or the telephone directory will soon be uncovered by supervising officers if they regularly check the work of their subordinates to determine its quality or by investigators conducting follow-up investigations.

Selective Field Contacts   Who should be the subject of a field interrogation? The general criteria are based upon time, place, and circumstances.

If criminals are to be prosecuted successfully, it is imperative that they be arrested in a manner and under conditions that will permit the use of evidence collected against them. This suggests the need for an appropriate basis for each field interrogation.

In determining whether a person has been properly stopped by the police for questioning, the courts have consistently ruled that factors such as recent reports of crime in the area; the time of day or

[2] Evelle J. Younger, "Stop and Frisk," *Law Enforcement Legal Information Bulletin,* Los Angeles County District Attorney, vol. IV, no. 6, June 1968, pp. 112–114.
[3] *McNabb v. United States,* 318 U.S. 332, 63 S. Ct. 608, 87 L. Ed. 819 (1943); *Mallory v. United States,* 77 S. Ct. 1356, 1 L. Ed. 2d 1479 (1957).

night; the type of information in the officer's possession regarding criminal activity in the vicinity; possession by the suspect of certain types of tools—especially when carried on his person—such as pry bars, channel lock pliers, small penlight, lock picks, etc.; knowledge of his past criminal record; traffic violations committed by him; or furtive acts and a suspicious manner are significant in determining whether there was reasonable cause for the detention.

The power of the police—charged with the apprehension of criminals and the prevention of crime—to stop persons on foot or in vehicles and inquire into the reason for their presence in a particular place or at a particular time is well established even when there is not enough cause to justify an arrest. Officers would be justly censurable if they did not make such inquiries. Accordingly, they should be alert for circumstances under which they should question persons on their beat.

At times they may decide that, rather than conduct an immediate field interrogation, a better course of action would be to wait a few moments and observe the suspect on the chance that he or she may commit an act that will eventually justify an arrest. Such observation may really provide a sound basis for the interrogation. A prowler in an alley is one thing. It is another thing if he or she tries to pry open a window.

Such specific facts should be clearly recorded for later reference in the event of a criminal prosecution. These may be the basis for drawing logical inferences which reasonably warrant the detention and search.

Persons who do not "fit" the neighborhood, such as a person loitering around playgrounds where children congregate, or a person wearing sneakers and dark clothing in an alley where adjacent buildings have been the target of recent burglaries who explains that he or she has been walking his dog even though he or she does not live in the area, would be examples of selective contacts.

Persons carrying boxes, bags, luggage, or unusual objects when this would be out of the ordinary may be burglars carrying away their loot. Persons who act furtively or take evasive actions by changing their course, crossing the street, etc., when they see a police officer approaching, or who dispose of an object when they think they have been seen by an officer, or persons between buildings—especially at night—who quickly move to the street and try to look like innocent pedestrians are also good subjects for interrogation.

Individuals—especially minors—loitering in unusual places, working on a car, or just sitting in it under unusual circumstances—sometimes trying to give the impression of a petting party—or persons sounding a horn or whistling may be lookouts for another criminal or may be waiting for an opportunity to commit a crime. These should be considered suspicious by the patrol officer, especially when the individuals are strangers in the area.

Contacts with persons such as these require a considerable amount of tact as well as an unusual amount of caution. The subject of the inquiry may be a law-abiding citizen who may or may not be able to give a convincing reason for being in the area because he hadn't thought that he might be asked to give one, or he may be a dangerous criminal who has prepared a convincing act or explanation knowing that he may be stopped by the police and questioned. An officer should view with suspicion a story that seems to be too "pat," as it may have been concocted to mislead him. Burglars and other criminals often carry a dog whistle and leash as cover to explain their presence in a dark alleyway. They may pretend intoxication or claim that they went there to relieve themselves, or they may resort to other devices to mislead the police in the event their activities are questioned. Male/female couples have been known to team up to commit burglaries and other criminal acts. Therefore couples should not be overlooked as suspects under certain conditions.

Whether the observations which formed the basis for the field interrogation were enough to establish reasonable cause to support an arrest or merely a detention will depend on the circumstances of each case. A search of a suspect in connection with a detention must be guided by the rules just discussed. A search incident to a formal arrest may generally be more detailed than one connected with a detention in which no weapon was found in a cursory frisk. It is appropriate at this point to include a brief discussion of the major legal aspects of arrests which often form the basis for a search.

Arrests and the Use of Force

Before a peace officer may arrest a person without a warrant, he must have probable or reasonable cause to believe that a criminal offense has been or is being committed by the person to be arrested. *Probable* cause has been defined by the courts as being that amount of trustworthy evidence which is sufficient to convince a man of reasonable caution that an offense has been or is being committed.[4]

In cases involving minor offenses or misdemeanors, the law of

---

[4] *Brinegan v. United States,* 338 U.S. 160 (1949).

most jurisdictions requires that the acts constituting such crimes be committed in the officer's presence. Such in-presence requirements can be satisfied through any of the officer's senses. Laws governing the more serious, felonious offenses ordinarily require only that the officer have probable cause to believe that such a crime has been committed by the person to be arrested.

In order to accomplish one of their major objectives, the control of crime through the apprehension and convictions of criminals, officers should have a good working knowledge of the laws of arrest in their own jurisdiction. These rules are their most valuable tools. To perform their duties effectively, they must also know what factors constitute probable or reasonable cause.

Probable cause may be established from evidence coming to the officer's personal attention through his senses, through information provided by informants, or through statements of the person arrested. Thus, the presence of a suspect at an unusual time and place, his known criminal record, his suspicious acts, or his evasive or contradictory statements or admissions may not by themselves establish probable cause for believing the person has committed a burglary or other offense; but in combination, coupled with the officer's ability, based on training and experience, to interpret the facts and draw inferences from them may be sufficient to justify an arrest on probable cause. A field interrogation often leads to an arrest.

Making an Arrest   When an officer in uniform has made a decision to arrest, he should substantially notify the person to be arrested of the intent to arrest and the charge. He must then place the person under physical restraint unless the person voluntarily submits to the officer's authority.

Use of Force in Arrests   Should the person refuse to submit to restraint or should he or she resist the arrest, officers are entitled to use whatever force is reasonably necessary to effect the arrest or overcome the resistance. They are not justified in using deadly force, however, to overcome minor resistance, nor are they justified in killing in any case involving a misdemeanor only.

In felony cases, the law is broader and gives officers more latitude in using force to accomplish the arrest or overcome resistance. They must, however, use force prudently and with due regard for the safety of other innocent persons.

Most agencies have established rules that are more restrictive than the law in governing the use of force by officers. The scope and intent of these rules should be clearly understood by every officer. He should decide how he will apply them. In this respect, he has only two alternatives—to apply the rules rigidly, adhering religiously to their scope and intent, or to apply them more restrictively. He cannot properly apply them more liberally than they were intended. Good judgment will determine the propriety of the force he uses in any particular situation. It is rarely possible to use precisely the amount of force necessary to overcome resistance, but the force must be somewhat equal to the resistance or it becomes excessive and illegal. The officer cannot use great force to overcome minor resistance. He is liable for the clearly apparent use of excessive force.

The techniques and procedures the officer follows in dealing with suspects in the field should be governed by established laws and regulations. Any substantive departure from these can only lead to criticism.

Techniques in Stopping Vehicles Containing Known or Suspected Felons

The history of law enforcement is full of accounts of police officers being seriously injured or killed because they were careless in dealing with dangerous suspects. Felony suspects should always be considered high risks by the officer. In some cases, persons who commit lesser crimes should also be considered dangerous and approached accordingly.

Officers can protect themselves adequately from these persons by applying some basic, commonsense techniques, but there are other risks they face that can be just as hazardous. They must guard against becoming the victim of perils such as those involved in operating their vehicle while trying to observe a suspect, communicate with headquarters, and perform a multitude of other tasks at the same time. Each is equally dangerous to them, yet they often tend to focus their attention on the suspects and disregard the other hazards.

One-Man Unit Car Stop Procedures—High-risk Suspects

Perhaps one of the most difficult decisions the officer working a one-man unit has to make is that which involves stopping and arresting the occupants of a vehicle who are strongly suspected of being dangerous felons or misdemeanants or who are known to be wanted for serious crimes. There are times when he might feel that he must take some positive action regardless of the danger or risk losing the suspects in traffic; however, he should restrain himself unless there are compelling reasons why he should not wait for a backup unit to assist him. The safest procedure is to follow the suspects until assistance arrives, then stop the vehicle using two-man car techniques to control them. If he chooses to follow the suspects while waiting for a backup unit, he should remain close enough so that he will not lose them if they make quick lane or direction changes or take other evasive action or if he is stopped by traffic or signal changes and cannot follow.

Prestop Procedures   Before deciding to stop such suspects without waiting for help, officers should check their hot sheet and the notations they have made concerning recent car thefts and wanted suspects. Any information they may be able to obtain about these will help them deal with the suspects more safely.

Sometimes, when an immediate stop is not essential, it may be practicable to make a "running want"—a check through the dispatcher while the car is being followed—to see if the vehicle or its occupants are wanted. This may provide additional data that will guide the officer in deciding what course of action to take. Some departments with electronic information retrieval equipment can readily provide much information to the field officer in such situations.

Once he has decided to stop the suspects by himself, he should notify his dispatcher of the action he has decided to take; request assistance; and give his direction of travel, the exact location where the stop is to be made, the probable reason the suspects are wanted or the reason for his suspicions, their description, the description of the vehicle, and its license number. If he is not familiar with the area and does not know the name of the street he is on, he should determine this fact before making the stop so that the dispatcher may pass on the new information to the backup unit assigned.

If circumstances do not permit the stop to be made at the location given to the dispatcher, the officer should transmit the correct location before he leaves his vehicle. When his call is acknowledged, he should activate his red light and siren and, at night, his high beams, focus his spotlight on the suspect's car, and pull it into any available space. This may be of advantage to him by giving him the element of surprise.

He should, whenever possible, make the stop in a well-lighted area, preferably in the middle of the block where he is most protected from traffic, and where he is most visible to other persons. If there is time to make a choice, the stop should be made away from low fences, bushes, alley openings, intersections, rough terrain, or other hostile locations, high-speed areas where he is exposed to traffic, or places which might afford cover for the suspects or make escape easier for them.

The front of the police vehicle should not be driven past the left rear of the suspect's car when the red light and siren are activated. The noise of the siren—especially when it is unexpected—causes some people to panic and may cause the driver to stop suddenly or swerve into the police car. The officer should be especially alert at this time so that he is not involved in a rear-end collision or forced to the left into oncoming traffic. If he activates the red light and siren when he is too far to the rear of the suspect's car, he may invite an attempt to escape.

When it becomes apparent that the driver understands that he is to stop at the side of the road, the police car should fall behind him when he sees that it is safe to do so and follow him to the curb. The left side of the police car should be about 3 feet to the left of the suspect vehicle and approximately one-half car length to the rear. In this position, the left rear of the car will provide a safety zone and protect him from the traffic flow. At night, if all available light from the police car is focused on the suspects, the officer will have the added advantage of being able to see them while their view of him is limited as long as he stays out of the light.

He should place his microphone on the car seat in an easily accessible position, leave his car from the left side with his shotgun at the ready position, and take a position behind his left front door where it and the motor will give him some protection in the event he is fired upon. His sidearm should be drawn if he has no shotgun. From this position, he should direct the suspects through his loudspeaker, if his vehicle is equipped with one, or in a loud, clear voice to look straight ahead and place their hands flat on the windshield with fingers spread. Those in the back seat should be directed to place their hands, with fingers spread, flat against the side windows, the back window, or atop the front seat with palms up. He should then command the driver to shut off the motor and throw the keys out the window. He should not try to remove the suspects from the automobile but should keep them in that position until assistance arrives.

Backup Unit Procedures   As the first backup officer approaches the scene, he should notify the dispatcher of his arrival and should park at the curb directly behind the first police vehicle. He should display his rear amber light and turn off his headlights to avoid being silhouetted by them as he advances if it is night. He should then slide across the seat and get out the right side of the car with his weapon at the ready. If the shotgun rack prevents this, he must go through the left door and cross to the right side of his car without being silhouetted. If his flashlight is needed, it should be held in his free hand. As he advances to a cover position past the lead vehicle, he should direct the spotlight of that car along the right side of the suspect's car. In this way, the area into which the suspects must move will be lighted while the officers can remain in a darkened area.

He should then move quickly and cautiously to a cover position at the right rear of the suspect vehicle where he can best view the occupants while their view of him is partially obstructed by the blind spot at the right rear top panel, a telephone pole, a tree, or whatever has been selected as cover. He should observe the lid of the trunk when he passes to ensure that he will not be surprised by someone lying there. The rear of panel trucks should be inspected for the same reason.

From his cover position, he should inspect the rear compartment and watch the suspects closely, especially their hands. He should indicate when he has all the occupants under observation. The other officer should then move quickly to the left rear of the suspect's vehicle where he can place the occupants under close observation. As he does so, the guard officer should move to the right several steps and direct the suspects in a loud, clear voice that they are to leave the car one at a time as he directs. He should move his position slightly from time to time depending on the direction in which the suspects' car doors open so that he can keep all the suspects under observation at all times. He should instruct suspects wearing seat belts to unfasten them with their left hand then exit as directed with both hands in front of them with fingers spread.

As he does so, the officer at the left rear should move forward to a position near the left center of the car where he can see the interior but far enough from the car that he will not be knocked over should the suspects suddenly open the door. From this position, he can observe the suspects as they leave the car. He should watch them carefully to be sure that they do not arm themselves while sliding across the seat by reaching for a weapon hidden between the cushions; under the seat, visor, or dash; or in the upholstery or door panel.

Removing Suspects from Car   The first suspect should be told to put both hands out the window, spread his fingers apart, and open

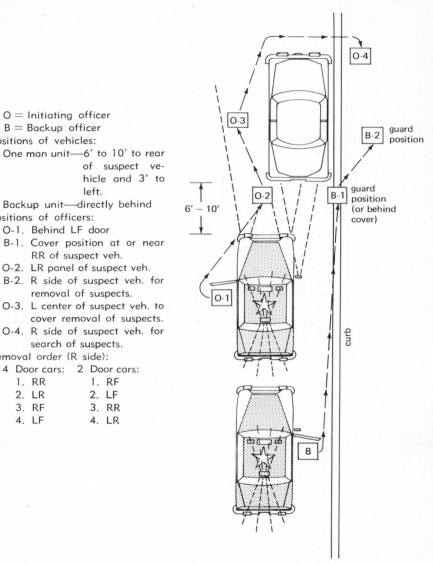

O = Initiating officer
B = Backup officer
Positions of vehicles:
  One man unit—6' to 10' to rear
            of suspect ve-
            hicle and 3' to
            left.
  Backup unit—directly behind
Positions of officers:
  O-1. Behind LF door
  B-1. Cover position at or near
        RR of suspect veh.
  O-2. LR panel of suspect veh.
  B-2. R side of suspect veh. for
        removal of suspects.
  O-3. L center of suspect veh. to
        cover removal of suspects.
  O-4. R side of suspect veh. for
        search of suspects.
Removal order (R side):
  4 Door cars: 2 Door cars:
    1. RR   1. RF
    2. LR   2. LF
    3. RF   3. RR
    4. LF   4. LR

Figure 6-1. HIGH-RISK STOP—ONE-MAN UNIT WITH BACKUP UNIT.

the car door from the outside. As the other suspects leave the car,
they should be told to face away from him, kneel with their legs
crossed and their fingers interlaced behind their heads, or if they are

believed to be highly dangerous, to lie flat on their stomachs, spread their legs, and place their arms to the sides, palms up. The wall search position described below may be used as a third alternative although it has certain disadvantages.

Ordinarily, the occupants should be removed from the right side of their car. The person in the right rear seat in a four-door car should get out first. The occupant in the left rear should follow. He should be told to close his door with his foot so that it cannot be used as a shield for those in the front seat. The occupant in the right front should then be removed, followed by the driver. In two-door cars, the passenger in the right front should be removed first, followed by the driver, the person in the right rear, and the person in the left rear.

The procedure for removing suspects from a car and putting them in a search position should not be inflexible but must be adaptable to unusual circumstances. While it is much safer to remove all suspects from the right side of the car to protect them from oncoming traffic, if one suspect leaves the car on the left side, all should use the left door so that they can be kept close together for best control. The less they are permitted to walk about, the less chances they will have to escape.

Alternate Procedures   In some cases, circumstances may dictate that neither officer leaves his cover position behind the front door of the police car. If the suspects are believed to be highly dangerous, it is better to park the police car directly behind theirs. The door of the police car can be used more safely as a shield as it will not project so far into the road and expose the officer to the danger of traffic from the rear. Also, at night, the spotlights can be used to best advantage to light the suspect car from this position. From that position, it may be most feasible to tell the suspects to leave their vehicle and take the desired position before they are approached for the search.

When all suspects have been removed from the car and placed in the search position chosen, the officer on the left side of the suspects' car should go to the right side to assist in the search. The terrain in which the stop is made may dictate which position is the most feasible under the circumstances. The search can then be carried out as described later in this chapter.

Wall Search   In some cases the typical wall search may be made. The suspects in this type of search should be directed to lean against the side of their car, a wall, fence, etc., with their feet as far away from it as possible. The search can then be made by one officer while the other stands guard. The searching officer should place his right foot inside the right foot of the suspect when searching from the right and his left foot inside the suspect's left foot when the search is made from the left. While the detailed search is being made with one hand, the other should be placed in the small of the suspect's back. Any motion the suspect makes will then be telegraphed, and the officer will be in a position to kick the suspect's feet from under him if he becomes aggressive. The officer should holster his sidearm securely before the search starts. He should be careful as he moves from side to side to avoid getting in the guard officer's line of fire. If there is more than one suspect, the officer can avoid positioning himself between them by searching one side of the suspect on one end of the line then moving him to the other end to complete the search.

The primary disadvantage of the wall search is that the officer is vulnerable to attack by an agile suspect, who, by slightly shifting his weight, can whirl and kick or strike the officer with considerable force. Criminals will often practice diligently how to assault officers from the wall search position. If this position is used, the suspect should be required to place his feet a distance from the wall equal to at least ninety percent of his height so that almost all his weight is resting on his hands.

Two-Men Unit Car Stop Procedures—High-risk Suspects

The prestop procedures followed by two-men units are substantially the same as those of single-man units except under some rather obvious circumstances noted below. Officers in two-men units should keep each other informed of their observations of the suspects, their location in the vehicle, what they appear to be doing, what they do after becoming aware that they are to be stopped by the police, etc. The same communications procedures of notifying the dispatcher and checking the suspects by radio and on the hot sheet should be followed as in the case of a single officer except that the passenger officer performs these tasks.

Ordinarily, in two-men units, the police car should be safely positioned to the left rear of the suspect vehicle before the red lights are turned on so that the movements of the occupants—especially their hands—can be observed during the stopping period. At night, the spotlight can be used to illuminate the interior of the car to observe the occupants. This sometimes is best accomplished by shining the spotlight in their rearview mirror. The single officer of a one-man unit may not be able to do this, since most of his attention must be devoted to driving—especially just before the stop is made.

The warning lights to the rear should be displayed to warn other motorists of the presence of the police car. The passenger officer in a two-men unit can also note the exact location where the suspects throw evidence from their car so that the evidence may be found later. Although the lone officer should make a mental note of such facts, he may be unable to pinpoint the exact location where this occurs, especially when the objects are discarded in rural areas where precise landmarks are not present. Curves in the road, trees, road mark posts, culverts, bridges, telephone or power poles, etc., often provide good reference points for such purposes and should be carefully noted for later use.

Stopping the Suspects   As in a one-man unit, the police car should be driven to the curb at a safe distance behind the suspect's car, parked with the left half of the police car to the left of the suspect's vehicle and from 6 to 10 feet to the rear as shown in Figure 6-2. The same consideration should be given in selecting the stopping place as in the one-man unit operation. The most dangerous time in this procedure is when the police car is being parked and *before* the passenger officer is in the guard position. It is then that the suspects are most likely to try to escape or take offensive action against the officers.

When the suspect's car has been stopped, the passenger officer should step quickly to the roadway with a weapon in hand and use the door as a shield. From here he should command the suspects, directing the driver to turn off the motor and throw the keys out the window. He should order the front seat occupants to place their hands flat on the windshield with fingers apart and rear seat passengers to place their hands in the same position on the door windows where they can be clearly seen.

The driver-officer should step out behind his open door and cover the suspects until the passenger-officer quickly moves to the guard position at the right rear of the suspects' vehicle to observe the occupants. The procedures to be followed in removing the suspects one by one and placing them in the search position are the same as for one officer assisted by a backup unit.

D = Driving officer
P = Passenger officer
Position of police vehicle:
   Same as initiating vehicle in Figure 6-1.
   (6'–10' to rear and 3' to L of suspect veh.)
Positions of officers (in sequence):
   1. P-1. Behind RF door.
   2. D-1. Behind LF door.
   3. P-2. To guard or cover position at RR of
        suspect veh.
   4. D-2. To guard position at LR of suspect
        veh.
   5. P-3. To R side of suspect veh. for removal
        of suspects.
   6. D-3. To L side of suspect veh. to cover
        removal.
   7. D-4. Search position.
Order of removal of suspects:
   Same as Figure 6-1.

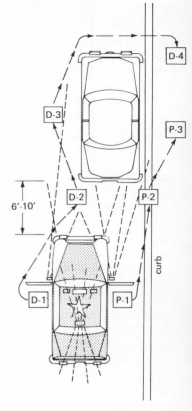

Figure 6-2.   TWO-MEN UNIT—HIGH-RISK STOP.

Traffic Stops—General Procedures

When the stop involves a minor traffic offender the officer should exercise the same care as in another case involving a more serious offense; yet an officer is often involved in so many of these incidents that he begins to consider them routine and of minor importance. It is then that he is most likely to become careless and wind up as a casualty when he encounters a truly dangerous suspect who has been stopped for a minor traffic violation. The officer is expected to use good judgment so that his actions do not become unreasonably offensive, but he is never expected to place public relations considerations over personal safety.

Traffic Stops—Two-Men Units

The general procedures discussed earlier in this chapter in the section on stopping vehicles containing high-risk suspects should be followed in all car stops by both one-man and two-men units. These techniques may require some modifications depending upon the circumstances of each case, however. The reason for the stop, the nature of the violation, the conduct of the occupants of the vehicle before and after they observe the officers, the time of day or night, and any unusual condition of the vehicle which might give rise to suspicions certainly should guide the officer in taking whatever measures are reasonable to protect himself during the contact.

As soon as practicable after the violation is observed, the officers should stop the offender, first getting his attention by short, sharp signals from the horn. He can then be directed by arm signals, or flashing movements of the spotlight at night, to stop at the curb. The siren should not be used to attract his attention except as a last resort. It often creates panic and may cause an unexpected and dangerous reaction by the driver.

Selecting Location for Stop   The suspect vehicle should be stopped in a legal position if practicable. Unlike incidents involving felony suspects, an immediate stop is not urgent when minor traffic violations are observed. Sometimes, however, even in these cases, the pullover should be made quickly so that the violator will not take advantage of a delay and try to evade apprehension.

Places for the stop which are safest for the officer and the motorist should be selected, such as a location out of the traffic flow where the opportunities for escape are least. Bridges, narrow roadways where off-highway parking is not possible, soft shoulders, freeway bottlenecks, and high-speed areas which do not afford good protection to the officer should be avoided if possible.

Position of Vehicles   The police vehicle should be positioned as in a high-risk stop. The officer should avoid overshooting the violator's vehicle. Should he overshoot, he should make a U turn and park behind the violator's vehicle. He is extremely vulnerable while in front of the motorist and should therefore avoid stopping there. Whenever possible, he should park well off the traveled portion of the roadway. If the violator is parked too close to the traffic, he should be asked to move to a safer position out of the traffic flow. After he becomes aware that he is under observation, he should be watched for any attempt to arm himself, to hide weapons, to conceal, discard, or destroy evidence.

Precautions in Approaching Violators   The officers should carefully watch the movements of the occupants of the violator's car at all times after their initial observations. As the police car is being stopped, the passenger officer should increase the volume of the radio so that broadcasts can be heard from outside. As soon as the police car stops, he should step from it and move to a position in the blind spot at the right rear panel of the violator's car. He should attract the attention of the occupants to himself either by using his flashlight or by tapping or bumping the fender as he approaches. He should position himself where he will be able to observe the movements of the occupants, watch the right side of the violator's vehicle, and cover his partner's movements as shown in Figure 6-3. An assault or an attempt to escape is most likely to occur while he is taking this guard position.

Meanwhile, the driver officer should open his car door and step out after looking to the rear to make certain that he will not be endangered by traffic. By following this procedure, only one officer moves forward at a time. The driver should delay his approach until his partner is in the guard position and should then position himself just to the rear of the front door of the violator's vehicle, checking the back seat before passing to make sure no one there poses a hazard to him. At the rear of the front door the officer can examine the interior of the car. This will force the violator to turn slightly to look back, and he will not be able to open his door and knock the officer off balance or move suddenly without telegraphing his movements. The officer should then move to the front of the front door and *face the rear* where he can talk with the violator while watching him, the other occupants of the car, and the approaching traffic which is usually the greatest hazard to him.

It is usually not necessary to remove the violator and his passengers from the vehicle when only a minor traffic law violation is involved. Nor would it ordinarily be necessary or appropriate for the officers to draw their weapons in such cases. However, they should not conclude that they are dealing only with a routine traffic stop until they reasonably satisfy themselves that the violator and his passengers are not a danger to them.

During this contact, the passenger officer should continue to watch the occupants of the violator's car. When the interview starts, he should move back a few steps, out of the light if it is night, and continue his observations while his partner concludes the contact.

D = Driving officer
P = Passenger officer
Position of police vehicle:
   Same as in Figure 6-2.
Positions of officers:
   1. P-1. In blind spot a RR of violator's veh.
   2. D-1. Inspect interior of violator veh. from
             position along L side.
   3. D-2. If safe, move to front of LF door of
             violator's veh., facing to rear to
             watch violator and traffic from the
             rear.
   4. P-2. Guard and observation position out
             of car lights.

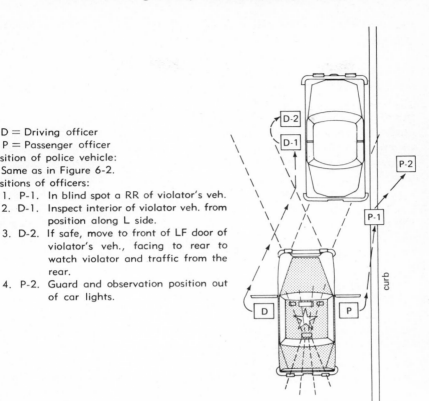

Figure 6-3.   TRAFFIC STOP—TWO-MEN UNITS.

One-Man Unit Traffic Stops

When an officer assigned alone to a patrol unit finds it necessary
to stop a motorist who has committed a traffic violation, he should
carefully evaluate the circumstances before committing himself to
a particular course of action. He should follow the same general procedures as for a two-men unit traffic stop with any modifications
needed. His main consideration should be his personal safety. If he
is doubtful that he should make the stop alone, he should call for a
backup unit even if this procedure entails following the violator
a considerable distance before that unit arrives.

If he decides to make the contact alone, his approach to the
violator should be very careful in the safest place available. Wherever

the stop is made, the officer should watch traffic approaching from the rear on his side of the roadway. This is his greatest hazard and he must be constantly alert so that if necessary he can jump onto the hood of the violator's car to avoid being struck by an intoxicated, sleepy, or inattentive motorist.

Police vehicles are struck from the rear by such drivers most frequently when traffic is light with considerable intervals between cars. It is believed that these drivers mistakenly think the taillights of the police car are those of a moving vehicle. They move over to follow it and do not realize until too late that it is actually stopped.[5] The frequent, tragic consequences of such incidents should be a constant reminder to officers that they must be alert to this danger.

On occasion, the officer should approach an interview position on the right side if traffic conditions are such that he would be unnecessarily exposed to danger by walking or standing on the street side. Ordinarily, traffic violators will expect the officer to approach on the left side. He should therefore vary this procedure from time to time and do the unexpected as a precautionary step.

Searching Suspects

Many officers have been injured or killed by suspects who supposedly were searched carefully but who had hidden weapons which were not found. If there is reasonable cause to believe a suspect is armed or if there is reasonable cause to arrest him, a thorough, meticulous search should be made of his person and immediate presence for additional weapons, evidence, or contraband.

In the Chimel[6] case, the United States Supreme Court ruled that a search without a warrant could not extend beyond the arrestee's person and his reach. Therefore the scope of a search incident to an arrest may be based on the arrestee's build, mobility, dexterity, and conduct. Should he attempt to escape, the search could extend to the places which have come or are likely to come within his reach. Likewise, evidence thrown by the suspect out of his reach could be seized under the rule permitting the seizure of objects in plain view.

The Chimel rule does not apply the same rigid standards of arm's length searches to automobiles. Also, a search could be made beyond arm's length without a warrant with a valid consent or in an emer-

[5] Department of California Highway Patrol, *Enforcement Tactics,* H.P.G. 70.6, Sacramento, 1969, pp. 3–8.
[6] *Chimel v. California,* 395 U.S. 752, 23 L. Ed. 2d 685, 89 S. Ct. 2034 (1969).

gency situation such as hot pursuit, or where it is necessary to aid a possible victim if there is imminent and substantial threat to life, health, or property.[7]

Cursory Searches—Male Suspects   Any suspect should always be frisked for weapons if there is any reasonable cause to believe he is armed. In the casual field contact, a pat-down search is ordinarily sufficient. There will be no need for a full body search. One is not legally warranted without reasonable cause to believe the person is armed. Such cause is ordinarily established by a frisk that indicates the suspect has a weapon.

Cursory Searches—Females   When a female becomes the subject of a field interrogation, the male officer should instruct her to keep her hands in sight and follow directions. He may at times deem it advisable to examine her handbag for offensive weapons and, if the handbag could be used as a weapon, he may take it from her and place it in the police car until the contact is concluded. Other items that might be used as weapons may likewise be removed from the female suspect. The officer can ask her to draw her slacks or dress tightly against her legs to reveal hidden weapons. If he must search other parts of her body for weapons, he should ordinarily do so with the back of his hand. The techniques of making thorough searches of females are discussed later in this chapter.

Detailed Field Search—Male Suspects   The most dangerous suspect is the one who has taken pains to conceal a weapon so that a superficial search will not reveal it. These are the high-risk suspects. Jailers making "skin searches" are constantly amazed at the number of weapons they find on prisoners who have supposedly been carefully searched by arresting officers.

One officer should conduct the search while the other guards the suspects. The search should begin with the suspect's hands since they pose the prime danger to the officer. Usually that is accomplished before the suspect is commanded to assume the search position. His hair should be examined for a weapon, if his hair style is such that it might conceal one. Then he should be directed to interlock his fingers behind his head if he is to be searched in the standing or kneeling position. The officer can then grasp the suspect's interlocked fingers with one hand and search from the rear with the other. The search should proceed down the arms, front and back, to

[7] *People v. Smith*, 7 Cal. 3d 282 (1972).

the armpits, around the body under the arms and across the chest and waist areas, across the back over the shoulder blades. It is very important that the entire waist area above, below, and under the belt be carefully examined for concealed weapons. The hip areas, the small of the back, the stomach, groin, and crotch areas should be given special attention as they are frequently selected as hiding places for weapons. These are sometimes hung from the belt inside the trousers and allowed to dangle between the legs into the crotch. They may be strapped, taped, or carried in holsters affixed to the upper or lower parts of the legs or hung from the neck under an arm, over the breastbone, or in the small of the back. Therefore, these areas should be thoroughly examined. One leg at a time should be searched from the front to the back and from the top of the groin area to the feet. The officer should carefully examine for weapons or contraband in the coat collar, hat, belt, belt buckle (which may itself be a dangerous weapon or may have been fashioned into a stabbing instrument), coat lining, shoulder padding, pants cuffs, shirt, socks, and shoes.

Cigarette packages should be examined. These are often used to conceal marijuana or hashish, or cigarettes impregnated with hashish oil. They may have a characteristic perfumed smell or telltale stains from the oil.

All seams on clothing and inside and outside pockets should be inspected. These often conceal razor blades, knives, wire, narcotics, and weapons of all sorts.

At times, the suspects should be handcuffed before the search is conducted if that can be accomplished safely. Suspects should be cuffed with their hands behind their backs. The handcuffs themselves become dangerous weapons if suspects can swing their arms freely in front of their bodies. Some persons can break standard handcuffs if the hands are cuffed in front.[8]

Whenever contraband or weapons are discovered, they should be called to the attention of the guard officer. He may then also testify in court where the evidence was found.

Arresting and Searching Female Suspects

When a male patrol officer finds it necessary to arrest a female suspect, he is bound by the same legal provisions in stopping, searching, and interrogating her as he is in dealing with males. In the

[8] Los Angeles Police Department, *Training Bulletin*, vol. III, issue 23, May 3, 1971.

majority of cases, he will encounter little or no difficulty; however, he should be alert, because women can be as dangerous as men. The male officer might tend to be overly lenient with a female suspect who appeals to his sympathies. There is also the possibility that the woman may threaten to accuse the man of attempted rape or other offensive behavior.

Once the officer has decided upon a course of action he should proceed with as little conflict as possible. Conversation with the suspect not bearing upon the arrest should be kept to a minimum. He should protect himself from a possible complaint by following the standard police procedures in making a body search of a female when this becomes necessary in the field. A male officer should avoid making the search himself if a female police officer or other female employee is available to make it, to assist, or to witness the procedure.

In the absence of either of these persons, he should solicit an impartial, private person—at least one female if possible—to witness the search. He should record the names, addresses, and telephone numbers of these witnesses for later reference should their statements be necessary to refute a claim by the suspect that she was molested or otherwise treated improperly. As a last resort if the male patrol officer is alone and deems it advisable to frisk her, he should do so.

In the frisk, it is seldom necessary to make a detailed body search of a female for evidence or contraband, although if he has reasonable cause to believe she is armed, he should protect himself by as extensive a search as is necessary. Each case must be decided on its own merits; however, sympathy for or fear of a suspect just because she is a female should not influence the male officer to a point where he becomes careless.

The field search made before transporting a female arrestee to the station should include some or all of the following procedures depending upon the circumstances of the arrest, the nature of the charge, whether the arrestee is combative or cooperative, and whether she is to be handcuffed or otherwise restrained.

If the subject has a handbag which could be used as a weapon, it should be taken from her. High-heeled shoes should be removed, especially if the woman is combative, since they can be used as dangerous weapons. Outer garments such as sweaters, coats, jackets, and the like should be removed, examined for weapons and returned. Packages should be taken from the arrestee and booked as her personal property or as evidence. Accessories such as belts with heavy buckles, large metal pendants, clasps, brooches, or pins should be removed from her person when circumstances dictate, as should magazines, rolled newspapers, and the like.

When a female is arrested on a serious charge and a detailed body search for evidence is indicated, ordinarily she should be hand-cuffed with her hands behind her back or otherwise securely re-strained, transported to the station, and searched there by a female under controlled conditions as may be provided for in the depart-mental rules. This procedure should be followed only when there appears to be no danger that she could destroy evidence while being transported.

Searching Vehicles

When reasonable cause exists to arrest persons in a vehicle, such cause ordinarily extends to the car and justifies a search for contra-band or evidence of the crime for which the arrest was made. Because of the mobility of vehicles, the courts generally have permitted more latitude in searching them than is the case with persons and premises.

Legal Aspects of Vehicle Searches   Although the rules of searches and seizures have changed swiftly in recent years, a few landmark decisions[9] have had such a vital bearing upon a large segment of the patrol officer's work—the stopping and searching of vehicles—that it is appropriate to discuss them at this point. Deci-sions of state appellate courts in search and seizure cases are not included because of their volume and inconsistency; however, the officers should acquaint themselves with current decisions that affect their particular jurisdiction.

Rules handed down by the U.S. Supreme Court in the Chambers case in 1970 and in the Coolidge case in 1971 provide a basis for searching a vehicle without a warrant under certain circumstances. These cases permit officers to make the search when there is an arrest and probable cause to believe the occupant has committed a criminal offense and the car contains weapons, profits, instru-ments, contraband, or evidence of the crime for which the arrest was made. Search of a car without a warrant is also permissible under this rule even though an arrest has *not* been made if probable cause exists that the vehicle contains evidence, profits, contraband, or

9 *Carroll v. United States,* 267 U.S. 132 (1925); *Harris v. United States,* 390 U.S. 234 (1968); *Chimel v. California,* 395 U.S. 752 (1969); *Chambers v. Maroney,* 399 U.S. 42 (1970); and *Coolidge v. New Hampshire,* 91 S. Ct. 2022 (1971).

instruments of an offense under investigation. The court said in Chambers,[10]

> For constitutional purposes we see no difference between on the one hand seizing and holding a car before presenting the probable cause issue to a magistrate, and on the other hand, carrying out an immediate search without a warrant. Given probable cause to search, either course is permissible under the Fourth Amendment.

The court also stated,

> The right to search and the validity of the seizure are not dependent on the right to arrest. They are dependent on the reasonable cause the seizing officer has for belief that the contents of the automobile offend against the law.

Nor need the search of the car be made at the time and place of the arrest. The court held that where an automobile could properly have been searched without a warrant on a highway, it could as well be searched without a warrant at a police station thereafter, since the probable cause continued in effect. As the court stated in the Coolidge case[11]

> The rationale of Chambers is that given a justified intrusion, there is little difference between a search on the open highway and a later search at the station. Here we deal with the prior question of whether the initial intrusion was justified.

The following examples illustrate the application of this enunciation: A suspect holds up a place of business. His car is described by witnesses. Investigating officers identify the suspect. While approaching his residence later, they see another party driving the car used in the holdup although that party is not known as a suspect in the robbery. The car may be stopped and searched since it may be assumed that it contains proceeds or instruments of the crime.[12] By

[10] *Chambers v. Maroney*, 399 U.S. 42 (1970).
[11] *Coolidge v. New Hampshire*, 91 S. Ct. 2022 (1971).
[12] *Carroll v. United States*, 267 U.S. 132 (1925); John B. Hotis, "The Warrantless Search of Motor Vehicles," *F.B.I. Law Enforcement Bulletin*, vol. 40, no. 1, March 1971, pp. 8–30.

the same reasoning, if the suspect were seen days later driving another vehicle, he could be arrested and his car searched without a warrant incident to the arrest; but the search would be limited by the Chimel rule to that area which is immediately accessible to the suspect unless there was independent cause to believe the vehicle contained evidence of the crime.

If circumstances permit a warrantless search, it should be made at the place where the vehicle is first stopped. The courts will probably continue to allow delay and removal of the vehicle to a more appropriate location if necessary in making a reasonable cause search when it is impractical to make the search at the scene; however, if the circumstances do not demand immediate action to prevent removal of the car or destruction or concealment of evidence in it, or if the car itself is not being used for some illegal purpose, then a warrantless search would not be justified. Because of the mobility of automobiles and the attendant difficulty in obtaining a warrant to search them within a short period of time, courts have usually been liberal in upholding emergency searches where there was no incidental arrest and the officer had reasonable cause to believe the vehicle contained incriminating evidence.

Despite the broad language of the opinions cited, officers should not conclude that the search warrant requirement no longer is applicable to automobiles. The Chambers and Coolidge decisions clearly indicate that search warrants may be required in some cases even though there is probable cause to believe the car contains contraband or evidence. The search may properly be made without a warrant only when the "opportunity to search is fleeting" and the car is readily movable. If it is practicable for the officer to secure a search warrant before making the search, then he must do so or risk having the evidence excluded by the court as having been improperly seized. It is practicable for him to obtain a search warrant if he knows where the car is, if he has probable cause to seize and search it, and if it is reasonable for him to take the time necessary to obtain the warrant.

Practical Aspects of Searching a Vehicle

Once reasonable cause to search a vehicle has been established, the officer is faced with the challenging task of finding the evidence. It is often hidden in the highly complex maze of compartments, hollow spaces, or recesses constructed in automobiles by the manufacturer or the criminal and used to conceal contraband, fruits of criminal acts, weapons, or other evidence. The success of the officer in finding these items will depend upon his knowledge of what to look for, how to look for it, and where it is likely to be.

Most field situations do not justify an exhaustive search involving dismantling of the car or parts of it, removing upholstery, or the like; but a cursory search, if organized and systematic, will often yield dividends that will more than reward the officer for his efforts.

First, if the vehicle's occupants have been arrested, the police officer must decide upon the scope and detail of the search. The arrestees should be placed under the full control of another officer to protect the searching officer while he focuses all his attention on making a methodical examination of the car.

If a detailed search is to be made, it should be done where the car can be placed on a hoist; it is not ordinarily undertaken in the field. This type of search may involve examining the motor exhaust system, radiator, gas or other tanks, etc., to locate contraband carefully concealed for smuggling or evading discovery.

The Cursory Vehicle Search   In many cases, a thorough search of a vehicle is not made in the field by an arresting officer because of the nature of the arrest. The ability of the officer to make discriminating judgments in these cases will depend in large part upon his experience. A drunk-driving offense, for example, would not usually require a search under the hood for alcohol.

The cursory search in the relatively minor cases will involve looking into the glove compartment, under, between, and behind seats, in map pockets, under the dashboard, behind the visors, in cigarette trays, in storage compartments, on top of the radio, heater, and glove compartment, in the ventilating system and the trunk, and in its various compartments and recesses.

The search, whether by one officer or by two, should be systematic to produce best results. It should start at the front on one side, proceed to the rear, then back to the front. The same search pattern should be followed for the other side. When two officers search, they should alternate sides so that the entire vehicle is searched twice. This provides additional opportunity for one of the officers to find items overlooked by the other. The most successful searches are made by those who follow such a systematic procedure. Officers whose searches are superficial often overlook evidence which could easily be uncovered by a more methodical procedure.

The Thorough Vehicle Search   When a thorough field search of the vehicle is indicated, a systematic and methodical examination should be made. Nothing should be left to chance. Every remote place in the vehicle must be examined. As previously discussed in *Chambers v. Maroney*, the U.S. Supreme Court has ruled that the removal of a vehicle to a garage for a search is not in violation of an occupant's Fourth Amendment rights once there is reasonable cause to make the search.

It is often best to search the car in a garage. The search should be systematic, unhurried, and thorough. Even though evidence is found before completion of the search, it should be continued until the whole vehicle is examined. All the places previously described in the cursory search should be inspected as well as the exterior portions of the car.

The front end search should include an examination of the front bumper, lights and light wells, radiator and surrounding area, grille, and motor area including the air filter and distributor. All four hubcaps and the underside of fenders should be carefully examined as should the gas tank area—especially around or under the filler spout. Evidence or contraband has even been dangled into the gas tank on a string or wire. The taillight recesses and reflectors should be examined. Contraband, fruits, or evidence of a crime is frequently taped or wired to flat surfaces and might easily be overlooked.

Inside the vehicle, the armrests, the bottom of door panels, under the dome light housing, behind the visor or rearview mirror, and all the seat belt housing, should be examined carefully. Additionally, seat cushions may have to be removed to inspect the webbing, padding, and springs. These areas are frequent hiding places for contraband. Removal of the floor mats may reveal narcotics or other evidence hidden underneath. Double walls in glove compartments sometimes are constructed to hide narcotics, weapons, or contraband.

Every article found in the car should be carefully examined to see if it contains evidence or contraband. In the trunk, the tire well, jack and accessory equipment, toolboxes, false panels, floor mats, etc., may conceal instruments of crime. Hollow places in the trunk lid should also be examined for contraband or evidence.

Evidence Handling Procedures   The officer should carefully describe evidence in his notebook, including a notation of the exact place where it was found. It should be marked appropriately and booked for later use. Names of persons present when it was located should be recorded so that they may be called as witnesses later in court if necessary.

Field Interrogations of Pedestrians—One-man Unit

A single patrol officer will often find it necessary to investigate pedestrians. Each case must be assessed according to its own merits; but if he will follow some basic guidelines, he will increase his margin of safety while conducting these inquiries.

Notification to Dispatcher   As with any contact with a suspect in the field, the officer in a one-man unit should, before leaving his car, notify his dispatcher if he plans to conduct a field interrogation. The place of the contact, the description of the suspect, and the reason for stopping him should be given. A backup unit should be requested if there is the slightest indication that the suspect or suspects are armed or dangerous. The danger inherent in all such contacts should be carefully considered in determining if assistance should be requested.

If the officer decides to make the field contact alone, he should promptly notify his dispatcher once it is concluded. A backup unit should be sent to determine if help is needed if this notification is not received in approximately ten minutes.

Location for Field Interrogation   If possible, the location for the inquiry should be in a lighted area selected to minimize the danger to the officer and to reduce the chances of escape if the suspect flees. A fence, a row of buildings, etc., do not provide as many avenues of escape as do alley openings, parking lots with rear exits, parks, yards, and driveways.

Approaching the Suspect   The immediate approach to the pedestrian suspect by the motorized patrol officer should always be made on foot, ordinarily from the rear. The officer should never direct the suspect to approach the police vehicle while the officer remains seated in it. This would place the officer in an extremely dangerous position if the suspect opens fire. It would also hamper pursuit if the suspect flees.

If the police vehicle is traveling in the same direction as the suspect, it should be stopped just before coming abreast of him—if possible without signaling the reason for stopping. The officer can then get out of the car and approach from the rear.

At night, the police car should be angled toward the suspect so that the lights illuminate him. The officer can then approach slightly to the side out of the main beam. He will thus have an advantage over the suspect who must look into the lights of the police car if he turns to face the officer. If the police officer is traveling in the opposite direction to a suspect on the opposite side of the street, he should drive past and then make a U turn and park so that the approach on foot can be made from the rear.

When the suspect is proceeding in the opposite direction to the police vehicle but on the same side of the street, the police unit should be parked far enough in front of him to give the officer time to leave the car and take a strategic position before the suspect can pass. As in the case of an approach from the rear, at night the headlights of the police car should be focused on the suspect forcing him to look into the light. The officer can stand or make his approach out of the beam in an advantageous position.

He should watch the suspect's hands closely at all times during the approach since the movement of his hands will likely signal what he is going to do. Additionally, the hands are the most obvious source of danger, and if they contain a weapon or an instrument that could be used as one, the officer should be prepared to take whatever action is necessary to protect himself.

The most dangerous time in the whole field interrogation is during the last few feet of the approach. This is when the suspect who is wanted for a crime or is armed feels that his freedom is threatened. It is at this time that he is most likely to take offensive action or attempt to flee. The officer must be alert to prevent such action.

Making the Contact   Once the subject has been halted with an appropriate greeting or command and the actual inquiry has started, the decision whether to frisk will depend on the circumstances. At times this may not be necessary; however, *if there is the slightest reason to believe he is armed, he should be searched for weapons* as previously discussed.

If the officer is dealing with a known felon or high-risk suspect— male or female—he should call for a backup unit to assist him. When it arrives, the two officers can proceed with the search as a team. Felony suspects should always be frisked. Objects that could be used as offensive weapons should be taken from them until the inquiry is concluded then returned if they are released. The frisk should not be discontinued if one weapon is found, but should be completed since many suspects carry two or more weapons. If the frisk provides reasonable cause that a suspect has a deadly or dangerous weapon concealed on his person, he should immediately be handcuffed with his hands behind his back. A full, detailed search should then be made as previously described.

Interrogating Suspects

The techniques of questioning suspects will vary somewhat with each incident as will the legal requirements relating to the taking of confessions and admissions. Adept questioning will be useless if the officer fails to comply with the rules handed down by the courts to protect individuals from involuntarily incriminating themselves.

Interview Position   When conducting the interview, the officer should stand in a position which does not expose him unnecessarily to an attack. A position in front of the suspect at arm's length with gun hip back or slightly to the suspect's right side ordinarily is the safest interview position for one suspect. If more than one suspect is involved, the officer should stand to the right of one of them, keeping that suspect between himself and the other.

The Miranda Admonishment   Any suspect who has been arrested after he has been observed committing an offense, or who is in custody or deprived of his freedom in any way, must be told his rights under the Miranda rule[13] if the officer intends to use his statement against him in a prosecution. The circumstances of each case determine whether the suspect has been deprived of his freedom of action in any way. If the interrogation is conducted in an atmosphere of coercion or the questions compel the suspect to respond, he is deprived of his freedom of action.

When circumstances of the inquiry indicate that the interrogation is to be custodial, the Miranda rule requires that the suspect be advised:

1. That he has the right to remain silent.
2. That if he gives up his right to remain silent, anything he says can and will be used as evidence against him in court.
3. That he has the right to consult with an attorney and to have that attorney present during the questioning by the police.
4. That if he is unable to afford an attorney, he is entitled to have one appointed to represent him during the course of the interrogation without charge.

The officer may solicit a waiver by the suspect of his constitutional rights to remain silent or to have an attorney. Once the suspect

[13] *Miranda v. Arizona,* 384 U.S. 436 (1966).

clearly understands his rights, he should be asked if he wants an attorney and if he wants to talk or remain silent. If he elects to talk, he should be asked if he wants an attorney present.

If the suspect elects to talk without first consulting an attorney and does not desire one during the inquiry, his response and the circumstances surrounding it should be noted or recorded as soon as practicable. If the suspect wishes to talk, he can exercise his right to remain silent at any time during the interrogation, or if he expresses a desire to have an attorney present during the questioning, the interrogation must stop.

If, however, the contact constitutes a general inquiry only and a particular investigation has not focused on the subject, the officer need not advise him of his rights, although the trend of the inquiry may indicate that one is desirable. In deciding whether to give the Miranda warning, the officer should be guided by developments in the questioning. The factors that will be considered by the courts in determining if the suspect was deprived of his freedom of action and thereby coerced into answering questions include the time of the questioning, its length, the presence of friends or relatives, the phrasing of questions, how many there were, their tone, how insistent or demanding they were, how much information the officer had regarding the guilt of the suspect, etc.

As long as the suspect is not deprived of his freedom of action, as long as no element of compulsion or coercion is present, as long as the questioning is *merely investigatory*, and if declarations of the suspect are spontaneous and voluntary, the lack of a Miranda warning is permissible; however, where doubt exists, it is better to give the advice before the inquiry begins. If officers properly stop a suspect and question him for a short time to determine whether or not a crime has been committed or to ask him if he has committed a crime—where there was a "momentary detention and questioning . . ."—a Miranda warning is unnecessary and the statements of the suspect are admissible against him if not otherwise defective.[14]

Interrogation Techniques   A cardinal rule in the interrogation of multiple suspects is that they should be immediately separated before questioning begins. Whenever possible, they should be prevented from talking with each other to reduce their opportunity to concoct a story or suggest an alibi to each other. When two officers

[14] Evelle J. Younger, *Admissibility of Out-of-Court Confessions—Law Enforcement Legal Summaries*, No. 3. California Office of State Printing, Sacramento, January 1972, pp. 7–9.

are working together and interrogate two suspects, separating them is simple. If two officers interrogate more than two suspects, one officer should question one suspect while the second officer controls the other subjects.

Likewise, a suspect or suspects should be questioned privately if uninvolved onlookers are present. The suspect should be asked, "Would you step over here and give me some information?" The necessary questions can then be asked in a low voice so that other persons cannot hear the conversation.

Names and addresses should be obtained immediately from each suspect, since much of the inquiry in the field may hinge on the place where he was observed in relation to his place of residence or employment. This forces him to give a reason for his presence. If he is lying, further questioning may provide clues to the real reason. He may produce cards or a driver's license from his wallet when asked to show evidence of his address. The officer should observe the wallet carefully as this is done. He may see pawn tickets or other items in it that may provide the basis for additional questions. The officer should *not* take a wallet for examination, however, until the owner has first removed all money from it unless, of course, the wallet and contents are evidence of a crime.

Accusations   Hasty accusations should be avoided generally, unless there is evidence to support the charge. A bluff in the form of an accusation may immediately weaken the officer's interrogation position since the suspect often will immediately recognize such a bluff when it has no merit.

Length of the Interrogation   Circumstances of each case will dictate how detailed a field interrogation should be. Sometimes answers to a few key questions will satisfy the officer that further inquiry is needless. The contact should be terminated at that point with a brief explanation of the need for such field inquiries if that seems appropriate. Usually the citizen will appreciate the necessity for such inquiries and will carry away a favorable impression of the contact provided the officer has conducted it in a professional, courteous manner and has not made the incident an offensive experience for the subject.

On other occasions, a thorough inquiry will be indicated. When a more detailed interrogation is indicated because of the suspect's evasive answers, inconsistencies in his responses may connect him with a crime. The officer should allow the suspect to talk if he is so inclined. In this way, he may make more contradictory statements.

Each may mean little by itself, but, when coupled with other such statements and pointed out to the suspect, may result in revealing admissions.

Evidence of Deception   Physical acts such as moistening the lips, yawning, sighing, deep breathing, rubbing the face, or rubbing the hands together do not necessarily indicate guilt feelings but may result from the nervousness attending the contact with the police. Such reactions should not therefore mislead the officer to false conclusions of guilt but should be pointed out to the suspect for the purpose of focusing his attention on his nervous reactions to distract him if he is concocting a story.

Field Report of Contact

If a formal report of the contact is made, it should be completed from information recorded in the notebook after the contact has ended. It should be made only when the information would serve some useful purpose as a follow-up tool for investigators or other officers. The suspect's full name, address, driver's license number, description, and companions, if any, should be included, as well as the time and place of and reason for the contact and the type of clothing he was wearing.

When the subject for a field interrogation is selected discriminatingly and the field report is properly reviewed by investigators, the data it contains may provide the lead needed to solve a crime. It may help them connect him with an offense in which the victim was able only to describe the suspect's clothing such as in a purse snatch case. It may disprove an alibi of a suspect under investigation by showing that he was observed at a place and time other than where he claimed to have been. It may place him near the scene of the crime, or it may identify his companions and connect them with the crime. If such a report is not prepared, a log entry should be made of the incident as may be required by regulations. The data in the officer's notebook will provide a permanent reference to the contact.

Foot Pursuits

Occasionally, a suspect on foot realizing that he is about to be questioned or arrested by the police will flee rather than be apprehended. Sometimes he will run because of sheer panic when an officer approaches even though he has committed no offense that has come to the attention of the police. At other times, he will flee because he has a guilty intent which would not itself constitute a crime in the absence of some act. The officer does not have any way of knowing

DRIV. LIC. NO.	1. NAME (last name first)		19. REPT. DIST.

RESIDENCE ADDRESS (if transient: from-to) | 23. SEX | 24. DESC. | 25. HAIR | 26. EYES

27. HGT. | 28. WGT. | 29. BIRTHDATE | 35. VEH. LIC. | STATE 42. | 45. MAKE/MODEL

52. MFG. | 53. VEH. YR. | 55. TYPE | 56. | COLOR 57. | 58. DRIV. ☐ PASS. ☐ | 59. DATE & TIME (24 hr. clock)

INTERIOR

67. ck. 68 if app.   70.
( ) UPHOLSTERY   ( ) STEREO TAPE
( ) BUCKET SEATS   ( ) MIRROR ORN.
( ) HEADLINER   ( ) FLOOR SHIFT

68.   71.
( ) CUSTOM   ( ) EQUIP. ADDED
( ) TORN   ( ) EQUIP. MISS'G
( ) COVER — OTHER   ( ) UNIQUE ITEM

69.
INSIDE COLOR(S)

FIELD INTERVIEW CARD

LAPD 15.43.0 (Aug. 69)

EXTERIOR

72.
( ) PAINTED INSC.
( ) STICKER/DECAL
( ) RUST/PRIMER

73.
( ) VINYL TOP
( ) DEC. PAINT
( ) LEVEL ALTERED

MODIFICATION

74.
( ) FRONT
( ) REAR
( ) OTHER AREA

BODY

75. ck. 76 if app.
( ) DAMAGE
( ) SIDE
( ) LEFT

76.
( ) RIGHT
( ) REAR
( ) FRONT

WHEELS

77.
( ) MAGS.
( ) CHROME RIMS
( ) UNIQUE SIZE

WINDOWS

78. ck. 79 if app.
( ) DAMAGE
( ) SIDE
( ) LEFT

79.
( ) RIGHT
( ) REAR
( ) FRONT

WINDOWS

80.
( ) TINTED
( ) COVERED
( ) PLAQUE/DECAL

RES. PHONE | SOC. SEC. NO. | LOCATION OF INTERVIEW

BUSINESS NAME, ADDRESS & OCCUPATION (juv.-school) | ☐ GLASSES ☐ MOUSTACHE

CLOTHING WORN | PHYSICAL ODDITIES/COMPLEXION

PERSONS WITH SUBJECT

CIRCUMSTANCES OF INTERVIEW

JUV. | ADULT | N. NAME/ALIAS

OFFICER(S) REPORTING (last name & serial no.) | DIVISION | DETAIL

Figure 6-4. FIELD INTERVIEW CARD. *(Courtesy of the Los Angeles Police Department.)*

the motives of this type of suspect. He sees the person run and can only assume there is a good reason for the flight, as flight is not ordinarily consistent with innocence.

Foot Pursuit Hazards   The officer may or may not be familiar with the neighborhood into which the suspect flees. He must make an instantaneous decision to pursue or call for assistance. If he decides to pursue, he should make every effort to apprehend the suspect quickly. If he doesn't, it is unlikely that he will be able to apprehend him at all without help.

In a pursuit on foot, especially in the dark, the officer should follow the same path taken by the fleeing suspect. The officer will find it extremely disconcerting if he takes what he believes is a short-cut through an unfamiliar backyard to head off the suspect and is caught in the throat by a low clothes line, falls into a hole, or is separated from the suspect by a wall.

If he finds it necessary to climb a fence or wall, he should quickly look over it to see what is on the other side. He should exercise great care when jumping to the ground to avoid a barbwire fence, cactus plant, thorny bush, or low-pointed picket fence on the other side. Any of these can be exceedingly dangerous. He should lower himself to the ground if he cannot see a clear place to jump.

Use of Flashlight   At night, the flashlight should be used. Although the beam of light cannot be kept on the suspect steadily, it can be used to illuminate him from time to time and to reveal hazards. It should be held away from the body if its light might make the officer a target for an assault.

The officer should be alert in a foot pursuit to the possibility of a planned ambush. He should also be on guard that the suspect does not double back or wait around a corner or in a shadow for his unsuspecting pursuer, attack and disable the officer, and make good his escape.

When two officers engage in a foot pursuit, ordinarily they should stay together if there is even a remote possibility of an ambush so that they will be able to protect each other.

Search Notifications   When a suspect is surprised while committing a crime or flees on foot when a police unit arrives, the officer should notify the dispatcher of the basic facts and summon assistance to search the area. The officer should describe the type of offense committed, the suspect, and the area into which he fled so that other officers can help seal off his possible escape routes.

Searching for the Suspect When the suspect has been pinned down, a methodical search of the area can be made. Officers should move inward once they have been stationed in strategic locations and remain in sight of each other during the search. Every possible hiding place should be examined. Shrubs, trees, roofs, open areas under houses, sheds, barbecue pits, storage areas, buildings, boxes, trash bins, etc., are often used as places of concealment by suspects. Criminals have a saying that police officers look everywhere but up, and so they frequently hide on roofs of sheds, patios, coverings of barbecues, etc.

A house-to-house or building-to-building search may be indicated depending upon the nature of the offense and other factors. Helicopters may aid to immobilize the suspect until foot personnel can find his hiding place. Vehicles should be assigned to patrol the perimeter in the event he slips through the search lines.

Apprehension of the Suspect If the suspect is apprehended, he should be handcuffed, searched immediately for weapons, and returned to the police car. Other units involved should be promptly notified so that they may terminate their search and return to their beats.

Breaking Door to Effect Arrest

There are times when a suspect will take refuge in a house or building where he thinks the police may not enter. If he commits a crime, he should not be permitted to escape responsibility for his deeds by taking sanctuary in any place. Therefore, it is the law in most jurisdictions that an officer may break a door or window of a house to effect an arrest for any crime under certain conditions: he must have reasonable grounds for believing the suspect is inside. The suspect must fail or refuse to open the door or window after the officer has identified himself, demanded that it be opened, and explained the purpose for the demand; a reasonable opportunity must be given the offender to open the door voluntarily to prevent destruction of the property. Only when the suspect refuses to submit to the processes of the law is the officer justified in making a forced entry. The rule is intended to protect the individual's right to privacy and to discourage confrontations conducive to violence.[15]

---

[15] *Miller v. United States,* 357 U.S. 301, 307–309 (1958); *Sabbath v. United States,* 391 U.S. 585, 589 (1968).

These rules apply also to felonies with several exceptions. The officer need not identify himself, demand entry, and state the purpose for which it is desired if he acts on a reasonable and good faith belief that to do so would increase the danger to him, would allow the suspect an opportunity to escape, or permit the destruction of evidence.[16] It has been held in some cases that the officer must have specific knowledge of a suspect's tendencies to violence, resistance, escape, or destruction of evidence before the exceptions apply.[17]

Field Identification

When a suspect is arrested in connection with a crime, it may be desirable to return him to the scene of the offense for identification by the victim under carefully controlled conditions; however, if he is only temporarily detained in a case where there is not sufficient cause to justify his arrest, he should not be taken to the crime scene without his consent unless there exists an emergency, such as the imminent death of the victim of an assault, and an identification or elimination of the suspect is possible.

Often a suspect is stopped on the basis of a description too general to justify an arrest or because he is leaving or is near the scene of a crime. The U.S. Supreme Court has ruled that it is necessary as a practical matter for the police "swiftly to determine whether they were on the right track . . . " in some cases and that the "one-man lineup" is not to be condemned unless it is "unnecessarily suggestive."[18]

A formal lineup of several people is not ordinarily feasible in a field situation nor is it more reliable than a one-man lineup there, since an identification in the field is made while the victims' memories are still fresh and not readily susceptible to contrivance by the police. However, to avoid the objection that a one-man lineup is unnecessarily suggestive, officers should procure a proper identification and minimize a misidentification in this way. While one officer talks with the witness or victim, another should remain out of view with the suspect. The witness or victim should be advised

---

[16] *People v. Rosales*, 68 Cal. 2d. 299, 305 (1968); *Miller v. United States*, 357 U.S. 301 (1958); *Ker v. California*, 374 U.S. 23 (1963); *People v. Gostelo*, 67 Cal. 2d. 586 (1967).

[17] *People v. Rosales*, 68 Cal. 2d. 305 (1968).

[18] *Stoval v. Denno*, 388 U.S. 293 (1967); *Gilbert v. California*, 388 U.S. 263 (1967); *United States v. Wade*, 388 U.S. 218 (1967).

that no inference of guilt should be drawn from the fact that the subject is in custody even though he may be handcuffed in the police car. The person viewing the suspect should be told that he is under no obligation to identify him as the one who committed the crime. It should be made clear that it is just as important to exonerate him if he is not the criminal as to identify him if he is, because the police will continue searching for the criminal if the wrong person is in custody. Witnesses or victims should view the subject separately without discussing the case with each other or indicating in any way that they have or have not made an identification.[19]

Transporting Arrested Persons

When a person has been arrested for a crime and is faced with the loss of his liberty, he will sometimes attempt to escape. Coupled with this attempt, he will often attack anyone standing between him and freedom. The mere fact that an arrestee appears docile when taken into custody does not mean that he will remain so. He may take advantage of any relaxation on the part of the arresting or transporting officer to make an attempt to gain his freedom. Sometimes he will use a weapon.

Pretransportation Search   When a suspect has been taken into custody, the first precaution that must be taken is a careful search and the removal from his person of *any* weapon or object that might be used to assault the transporting officer or others who will process him. Such items as heavy purses, high-heeled shoes, belts with large buckles, pen knives, metal fingernail files, pens or pencils, etc., should be taken from prisoners.

No officer receiving an arrestee should rely upon the search supposedly made by another person. To do so may invite tragic consequences.

Restraint of Prisoners   All persons—males or females, adults or juveniles—who have committed serious crimes and those who are likely to be combative should be handcuffed with their hands behind their backs, or otherwise securely restrained by straps or other approved devices as departmental rules may require.

[19] Evelle J. Younger, "Field Interrogation and Identification," *Law Enforcement Legal Information Bulletin*, Office of the District Attorney, Los Angeles, vol. 6. no. 1, 1970, pp. 10–19.

The slight added discomfort to the arrestee from this procedure is more than offset by the added safety to the officer since handcuffs can be an extremely dangerous weapon when swung freely by a person whose hands are cuffed in front. Proper adjustment and double-locking of the handcuffs are necessary to prevent undue chafing and bruising of the wrists and to insure that the arrestee cannot slip out of them and use them as a weapon. Restraining belts and other devices may provide alternate methods for the officer to follow.

Transportation Safeguards   Ordinarily a lone officer who must transport a prisoner should request assistance, although modern police vehicles often have a prisoner compartment that provides considerable safety to the single officer *if he properly searches* the prisoner and takes other security measures as may be indicated.

When it becomes necessary for a single officer to transport a prisoner, he should notify his dispatcher of the name and description of the prisoner, the charge, the location, and his destination. When the police vehicle does not have a prisoner compartment, the arrestee should be placed in the front seat, handcuffed with his hands behind him, and the safety belt securely fastened.

Two prisoners should not ordinarily be transported by one officer. When the police car is equipped with appropriate safety straps and a prisoner's compartment, one officer can, with reasonable safety, transport two prisoners in some situations when assistance is not available.

If assistance is available for the transportation of more than one prisoner, both officers should ride in one police vehicle. The second officer's car should be parked legally and locked. The assisting officer should then ride in the left rear seat with the two handcuffed prisoners to his right if the police car has no prisoner compartment. If there is one, both officers should ordinarily sit in the front seat.

Handcuffing the prisoners with their arms interlocked provides additional security. To do this, the first prisoner's hands are cuffed, palms out, behind his back. The second prisoner's left arm is passed under the right arm of the other prisoner before the handcuffs are affixed. The safety belt should then be fastened securely around at least one of the prisoners.

The feet of a prisoner in the rear seat are a constant source of danger to the driving officer if there is no separation screen between compartments. Leg cuffs or belts should be used, if they are available, on felon arrestees or combative prisoners. The prisoner's shoes should be removed and the passenger officer should be especially alert to prevent either prisoner from suddenly kicking the driver behind the head.

Transporting Females   While it is desirable that two officers transport a female prisoner from the place of arrest to the jail, often a lone male officer will find that he must transport her because assistance is not immediately available. When this occurs, he should take several precautions to avoid unjustified criticism. He should obtain the names of responsible witnesses who will be able to show what happened from the time of the arrest until the time he left the scene on his way to the station or jail.

Also, to protect himself from false accusations that he molested her while she was being transported to jail, he should request a time and mileage check from his dispatcher. These data should be recorded in his notebook. He should then proceed by the most direct route available to the station.

Ordinarily, delays for any purpose should be avoided en route to lessen the chances for a complaint of misconduct. If a delay cannot be avoided, it should promptly be brought to the dispatcher's attention so that he can make a record of the time and activity involved. Only when the arrestee has been delivered to the booking office and accepted into custody by another person, is the arresting officer relieved of his responsibility for controlling his prisoner.

In all cases where children will be left unattended as the result of the arrest of their mother, appropriate arrangements must be made to care for them. Another officer should be summoned to help make such arrangements so that the arrest will not be complicated by an unreasonable delay at the scene.

Preventing Conversation between Prisoners   Prisoners should not be allowed to converse with each other while being transported to jail, nor should the officer attempt to interrogate them during this time. Questioning them can be done more effectively at the station under controlled conditions.

Prebooking Medical Treatment   Injured, ill, or unconscious prisoners should be taken before a department-employed or -retained doctor for examination before they are taken to the booking office. Most agencies will not accept a prisoner who is in need of medical attention until he has been treated.

Prebooking Vehicle Inspection   When the transporting officer arrives at the station or jail, he should carefully inspect the police vehicle for evidence, contraband, or weapons the prisoners might have attempted to conceal in it. Drugs, narcotics, pawn tickets, knives, stolen property such as rings, watches, money, weapons, and even firearms, have often been found hidden in upholstery, behind seats, cushions, or in other parts of the police car by suspects. A common practice by disgruntled arrestees—often even minor offenders—is to hide their money in the police car, then accuse an officer of stealing it from them. When such items are found, they should be identified and processed as in the case of other property or evidence. If they can be connected to the suspect, appropriate reports should be made, clearly describing the circumstances under which the items were found.

Summary

It is constitutionally permissible for a police officer to stop, search, detain, and question an individual even though there is not sufficient cause to justify an arrest; however, there must be reasonable grounds based on specific objective facts that the detention and inquiry were necessary in the interests of public safety or crime detection and prevention.

When the officer has reasonable grounds to believe that the person is armed and dangerous, he may require the person to submit to a frisk or pat down for weapons or offensive instruments. Should the officer find in his frisk an object that feels like a weapon, he may then go further and remove the weapon from the suspect's possessions. The fact that the suspect is armed may also establish the reasonable cause for an arrest based on possession or concealment of the weapon if it is an illegal instrument.

If there is no reasonable cause for stopping the individual, then the frisk is unreasonable and evidence it turns up cannot be used against the suspect. Likewise, when the frisk goes beyond what is necessary to discover weapons, then it is unreasonable in scope and evidence found as the result of it is not admissible against the defendant.

A detention for a field interrogation cannot lawfully extend in time beyond reasonable bounds, but it can be continued when new facts are turned up during the inquiry to justify further investigation. The McNabb rule that evidence seized during a period of unlawful detention is not admissible against the suspect should guide the officer in the conduct of his field inquiries.

The general criteria for selective field interrogations should be based on time, place, and circumstances. Persons observed under suspicious circumstances, at unusual times, and in unusual places and those whose actions give rise to reasonable suspicions can be considered suspects who should be brought under police scrutiny.

All suspects on foot should be approached on foot by the officer from the rear. He should take advantage of the illumination his vehicle provides by directing his headlight beams at the subject while making his approach. He should then position himself strategically to the subject's right side where he can better physically control the person in the event of a sudden offensive act.

Some field interrogations do not justify a frisk of the suspect's person; however, each case must be decided on its own merits. Should there be any doubt about whether the suspect is dangerous, however slight the doubt he should be frisked for weapons. Should he be a felony suspect or a known felon, a frisk should be made in every case. If there is sufficient cause to arrest him, a search should be made of his person.

When the suspect is subjected to custodial interrogation or deprived of his freedom of action in any way and the officer desires to use his statements against him in a criminal proceeding, a Miranda admonishment must be given before the questioning begins. If the contact constitutes a general inquiry only and investigation has not focused on the subject, the warning is not required.

The suspect should be required to identify himself and explain the reason for his presence. Hasty accusations should be avoided, although contradictory or inconsistent statements should be evaluated in determining the suspect's truthfulness. If he is released upon the conclusion of the inquiry, the reason for stopping him should be explained. When the contact has been professionally conducted in a businesslike manner, he will usually carry away a favorable impression of the police.

When an arrest is made based upon the evidence obtained during the contact, a careful search of the subject should be made. If a field search of a female by a male officer is necessary, it should be made in the presence of witnesses whenever possible. Objects that could be used as weapons such as her handbag, high-heeled shoes, and the like should be taken from her. When a full body search is indicated, it should ordinarily be made at the station by a female officer or employee under controlled conditions.

On occasion, a suspect will flee when he believes he is about to be arrested. The officer should be alert if this occurs to avoid being led into an ambush. If two officers are involved, they should usually stay together during a foot pursuit to protect each other. During a pursuit at night in a residential district, an officer should follow the path taken by the suspect to avoid hazards such as low clothes lines, thorny bushes, picket fences, or barbed wire.

Frequently when a suspect is arrested with good cause for a particular crime, he should be returned to the scene for identification by the victim or witnesses. One-man lineups have been held reasonable by the courts, provided they are not unnecessarily suggestive of guilt. To avoid such possibility, the officer should admonish the victim and witnesses to avoid drawing any particular inference for or against the suspect merely because he is in custody.

Before an arrested person is placed in the police car, he should always be searched for weapons personally by the officer transporting him to the station for booking. No officer should assume that a prisoner has been carefully searched by someone else. The arrestee should be appropriately restrained with straps, handcuffs, or other devices and placed in the police vehicle in a position where he can best be controlled. Female arrestees should be transported from the field to the station by a male officer by the most direct route and only after the transporting officer requests the dispatcher to make a time and mileage record.

After the arrestee arrives at the station, the transporting officer should carefully check the police car for evidence or contraband which may have been hidden in it by the prisoner while he was being transported. Reports made in connection with the incident should clearly describe the circumstances under which the property was found.

Review

Questions

1. What is the distinction between an arrest and a detention?
2. Upon what circumstances should a field interrogation be based?
3. How long may a detention be continued?
4. What is the McNabb rule?
5. What is the Miranda rule?
6. What is a cardinal rule of interrogating more than one suspect?
7. Why should the circumstances leading to a field interrogation be recorded when the suspect is arrested?
8. Why should officers usually stay together in a foot pursuit?
9. What is the prevailing rule relating to field identifications or one-man lineups?
10. Why should a transporting officer never assume that another has searched the prisoner he is to transport?
11. Why shouldn't an officer ordinarily interrogate a prisoner on the way to the station?
12. Why should a check of the police car be made upon arrival at the station with an arrestee?

13. What is the Chimel rule?
14. Define probable or reasonable cause?

Exercises

1. You observe a person in an alley at 3:00 a.m. under suspicious circumstances which in themselves are not sufficient to justify an arrest for a particular crime. Explain how you would proceed.
2. What is meant by the principle "a search for weapons made without reasonable cause to arrest, must be limited by the circumstances which makes its need apparent"?
3. Enumerate some of the factors that may justify a search of a suspect in a field interrogation.
4. Is there any distinction between a search, a pat down, and a frisk? Explain.
5. Describe the best location in the field for a field interrogation if there is a choice.
6. Describe how you would approach the subject of a field interrogation: when he is walking on the same side of the street in the same direction you are traveling; when he is on the opposite side of the street walking in the opposite direction to that in which you are traveling.
7. Demonstrate the field interrogation position.
8. Explain how a waiver of the suspect's Miranda rights might be obtained.
9. Describe how a female suspect should be searched for weapons generally.
10. Describe how a detailed body search of a female should be conducted.
11. Describe what you should do and how you would proceed in a foot pursuit.
12. What instructions should you give the victim and witnesses before they view a suspect in custody in a one-man lineup?
13. Describe how one officer should restrain an arrested felon while transporting him in a police car without a prisoner compartment.

7

Preliminary
Investigation

A criminal case is brought to a successful conclusion when the perpetrator of the crime has been identified, apprehended, and successfully prosecuted, and when any stolen property has been retrieved and returned to its rightful owner. The extent to which this can be accomplished is in direct relation to the effectiveness with which the officer first at the scene performs his initial work. This initial activity of processing and recording all factual data about the offense and arresting the perpetrator at the scene or in flight is called the preliminary investigation. It consists of everything the officer does initially and does not involve any follow-up investigation away from the scene or in the future.[1] The follow-up is usually the responsibility of detectives or other investigators who prepare the case for prosecution.

The preliminary inquiry into a police incident is ordinarily the

[1] Paul B. Weston and Kenneth M. Wells, *Criminal Investigation; Basic Perspectives,* Prentice-Hall, Inc., Englewood Cliffs, 1970, pp. 25–26.

responsibility of the patrol officer, since he or she is usually the first person at the scene. Traffic accident investigators serve much the same purpose when they are organized to investigate traffic collisions.

Preliminary Action at the Crime Scene

When an officer responds to a call, usually his first responsibility is to render aid or secure any medical attention needed by injured persons. If a felony has been committed, the perpetrator must be promptly arrested when he is still at the scene or immediately available. When officers are not empowered to make an arrest, they must secure sufficient details to enable them to later obtain a criminal complaint.

If the suspect has left the scene, a broadcast of his or her description may be indicated to alert other officers in the vicinity. The officer must protect the scene and evidence from contamination or destruction, collect and preserve evidence which may be useful in a later prosecution, recover and safeguard property, and interview victims and witnesses present or obtain sufficient information about them so that the follow-up investigators may interview them.

Aid to Injured   The first responsibility of the patrol officer at the scene—with few exceptions—is to insure that injured persons are cared for. Sometimes first aid treatment can save lives. The officer should request ambulance services immediately if medical attention is required. Usually ambulance attendants are trained and equipped to render first aid and thus relieve the officer for other important duties.

If there is the slightest doubt that an injured person is dead, the officer should be sure he gets to a place where professional medical attention can be given. His removal may sometimes hamper the initial investigation, but this factor is far outweighed by the officer's responsibility to do everything possible to save a life even if the chances are remote.

Dying Declaration   If an injury caused by the criminal may cause the death of the victim, the officer should make an effort to obtain a dying declaration without delay. By the time the follow-up investigators are available to obtain this valuable evidence, the victim may have died and what might have been critical evidence of the cause of death will have been forever lost. If the injured person is transported to a hospital, an officer may ride in the ambulance to obtain further details of the offense or a dying declaration. Every officer should become familiar with and adhere to the laws of his state governing these statements.

Dying declarations are exceptions to the rule which ordinarily excludes hearsay statements as evidence against a defendant. The person to whom a dying declaration is made ordinarily can testify to what the dying person said about the cause of his death when the person believes he is going to die and has given up all hope of recovery. Details of the offense should be obtained even if the victim thinks he is going to recover. He should be asked who inflicted the injuries and why. Motive is often important in homicide cases. If a doctor at the hospital confirms that the victim is going to die and the victim then expresses his feeling that he cannot recover from the injury, the officer should again cover the details needed for a dying declaration.

The response of the victim to a question by the officer regarding the cause of the injury may be written or oral or may be by any act, sign, or signal equivalent to an oral statement. The declaration alone may support a guilty verdict.[2]

The person giving the declaration must die before the person witnessing it can testify to the *content* of the deceased person's statement. If the person does not expire, he can testify himself regarding the cause of injury. There is no legal necessity then for admitting hearsay evidence—that which a witness heard the victim say regarding the injury. The accused person thus has the opportunity of facing his accuser and cross-examining him in person, under oath, in a legal proceeding involving the infliction of the injury.

It is often difficult to prove that the dying person knows he is going to die at the time he makes his declaration; but unless the court is convinced that the sense of impending death was present and that there was no hope of recovery, his statement is not admissible as a dying declaration. Under Anglo-American law, a dying declaration has the sanctity of an oath on the witness stand. It is reasoned that a person who knows he is about to die will state the truth. This sense of impending death may be proved by signs, by asking for the last rites of the church, by writing a will, etc. An officer witnessing these conditions should carefully note their significance and record his precise observations in his notebook in case he must later establish a foundation for the actual declaration made.

Only those statements of the deceased relating to the cause of

[2] *People v. Amaya*, 134 Cal. 531 (1906).

death are admissible in evidence. Statements relating to other matters are not admissible as part of a dying declaration.

Preserving the Scene

The first officer at the scene of a serious crime should touch nothing himself, nor should he allow anyone else to do so unless absolutely necessary. Some special circumstances make it imperative to touch or move items of evidence. A limited exploratory examination may be needed to ascertain whether a person is dead, to render first aid, and to protect evidence from contamination or destruction by the weather, atmosphere, or persons.

The identity of all persons at the scene should be recorded. Curious officers not participating in the investigation, news media reporters, and other persons not directly involved must be kept away.

Marking Alterations   It may be necessary to move a victim of a crime to a hospital for medical aid or the coroner may cause the deceased to be moved, but, before this occurs, the officer should note the exact position of the body in his notes, and outline with chalk or otherwise mark its position. The position of pertinent articles of clothing, surrounding objects or other evidence on the floor, bed, etc., should also be marked and recorded. Photographs should be taken if possible before the scene or evidence is moved or altered. When this procedure is completed, a sketch should then be made so that the original positions of moved items may be related to the investigation by others assigned to the follow-up.

Photographing the Scene   An important crime scene should be photographed before it is altered or evidence is moved or before any detailed examination is made. However, as previously described, there are cases where this is impractical such as when a victim must be moved to save his life or an explosive device must be moved to prevent an explosion. In such cases, the exact position of the evidence can be marked in relation to the rest of the scene. Photographs can then be taken. They can be used as evidence if they are otherwise relevant, if they are a fair representation of the scene, and if any alterations can be satisfactorily explained to the court and jury.

Photographs supplementing sketches are especially useful in depicting a crime or accident scene. They are also valuable in showing where and how the criminal entered a particular place. The jurors have no other way of observing such details. Photographs permit the jury to see evidence which cannot be brought into the courtroom. They shorten trial time because they reduce the need for lengthy descriptions of places and things. They help the officer in reconstructing the crime or accident scene after it has been changed. They can show injuries to persons, damage to property, positions of evidence, etc., better than a witness can describe them.

Black-and-white pictures are usually perfectly acceptable although color sometimes depicts the scene better. Self-developing cameras are enjoying increased popularity because they permit the officer to see the pictures before he leaves the scene; however they do not ordinarily provide a negative from which an enlargement can be made nor do they give the detail obtainable from a conventional picture. Therefore the officer should take conventional photos to supplement quick-developing pictures. At least two pictures should be taken of each view in case one does not turn out well. It is better to have too many than too few pictures.

The position of the camera should be shown on the crime scene sketch. Notes should show the time and place of each picture. Flash equipment should be used indoors to provide proper lighting and eliminate shadows. Care should be used so that the film manufacturer's specifications are followed in setting the camera for use in taking flash pictures.

Indistinct features of the scene may require some sort of marking to make them visible in a photograph. Photographs should be taken first without such markings then with the markings. For example, skid marks may be very vague in photographs but may be clearly visible to the naked eye. The officer should photograph them as they initially exist, outline them with chalk, and photograph them again from the same position. The jury will then be able to use the pictures to supplement the officer's testimony. Tire impressions should be similarly photographed—first without treating them then again after they have been powdered with an appropriate dust to improve the contrast and make them more readily visible.

Perimeter Security   In securing the crime scene, the officer should also consider safeguarding the area around it. Evidence there might reveal the identity of the suspect. Footprints, tire tracks, discarded clothing, fibers, etc., may be found many yards from where the crime was committed. Rope, stakes, signs, and flares are often useful to warn away curious onlookers. Two 100-foot ropes, metal or wooden poles with bases to hold them, signs prohibiting entry, and flares are the usual equipment which should be available to the officer for such purposes. When the scene and the perimeter have been secured, he should proceed with locating and collecting evidence.

Collecting and Preserving Evidence— General Considerations

Although the patrol officer usually is not expected to be a specialist in collecting evidence, the obligation to prevent it from being destroyed, contaminated, or carried away by unauthorized persons ordinarily falls upon him. If a crime scene technician is available, he or she should gather and preserve that evidence which requires the attention of a specialist. If one is not available, the patrol officer performs the task himself.

He should concentrate first upon protecting the most fragile and easily destroyed evidence, such as latent fingerprints and traces of hair, fibers, imprints, etc. Stains from semen or blood are not as high risk as trace evidence but these and latent fingerprints may easily be contaminated or obliterated if they are not protected.

Physical Evidence   Any material object left at the scene of a crime by the perpetrator or victim and anything removed from the scene, altered, or contaminated by the perpetrator or victim is physical evidence. It consists of all materials, however small, which are connected directly or indirectly with the crime and which tend to establish the offense, incriminate or exonerate a suspect, or explain what happened.

Inanimate objects and articles are silent witnesses to many occurrences that must be reconstructed by the police and are therefore valuable indicators of what happened. Physical evidence properly collected often tells a story that people are unable to provide. Fingerprints at the scene of a burglary may positively prove that a particular suspect was on the premises. Many other types of physical evidence will conclusively demonstrate a defendant's part in a crime even when witnesses cannot.

Physical evidence—unlike a witness—does not depend upon a memory to speak the truth. Neither does it forget. It does, however, have some of the same shortcomings as witnesses. It sometimes does not provide all the facts that it might because the officer often fails to collect and preserve it properly. Usually this results from a lack of training or a failure to employ the correct techniques. This may invalidate its potential value.

It is often the patrol officer's responsibility to build a case without assistance from a specialist. He must therefore recognize what evidence is needed to prove that a crime was committed, what evidence will be required to disprove an alibi or establish the degree of a crime, and what facts can be established by witnesses or physical evidence. He must be prepared to recognize physical evidence when he sees it, properly collect and preserve it for later presentation in court, and prepare appropriate records concerning what he finds.

Chain of Continuity   Before evidence can be properly received in court, a witness must show its relation to the case, how and when it came into his possession, to whom he gave it, and who had custody of it from the time it was collected to the time of its introduction in court. This principle is called the *chain of custody* or *chain of continuity*. Proof of this chain is necessary to establish that the evidence is indeed the same that originally came into possession of the witness. If he cannot prove this, the court may exclude the evidence and, if it is vital, the case may be lost. Complete notations by the officer taking custody of evidence indicating where and when it was found, how or from whom he received it, and to whom he transferred it will help establish a proper foundation for its use in court.

Materials Needed   In searching a crime scene, officers should have some basic materials and supplies to aid them in locating, tentatively identifying, and collecting evidence. Good illumination is necessary in searching for stains and latent fingerprints. Simple magnification equipment will aid in identifying scratches, pry marks, etc. Some chemicals and powders will often reveal hidden or concealed traces of blood or fingerprints, and an ultraviolet light will cause some stains such as those left by semen to fluoresce. Chalk to mark positions of evidence should be available. Paper bags, envelopes, plastic bags, glass vials or jars also are useful to preserve evidence or samples. These may be necessary for comparative purposes to prove that evidence from a suspect came from a particular source. For example, paint scrapings or chips from a particular window through which a burglar entered may be needed to prove that paint traces or chips found in the suspect's cuffs came from the same source. Both samples should be carefully preserved and should be kept free from contamination.

If the proper equipment or materials are not available when the officer needs them and he fails to perform his preliminary investigation correctly, he may never be able to remedy his failure. The original crime scene may be altered to such a degree by clean-up or repair activities that it becomes valueless as evidence, or the chain of custody may not be intact making the evidence inadmissible.

Bindles   If envelopes, jars, vials, or other containers are not available to package evidence—especially small samples of paint, dust, debris, or residue—the evidence may be preserved for laboratory analysis in a *bindle*, as shown in Figure 7-1. All you need to construct a bindle is a clean sheet of paper, as from a tablet or loose-leaf binder.

When the officer places evidence in a bindle, he should seal it in an envelope and label it with his initials, the exact place where the evidence was obtained, the date, and the type of contents. He should not tape or staple the bindle closed, because that would make opening the packet difficult and might cause the evidence to be damaged or contaminated when it is removed at the laboratory. A carefully constructed bindle will remain closed and can be opened readily. Separate bindles containing evidence should not be packaged together if there is danger that the contents from one may contaminate the

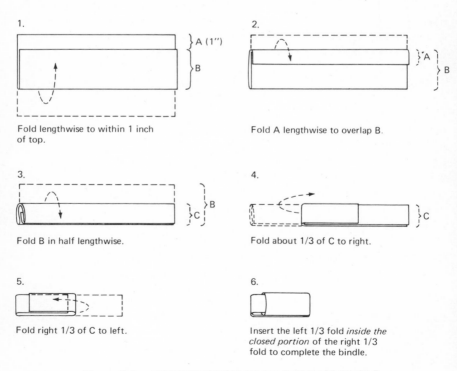

1.

{ A (1″)

B

Fold lengthwise to within 1 inch of top.

2.

A

B

Fold A lengthwise to overlap B.

3.

B

C

Fold B in half lengthwise.

4.

C

Fold about 1/3 of C to right.

5.

Fold right 1/3 of C to left.

6.

Insert the left 1/3 fold *inside the closed portion* of the right 1/3 fold to complete the bindle.

Figure 7-1.   CONSTRUCTION OF AN EVIDENCE BINDLE.

other. For example, bindles containing paint chips found on a burglar's clothing should not be placed in the same package with bindles containing paint chips from a window through which he climbed at the place of the crime.

System of Searching for Evidence

There are several methods which help the officer to completely search the crime scene and still prevent unnecessary duplication of effort. The search should be made thoroughly and systematically of the entire crime area, indoors and outdoors, whenever there exists a possibility that evidence may be found.

The officer should adopt a system to conduct his search. This system may vary from case to case but may prevent him from overlooking some vital evidence. Indoors, he should usually start at a certain point, proceed around the room searching the floor first so that vital trace evidence left there may be recovered before it is stepped on. He then should examine the rest of the room. This type of search may reveal what happened or may indicate the existence of evidence that should receive prompt attention. For example, it may be more important to determine immediately a dead person's body temperature and other evidence indicating the time of death than to look for the murder weapon.[3]

Techniques of Collecting, Marking, and Preserving Evidence

As an officer gains experience in searching for, collecting, and preserving evidence, he will learn to proceed systematically, carefully looking for that which may serve to identify the criminal. He will make a record of what he does, knowing that mistakes he makes during the investigation can rarely be corrected. Too much attention to details is better than too little. Careful attention to his methods of collecting and marking evidence will enable him to establish a proper foundation for its admission in court. He should carefully preserve the evidence he gathers in a vial, envelope, or bindle and tag or mark it for later identification.

[3] Arne Svensson and Otto Wendell, *Techniques of Crime Scene Investigation*, 2d ed., American Elsevier Publishing Company, Inc., New York, 1965, pp. 20–21.

Clothing   Clothing is one of the most productive sources of physical evidence because of its construction. Cuffs, fabric, and pockets often will produce vital evidence not even suspected by the criminal. Dust, debris, and the like will adhere to the fabric and may positively place the defendant at the scene of a crime in the face of his denials.

No special techniques are required in the collection of this type of evidence. When it seems to be pertinent such as in some rape or burglary cases, clothing should be taken from the suspect, one garment at a time. It should be handled gently to prevent the loss of trace evidence it may contain. It may be necessary to cut clothing from victims because of their condition. When this happens, care should be exercised to avoid cutting the clothing in areas which have been burned, damaged, or stained by powder, bullets, chemicals, blood, semen, and the like. Buttons should not be cut off or moved, and no unnecessary changes should be made in the articles.

Each item of clothing should be packaged separately. Notes should be made describing some distinctive mark made on the garment and indicating the time, the place, and from whom it was collected.

A ball-point pen should be used for marking clothing, as the ink usually will not smear or run. A marking place should be selected which will not injure or deface the article or destroy its value as evidence. Obviously, markings should not be made so near a blood or semen stain as to interfere with their chemical analysis. Markings should include the officer's initials and the date or whatever is required by department rules.

Trousers, skirts, and dresses should be marked on the inside waistband at the back. Shirts should be marked on the lower seam of the tail. Coats and other clothing should be marked on the label or in some other inconspicuous place if the article does not have a label. An attempt should be made to show if the garment was worn at the time of the crime. In rape and other sex cases undergarments may be especially productive as evidence and should be obtained from the female victim and the male perpetrator.[4]

Blood   Blood and stains at the scene of a crime are vital to the investigation and careless or improper handling can sometimes destroy their use as evidence. Blood may not positively connect a suspect with a crime, but it might positively exclude him as the person from whom it came.

[4] Los Angeles Police Department, *Daily Training Bulletin*, Charles C Thomas, Publisher, Springfield, Ill., 1958, p. 210.

Blood corpuscles are of major importance because they can be classified in so many ways.[5] To completely determine the blood type, the corpuscle must be intact and fresh. It will be destroyed when the blood dries if it is not preserved in a saline solution. Blood grouping factors are also destroyed by putrefaction; however, if the blood is dried but not putrefied, it can be partially typed to establish the principal blood factors. This may be sufficient to exclude some persons as suspects.

Wet blood of possible evidentiary value should be collected in a saline solution to permit a complete typing. If no saline solution is available, a teaspoon of blood in a quart of water may permit useful laboratory analysis. Such exemplars should be refrigerated as soon as possible after they are collected to prevent putrefaction.

When clothing is bloodstained, the entire article should be submitted to the laboratory. If the blood is wet, it should be dried before the article is packaged, otherwise the sample may be ruined by putrefaction. Blood on the article should be permitted to dry in such a manner that the pattern of the stain will be preserved.

When bloodstains are found on other objects, the entire article should be submitted to the laboratory if possible. If the item is too large for transportation to the laboratory, or is nonabsorbent, a sample of the blood should be scraped from the object and preserved in a clean glass container. Each scraping should be kept separate, and, for each blood scraping, another scraping the same size should be taken from an unstained adjacent area. This material can be used as a control standard.

When the article containing the stain is absorbent and too large for transmittal to the laboratory, the stained area should be cut from the article. Materials from unstained, adjacent areas should also be submitted for control purposes and comparisons.

It is imperative that blood samples be obtained from suspects and victims for purposes of comparison or elimination. Such analysis can provide a link in the chain of evidence against a suspect.[6]

Semen   Like blood, semen can be typed to determine the major blood factors, if the donor is a secretor—that is, if his body secretes

---

[5] Harry Soderman and John J. O'Connell, *Modern Criminal Investigation*, 5th ed., Funk and Wagnalls Company, New York, 1962, pp. 242–248.
[6] Bryan J. Culliford, *The Examination and Typing of Bloodstains in the Crime Laboratory*, National Institute of Law Enforcement and Criminal Justice, Washington, D.C., 1971, pp. 15–17.

his major blood factors in his semen.[7] Most Caucasians are in this group. A saliva analysis can also determine if a person is a secretor. Saliva samples and blood samples from suspects and victims can be valuable in cases involving sexual offenses where semen is present.

Areas containing semen stains or samples from such areas should be obtained for analysis. Investigating officers should obtain clothing from all suspects and the victim, much as in the case of clothing containing bloodstains. Underclothing is especially important. The laboratory should receive car seats, blankets, sheets, cloth from furniture, towels, etc., intact wherever possible. Vaginal and penis smears are also valuable for laboratory comparisons.

Semen stains are usually easily detected by touch or smell. A stiff, starchy area should immediately be suspected and preserved for microscopic and chemical analysis. Semen shows up under ultra-violet light, and its presence may be detected by this device, but laboratory analysis is needed for proper, reliable identification of the substance. A male who has had a vasectomy still produces semen that can be readily identified.

Before the laboratory analyst can properly interpret the results of his test of semen in connection with a sex crime, he must know when the victim last had intercourse, with whom (if other than the suspect), whether the male wore a condom, whether she showered or douched after intercourse, and whether she changed clothes—especially her undergarments—since last having intercourse. The police officer should obtain this information.

The male suspect should be asked when he last had intercourse, with whom (if other than the victim), when he last masturbated or experienced a nocturnal emission, if he bathed or changed outside clothes or undergarments in the meantime. These data may dispute an alibi or support it and should be ascertained to aid the analyst in arriving at his conclusions.

Hair Hair samples should be preserved for examination in cases involving sex crimes such as rape, child molesting, bestiality, and sodomy. While hair is rarely useful for positive identification of a suspect, the analyst may be able to demonstrate a high likelihood or absolute impossibility that it came from a particular person. Hair can be identified according to its species. This identification may be vital in bestiality and other sex cases. Sometimes racial origin can be determined, but these determinations are questionable in cases where

---

[7] Soderman and O'Connell, *Modern Criminal Investigation,* pp. 248–252.

racial mixtures are present. Color of hair can be determined within limits, and dyeing by chemical treatment can be detected. These factors can constitute circumstantial evidence which may support other information collected.

The officer should keep hair found in different places separate, and he should note the area where each sample was found. Bindles or small envelopes, instead of vials, should be used to preserve hair, because vials tend to cause it to curl.

Hair samples should be collected from the victim and the suspect for comparisons. They should be pulled or cut close to the scalp or body. At least five samples of hair from the head should be obtained from each of several areas—the temples, crown, and front. They should be packaged separately by area and identified according to the place where they were obtained.

Pubic hair of the victim of a sex crime may become contaminated by hair from the perpetrator. By combing the pubic areas of each with a clean comb, loose native hair, and hair transferred during the crime, may be obtained for examination. Samples of native hair should then be obtained from the parties so that two samples will have been obtained from each. Both samples from each individual should be packaged separately to avoid contamination.

Fingernail Scrapings   Scrapings of materials from under the fingernails often provide valuable clues that might lead to the solution of a crime. The types of evidence normally found are fibers, hair, blood, flesh, fecal matter, etc., and may serve to connect the suspect with the crime.

The fingernails of the suspect and victim should be cleaned with a clean fingernail file. The debris obtained from each finger should be placed in a separate, labeled, container. If the fingers are obviously contaminated with the victim's or suspect's own blood, such facts should be noted on the appropriate container for the criminalist's consideration in his examination.

Fibers   Trace evidence consisting of fiber or fiber imprints may be excellent evidence to prove a criminal offense against a burglar, hit-and-run driver, or assailant. Fibers may be found snagged on projections, or in such places as screens, window sills, rough surfaces, automobile bumpers or fenders, clothing or wet paint.

Imprints clearly showing the pattern of weave of clothing will often be found etched on hardened paint surfaces. These imprints may provide positive proof that a certain vehicle struck a particular hit-and-run victim or that a person wearing certain clothes leaned against, knelt on, or touched an object in another type of crime. Sometimes, the fibers will be "burned" into the paint where the impact between the fabric and a particular surface was sufficient.

Laboratory analysis of fiber imprints will often reveal whether the impression was made by a certain fabric. Analysis of the fibers themselves may reveal if they are natural or synthetic, whether the color is natural or dyed, and whether the fibers are from a particular source. The criminalist can often prove that the fiber evidence is the same in all respects as the cloth in a particular item of clothing.

Fabric strands or imprints will sometimes show up on hard surfaces under strong oblique illumination. If fibers are found, they should be carefully retrieved. The entire article to which they have been transferred should be submitted to the laboratory if practicable. If not, a clean piece of paper should be placed under the object while the fibers are removed to prevent loss or contamination of critical trace evidence. Fibers should be preserved in clean envelopes, bindles, or glass containers properly identified for later reference. The article from which the fiber is believed to have come should be submitted to the laboratory for comparison with the trace evidence if possible.

Fabric impressions on articles should be photographed when the article itself cannot be submitted to the laboratory because of its size or construction. Special photographic equipment and techniques may be required, however, which are not readily available to the patrol officer. In such cases, when the evidence is important enough, the officer can usually obtain assistance from private sources.

Paint   Paint is often found on objects such as clothing, tools, and automobiles involved in hit-and-run accidents. Laboratory analysis of paint usually involves an examination for color, surface texture, and sequence of layers. Infrared and spectrographic analysis can determine how the samples collected at the scene of a crime compare with those collected from the suspect. Therefore, it is imperative that samples of paint be collected from the scene when paint chips or transfers are found on the suspect, his tools, or his automobile.

Paint particles found at the scene may be matched physically with areas where paint is missing on tools or on an automobile in the suspect's possession. In cases where paint has transferred from a suspect's tool, weapon, or vehicle to a particular object, a sample of the transferred paint should be collected as well as a sample of the uncontaminated paint from the object that received the transfer. The paint from the uncontaminated surface should be cut or chipped from a place close to the area where the suspected paint is found. Two samples should be collected from separate areas of damage for control purposes. Each sample should be packaged in a separate container and clearly labeled with a description of the exact area from which it was taken.

Wood   Wood does not have the same relatively high evidentiary value as glass and paint unless it contains paint or other identifiable material. A piece broken or cut from a particular source can, however, be easily compared physically with that source if both parts are available for comparison. This factor makes wood an important type of evidence in roof or wall burglaries, and in hit-and-run cases involving property damage. The most common sources of this type of evidence are clothing, tools, and automobiles. Wood samples should be taken from near the area involved. Large samples should be obtained and should contain all alien materials such as tar and paint that might help in identification or comparison. Nail holes, weathering, natural grain, bleached spots, and the like may reveal that a sample of wood came from a particular source. Broken ends are particularly important for comparison with the source. These should be preserved in a clean paper bag for transmittal to the laboratory. The bag should be clearly labeled to show where the samples were taken, when and by whom collected, the case number, and the officer's name.

Tool Impressions   Tool impressions in wood may be sufficiently clear to enable the criminalist to make a positive identification of the tool that left the impression if it is available. Such evidence should not be overlooked and it may be a simple task to remove the wood with its impression to the laboratory for examination. Usually, however, special on-scene procedures using special techniques are necessary.

Soil   Clothing, shoes, tools, fingernails, etc., often contain soil which may be readily identified by laboratory analysis. When a crime indicates that soil from the suspect's shoes or clothing should be compared with soil from a particular area, it is important to collect sufficient amounts to permit proper laboratory analyses. Approximately one ounce of soil in each of four or five samples should be collected from the area where the suspect might have walked. Samples from different areas should be packaged separately in tight containers such as glass jars. Samples of soil from vehicles should be collected from different places on the car and packaged separately. Care should be taken to avoid crumbling the samples.

Glass   Glass fragments can ordinarily be matched with their source by an analysis of the physical properties alone. The criminalist may be able to positively identify glass as having come from a particular source—if that source is available to him—by a physical comparison. Glass breaks into distinct, individual pieces, and therefore even small pieces might be matched physically with the parent piece. When this cannot be done, the density and refractive index or a spectrographic analysis may identify the samples. Other examinations may determine which side of the glass was subjected to the breaking force. Rib marks or striations may reveal the direction of the force. Glass broken by fire will show a different pattern because the breakage is due to different speeds at which the glass expands.

It is not practicable to attempt to mark glass; therefore an outline of pieces of glass should be traced in the notebook with each tracing numbered, initialed, dated, and otherwise identified. Pieces should be packaged separately. If practicable, they should be placed in glass vials, envelopes, or bindles.

In traffic accident investigations—especially in hit-and-run incidents—broken glass from vehicles is often extremely important in the positive identification of a suspected vehicle. All pieces from headlights or taillights should be collected to insure a physical match in the event fragments are found on the suspect's vehicle.

Incendiary Materials   Arson, the malicious burning of property, often cannot be proved without establishing how the fire started. Usually some combustible material is used by the arsonist to start the fire and, when witnesses are unavailable to prove how it started, physical evidence left at the scene may help do so. In the area where it appears the fire started, the officer should collect samples of burned and partially burned materials from the floor or the places below the point of origin. He should also collect samples of incompletely burned or unburned flooring material, furniture, etc., over which flammable materials might have flowed. Even soil under the place at which the fire originated should be collected, as it might reveal what materials were used to start the fire and thus help in identifying the arsonist.

Residue such as melted glass may indicate that the flammable material was carried to the scene in a jar or bottle, while ashes might reveal that a common flare or a magnesium substance was used as a starter. Samples of such residue should be collected for laboratory analysis.

Clocks or clocklike devices or partially burned matchbooks or cigarettes might have been used as starters. They should be collected as possible evidence leading to the identification of the suspect.

Materials should be placed in a clean, airtight jar to avoid contamination of the evidence. A separate container should be used for each location where charred material is found. Each should be appropriately labeled showing where the sample was obtained and the usual identifying data.

In order for the criminalist to make an appropriate analysis of the samples submitted from the scene of the fire, he should be provided comparison samples from the source of the material if these are obtainable. Samples of incendiary materials from the place where they were obtained or from containers in the suspect's possession may enable the criminalist to make a positive comparison of the evidence samples and their source and may help in proving the case against the arsonist.

Cartridge Cases   Empty cartridge cases found at the scene of a crime often will yield fingerprints of the criminal. They may also contain markings left by the firing pin, ejector, extractor, breech, etc., which will serve to identify his weapon as the one which fired the bullet. Considerable care should be exercised so that such evidence on a cartridge case is not destroyed by careless handling.

Empty cases should be packaged separately from a weapon believed to have fired them. They can be transported to the laboratory safely if they are wrapped in soft tissue and sealed in a coin envelope. The officer's initials and a list of the contents should be recorded on the envelope before the evidence is placed in it, rather than after, to prevent undue chafing of the cartridge cases.

Bullets   Expended bullets can often be positively identified as coming from a particular type of weapon. When the suspected weapon itself is available, often it can be shown if the bullet was fired by that weapon. Striations left on the bullet sides may at times be positively matched with the barrel from which it was fired if the bullet is not too badly damaged. Bullets should be packaged like cartridge cases for transmission to the laboratory. If it is necessary to mark directly on a bullet for identification, the markings should be placed on the base.

Special Problems of Marking Evidence for Identification

When evidence is packaged and is of such a nature that marking the item itself is impractical, the container should be clearly labeled so that when the article is introduced into evidence at the trial, it can be identified by the witness who collected it. Sometimes the article itself should be marked for later identification, as described in the following paragraphs.

Evidence with Serial Numbers   Articles bearing serial numbers ordinarily need not be marked for identification; however, other characteristics should be described in the appropriate reports made in conjunction with the case and in the officer's notebook to aid him when he is later required to identify the evidence in his testimony in court. For example, the serial and parts numbers, make, model, caliber, and other descriptive characteristics of a firearm may all be required for positive identification. Partial numbers may not be sufficient without other descriptive data, because some of the same numbers have been used in the past on different models of firearms by some manufacturers.

When markings are needed for firearm identification, they should be made unobtrusively, such as under grips or inside slides on automatics. Removable major components such as the frame, slide, and barrel should each be given a distinctive mark that may be later identified in court. Unusual nicks, scratches, etc., should also be described in the notebook to aid in identification.

Watches   Numbers on watches should be recorded when practicable, although serial numbers are often not available unless the watch is opened. Opening a watch without special tools or training may damage it unnecessarily. In this case, the officer should mark the item so that positive identification can be made later. If a distinctive, permanent scratch is found, the officer should describe it and its location on a sketch in his notebook. If no distinctive markings is found on the watch, a small mark should be placed in an inconspicuous place and described together with its location in a sketch in the notebook.[8]

The mark made on items to identify them should be as small as possible. A pinpoint sometimes is useful for this purpose. The mark

[8] Los Angeles Police Department, *Daily Training Bulletin*, p. 210.

should be unique so that the officer will later recognize it immediately when he sees it. In every case, he should describe it and its location in his notebook.

Jewelry   Jewelry should be identified like watches and then sketched in the notebook with a description of a distinctive mark and its location. Rings should be marked on the inside of the band furthest from the setting if possible without defacing any inscriptions. These inscriptions may themselves be sufficient to identify the ring without other markings being made. Pins, brooches, and other jewelry should be marked on the back if such marking will not damage the item.

Cigarettes, Narcotics, and Drugs   Each marijuana cigarette should be numbered if more than one was seized as evidence. Necessary information describing the exact place each cigarette was found should be recorded in the notebook along with other pertinent details of the incident.

Packages in which narcotics are found should be initialed and dated by the officer finding them. Narcotics in powder form should be preserved in glass vials or bindles, properly labeled or identified to show their source and other necessary details.

Fingerprint Evidence

Visible or invisible prints from fingers, palms, or feet found at the scene of a crime often make the difference between success or failure in an investigation. These are frequently the only evidence available to prove the suspect was ever at the scene.

Latent Prints   Latent prints are those which are invisible to the naked eyes or which are visible but cannot be examined properly until they are developed.[9] They are marks of perspiration or oily material left on a surface by ridges on the fingers, palms, or feet.

Plastic Prints   Plastic prints are the impressions left in soft material by the friction ridges of the fingers, palms, hands, or feet. A negative or reverse "cast" is produced by the pressure of a person touching the plastic material. These should be photographed in the

[9] Svensson and Wendell, *Techniques of Crime Scene* Investigation, p. 44.

condition in which they are found. The object containing them should be taken to the laboratory, if possible, for examination.

Visible Prints   Sometimes the ridges pick up foreign materials such as grease, oil, blood, dust, ink, and the like and leave visible prints which might have great value in identifying the criminal. Glove print evidence should also be collected; these prints may be matched with the gloves involved should they be found.[10] Visible glove prints should be photographed where they are found if the object on which they are located cannot be properly safeguarded for transmittal to the laboratory.

Searching for Print Evidence   In searching for latent, plastic, or visible print evidence, the officer should isolate and protect surfaces receptive to prints to prevent handling which might contaminate the impressions. Surfaces on which prints are most likely to be found include those which will not absorb or spread the oily material deposited by fingers, palms, or feet. Hard objects with glossy, polished, or smooth surfaces usually are the most receptive to print evidence. Oily, damp, soft, or rough surfaces rarely produce good latent prints but should not be overlooked because of the possibility that they may contain plastic impressions. Paper often retains latent prints well and can usually be easily safeguarded for special processing in the laboratory.

Prints may be unidentifiable if they were made with too much pressure. The patterns tend to run together and lose detail. When pressure is light, sweat and oil on the ridges may not be transferred sufficiently to leave a good latent print, although the light pressure may tend to improve a plastic or visible impression. Prints may be smeared by movement of the fingers, hands, or feet at the time of contact with the surface; however, an imperfect print may not be impossible to identify, since the pores and other features of print patterns sometimes permit positive identification without a ridge pattern. Partial prints should therefore be collected if their characteristics are clear.

In searching for prints at the crime scene, the officer should attempt to reconstruct what the suspect came in contact with while there and what he did. Those surfaces capable of holding print evidence and possibly touched by the suspect should receive careful attention. If a window was broken in a building or automobile by a

10 Soderman and O'Connell, *Modern Criminal Investigation*, pp. 149–151.

thief or burglar, for example, the criminal may be identified positively by a clear, partial print on the glass. Broken window parts should therefore be carefully examined for prints. A thorough visual examination should then be made with direct and oblique light. A strong beam from a flashlight is usually adequate.

Handling Print Evidence

When examination at the scene reveals plastic or visible prints, they should be photographed before any attempt is made to remove them from the surface. Ideally, the material containing such impressions should be protected and transmitted to the laboratory for examination. If it appears that latent prints possibly are present, they should be developed with dust or chemicals, then photographed and lifted for laboratory examination.

Latent Print Development Materials   Latent prints, invisible without close examination, must be developed before they can be processed further. When they are made visible, they can be examined, photographed, and lifted by the use of clear lifting tape or rubber lifters.

Powder is ordinarily used to develop latent prints on most hard, smooth surfaces to improve the contrast between the print and the surface. Black powder enjoys the widest use because it works well on so many different types and colors of surfaces. Gray or silver aluminum powder is more adhesive than black powder and is therefore sometimes better. Other colors are available for developing prints to provide wide contrast; but, for ordinary purposes, black, gray, and silver will serve most of the field officer's needs.

Soft camel hair brushes have proved highly useful in powder application although brushes with fiberglass bristles are becoming popular. Ostrich feather brushes, called dusters, are commonly used on large surfaces. Other brushes employ a magnetic principle to control the application of iron base powders.

Developing Latent Prints   Before attempting to develop a latent print, a trial print should be made to test the brush, powder, and techniques. This test will help in determining if the powder will adhere properly to the print and will provide an adequate contrast between the developed print and the background.

The brush must be absolutely dry. By dipping it lightly into the powder chosen and gently tapping the handle, excessive powder will be removed. This will reduce the chance of damaging the latent impression by applying too much powder. Damage to the print often happens if the powder is tapped or sprinkled directly onto it.

The brush should then be held perpendicular to the surface and moved lightly over the area being dusted. When a print becomes apparent, its development should be finished by gently moving the brush following the general pattern. Excess powder can be removed by blowing. Additional powder may be added if necessary to improve the quality of the developed print.

Lifting Developed Prints   Once the latent print has been powdered and brushed, photographs should be taken. This will insure that a picture of the developed print will be available in case the print is damaged during lifting.

If the lift is to be made with tape, several inches should be pulled from the roll but left attached to it. The end of the tape should be anchored immediately in front of the developed print. The tape should then be brought down slowly and steadily over the print to avoid trapping air bubbles between it and the tape. Once the tape has made contact with the print, any attempt to change its position may damage the developed impression. When contact has been made, the tape should be rubbed with the fingertip so that it firmly contacts the print, then lifted slowly and carefully without removing the anchored end. Next, a latent print card is slipped under the tape, and the tape is carefully pressed onto the card so that no air is trapped. The anchor is then removed and the excess tape trimmed at the ends of the card. The card should be completed to show precisely where the print was lifted, its position on the surface, and its source if possible.

Chemical Developing of Prints   On rough surfaces, unfinished wood, paper, or cardboard, the development of latent prints can best be done with chemicals. Powder will not ordinarily provide satisfactory results on such surfaces.

Iodine fuming, silver nitrate, and ninhydrin development procedures are not as simple as the development of prints with powder and a brush but must be used when powder would be unsatisfactory. These procedures should be performed by a laboratory technician unless the patrol officer has had special training in their application.

Iodine fuming is relatively simple and produces satisfactory results in the development of latent prints up to about three days old. The development can be done quickly but the developed print will remain visible for only a short period. During this time, it must be photographed if its image is to be preserved. This procedure is often used for development of prints on paper or new wood.[11]

Ordinarily, paper should be submitted to the laboratory for iodine fuming because of the bulky equipment required. When the process must be applied at the scene, special equipment built for the process should be used. If an iodine fumer is available, the investigator should hold the opening of the glass tube close to the surface being processed and blow through it.

Elimination Prints   Plain ink impressions should be obtained from persons other than the suspect, who had access to the area and may have legitimately left some of the latent prints found there. These standards of comparison are used to eliminate prints so that the examiner can concentrate upon identifying those which might have been left by the criminal.

Packaging Potentially Dangerous Items

Objects that are potentially dangerous such as ice picks, razors, knives, and broken glass must be protected when packaged or wrapped to prevent injury to persons who have occasion to handle them but are unaware of their nature. Such safeguards must be taken whether the objects are evidence or are merely being held for the owner. Items which must be analyzed or examined in the laboratory should receive the special attention we have described.

Stabbing or Cutting Objects   The point of an ice pick should be protected by a cork or several thicknesses of cardboard or taped inside a small box. Straightedged razors should be folded if possible and tied. Fixed bladed knives, bayonets, stilettos, etc., should be protected with cardboard stapled around the blade and wrapped with paper. Razor blades should be wrapped and placed in an envelope with a notation describing the contents on the outside.

Explosives and Ammunition   Firecrackers should be boxed and securely tied. The contents should be clearly identified in large red letters on the outside. Cartridges and clips should be removed from a

[11] Svensson and Wendell, *Techniques of Crime Scene Investigation*, p. 49.

firearm before it is booked, unless the weapon and cartridges are to be examined for latent fingerprints, in which case the weapon should not be unloaded until after the examination to prevent contamination or destruction of prints. The evidence tag attached to the weapon or the package containing it, however, should contain a distinctly marked notation alerting the laboratory technician that the weapon is loaded. If possible, a loaded weapon should be delivered to the laboratory in person.

Flammables   Gasoline coming into the possession of officers should be returned to the owner immediately if possible. When it is to be held for evidence, a small sample—approximately one pint—should be retained in a tightly capped, metal container for laboratory analysis. A larger empty container should be capped before booking. The total amount of gasoline involved in the case should be described in the notebook and in appropriate reports.

Booking of Property

At times during the course of the preliminary investigation, the officer will collect numerous items of potential evidentiary value. To prevent one piece of physical evidence from contaminating another or from becoming lost or damaged and to reduce the amount of handling when laboratory examinations are indicated, evidence should be wrapped or otherwise preserved in separate packages or containers and tagged for identification. Methods of collecting evidence and packaging it at the scene of a crime have been discussed previously. The following standards for handling other types of property and preparing it for booking with the laboratory or the property officer are minimal; some agencies will require that additional procedures be followed.

Preparing Property for Booking   All items booked for safekeeping, as found or recovered property, or as evidence should be securely packaged and, when necessary to protect them, tied securely and tagged for identification. Every tag should contain the property report or case number, the date, time, and place where the property came into the officer's possession, the officer's name, and a list of the contents. A copy of the report listing and describing the property should be firmly affixed to the tag. At times, it is impracticable to list all items contained in a package. For example, a large tool box containing numerous hand tools should be described on the tag in general terms, such as, "twenty-one assorted mechanic hand tools and metal box." All tools would then be listed and described on the appropriate police report, a copy of which should be attached to the tag.

Small Articles An officer taking possession of property must exercise reasonable care to safeguard it against loss or damage. Small articles like jewelry or money should not be placed loose in a package with other articles, as they may be lost when the package is opened or damaged by the other objects when the package is handled. Rather, they should be placed in an envelope, small box, or wrapping with the contents listed on the outside. This will eliminate the need for opening several packages when one specific item is sought for presentation in court or analysis at the laboratory.

Bulky Items Bulky items or an assortment of clothing belonging to one person and not of value as evidence or items which require no laboratory analysis should be neatly bundled, securely tied, and tagged for identification purposes. Sturdy cartons and firearms ordinarily need not be wrapped but should be tagged. Ammunition belonging to a weapon may be packaged and attached to it. Handbags, patent leather shoes, etc., should be wrapped to protect them from damage.

Perishable Materials Perishable items such as ice cream, frozen or fresh meat, vegetables, and fruit, pose a special problem for the officer, since most police agencies are not equipped to preserve them. If an arrest is made in connection with such perishables, the arrestee or if possible the owner should be permitted to make arrangements for their disposal. When the perishables are needed as evidence, private storage lockers may be found to accommodate them. Small samples which must be kept for laboratory analysis can usually be refrigerated at the police station or a private facility until they can be delivered to the laboratory for analysis and preservation. Care must be exercised in the transfer of the property so that the continuity of evidence is not destroyed.

Explosives Explosives other than firecrackers and fixed ammunition should be handled as described in Chapter 12. Most police agencies will not permit the storage of dangerous explosives within a police facility; therefore, handling such items must be accomplished according to local procedures.

Large Objects   Large items such as automobile tires, television sets, radio or stereo consoles, or suitcases need not be wrapped but should be tagged. Tires should be tagged separately. Several items belonging to one person or coming into the possession of the police in connection with a particular case should be tied together and tagged unless it is impractical to do so because of their shapes and sizes. In such cases, they should be tagged separately.

Liquor   Liquor containers should be corked or capped with the original caps or soft drink bottle caps and sealed with wax. Officers seizing the evidence should place their thumbprint in the wax so that the evidence can be positively identified by them when they testify. Cellulose tape and sealing wax may be used when a cork or cap is not available. Paper or cloth should never be used to seal a bottle, because they may contaminate the material or allow it to evaporate.

Narcotics   Narcotics or drugs should be placed in a glass vial— or a bindle if the vial is not available—to prevent contamination, destruction, or loss and to maintain the continuity of evidence. When several samples of narcotic evidence are found in connection with a case, each should be placed in a separate vial or bindle. Each should then be placed in a small envelope and sealed. The envelopes should be initialed and dated. The several samples should be placed in a large envelope and carefully sealed. The contents and the place found should be noted. Some agencies require that wax be placed on the seal and that the officer who found the evidence impress his right thumbprint in the warm wax for future identification. The envelope cannot be opened without removing the wax seal. This procedure has been found to be especially important in cases where evidence must pass through several hands in transmittal to a laboratory for analysis. Laboratory technicians analyzing the samples for court presentation will retain the wax impressions to establish a chain of evidence.

Summary

When a patrol officer is assigned to handle a call involving a crime which requires some investigation, his initial responsibility involves giving aid to or securing medical attention for an injured victim, apprehending the suspect if he is still present, and safeguarding the scene so that evidence which might be vital to a prosecution is not damaged, altered, contaminated, or destroyed. The initial action taken by him at the scene will usually determine how efficiently the incident can be brought to a successful conclusion.

One of the first acts the patrol officer should take upon responding to a call, if no one has been injured and an immediate arrest cannot be made, is to protect evidence at the scene from curious onlookers, other officers not involved, members of the press, etc. If a specialist is not available to collect physical evidence, the officer must assume this responsibility. He should photograph the scene to preserve a representation of it in its original state before collecting physical evidence. He must note how, when, and from whom evidence comes into his possession and to whom he releases it to preserve the chain of custody. The officer will ordinarily be required in court to establish that evidence found at the scene of a crime was passed from the finder through a continuous chain of persons to the laboratory technician who processes it in the crime laboratory and testifies regarding his findings.

The search for physical evidence should be thorough and systematic. When it is found, it should be carefully collected, marked, and placed in a protective container for whatever laboratory analysis may be indicated.

Clothing is one of the most productive sources of evidence in certain crimes. In or on it will be found trace evidence that adheres to the fabric or is caught in the cuffs or pockets. Such evidence is simple to retrieve and often leads to the identification of the suspect or can be used to show his participation in the crime.

Blood, wet or dry, can often be used to connect a person with such crimes as assaults and homicides. Semen, hair, and the like can also be of value to the investigation to show the likelihood that a crime was committed by a particular suspect.

Trace evidence, such as that obtained from fingernails, fiber strands, and impressions left by fiber patterns in sofe materials or etched on painted surfaces may be helpful in pointing to the perpetrator of such crimes as rape, burglary, and hit and run. Wood particles or tool markings in wood may lead to the identification of burglars who attack through roofs or use tools to pry open windows.

Physical comparisons of glass found at the scene of a crime may provide clues leading to the identification of the vehicle involved in a hit-and-run collision or a homicide. Analysis of paint chips or paint traces may provide similar clues. The identification of incendiary materials may lead to their source and to the perpetrators of arson.

Latent prints left by the fingers, palms, or feet of criminals at crime scenes are perhaps some of the most valuable types of physical evidence available. Such evidence is not only generally the easiest to obtain, but is the easiest to compare with impressions available from a suspect.

Latent prints can be located by the use of strong, oblique illumination. They generally adhere best to smooth, hard surfaces. When found, they can readily be developed by the use of powder applied with a soft brush. Chemicals, while not as simple to apply as powder, can be used on paper or on rough surfaces where the use of powder may not be appropriate. Developed prints should be photographed to preserve them on film permanently before any attempt is made to lift them. They should then be mounted on print cards for examination. Inked prints of persons who have a legitimate reason for being on the premises should be obtained for comparison with the developed latent prints for purposes of eliminating those left innocently at the scene.

Physical evidence collected in connection with an investigation should be carefully packaged and labeled. In some cases, the evidence itself should be marked. Distinctive markings should be used which will later enable the person who collected it to identify it from notations he made in his notebook describing the markings.

Clothing, cigarettes, and occasionally jewelry can be marked for identification by the officer for future use. Other articles such as motors, weapons, and some power tools may be identified by serial numbers. Articles of evidence such as narcotics and trace evidence should be carefully labeled on the packet in which they are preserved.

When property is packaged for booking with the laboratory or property custodian, dangerous articles such as cutting or stabbing instruments should be carefully wrapped with protective coverings to prevent injury to other persons. When loaded weapons are packaged and transmitted to the laboratory for examination, their container should clearly indicate that they are loaded to alert the criminalist.

Review

Questions

1. Define *dying declaration* and discuss what is needed to make one acceptable as evidence.
2. When might it be necessary to move an article of evidence at the crime scene before pictures are taken?
3. Why should photographs be taken if possible before the crime scene is altered?
4. What is trace evidence? Give an example and describe how it might be of value to an investigation.
5. What are latent prints? Plastic prints? Visible prints?
6. What is some of the equipment that might be needed to protect a crime scene?

7. What are some of the materials needed by a patrol officer for collecting and preserving physical evidence?
8. Define *chain of custody* and give an example of how it is important in court.
9. Explain how you would collect samples of paint, hair, wood, soil, glass.
10. How would the items in question 9 be matched with samples of material believed to be the source from which these materials came?
11. How should the following articles be marked for identification at the time they are found: watches, jewelry, marijuana cigarettes?
12. What do you do with perishable items needed for evidence?

Exercises

1. Assume you are assigned a call involving a criminal homicide which has occurred in the bedroom of a typical medium-sized home (about 2,000 square feet). You are responsible for the preliminary investigation including the collection and preservation of physical evidence at the scene. The perpetrator has left the premises and is not known at the time you arrive at the scene. Describe in sequence what you would do in fulfilling your responsibilities.
2. Describe in detail and demonstrate how you would prepare an evidence bindle if no other type of container were available for the packaging of small bits of trace evidence such as paint chips.
3. Describe how you would mark a shirt for identification; a pair of trousers; a dress; a coat.
4. Describe how you would examine an automobile that is suspected of having been used in a hit-and-run felony accident, what physical evidence you would look for, and where you would look.
5. Demonstrate and explain how and where you would search for latent prints and how you would process them as physical evidence. Describe the process of dusting, lifting, and preserving such prints.
6. Describe how you should package items such as ice picks, razors, sharp knives, firecrackers, gasoline, or loaded firearms for booking.
7. Describe how you would take photographs of indistinct tire impressions in dirt and of light skid marks leading to the tires of an automobile that caused a fatal traffic accident.

8

Incidents Involving Vehicles

The motor vehicle has contributed greatly to the mobility and efficiency of the patrol officer but it has at the same time become the source of many new problems and considerable danger to him and to society. It is very often a tool of the wrongdoer. It is attacked more often than any other type of property and causes unparalleled injury and loss of life and property on the highways. The time loss and resultant economic loss to thousands of motorists due to congestion caused by a single traffic accident on a major freeway is beyond calculation. Therefore, the patrol officer must devote a major share of his or her time to handling situations involving vehicles.

The amount of time absorbed by these incidents will vary greatly. The routine direction of traffic required to prevent unnecessary and costly delays at the scene of a minor traffic accident on a busy thoroughfare may take a few minutes or may consume a good part of the patrol officer's day. The routine investigation of a vehicle theft or a theft from a vehicle will require a considerable expenditure of his time. Investigating a traffic accident, arresting an intoxicated or hit-and-run driver or a bandit using a vehicle to flee, stopping and searching vehicles in connection with the commission of crime, and the dangers resulting from such activities place an added burden upon the patrol officer in the performance of his complex tasks.

Studies have indicated that as much as 42 percent of police time is taken up in one way or another with automobile use.[1] The officer must therefore familiarize himself with a vast field of law regulating motor vehicles and become adept at the techniques for dealing with vehicles and the problems arising from their use if he is to perform his work safely and efficiently. He must recognize and accept the enormous traffic problem as an inseparable part of the police function.

Traffic Accident Investigation

In most police agencies, the patrol officer is required to investigate traffic collisions and actively engage in traffic law enforcement because the size of the agency does not permit the use of specialists for these tasks. The techniques of traffic accident investigation may involve the whole spectrum of procedures common to other kinds of investigation. The patrol officer is responsible for collecting oral evidence from the parties involved and witnesses. He must collect physical evidence from the scene and attempt to determine what happened and who was to blame.

The patrol officer often looks with apprehension at a complex traffic accident. Since he has no option but to make the best investigation possible, some basic guidelines are presented here to assist in this important task.

Response to Traffic Accident Calls   Using flashing lights and the siren when responding to a traffic accident call is appropriate only under certain conditions. When the dispatcher gives the authority or there is evidence indicating that an incident is a bona fide emergency, use of the red or other authorized lights and siren is ordinarily legally justified and the officer has certain exemptions from the rules of the road. He is also generally given some immunity from

[1] John A. Volpe, "Drunken Driving," *The Police Yearbook*, International Association of Chiefs of Police, Washington, D.C., 1971, p. 35.

civil liability provided he does not arbitrarily exercise his rights and drives with due caution and regard for other persons.

When the officer learns that a legal emergency exists and requires police attention, he should notify the dispatcher of the facts justifying the emergency response so that a record may be permanently made in the event questions are later raised concerning the need for urgency. In the absence of such conditions, the officer should proceed without delay to the scene obeying all traffic regulations. He is not exempt from the rules of the road in nonemergency situations. Every officer should acquaint himself with the laws of his state and the rules of his organization as they relate to his liabilities and immunities when he drives under emergency conditions.

Action upon Arrival at the Scene When the officer arrives at the scene of a traffic accident, he should activate the blinker lights on his vehicle and park it safely off the roadway. Circumstances may indicate that it should be positioned to protect injured parties who cannot be moved safely. He should make a quick evaluation of the accident to determine if a hit-and-run violation has occurred, what assistance will be required to control traffic, remove injured parties, and clear the scene of disabled vehicles, debris, and hazards so that the flow of traffic can be restored as soon as possible. If a power pole is involved, he must take steps to keep persons in the area a safe distance from any electric wires that may be charged. He should treat all wires as live.

Persons in cars with power wires draped over them should be told to remain inside, to keep their windows closed, and to avoid touching any metal. Once the power company has turned off the current, occupants can be removed to safety. To attempt this before the power has been shut off may cause electrocution.[2]

If there are no injuries, the patrol officer must decide if a traffic accident or other report is required by law or department regulation. If not, he should assist the parties in exchanging information they will need for insurance or other purposes. The fact that he is not required to make a report does not relieve him from the responsibility to keep the peace and alleviate congestion or some dangerous condition at the scene.

The police officer's priorities will be dependent upon the nature

[2] J. Stannard Baker, *Traffic Accident Investigator's Manual for Police*, The Traffic Institute, Northwestern University, Evanston, Illinois, 1970, pp. 111–112.

of the accident, the injuries, and the extent of damage to vehicles. After his initial assessment of the accident, he should ordinarily give high priority to notifying his dispatcher of the need for an ambulance, a tow truck, additional flares, fire equipment, barricades, or other officers to assist at the scene or divert traffic.

Warning Devices   He should first take whatever action is needed to prevent the existing conditions from becoming more aggravated. He can do this by setting out reflectors or flares to warn other motorists that caution is needed in the vicinity. Spectators may be solicited to help in placing these in a pattern for several hundred feet along the highway as needed at the approach to the scene. Obviously, if gasoline or some dangerous, explosive substance is a hazard in the vicinity, flares or other equipment that may increase the danger should not be used.

Flares should be considered as warning devices only. An officer should not depend upon them for his personal safety. They are in themselves dangerous when carelessly used; therefore, he should be very careful when he uses them or has them placed on the roadway by an onlooker unfamiliar with their potential for causing injury. They burn at about 2,200 degrees Fahrenheit. Hot slag dripping from them can seriously burn the skin if lighted flares are held upright. They should be held horizontally or with the burning tip down. Waving them over the head or in front of the face can be exceedingly dangerous.

When they burn to a point where they are less than 3 inches long, they should not be handled. Officers kicking or stomping out burning flares have been badly burned when the slag entered their shoes. A flare should be extinguished by snuffing the lighted end on the pavement or covering it with dirt.

Rendering Aid to the Injured   Any first aid needed to preserve life must be given as soon as possible. Persons trapped in wreckage should be extricated promptly and with reasonable care to avoid injury or aggravation of an existing injury.

Injured persons should not be placed in the police vehicle if it has been parked in the roadway to protect them or the scene. They should be moved to a safe location at the roadside if this can be done without the risk of worsening some injury to the spine or internal organs. If not, they should be left in a protected position until they are removed by an ambulance. Officers should be guided by accepted medical practices in determining the course of action they should take in such cases. Sometimes, the risks of moving an injured person are greater than the danger from traffic.

Accidents Involving Dangerous Substances

Occasionally, a vehicle containing some dangerous substance is involved in a traffic collision. The material is sometimes spilled on the highway and poses a special problem to the police. If gasoline spreads over the roadway, the officer should not allow smoking or other acts which might cause the fumes to ignite. He should immediately request fire equipment to wash the street or take other necessary action to prevent a fire. Measures to remove other hazardous materials such as flammables, explosives, or poisons spilled or deposited on the highway must be taken quickly because of the threat they pose to the public. If the substance remains in its container and is not exposed to some unusual outside influence such as fire or heat, it is not ordinarily a hazard; however, its stability cannot easily be predicted once it is released. It may be affected by temperature changes, wind, heat, other materials with which it comes in contact, etc., or a chemical change may occur upon release and create a toxic gas, a fire, an explosive potential, or a combination of these hazards. Therefore, the officer must take extreme precautionary measures to protect himself and others. He should rescue persons exposed to the hazard if reasonably possible. In doing so, he should avoid touching the substance or breathing dangerous, toxic fumes.

If the driver is available, the officer should have him identify the substance and its characteristics so that protective measures can be taken to avoid the hazard it creates. The dispatcher should be requested to notify the concerned shipping or receiving agency of the incident. When the driver is not available to provide this information, the officer should examine the vehicle, especially the cab, for emergency instructions which ordinarily will be present.

An accurate description of the situation and of the substance should be relayed to fire personnel when they are called to assist. Assistance for traffic and spectator control should also be summoned if needed. Even though no fire has occurred, firemen should be available for control work if needed. The officer should confer with the firemen and assist them until the hazard is eliminated.

Some incidents may require clearing nonessential control personnel from an area at least 500 yards in all directions from the hazard and excluding them until the hazard is eliminated. As with gasoline spillage, precautions must be taken to control the use of flares, cigarettes, vehicles, and fire within the area. Many vapors are heavier than air and can spread along the ground creating a fire and explosion hazard. When a cloud of toxic, flammable, or explosive gas drifts from the scene, persons in the area likely to be affected should immediately be evacuated for whatever distance or time appears to be necessary for their protection. If radioactive materials are involved, the dispatcher should be alerted immediately so that the appropriate agency may be notified and control action taken without unnecessary delays.[3]

Clearing Wreckage, Spillage, and Hazards   The likelihood of other traffic accidents increases where roadways are blocked or restricted by vehicles and debris at the scene. These attract the attention of passing drivers, impede traffic, and often lead to more crashes. Such hazards are a major cause of congestion, particularly on freeways, and should be removed promptly to assure resumption of the normal traffic flow.[4]

Mobile vehicles should be moved to the side of the roadway as soon as possible to reduce congestion after they have been photographed in their original positions, if necessary, and have been outlined with chalk on the pavement to permit taking measurements later. Approaching drivers must be warned of the hazards and detoured safely past wreckage, control equipment, exposed pedestrians, etc.

Protecting Property of Parties   Property of persons incapable of caring for it because of injuries should be gathered and securely stored in the police car to prevent theft during the investigation. Thereafter, if it is not properly released to relatives or friends, it should be booked at the station for safekeeping. If the investigating officer is negligent in safeguarding this property, he is liable for any loss due to his negligence.

When preparing an inventory of accessories and other items before the vehicle is released to the tow truck operator, the officer should carefully record all items which might be improperly removed before

---

[3] Los Angeles Police Department, *Training Manual of the Accident Investigation Division,* 1971, pp. 45–46.
[4] Insurance Institute for Highway Safety, "Debris Hazard Control and Cleanup," *Highway Safety Program Standard 16,* Washington, D.C., November 2, 1968, p. 31.

the car is claimed by the owner or his insurance representative. He should either personally prepare the inventory or check it carefully if the tow truck operator prepares it, to protect himself from liability for missing property or the embarrassment the loss might cause.

Investigation While awaiting arrival of the tow truck, the investigating officer should obtain the operator's license from each of the parties involved in the accident, and he should keep them until the parties have been interviewed. He should then locate and interview witnesses immediately, asking their names and obtaining other pertinent information and their version of the accident. Failure to do so at this time may unnecessarily complicate the investigation. Witnesses seldom come forward to provide information once they leave the scene because of reluctance to become involved in a lengthy court case. The alert investigator can usually tell which onlookers appear most knowledgeable about what happened. Witnesses often claim ignorance about what happened because they are reluctant to admit that a relative or friend was at fault. If this claim is recorded, it may later be used to discredit a concocted story by these witnesses.

Involved parties and witnesses should ordinarily be interviewed separately to avoid arguments, contradictions, and interruptions. There are times, however, when an accusation by a disinterested witness in the presence of a driver believed to be responsible for the accident has the effect of causing him to admit—tacitly or verbally— his responsibility. The patrol officer should carefully observe each party during the interview to detect any insobriety or other condition that may have contributed to the accident. If intoxication is suspected, its degree should be determined as we will discuss later.

Each party should be permitted to give his account of the incident without interruption. Pertinent questions should then be asked to clarify any legal issues involved. Such elements as speed and the relative positions of the vehicles at critical moments when right-of-way arises are vital and must be determined in such violations. In his interviews with parties and witnesses, the officer must cover those elements of the suspected traffic law violation which are not obvious from the physical evidence.

Physical Evidence at the Traffic Accident Scene The investigator lastly examines the scene to obtain physical evidence that often reveals the cause of the accident and makes proof of a violation possible. Careful notes should be taken and sketches made showing such details as the place of impact, damage to property, injuries to parties, statements of witnesses and parties, and the type of paving (for use in determining speed from skid marks). The point of impact is usually revealed by broken glass, debris, broken skid marks, and statements of parties and witnesses; it should be carefully measured from fixed points such as curbs or the edge of the roadway paving.

Skid Marks   Vehicles' minimum speed can be determined from skid marks left on the pavement. They are often invaluable for determining what took place before and during the accident. The officer should thus accurately measure and describe them. The type of skid marks, location on the pavement, point of origin, direction, length, and point of termination should be clearly noted.

The point of origin of the skid marks indicates the position of the vehicle when the brakes locked the wheels. Thus, if the skid marks originated on the wrong side of the street, the vehicle had to be on that side *before* the driver perceived danger and applied the brakes. If they started before a stop sign or signal and extended into the intersection, they indicate that the driver did not stop as required.

Their direction, length, and termination will reveal at least the probable place of impact and the minimum speed of the vehicle at the time it started to leave skid marks. Usually this minimum speed is considerably less than the actual speed, because the impact stops the car sooner than normal, and thus it leaves shorter skid marks. Skid marks may also be used to refute a driver's statement that he had brake failure.

Skid marks should be measured to the nearest half foot. Each skid mark should be measured. All of them from one car should be added together even though less than four wheels left marks. The total is then divided by the number of wheels on the vehicle to find the average length of the marks. Minimum speed can then be computed by using a device such as the Skid-Speed Chart.[5] A typical chart is shown in Figure 8-1. Light tire patterns, sometimes called impending skid marks, should be measured like regular skid marks. Brush marks are caused by a spinning vehicle with or without evidence of braking or by a vehicle being pushed by another vehicle in a collision. They should not be used in calculating the length of skid marks.

The minimum speed shown on the chart will only be approximate

[5] Traffic Institute, Northwestern University, *Charts and Tables for Stopping Distances of Motor Vehicles,* Evanston, Illinois, n.d., p. 12.

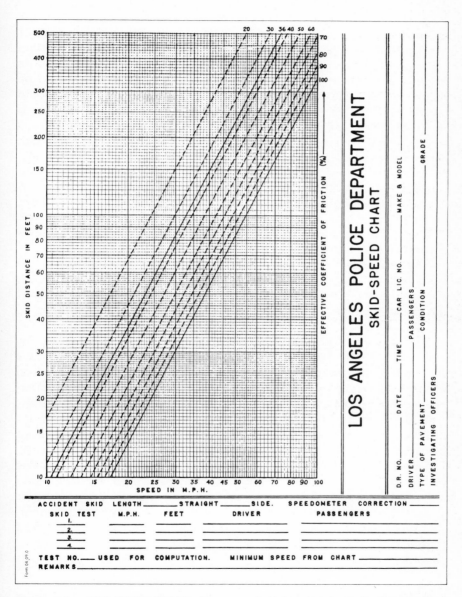

Figure 8-1.   SKID-SPEED CHART. *(Courtesy of the Los Angeles Police Department.)*

but will always be less than the actual speed at which the vehicle was traveling. When the officer is in doubt about the use of skid marks, an expert should be consulted if the case warrants it.

In the event four locked-wheel skid marks overlap, and if the pattern indicates the wheels were locked over the entire length of the skid marks, they should be measured from their point of origin up to the center of the rear wheels if the car leaving them is in its original position. If it has been moved, the overall length should be measured, but the wheel base (about 10 feet on most cars) should be subtracted from the overall length of the marks before computing the minimum speed from the chart.[6]

Equipment violations related to the cause of the accident can often be ascertained by examining the brakes, tires, lights, etc. Measurements to determine the pertinent dimensions of streets and intersections usually should be verified by two officers; however, modern roller measuring devices permit accurate measurements without a tape. Onlookers can be solicited to assist in holding the tape if the officer does not have other devices available. Such measurements are adequate for most investigations.

The officer's responsibility at the scene ends only when traffic has been restored to normal and the parties are informed of any procedures with which they must comply. At times, he should remain until the scene has been cleared of wreckage and hazardous conditions.

The Traffic Accident Report   Traffic accident reports are invaluable for quick, fair adjudications of civil actions and are bases for the identification and prosecution of negligent drivers. The stamp shown in Chapter 4 is a guide for collecting the essential information needed for a traffic accident investigation report. The officer's accident diagram and his notes in his notebook concerning the parties involved, their statements and those of witnesses, and the physical evidence should be used as a basis for the necessary accident reports.

The diagram of the accident should show the number of vehicles involved, the place they collided accurately measured, their direction of travel before and after the collision, the names and widths of streets, and the locations of traffic control devices. When pertinent, the existence of painted lines showing lanes, marked or unmarked crosswalks, stop limit lines, length and place of skid marks, etc., should be shown.

[6] Los Angeles Police Department, *Training Manual of the Accident Investigation Division*, pp. 110, 141–152; J. Stannard Baker, *Traffic Accident Investigator's Manual for Police*, pp. 257–261, 379–381, 509–514.

A brief reconstruction of the accident should also be written on the accident diagram summarizing the details shown. This summary should also include pertinent information about the lighting at the time of the accident, a description of injuries, the condition of the parties and vehicles that might have contributed to the accident. It should also contain a description of pertinent physical features of the scene that might require repair or correction as well as any other details not elsewhere described which may be essential in a later prosecution.

Notifications in Traffic Injury and Death Cases   The investigating officer should notify the next of kin of injured or deceased victims of the accident whenever feasible in the interests of good public relations. If this is not practical, he should have notification made according to the rules of his agency.

Traffic Direction

Patrol officers frequently find it necessary to direct traffic to relieve congestion or protect persons or property. They may have to detour traffic around a collision, a construction project, or disruptive articles that have spilled on the street. Frequently they will be required to direct traffic at intersections where the signal system has broken down or near schools or other places where pedestrian and vehicular traffic warrant such police activity.

This function provides an excellent opportunity for the police officer to promote good public relations in the community. If he performs efficiently, expedites traffic, and increases safety, his entire agency will profit by the image he presents.

Traffic direction is an important task. All officers required to perform such duties should acquaint themselves with the simple techniques involved so that they do not create a greater problem than the one they are trying to alleviate.

Standard Techniques of Control   Since pedestrians and drivers will not usually be able to hear oral commands, especially at a noisy intersection, signals must be used to let them know exactly what they are supposed to do. The signals must be visible for considerable distances and must be easily understood.

Motorists and pedestrians will comprehend standard gestures and signals more clearly and quickly than carelessly improvised signs. The officer most proficient in this standard sign language will move traffic more smoothly, swiftly, safely, and easily than the officer who thinks he can carry out his task in a slovenly fashion.

Position in Intersection   Usually the officer should stand in the center of an intersection to be most easily observed by motorists. From here he can stop approaching vehicular traffic and then he can move nearer a crosswalk to control pedestrian traffic while permitting vehicles caught within the intersection by a signal change to make or complete right or left turns.

His position will depend, of course, upon the physical characteristics of the intersection and the specific task he wishes to accomplish. His posture and demeanor should clearly indicate that he is in charge and can control traffic movement at all times. He should stand erect with his weight evenly distributed on both feet and with his hands at his sides when not giving signals. He should avoid waving his arms like a windmill. Rather, his movements should be precise and positive so that they will not be misunderstood.

Standard Direction Signals   In starting one line of traffic, the officer should stand with his side toward the traffic he wishes to move, and point his arm and finger at the vehicle that must move first. Then, when the driver's attention has been attracted, the arm should be moved up and in front of the chin in a circular motion with the elbow bent. The arm should then be dropped and the same procedure is followed in starting vehicles from the opposite direction.

When stopping two lanes of traffic approaching from opposite directions, the officer should stand sideways to vehicles approaching, hold up his arms at shoulder level, and point at the lead motorist approaching from one direction until his attention is attracted. Then he should raise the pointing hand so that the palm is upright facing the driver. This is the stop signal. When it is clear the driver has seen it and applied his brakes, the officer should turn his head toward the traffic approaching from the opposite direction and repeat it, holding both arms at shoulder height with palms in a vertical position until the vehicles have stopped. Both lines of traffic can thus be stopped at about the same time with relative safety.

The officer can move forward or backward to see and be seen by vehicles approaching on inside lanes from either direction. Once approaching traffic has been stopped, he should turn his body 90 degrees to the right or left so that he can signal vehicles which have been awaiting a signal change to proceed.

Left turning vehicles should be assisted with great caution to avoid

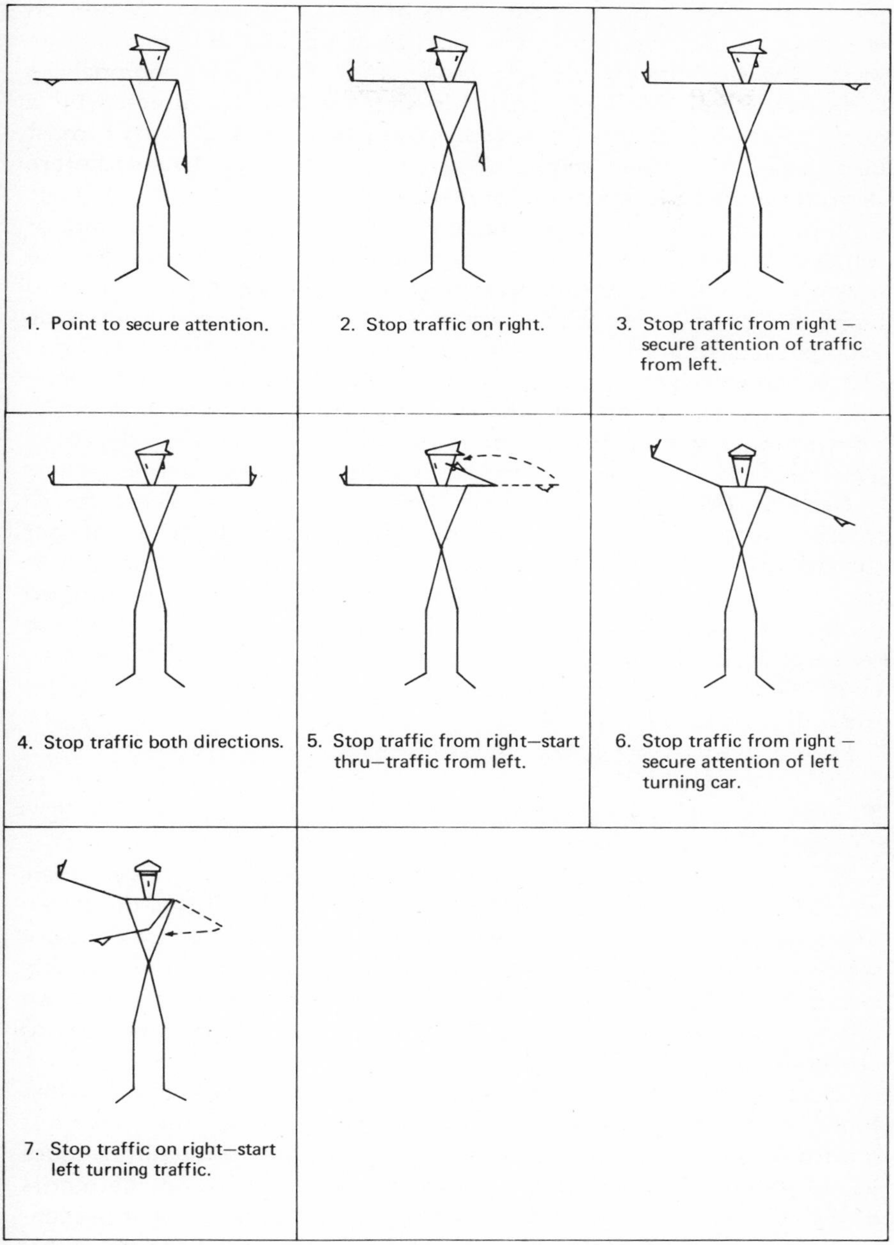

1. Point to secure attention.

2. Stop traffic on right.

3. Stop traffic from right — secure attention of traffic from left.

4. Stop traffic both directions.

5. Stop traffic from right—start thru—traffic from left.

6. Stop traffic from right — secure attention of left turning car.

7. Stop traffic on right—start left turning traffic.

Figure 8-2.   STANDARD TRAFFIC DIRECTION SIGNALS.

the conflict which often occurs in right-of-way situations. When an appropriate break occurs, traffic must be stopped in the lane through which the left turning vehicle must cross. Once the approaching vehicle has stopped, the turning driver may then be directed by a clear pointing motion to proceed. When two lanes of traffic must be stopped, the officer should be sure that both have done so before permitting the turning car to commence its turn.

In periods of low visibility, such as during darkness, dusk, rain, or fog, the traffic officer should wear high-visibility equipment and use a warning light, and he should take exceptional precautions to avoid being hit by a driver whose vision is obscured. Signals should be exaggerated so that each driver will clearly understand what the officer expects him to do. The use of lighted flares to direct traffic should be a last resort because of the danger discussed previously. They should never be relied upon to protect him from being struck.

Use of a Whistle   A whistle, properly used, is an excellent device to supplement hand and arm signals. Short, sharp blasts will attract the attention of pedestrians who do not react to arm signals. It is also useful to attract the attention of motorists who are stopped awaiting a signal change or a motion to move. It should never be relied upon as a signal to a motorist in a moving vehicle, however, as it seldom can be heard inside a car when windows are closed or the radio is playing.

Traffic Law Enforcement

In enforcing traffic law, patrol officers perform one of their most important functions in dealing with the public. This is the phase of police work in which they will have the most contact with every segment of the population. Their primary objective in these contacts is to achieve the voluntary compliance of motorists with driving regulations, but one result is usually a degree of resentment toward authority.

Motorists often feel they deserve some special consideration. When this consideration is not forthcoming, they will feel the officer is arbitrary, unfair, and inconsiderate. They at times complain because he refuses to become involved in an argument regarding the merits of the case. If he discusses the offense, he is often accused of preaching, being rude, or of "holding court on the street" because of his

Enforcement Policies and Practices

temerity in even assuming that the motorist could violate a traffic law.

Violating a minor rule of the road does not mean that the violator is a criminal in a true sense of the word. He may have been careless and inattentive to his driving, as is usually the case, or he may be incapable of correctly assessing risks. However, he may be the motorist who evades the rules if he thinks he can get away with it.

Sometimes drivers' violations result from excessive confidence in their own driving skill. This, coupled with a lack of knowledge about basic physical laws, causes them to drive beyond their capacity without recognizing the hazards involved.[7] Sometimes they don't know that they have violated the law. Whatever the cause of the violation, when it results in a traffic accident, the effect is injury, death, property damage, inconvenience to others, economic loss, or congestion, or a combination of these.

Traffic violation contacts involving warnings, citations, or arrests should have one major objective—to change the driving behavior of the motorist. Accordingly, the attitude of the driver is very important, since traffic law violations usually involve attitude problems. An officer should not base his decision to issue a citation, give a warning, or make an arrest upon whether the offender fails the attitude test; yet the driver who violates the traffic laws should be encouraged to react constructively when he is stopped. This is the objective of the officer. How it is accomplished is a decision only he is in a position to make. Certainly, not every traffic law violator should be arrested or issued a traffic citation or a summons to appear in court, especially when all the evidence indicates that a warning would suffice to correct his driving behavior. Reliable judgments of the violator's long-term reactions are difficult in such situations.

The written warning has considerable deterrent value. It allows the motorist to profit from his error without a penalty. The emphasis is placed on education rather than discipline. Visual warnings such as a nod of the head, a toot on the horn, or a wave of the hand to let him know his violation has been observed also has considerable deterrent value.[8] When other motorists see the enforcement action

[7] Traffic Institute, Northwestern University, *Background for Traffic Law Enforcement, Publication No. 2022,* Evanston, Illinois, 1959, p. 5.
[8] Traffic Institute, Northwestern University, *Taking Enforcement Action, Publication No. 2017,* Evanston, Illinois, 1959, p. 2.

being taken or hear about it from the offender, it will also have a deterrent effect upon them. They will often learn to avoid offensive driving practices by observing the unpleasantness others experience for committing prohibited acts.

Officer-Violator Contacts

When a motorist is stopped for a traffic law violation, the contact should be professional and businesslike from start to finish. The officer should address the offender politely with an appropriate greeting such as "good morning" or "good evening" and then immediately inform him of the reason he was stopped. If members of the driver's family are passengers, especially if they are young children, and the offender seems likely to argue, the officer should explain the violation out of their presence on the sidewalk or in a safe position off the roadway. There is little to be gained by lowering the image of the driver in the eyes of his children unless he insists on an explanation of the law in their presence. The officer may expect any type of emotional reaction at this time from impassiveness to rage or hysteria. He must, however, remain calm himself.

An immediate appraisal should be made to determine if the motorist is possibly under the influence of liquor or a drug. If he appears to be, the inquiry should proceed as described later in this chapter. If not, his operator's license and vehicle registration information should be promptly requested. If the officer decides to issue a citation, he should so inform the motorist, then return to the curbside or his vehicle to prepare the citation. A prolonged debate over the merits of the case may thus be avoided. The officer will also have an opportunity if the circumstances warrant to check through his dispatcher to determine whether there are outstanding warrants for the motorist.

The officer should then return to the motorist, obtain his signature on the citation, give him a copy of it, and explain what is required of him in responding to it. Once the driver fully understands, his operator's license and registration certificate should be returned. Any information regarding general procedure in adjudicating the matter should be provided courteously; however, the officer should avoid quoting bail, guessing at the fine, or speculating upon what action a court might take in the case. These are matters which may depend upon many factors not known to the officer such as the prior driving record of the offender, previous punishments imposed, and whether the violator is on probation.

Notes concerning important details of the contact can be placed on the back of the file copy of the citation for possible later use in court. The specific actions of the violator that increased the hazard of his violation, the names of witnesses, the position where the violation was observed, the place he was stopped, what he said at the time or during the ensuing conversation, the distance traveled during a pursuit if there was one, and the violations observed during this time should be noted.

The officer's last act in the sequence is to help the motorist re-enter the traffic flow safely. Ordinarily, he should then wait until the motorist is safely on his way if he decides to go in the same direction. This delay will enable him to avoid giving the appearance of following the motorist. In some cases, the circumstances of the contact may indicate that the officer should leave the scene in the opposite direction if he can do so safely and properly. After he has taken enforcement action, he should promptly clear with his dispatcher. The communications center will then know that the incident has been concluded safely.

The Intoxicated Driver

Intoxicated drivers are responsible for a large percentage of traffic accidents. They are involved in about one in every four of those resulting in fatalities. Some studies indicate that two of every three fatally injured drivers had been drinking.[9] Driving under the influence of an intoxicating liquor is the cause of more traffic accidents than any other traffic law violation except those involving right-of-way. Drinking is a factor in at least half of the total motor vehicle accidents in the nation.[10] It is estimated that it is responsible for over 30,000 deaths and 800,000 injuries every year in this country.[11]

[9] R. G. Mortimer, M. W. Kenlan, L. D. Filkins, and J. S. Lower, "Identifying a Major Hazard on The Highways—The Problem Drinking Driver," *Police*, vol. 16, no. 8, April 1972, p. 17.

[10] Los Angeles Police Department, "Drivers Under the Influence," *Training Bulletin*, part IV, vol. II, issue 13, 1970, n.p.; *U.S. House of Representatives 89th Congress, Report No. 1700*, 2d Sess., July 15, 1966, p. 26; Minnesota Department of Public Safety, *The Alcohol-Impaired Driver and Highway Crashes*, St. Paul, 1970, p. 8; U.S. Department of Transportation, *Alcohol Safety Countermeasures Program*, National Highway Safety Bureau, Washington, D.C., 1970, p. 2-2.

[11] John A. Volpe, "Drunken Driving," p. 36.

Although the laws governing motor vehicle operation will vary somewhat from state to state, the techniques of detecting and removing intoxicated drivers from the highways and collecting evidence for prosecution are substantially the same everywhere. Since it is not feasible for the police to control drinking drivers by controlling their drinking habits, the patrol officer must rely upon traffic law enforcement to reduce the slaughter caused by intoxicated motorists.

Drinking drivers are most common in the early morning, particularly on weekends, on medium volume roads.[12] If the officer learns where and when the problem is greatest, he can concentrate his enforcement efforts there with best results.

Legal Definition   "Drunk driver" is a common term; however, the law differentiates between the drunk or intoxicated person and one who is under the influence of intoxicating liquor. The courts have consistently held that a person who is under the influence of an intoxicant is not necessarily drunk. The term *drunk* refers to a person's condition when he is so affected by an intoxicating liquor that he is unable to care for himself or his property. The term *under the influence of an intoxicating liquor*, as it refers to a driver, means that liquor has so far affected the nervous system, brain, and/or muscles as to impair to an appreciable degree the person's ability to operate a vehicle as would an ordinary, prudent, and cautious person in full possession of his faculties and using reasonable care under similar conditions.[13] Thus, if the person's driving efficiency is appreciably lowered by an intoxicating liquor, he is under the influence and in violation of the statute which prohibits driving in such a condition. Often the statute will also prohibit driving under the influence of any drug. In this case, the term *under the influence* also refers to the driver who is under the influence of drugs.

Recognizing the Drunk Driver   Many officers have had wide experience in dealing with drivers whose driving efficiency is definitely lowered by alcohol or drugs. They have found that these drivers often exhibit certain easily recognized characteristics. These driving irregularities tend to provide objective evidence of an offense.

---

[12] R. G. Mortimer, et al., "Identifying a Major Hazard on the Highways—The Problem Drinking Driver," p. 17.
[13] *People v. McKee*, 80 Cal. App. 200 (1926); *People v. Dingle*, 56 Cal. App. 445 (1922).

The physical appearance of the driver whose head bobs up and down may be a giveaway that he or she is intoxicated. Drooping or squinting eyelids often reflect his attempt to improve vision impaired by alcohol. Clothing in disarray may give the initial clue of his condition. This may later be confirmed by other observations.

Some drivers who are under the influence drive unusually slowly, hold to the curb lane, or make obvious efforts to drive inconspicuously focusing all their attention straight ahead. If someone drives slowly in the center lane apparently unaware of what's happening around him, he should be watched closely for other evidence which may indicate that he should be stopped.

Occasionally, the driver under the influence of alcohol or drugs will see a stop sign only in time to skid abruptly to a stop or he will approach the sign very slowly, misjudge the distance, and stop in or beyond the crosswalk or intersection after a series of jerky motions. He may reveal his condition by an unusually slow or jerky start from a signal, by overdriving in passing other vehicles—swerving far to the right or left—and taking an unusually long time to return to his lane after passing. Some such drivers give their condition away by erratic or high-speed driving, constantly changing lanes, or swerving from side to side of a lane causing other motorists to swerve, changing lanes or stopping suddenly, or straddling double lines and interfering with oncoming traffic.

Officers should carefully observe these physical conditions and driving irregularities as well as other conditions which will provide the necessary reasonable cause to stop the driver for further inquiry. These observations are very important to supplement other tests that may be given to determine the extent to which the driver is under the influence of liquor or drugs.

Car Stops—the Intoxicated Driver   As in the case of other car stops, an officer should consider the driver who is suspected of being under the influence of alcohol or drugs as potentially very dangerous but for a different reason. An intoxicated driver may be just as capable of committing a violent assault upon the officer as the felony suspect, with the additional danger that he has a dangerous weapon —his vehicle—which he is usually unable to control prudently.

The officer should therefore exercise extreme caution and maintain sufficient clearance between vehicles to have room to maneuver in the event of a sudden, unexpected action by the suspect. Otherwise, the same precautions and techniques for stopping other vehicles (as described in Chapter 6) should be used. Furthermore, no officer should ever assume that an intoxicated driver is not armed.

If the suspect stops his vehicle in a traffic lane, he should not be allowed to drive it to the curb because of the possibility of his damaging other vehicles, injuring another person, or attempting to escape. He may even later try to establish a defense in court by contending that the officer apparently did not believe he was under the influence because he was allowed to drive after he had been stopped. The officer should move the vehicle himself if necessary.

When the stop has been made, the officer should make certain that the brakes on the suspect's vehicle are set and the motor turned off. This is especially important when the suspect's driving behavior has led to the belief that he is intoxicated.

Gathering Evidence of Intoxication

The officer should gather supporting evidence of the suspect's condition after he or she is stopped. Any objective symptoms of his being under the influence of alcohol or drugs should be noted. While talking to him, the officer should observe his clothing, speech, coordination, eyes, and general ability to react to questions. Does his breath smell of alcohol? Are his clothes disarranged? Is his speech slurred? Is his coordination impaired? Are his eyes bloodshot or do they react more slowly than normal to light? Has he taken medication recently? Is he diabetic? Can he remove his operator's license easily or does he fumble abnormally?

It may be advisable to have the suspect get out of the car from the passenger side to see if he staggers or loses his balance. Caution should be exercised at this point to avoid an attack by the suspect or to prevent him from arming himself while sliding across the seat. He should then be taken to a position of safety on the sidewalk or some level portion on the shoulder off the roadway. The officer should be cautious that the driver does not fall or walk into oncoming traffic. He should be kept under constant observation to ensure his and the officer's safety.

By this time, even in cases which were doubtful at the beginning, the officer should have reached a definite conclusion regarding the sobriety of the suspect and whether his driving, behavior, and physical condition warrant an arrest. If so, he should be advised of his rights under the Miranda rule before he is engaged in a conversation in which he is likely to make admissions against his own interest.

This admonishment does not apply to sobriety tests. It applies only to his responses to questioning, such as his admission that he has been drinking, how much he has imbibed, when, and where.

The Sobriety Test   The place selected for the sobriety test should be well-lighted and away from distracting noises or onlookers. Each test should be explained to and demonstrated for the subject before he is asked to perform it. The officer should not close his eyes while demonstrating tests which require that the eyes be closed. To do so might invite an attack by the suspect.

The officer should closely observe the results of all tests and describe the results accurately on the sobriety report or in his notebook. The subject's coordination and balance should be tested by having him stand erect with his eyes closed or walk along a straight, smooth line in the sidewalk, a chalkline on the pavement, or a line scratched in the dirt. The subject should be directed to walk the line by placing the heel of one foot against the toe of the other for approximately ten steps. This is called "Frankel's test." He should then be told to turn, keeping one foot on the line, and walk heel to toe back to the starting point. The officer should note his balance in walking and turning. This is called "Fournier's test." These tests are a better examination of disorder in a subject's gait than just observing his walk.

The suspect should then be directed to stand erect with his feet together, his head tilted slightly back, arms at his sides, and eyes closed. Any inability to avoid swaying without shifting feet should be noted. The inability to maintain equilibrium is known as the "Romberg sign"—a neurologic reaction arising from impairment of the sensory phase of muscular coordination.[14] In cases of marked impairment of coordination, the subject may fall. In observing the test, the officer should therefore stand near him to prevent this. Swaying due to nervousness may be overcome by having him stand erect with his head tilted back slightly, his eyes closed, his arms extended horizontally to the sides, fingers closed, and index finger extended and touch the tip of his nose with one finger then the other. A false Romberg sign will then be avoided.[15] Any lack of balance and coordination as reflected by his inability to touch his nose as directed

[14] Aaron J. Rosanoff, *Manual of Psychiatry and Mental Hygiene*, 7th ed., John Wiley and Sons, Inc., New York, 1938, p. 1079.
[15] T. R. Harrison, Raymond D. Adams, Ivan L. Bennett, Jr., William H. Resnick, George W. Thorn, and M. M. Wintrobe, (eds.), *Principles of Internal Medicine*, McGraw-Hill Book Company, New York, 1958, p. 278.

should be noted. The test should be repeated several times to eliminate the accident factor. A staggering gait is characteristic of alcoholic and barbiturate intoxication.[16]

At night the reaction of the suspect's eyes to light should be tested
last. This will prevent the possible defense that he was blinded by the
light and therefore couldn't perform the other tests normally.

The eyes of an intoxicated person will ordinarily react slower and
to a lesser degree than those of a sober person. The suspect should
be directed to stare at a fixed point. The officer should then direct
the beam of his flashlight from the side of his face to his eyes and
note the reaction of the pupils. This less intense circle of light *around*
the central beam should be used as it causes a slower and more
readily distinguishable pupil reaction than does the direct beam.
The same test should then be performed on another officer and a
comparison made of the relative time and intensity of reaction
between the two. When the test is made during daylight, adequate
results can be obtained by placing a cupped hand over the suspect's
eyes, removing it rapidly, and noting the pupil change.

Results of all these tests and other observations of objective physical symptoms that support the conclusion that the driver is under the
influence of intoxicating liquor or drugs should be carefully described
in the officer's notes. These will be the basis for arrest and related
reports and for the officer's testimony in court if required.

A systematic and thorough examination at the scene coupled with
complete reports of the circumstances have a strong effect upon the
suspect and his legal counsel. Guilty pleas are more frequent when
cases are completely investigated and reported than when the officer
is neglectful in his investigation and superficial in his reports.

Pursuit Driving

All available evidence indicates that up to a half-million hot pursuits occur in the nation each year. Six to eight thousand of these
result in crashes—most of which involve injuries or death.[17] These
data indicate the seriousness of the problem.

The Decision to Pursue   Every pursuit of a fleeing suspect is
potentially very dangerous to the officer because of the high speeds

[16] T. R. Harrison, et al., *Principles of Internal Medicine,* p. 276.
[17] The Center for the Environment of Man, Inc., *A Study of the Problem of Hot
Pursuit by the Police—Final Report,* Hartford, Connecticut, July 1970, p. 2.

involved, the violation of the rules of the road with which he ordinarily complies, and the accompanying nervous tension which reduces his capacity to react to hazards easily avoided under normal operating conditions. Consequently, the decision to pursue an offender should not be made lightly. An officer should become involved only as a last resort after considering the personal and financial risks to himself, danger to the public, condition of the roadway, weather, time of day, capacity of his automobile, type of vehicle and pedestrian traffic, and seriousness of the offense. It would be foolhardy for an officer to jeopardize his safety and that of the public to apprehend a minor traffic law violator; the gravity of the offense would not be commensurate with the risk.

Other factors which the officer should consider but often does not are his own physical limitations. Poor vision, slow reaction time, night or glare blindness, or impaired depth perception or peripheral vision may be present but not recognized.

The normal reaction is to pursue the offender until he is apprehended; yet this course of action may be neither safe, nor practicable, nor judicious. Therefore, each case must be decided on its own merit. Often it is more practical to forego an immediate apprehension where the hazards are unreasonable. If the offender is identifiable, he can be easily and safely apprehended at another time under controlled conditions.

Sometimes, it may be wise for the patrol officer to merely follow a suspect without becoming involved in a pursuit. He should follow the same prestop procedures as in the case of a person suspected of a felony—checking the license number against the hot sheet, recording it on a paper that will remain in the police car, and notifying his dispatcher of what action he is contemplating, the description of the suspect and the vehicle, the location, whether the stop is to be made, and whether assistance will be needed. Circumstances may justify a "running make" on the license number to determine if it is stolen.

If the violator does not become aware of the officer's presence, a good opportunity is available for making a quick stop to avoid a pursuit. The offender may be stopped in traffic by other vehicles thus enabling the officer to apprehend him without a chase.

Studies show that traffic violations initiate over 90 percent of pursuits; that males under twenty-four years of age with poor driving records are most likely to be involved; that alcohol is involved in over half the incidents; that over 15 percent of the offenders are driving without a valid driver's license; that over half the apprehended offenders have at least one previous license suspension or revocation; that only 3 to 8 percent of the cases involve stolen vehicles; and that the majority of the pursuits occur at night and on weekends.[18]

These data indicate rather conclusively that the offenders are likely to lead pursuing officers into unreasonably high-risk situations. Therefore the officer is well advised to reduce the hazards of pursuit by stopping the suspect as soon as possible after observing a violation. Circumstances may indicate in some cases that this course of action should not be attempted by a one-man unit until assistance arrives.

Broadcasting the Pursuit

When a violator fails to respond to the flashing light and gestures or oral directions to stop, but instead increases his speed or takes other evasive action, the officer should activate his siren and emergency light. This *may* give him some protection against liability if he drives with reasonable prudence and becomes involved in an accident. The laws of most states make him exempt from the rules of the road under such conditions.

All such incidents will not necessarily require a pursuit broadcast and assistance. Unless a one-man unit or a serious offense—actual or suspected—is involved, or the chase is prolonged and fast, the officer should not broadcast that he is in a pursuit; the broadcast may involve unnecessarily many other police units in a dangerous situation.

When pursuit does begin, however, the patrol officer should immediately identify himself and notify his dispatcher of the situation. If the communications load permits, he should then wait until the dispatcher directs other units to stand by so that pursuit information can be broadcast. The officer should then indicate the direction of travel, the name of the street upon which he is driving, and the name of the last street crossed. In addition, he should give the make, model, color, and license number of the violator's car; the number and description of suspects; and any other pertinent information.

It is imperative that the dispatcher be notified of the offense for which the suspect is wanted so that other units may be informed. They will then have some substantial information upon which they might rely should they need to decide whether to shoot at the offen-

---

[18] The Center for the Environment of Man, Inc., *A Study of the Problems of Hot Pursuit by the Police*, p. 2.

der. The reason specified for the "want" should be based upon *facts* known to the officer instead of speculation and probability. Other officers must not be misled into thinking that the suspect is wanted for a felony when in fact he might be wanted only for a minor traffic violation in which he panicked and tried to evade apprehension.

There are a multitude of minor violations that could result in disastrous pursuits if other units did not receive adequate or accurate information and drew conclusions that were not supported by facts. Other officers might take forceful action such as shooting which they assumed was justified in apprehending a fleeing felon only to learn too late that the suspect was wanted for a misdemeanor.

Any unusual occurrences observed during the pursuit such as objects being thrown from the car or hit-and-run traffic accidents should be broadcast so that other units can follow up these incidents to collect evidence or make necessary investigations or reports. Exact locations where objects were discarded should be reported. When possible, a description of the objects should be given to help other units locate them. Even general descriptions of the size of objects or packages are helpful and may be crucial to later identifications.

Pursuit Broadcasting Techniques   All pursuit broadcasts should be made slowly and clearly during periods of low siren pitch. The receiver should be turned up so the officer can hear rebroadcasts of the information he transmits to the dispatcher.

In one-man units, the driver should not attempt to transmit information while turning because the microphone cord may become tangled in the steering wheel or gear shift lever and cause him to lose control of his car. Furthermore, at such times he should concentrate on his driving rather than on his radio transmissions.

Two-men units will encounter few broadcasting problems during pursuits; but a single patrol officer will have little time to broadcast his messages and should do so when he is on a straight road. Turning and maneuvering through traffic is a full-time job and little time can be safely diverted to radio broadcasts during these periods. The officer should place the microphone on the seat under his right leg so he will not have to reach for it or hang it up before or after using it.

He should make frequent transmittals to his dispatcher keeping him informed of new directions of travel, locations, and instructions or suggestions that may be relayed to other units to help them be of the greatest help. If he finds it necessary to leave the police vehicle to pursue the suspect on foot, he should notify the dispatcher of this fact and the location. These procedures require very little time, and they give other officers information to enable them to provide swift assistance when time is precious.

Coordination of Efforts through Communications   Apprehension of a pursued suspect is usually the result of a team effort on the part of many police elements. Sometimes a pursuit will involve police agencies from other jurisdictions. Therefore, the key to the coordination of a pursuit is the dispatcher. Ordinarily, it is his responsibility to limit the number of units directly involved for reasons of safety. He should relay broadcasts and otherwise notify other police units of details of the incident as they develop so that the other officers can be most effectively deployed to assist in apprehending the suspect.

Pursuit Driving Techniques

Just as in any other patrol activity, the officer should apply defensive driving techniques to pursuits. His driving skills are tested at this time perhaps more than at any other because he must either respond rapidly to the evasive tactics of the suspect or lose him or become a traffic accident casualty.

Use of Safety Equipment   At the outset of a pursuit, the officer should check his seat belt and shoulder harness and tighten them securely with one hand if they are loose. During the daytime, headlights should be turned on in addition to the red light and siren as an additional warning to other motorists and pedestrians. He must be constantly alert for unexpected maneuvers designed to mislead him, such as sudden slowing, quick acceleration, or unexpected reversals of direction.

Overdriving is a frequent cause of accidents and is most prevalent in emergency operations. If the officer fails to recognize his driving limitations under pursuit conditions and if he does not familiarize himself with the performance capacity of the car he is driving, he will eventually become involved unnecessarily in a traffic accident. The result may be a serious injury or death to himself or another innocent party or, at least, serious damage to his police vehicle.

Use of the Siren   The siren should be used so that its pitch alternates during the pursuit. The officer should bring it to its highest pitch sufficiently before entering an intersection so that pedestrians and other motorists will have maximum warning. The limitations of the siren as previously discussed must be constantly kept in mind.

Use of Brakes   When it becomes necessary to use the brakes, they should be applied with a hard, short, pumping motion rather than with a continuous hard pressure which causes overheating and glazing of bands and expansion of drums resulting in skidding and loss of control. Brake "jabs" will also tend to prevent wheels from locking. Skidding resulting from locked wheels causes almost full loss of control. A vehicle with all four tires skidding will usually move in a straight line. By jabbing and releasing brakes sharply, the driver can maintain considerable steering control because the wheels will turn between jabs.

Transmission Use   The tremendous strain generated in an automatic transmission when it is quickly shifted from high to low at high speeds is likely to cause serious damage to it. Decelerating by this means should therefore be avoided.

Turning   At high speeds the officer should brake hard without skidding *before a turn*, then release the brake pressure and *accelerate out of the turn*, to maintain much better control of his vehicle.

Often the violator will suddenly turn and proceed in the opposite direction hoping to escape. Ordinarily he will do so at places where he can turn suddenly and cause his pursuer to overshoot a favorable turning location and be forced to proceed on and waste time while looking for another turning place. The pursuing officer should watch for wide driveways such as those constructed for filling stations, drive-in businesses, or parking lots, and places without curbs where the shoulders are sufficiently wide and strong for use in turning. These places are preferable to intersections, curves, or areas where vision is restricted or the hazards from other cars are great.

When the roadway is wide enough for a U turn without using a driveway or shoulder, the turn should be made from the lane nearer the center of the street. This type of turn is safer than one made from the right lane since it eliminates most of the hazards of vehicles approaching from the rear and passing on the left into the path of the turning police car. On narrow roadways where a front or U turn is not practicable, the "bootleg" turn shown in Figure 8-3 can be employed effectively. This turn involves stopping at the extreme

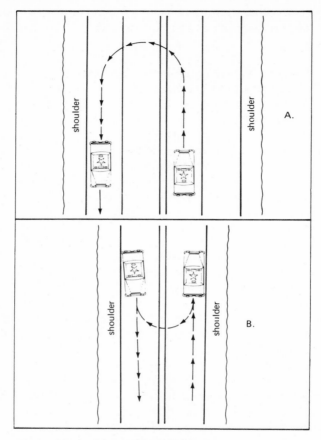

Figure 8-3. TURNING MOVEMENTS. A. U Turn from center lane to proceed in opposite direction. B. Bootleg Turn. Back 180 degrees from extreme right of roadway. Proceed in opposite direction.

right side of the roadway, cramping the steering wheel as far to the left as possible, backing up until the car is facing the opposite direction, straightening the wheels, and continuing the pursuit.

Maintaining Maneuvering Position The pursuing officer should anticipate unfavorable traffic or roadway conditions and try to turn them to his advantage. Signal changes can be anticipated ahead of time so that he can prepare to clear an intersection most safely even against a stop signal. Proper use of the siren will aid him without aiding the violator. If caution and good judgment are not exercised in the use of the siren, it may clear the way for the person being pursued. Motorists may yield to the suspect because they hear the siren then quickly close in behind him not knowing that the police car is following. The officer is often effectively cut off from the suspect who is able to make his escape.

Right turns are far more frequent than left turns in a pursuit because they can be accomplished faster. The position of the police car in these cases is most important. A right turn from a left lane in even moderately heavy traffic is usually slower and far more dangerous than a right turn from the right lane.

Shooting during Pursuit   The futility of shooting at a moving vehicle, especially from behind, when the shooter does not have a steady aim, is apparent. Studies have indicated that bad judgment shootings occur nearly twice as often when a pursuit is involved in an apprehension than when there is no pursuit. From these studies the unmistakable conclusion was drawn that a decrease in the quality of an officer's judgment occurs during pursuits.[19] A detailed discussion of the use of firearms against vehicles is contained in Chapter 11.

The obvious conclusion the officer should draw from these studies is that, under the stress of pursuit and closely connected activities, he is more likely to overreact and make judgmental mistakes than under ordinary conditions. This characteristic reaction may be at least partially overcome by preconditioning. The officer should prepare himself emotionally beforehand so that the stress of a pursuit will not be entirely unexpected. He will then be able to temper his reactions to given stimuli.

Assistance by Other Units

Units not directly involved in a pursuit should refrain from making unnecessary or unrelated broadcasts if their transmissions may interfere with the dispatcher's efforts to coordinate pursuit activities or if such transmissions will interrupt other pursuit-connected broadcasts. Loss of vital information such as a change in direction may result from such interference. Units should use their radios, however, if

[19] Los Angeles Police Department, *Physiological and Psychological Effects of a Pursuit Situation Upon a Police Officer*, March 1970, p. 1.

they have information that is pertinent to the pursuit and is not available to the units involved.

Other units should not immediately move toward the apparent pursuit course to intercept the suspect when they first hear the broadcast. They should wait until they can determine which direction it will take before moving to an intercept position along its course. Once this position is reached, no attempt should be made to take the place of the officer then most directly engaged unless it is apparent that he has lost the suspect. Rather, the assisting officer should fall back behind the pursuit unit and remain there until his help is needed. He should remain a reasonably safe distance behind and should be alert for any sudden movement of the vehicles ahead. He is thus in a position to recover evidence discarded from the suspect's vehicle or take whatever action may be necessary if a hit-and-run accident or some other incident occurs that requires a follow-up. In addition, he may be a vital witness to a criminal act by the suspect.

Terminating the Pursuit

Supervisors rarely have difficulty motivating officers to do things that are dangerous but they sometimes have difficulty discouraging them from action in which the risks far outweigh the benefits to be gained. So it is with pursuits. Officers should seriously weigh the hazards of continuing a dangerous pursuit against the advantages of apprehending the suspect. When the risks clearly exceed the benefits, the officer should terminate the pursuit. The offender will sooner or later outsmart himself or become a traffic statistic or the police will gain enough evidence during the incident to identify him, secure a criminal complaint and a warrant of arrest, and take him into custody at a more convenient and safer time.

The decision can properly be made only if the officer recognizes the risks of overdriving, his personal limitations and those of his vehicle, and the highway conditions. When he decides to terminate the pursuit, he should so notify his dispatcher indicating the direction taken by the violator and any further details that may be useful to other concerned units so that the information can be transmitted to them.

Roadblocks

Courts have consistently held that the police may use reasonable means and force to apprehend lawbreakers. The extent and kind of force will determine the legality of an arrest or a seizure of evidence. They may also establish a civil liability. Thus, when using a roadblock to make an arrest or seize evidence, the officer must consider both the legal limitations imposed upon him and the possible civil liability incurred if it is eventually determined that the techniques he used constituted an unreasonable risk to public safety.

Legal Considerations in the Use of Roadblocks When a major crime has been committed, the police often find it desirable to set up a roadblock to prevent the perpetrator's escape and capture him as soon as possible. However, they may not without any provocation indiscriminately stop and search automobiles hoping that such a search will result in the discovery of contraband or the apprehension of law violators.[20] This is the accepted federal rule and is generally followed by the states.

This does not mean that all searches of automobiles must be based upon a search warrant. The automobile's mobility has consistently been recognized as an important consideration in determining what would be a legal search of an object of transportation.

Legal Authority to Search Vehicles for Suspects If a police officer receives information regarding the commission of a serious crime and is given a description of an automobile in which he has probable cause to believe the suspects may be found, he must be given the authority to do those acts which are reasonably necessary to apprehend the perpetrators. Therefore, he should have authority to regulate traffic in a way that would permit him to inspect properly the occupants of all passing automobiles reasonably meeting the description of the wanted vehicle. The only feasible method of accomplishing this is often a roadblock.

Authority to Search and Arrest—Emergencies In an emergency, certain acts are justified which might not otherwise be so. The courts have stated that the reasonableness of a search will be based upon the conditions existing at the time. In the past, the rule was that an officer could stop a train or stagecoach to arrest a person on it. When police establish a roadblock, they are, in legal contemplation, in "fresh pursuit" of the criminals who are the object of the search. Officers within the immediate area of the search can now be

---

[20] *Wirin v. Horrall*, 85 Cal. App. 2d. 497; see also *People v. Fidler*, 117 N.Y.S. 2d. 313.

almost instantaneously alerted to these emergency occurrences and can form a trap to capture the offender. They can do so only if they are allowed to control and search all modes of transportation from the area. If they are in fresh pursuit of a felon who is in an automobile, they must have rights at least equivalent to those which they possess when in fresh pursuit of one who has attempted to seek refuge in some building.

Arrests of Suspects in Vehicles   By legislative and judicial authority, the police may enter, search, and apprehend a criminal who has taken refuge in a building under certain conditions. When they have proper cause for the arrest and reasonably believe he is inside, they may break in if he fails to respond after they have given him proper notice of their intent to arrest him. They do not need the permission of the owner to enter and make the arrest. They may do the same with an automobile. Because a vehicle can carry the criminal or evidence of the crime out of the grasp of the police, they should have even greater power in attempting to apprehend him when he is in an automobile.

Roadblocks and Civil Negligence   Officers are held accountable for the amount of force they use in enforcing the law. If the force is excessive when weighed against the nature of the crime involved, they become liable for their acts. Therefore officers should consider the likelihood of creating an unreasonable risk to public safety and exceeding common and accepted good police practices when they establish roadblocks. When they are positioned in such a way as to create an unreasonable risk, their use constitutes negligence if injury to others results.

The Myers decision involved a pursuit of a minor traffic violator at high speeds and under dangerous driving conditions.[21] In an effort to stop the fleeing suspect, an officer set up a roadblock by positioning his squad car across the roadway 600 to 800 feet below the top of a steep hill. The fleeing driver came over the hill at 90 miles per hour, crashed into the police car and a taxicab which had been stopped by the roadblock, and killed the cab driver. At the speed of the chase, a vehicle would not have been able to come over the hill and stop in less than 1,750 feet. Thus there was sufficient evidence, considering the speeds involved in the pursuit and the position of the roadblock, to constitute negligence. The United States Supreme Court

[21] *Myers v. Town of Harrison,* 438 F. 2d. 293, 30 L. Ed. 2d. 57 (1971).

refused to reverse the judgment of $481,250.00 against the officer and the town that employed him.

Types of Roadblocks   Some agencies have used a "spikeblock" or a modified version of it with considerable success although many types of such devices have a limited capacity for stopping vehicles. Historically, the use of spikes in various forms across a highway as a roadblock has not been efficient.[22] Such a device should not be used —even if available—to stop a minor traffic law offender, as the damage to his vehicle would exceed the benefits to be derived from the apprehension; yet, when used for more serious offenders, these blocks are relatively safe and are preferred to gunfire, solid roadblocks or forcing the fugitive off the road with the police vehicle. Appropriate signs should be used to inform motorists of the presence of roadblocks.

Police vehicles should not be used as roadblocks on or across roadways except in the most serious cases and then only if the rules of a particular agency permit such use. The destruction of a police vehicle by a fugitive and the danger to inattentive drivers can rarely be justified.

Wooden barricades, rubber or plastic cones—well-lighted or reflectorized—and appropriate signs notifying motorists that a roadblock is ahead are most useful in blocking roadways, yet these are seldom available to the patrol officer on short notice. When time is available for obtaining and arranging them, they offer the safest and most economical means for stopping traffic.

In rural or sparsely settled areas, narrow roadways with steep embankments on both sides, roads bordered with storm drains, fences, trees, soft shoulders, and the like should be considered in selecting a site for a roadblock. Motorists can then be confined to the roadway and passed through the barricades after inspection. In urban or densely populated areas, the blocks should be established away from intersections, off ramps, entrances to alleys, parking lots, etc., which might permit a suspect to turn off the road before entering the roadblock area thereby escaping inspection.

Thefts from Vehicles

Nelson and Smith contend that thefts from vehicles in the United States account for an economic loss of at least three times that re-

---

[22] Federal Bureau of Investigation, "Spikeblock," *F.B.I. Law Enforcement Bulletin*, vol. 41, no. 20, February 1972, pp. 24–25.

sulting from auto thefts, which rank near the very top of America's major police problems.[23] The conclusion is unmistakable that thefts from vehicles, commonly called car clouting, constitute a problem of major proportions for the patrol officer. For this reason, he must constantly strive to gain expertise in this area of crime prevention to better enable him to take more effective repressive action. If he lacks an interest in the problem of car clouting and is not alert for this type of crime, he will accomplish little in its control; but he can do much if he will train himself to recognize the earmarks of the car prowler.

The narcotics addict has long favored this crime as a ready source of income to support his habit. It can be extremely lucrative for him and also for the professional thief and the opportunist. The criminal finds it even more attractive because much of his loot is never reported to the police and, when it is, they have difficulty in identifying it—even if it is recovered—because packages, clothing, and accessories seldom have recorded identifying features. This fact gives the car clouter an opportunity to steal almost with impunity. The ease with which he can operate and the apathy which often exists in connection with this offense make the patrol officer's efforts to repress car prowling doubly difficult.[24]

Car Prowling Methods   Some of the criminals who steal from vehicles work on foot while others work from automobiles. Some concentrate upon cars parked on the street while others concentrate on cars parked in lots; they ordinarily stick to their specialty. Neither can ordinarily "case"—or look over beforehand—his or her target.

The Foot Thief   The thief who works on foot usually betrays his interest in parked vehicles by "shopping" for a target—trying door handles, leaning against cars while feigning drunkenness, glancing subtly into cars looking for loot. When he discovers possible loot, he may lounge against the car or move away from it to lounge against the adjacent building, or he may move on and double back to determine if he is being watched. His interest then shifts from the loot to people on the street or sidewalk to assure himself that the victim or an officer does not have him under observation. Ordinarily he will carry a simple tool—a can opener, screwdriver, thin-bladed knife, etc. These tools are usually thin enough to insert between the rubber

[23] Alfred T. Nelson and Howard E. Smith, *Car Clouting*, Charles C Thomas, Publisher, Springfield, Ill., 1958, p. 11.
[24] Nelson, *Car Clouting*, pp. 17–18.

molding around the wind-wing and strong enough to pry it open. Entry by a skilled thief can be made more quickly by prying a wind-wing or breaking it with a short, hard blow of the elbow than by using a key. He may then move away and return later to take the loot as if he were the owner. He often leaves the scene by cab or bus.

The foot thief specializing in stealing from cars in parking lots usually enters from the sidewalk but often gives himself away by a sidelong glance behind him just as he enters. He moves through the lot looking for loot and persons without going directly to a car. He then returns—often furtively—to a potential target. Because he must operate in the open, he is especially vulnerable to interrogation by an alert officer and therefore hesitates to carry a tool. He usually smashes a window with a rock, elbow, etc., takes the loot and leaves at the front entrance.

Mobilized Thieves   Car clouters operating from vehicles often prey upon cars parked in residential or apartment areas, or at conventions, sporting events, theaters, etc. where large groups of cars are parked. Apartment and hotel areas are especially attractive because valuable merchandise is often left in vehicles parked there. The thieves cruise these areas at night looking for a safe target. When one is discovered, they park legally to avoid attracting attention, commit the theft, place the loot out of sight in their trunk or glove compartment, and leave.

If two cars are used, one is parked legally near the scene of the theft. The stolen property is placed in this vehicle which is left locked. He is thus able to leave the vicinity of the theft in a second vehicle containing no evidence of the crime. The thief later returns and drives the first car away. Delivery trucks are often attacked in the same manner.

Arrest Tactics—Car Clouters   When an officer observes suspected car clouters and has reason to believe that he has not been observed by them, he should notify his dispatcher of the circumstances and request assistance. He should direct the assisting unit to wait in the vicinity and not approach the immediate scene until needed for the arrest. He should then leave his vehicle, take a vantage point close by and observe from concealment. He should remove his hat which often is identifiable if it is silhouetted and stand in the darkness, in a deep shadow, or in a doorway where he is least likely to be seen by the thieves. When they commit an act sufficient to constitute a crime and attempt to leave in an automobile, he should quickly return to his car, and notify the assisting unit of the direction taken by the suspects and the description of their car. Both police units should then take steps to make the apprehension.

The thieves usually prefer to leave the scene of their crime without attracting attention—not by fleeing in such a manner as to encourage arrest. If they are allowed to drive away normally, followed a short distance until they are stopped at a traffic signal or in traffic, then approached quickly by the officers on foot, apprehension can be made more safely than by pursuit.

Stolen Vehicles

Automobile theft has shown one of the most pronounced and consistent increases of all the major crimes in recent years throughout the country, having increased 69 percent since 1966. Almost a million motor vehicles are reported stolen each year; yet the crimes solved by arrest for this offense have been among the lowest of all major crimes.[25] Probably, the number of thefts can be accounted for in part by the increase in vehicles on the streets, the increased workloads of law enforcement personnel giving them less time to engage in repressive patrol, and the general increase in other crimes related to such thefts.

The patrol officer must become thoroughly familiar with the problem and the means of coping with this crime if the trend is to be reversed. He should become informed of the numerical sequence of vehicle licenses issued by state vehicle registration agencies, the color of temporary plates issued for the current year, and the patterns of thefts. Knowing where stolen cars are being abandoned on his beat or in adjacent areas may give him a clue to the routes most commonly used by auto thieves and indicate where his patrol activities would be most productive. He should also become familiar with the system used by manufacturers in placing vehicle identification numbers in automobiles so that he may readily identify a stolen vehicle that is brought to his attention.

A knowledge of the habits of car thieves will be very helpful to officers in countering such crimes. An ability to recognize the indicators that often suggest a vehicle is stolen, even though some of these are subtle, will be of inestimable value to him in performing

---

[25] Federal Bureau of Investigation, *Uniform Crime Reports*, U.S. Government Printing Office, Washington, D.C., 1971, pp. 25–32.

his duties. Circumstances which should arouse the officer's suspicions may involve the acts or appearances of the driver, the passengers, or the vehicle itself.

Driver or Occupants   If a driver's appearance indicates that he is too young to be eligible for a driving license or if he or his passengers do not "fit" the vehicle, the officer should make an inquiry to determine if they are rightfully in possession of it. Young thieves often take vehicles just for joyriding or for transportation, but the officer should not overlook the possibility that a stolen vehicle has been used in another crime such as robbery. The thief who steals a car for that purpose is one of the most dangerous of criminals and should be approached accordingly.

When the driver or his passengers display an unusual amount of nervousness or interest in the police, they should be investigated. This is especially important when they have been stopped for a minor traffic violation or detained for inquiry because they were in an unusual place at an unusual time under unusual circumstances. Careful questioning may reveal that the car has been recently stolen, even if not yet reported by the victim.

Often an auto thief will show no nervousness when he observes the police but will immediately turn into a side street, slow down to avoid passing the police vehicle, park, or accelerate. If he appears to be unfamiliar with the operation of the vehicle, he should be stopped to determine if he is properly in possession of it. Excessive speed and recklessness are often characteristic of the joyrider who steals a car for pleasure and cares little about driving it prudently.

Vehicle Irregularities   Broken wind-wings or signs indicating tampering with the license plates or door locks should cause the officer to become suspicious. He should particularly scrutinize vehicles that have been recently repaired or repainted and new automobiles that have unrepaired damage. Owners of new cars usually have damage promptly repaired.

In most cases involving stolen cars, the license plate is the clue which leads to the suspect's arrest. For this reason, car thieves sometimes change or alter plates, using tape or paint to make an 8 from a 3, a 7 or 4 from a 1, an E from an F, an N from an H, a Q from an O, a B from a P, and the like. They may attach one license plate— often a stolen one—over another, or use an old, damaged plate on a new vehicle. Sometimes a license plate attached loosely with wire or cord is a sign of a stolen vehicle. Expired out-of-state plates or out-of-state plates with a local car dealer's frames would likewise bear checking. Obviously, when the front license plate differs from the rear one, a violation has been committed and the car and driver should be thoroughly investigated. The absence of a current registration tab on the rear plate in a state requiring these tabs or a bug-spattered plate on the rear indicates a suspicious circumstance to be checked.

Stopping Procedures—Stolen Vehicles The techniques and procedures discussed in Chapter 6 for stopping a vehicle known to contain high-risk suspects may require some slight modifications when applied to a vehicle which is suspected of being stolen. Circumstances of each case will generally dictate what precautions the officer should take. In any event, his safety is of prime importance. It is far better to be overly cautious and safe than to be careless and risk death or injury needlessly at the hands of a dangerous criminal.

Follow-up Inquiry Once the vehicle is stopped, the officer should check the registration certificate to determine if the driver is the owner. If he is unable to locate it or does not know where to look for it, other evidence of identity may be secured from him to prove or disprove ownership. If the officer suspects that the driver is possibly a car thief, evidence indicating hot wiring such as loose wiring; the absence of keys to the ignition, doors, or trunk; or tampering with ignition tumblers may suggest that an intensive investigation be conducted.

Most car thieves do not acquaint themselves with details about a car that the owner would know. Therefore, the officer should try to determine how familiar the suspect is with the vehicle. He should be taken to a safe position away from it and asked how many miles were shown on the odometer. The owner probably would recollect this figure quite accurately. The contents of the trunk, glove, and other compartments would likewise be known by the owner. A thief would likely be unfamiliar with this information and would probably not know when the car had last been lubricated and when the oil was last changed. A sticker on the door or motor will ordinarily reveal this information. A thief will often not be familiar with the location of all dashboard switches or instruments and their operation. The owner generally will be quite familiar with these and will be able to describe what special equipment the car has, if any.

Summary

The control of vehicles has become a primary activity in the patrol officer's daily life. The economic losses to the nation from traffic accidents and congestion alone are staggering, even without consideration for the vast number of criminal offenses in which vehicles are involved.,

The patrol officer in those police agencies which have no specialized traffic units must be as proficient in making traffic accident investigations as he is in performing a multitude of other duties. The basic techniques of accident investigations are similar to those of most other investigations. The officer responds in much the same way but has the added obligation to protect persons and property from further injury and to control pedestrians and vehicles to prevent congestion, or destruction or contamination of evidence. After attending to these matters, he can conduct his investigation, see that damaged property is removed from the highway, and prepare the necessary reports. If hazardous substances are involved in the accident, he must not only have them removed but must take appropriate measures to protect the public from their effects.

The patrol officer must develop a technique of directing traffic so that he may prevent congestion at scenes of accidents and where vehicle conflicts occur at peak traffic hours. A mastery of standard traffic control procedures will enable him to move automobiles and pedestrians smoothly, swiftly, safely, and easily. These simple techniques can be learned quickly and should be part of every patrol officer's training.

One means of reducing the number of injuries and deaths and the economic losses from traffic accidents involves an effective traffic law enforcement program. Much can be done by the patrol officer in encouraging voluntary compliance by motorists with the rules of the road. He should take advantage of every contact he has with them to achieve the major objective of a selective traffic enforcement program—to change the driving behavior of those who commit offenses that cause accidents.

A high percent of all accidents on the highways involve drivers under the influence of intoxicants. Their control will materially influence the accident rate in a community. Therefore, the officer must learn to recognize the symptoms of the drinking driver so that appropriate action can be taken before he becomes or causes another traffic accident statistic. Once he has been removed from behind the wheel of his automobile, he no longer is an immediate threat to other motorists. The next step is to determine the extent of his insobriety. The collection of evidence to support a prosecution will follow the same general pattern applicable to other cases.

Frequently, officers will be confronted with a motorist who decides to flee rather than submit to an investigation or arrest. The decision to engage in a pursuit is one that should not be made lightly. The officer should consider the physical risks to himself, other officers who might become involved, and the public. He should also weigh the seriousness, time, and place of the suspected crime. Any pursuit should justify the risks involved. In some situations, pursuit is neither safe nor wise. Consideration should be given to alternate courses of action available such as securing enough information to support a request for a warrant of arrest or following the offender until he is stopped by other traffic.

Should the officer decide to pursue the suspect, standard broadcast techniques should be followed so that other police units may be informed of the nature and course of the pursuit. Pursuits often extend beyond a reasonable point. They should be terminated when the risks to the officer and the public clearly exceed the benefits to be gained from the apprehension.

Vehicles are often not only a means of commiting crimes but also the objects of thefts. Crimes committed against articles in the car or accessories have become a major police problem. Car clouters are usually easily recognized by anyone who has studied their methods.

Places where many cars are parked such as scenes of special events, apartment house areas, parking lots, and the like are especially vulnerable. They should therefore be given attention by the patrol officer. When theft patterns develop in particular areas, the officer should be alert for the car prowlers working there. The thief is on foot when taking the property, but usually he will leave the area in an automobile. A thief who comes by car may park close to the target, commit his theft, place the stolen property in his trunk or glove compartment and drive away. Other car clouters pick the target on foot, commit the theft, then carry the stolen property some distance to their cars.

Restrictive search and seizure rules will not usually permit a car search unless the officer has reasonable cause for it. This cause can be based on an observation of an attempted or completed theft.

The thief who steals the vehicle itself often can be detected by an alert officer. Such criminals often do not fit the vehicle, they frequently will give themselves away by their acts, or certain irregularities about the vehicle will give the officer sufficient cause to stop and question the driver. Inspection of the car and questioning of the operator about the vehicle will often yield clues that it is stolen, because the thief will not ordinarily be familiar with certain characteristics of the car known to the owner.

Review

Questions

1. What is the first thing an officer should do at the scene of a traffic accident involving an injury?
2. What precautions should be taken in moving injured persons from the road?
3. Why are flares so dangerous?
4. What can be determined from skid marks at a traffic accident scene?
5. What are brush marks?
6. Why should investigators of fatal traffic accidents notify next of kin whenever practicable rather than have other officers do so?
7. What is the major objective of a minor traffic violation contact between an officer and an offender?
8. Why should an officer not allow an intoxicated driver to move his car to the curb if he stops in a traffic lane?
9. What questions should be asked an intoxicated driver as part of the field sobriety test?
10. What factors should an officer consider before pursuing a vehicle?
11. As a general rule, when should a pursuit be terminated?
12. How should a vehicle with an automatic transmission be slowed when being driven at high speed?
13. What is a bootleg turn?
14. When might the use of a roadblock give rise to civil liability?

Exercises

1. Describe how the basic procedures in traffic accident investigation differ from those of other types of investigations.
2. Describe what should be done at the scene of a property damage accident if the following substances are spilled on the roadway: gasoline; explosives in metal drums; radioactive materials; toxic, flammable gases released from transporting containers.
3. Explain how locked four-wheel skid marks which overlap would be measured for purposes of determining speed.
4. Explain briefly what a traffic accident diagram should contain.
5. Describe how the whistle should be blown to assist hand signals in the direction of traffic.
6. Distinguish between the terms *under the influence* and *drunk*.
7. Explain some of the characteristics of the drunk driver which are easily recognizable.
8. Explain the objective symptoms of intoxication that should be

noted and recorded by an officer giving a motorist a field test for sobriety.

9. Describe the procedures that should be followed in broadcasting a pursuit.
10. Describe how the siren should be used in a pursuit.
11. Describe some of the practical types of roadblocks.
12. Describe how the car clouter on foot generally operates.
13. How does the car clouter operate from a car?
14. Describe some of the things about a vehicle and its driver that might indicate the car is stolen.
15. Explain how you might best question the driver of a car you believe to be stolen.

9

Nonemergency Calls

A large part of a patrol officer's time is taken in handling matters that are not emergencies and often do not involve a violation of the law. These incidents may require assistance, service, or merely advice and counsel. They may involve crimes as a side issue or problems that require resolution through civil processes. Fortunately, they usually can be solved by the application of sound judgment and common sense.

At times there is considerable information which can be evaluated beforehand to determine how to proceed. Frequently, however, there are virtually no details available to the officer until he arrives at the location of the call. Only then is he able to choose an appropriate course of action.

If the incident involves an unknown problem, he must anticipate the unexpected so that he will be able to avoid becoming the victim of a violent, surprise attack. If there is a breach of the peace, he must restore order. It is part of his duty to calm fears, reduce tensions, and prevent conflicts whenever he can. In doing so, he must exercise discretion of the highest order. No one can tell him how he can do this perfectly in the multitude of situations he will face; but basic operational guidelines will usually provide a point of departure from which he can improvise effective solutions to these many daily problems.

The adjudication of minor disturbances involving conflicts between neighbors, family members, or landlord and tenant, or those which occur during the repossession of property is not within the realm of the patrol officer's responsibilities when they involve strictly civil matters. His primary function in these cases is to restore order if it has been breached and maintain the peace. If the matter involves a criminal offense, he may be duty-bound to make an arrest, receive an arrestee who has been arrested by a private person, or take other police action.

Unknown Trouble Calls

If the general nature of the incident is known, the officer assigned will have some clues so that he can decide upon a basic course of action in approaching the scene and handling the matter. Occasionally, however, he will have no information except that some police attention is needed at a particular place. This is an unknown trouble call. In no case should he treat it as just another routine matter. The consequences might be serious. These calls and others in which only scant information is available should be approached with extraordinary caution because of their potential danger. They may involve a relatively minor problem or an extremely dangerous incident.

The lack of information may be due to nothing more than that the caller did not have time to describe what was happening or would not or could not give sufficient detail to the police to permit the dispatcher to describe the call more specifically—perhaps an angry spouse interrupted the caller.

However, the call may be an attempt to lure an officer into an ambush. He should be extremely cautious. A backup unit should be dispatched in all of these cases. When it arrives, both officers should approach the scene as if they were handling a case involving a felonious crime. Someone may have gone berserk with a gun or merely locked himself out of his car. The officers should therefore be alert and expect the worst so that they will be prepared to protect themselves if necessary. They should both remain present and not relax their guard until they are satisfied that the call does not pose a hazard to them.

The extreme hazards involved in such calls is well emphasized by the incident in which four California Highway Patrol officers lost their lives in a 4½-minute gun battle when they were responding to a radio broadcast that presented them incomplete information about a minor incident committed by extremely dangerous suspects. The California Highway Patrol dispatcher had received a complaint from a motorist that a suspect had brandished a weapon at him after an exchange of remarks following a traffic violation by the suspect. Only one person was observed in the suspect's vehicle at that time although later events revealed that there were two occupants. Radio reports were relayed to a two-men patrol unit along with a description of the suspect's car and a report that it was not wanted in connection with any crime. Law enforcement personnel in this area often considered this type of incident fairly routine because of the rural geography where the possession of firearms for hunting was common.

Exhaustive inquiry revealed that the officers took reasonable precautions in attempting to gain control of the occupants of the vehicle. Before the passenger could be restrained, he opened fire on the officers without warning. In the ensuing battle, he and the driver killed both officers. When follow-up officers arrived at the scene, they also were fired upon immediately and without warning. Having little opportunity to seek effective cover, both of them were also killed.[1]

Neighborhood Disturbances

Disturbance calls are among the most frequent of all police calls and perhaps test the officer's capacity for diplomacy more than any other type of incident. He will usually not attain desired results by a threatening, belligerent manner. He will find, however, that he can resolve most of these issues with a friendly, professional approach.

In handling disturbances of the peace, he should carefully assess the matter before committing himself to a course of action. He may conclude that he alone is fully capable of handling the situation safely, or he may decide to summon assistance and wait for it before acting. Many officers have been injured because they have misjudged the incident and failed to ask for assistance when they should have.

[1] Department of California Highway Patrol, "Shooting Incident, Newhall area," *Information Bulletin*, July 1, 1970.

If the disturbance involves a loud radio, party, musical instrument, or social event, a racing motor, or noisy animals, the responsible persons will ordinarily remedy the problem after a polite explanation that a complaint has been received about the noise. The name of the person who called the police, even if known, should not be revealed because of the possible bad effects the complaint may have on the future tranquility in the neighborhood.

If the offending parties fail to comply with the request and other complaints are received, the officer may be required to arrest the offenders. He should do so, however, only after he has determined that the complainant is willing to pursue the matter later in court as a witness. If a person who complains of such a disturbance is reluctant to make a private person's arrest of the offender—with or without the help of the officer—or to testify later in court that the peace and quiet of the neighborhood had been disturbed, the case will have little chance of being successfully prosecuted. However, when the offender maliciously and willfully continues the disturbance after repeated requests to abate it, the officer may have sufficient cause to make an arrest. He often can, by himself, establish the elements of the offense for a successful prosecution. His chances, however, are considerably better if he can prove that the offense continued after a warning, that the conduct of the persons responsible for the noise indicated they had no intention of complying with repeated requests to reduce it, and that there were other people who were obviously annoyed by it even though they did not complain.

Procedures in Neighborhood Disputes   Often neighbors who are ordinarily peaceful, cordial, and law abiding become incensed over matters which they can usually resolve themselves if they will cool their emotions and apply common sense. Such things as spite fences, property line disputes, throwing trash on each other's property, and cutting of a neighbor's shrubs or tree limbs projecting over the property line are the prime causes 'of flare-ups between them. The acts in question may cause justifiable anguish on the part of one or both of the disputants. Usually neither will consider an amicable settlement of their differences. The matter progressively becomes more tense. Eventually one neighbor threatens to retaliate or calls the police. The patrol officer then becomes involved.

The officer's first alternative is to attempt to calm the parties and have them reach a peaceable solution. Failing in this, more drastic measures may be indicated. If the acts in question are the basis for a criminal complaint, the officer may refer the complainant to the local prosecutor who may call the parties to his office where the conflicts often can be resolved without prosecution. In some cases, he may decide to prosecute the offender.

When a misdemeanor has been committed before the officer's arrival and when an arrest is appropriate, he may advise the victim of the authority to make a private person's arrest. The officer is then obliged to assist in the arrest if called upon or to receive the arrested person and proceed according to the legal requirements in the jurisdiction. In some cases, the officer may find it necessary to make an arrest himself after an offense is committed in his presence.

When one of the parties has committed a felony the patrol officer should proceed as usual in felony arrests. Whether an arrest is made by one of the disputants or by himself, he should collect all the facts and evidence reasonably available from participants and interested parties to support the criminal action to be taken. He should never issue a warning or an ultimatum that he cannot enforce. When the dispute involves a purely civil matter, he should advise the parties to consult their attorneys, have property lines surveyed if the controversy involves land boundaries, or seek redress in civil court as a last resort.

Family Disputes

Disturbances arising from family disputes are among the most difficult of all calls to handle—and sometimes the most distasteful to the police officer. They may be loud nonviolent quarrels or deadly altercations. The officer can never be sure what to expect. This type of call is one of the leading causes of job connected police fatalities,[2] and therefore most departments send backup units to every call of this nature.

The person receiving a dispute call, especially one involving a family squabble or unknown trouble, should ask the complainant to remain on the telephone to give all available information. It may be possible to discover whether the parties are armed, the exact nature of the dispute, if violence is involved, the exact location of the assailant, his past reputation for violence, etc. This information should then be transmitted to the officers assigned.

[2] National Institute of Law Enforcement and Criminal Justice, *Training Police as Specialists in Family Crisis Intervention*, Washington, D.C.: United States Department of Justice, 1970, p. 3.

Approaching Family Dispute Calls   In approaching the location, the officers should make a mental note of places they could use for cover if attacked unexpectedly by gunfire. They should avoid walking together when nearing an entrance to the premises. One officer should attempt to look in a window and describe what he sees to the other officer, who should stand to the side of the door in as protected a position as possible while knocking.

Initiating Family Dispute Investigations   Upon entering the premises, one of the officers should question the participants to learn what the incident is about. The second officer should witness the interview. Only one person should be allowed to talk at a time. If one of the parties tries to monopolize the conversation, they should be interviewed in different rooms. To reduce the chances for a complaint of improper conduct and to avoid any appearance of wrongdoing if children are present, an officer of one sex should not interview a person of the other sex in a bedroom. The officers should hear both stories before attempting to resolve the situation.

The patrol officer is expected to act as peacemaker, referee, judge, lawyer, and marriage counselor. He is expected to advise the victims of their legal rights—often only to become a victim himself. He should be alert for a sudden attack at any time from either party under these emotionally tense situations.

Family Dispute Arrests   Officers should try to avoid making arrests for minor offenses committed by a family member during a quarrel. When the dispute involves an offense by one spouse against the other, usually the officer must contend with both of them. The victim will often suddenly change his or her mind and side with the offender against the officer. Experience shows that an arrest for a minor crime in these disputes is frequently followed by the victim's refusal to sign the criminal complaint the next day.

Prearrest Detention   The better procedure to follow in family dispute cases is a prearrest detention. It permits making a reasonable investigation without placing someone under arrest. As these disputes frequently resolve themselves at the scene, the officer can usually restrain the parties from violence, conduct his investigation, and allow tempers to cool without an immediate physical arrest.

He must make a quick decision if it appears that the quarrel will resume, perhaps violently, as soon as he leaves. He may find it necessary to arrest one party, if this is legally permissible. Alternatively, he may suggest that one person should leave until tempers cool. The latter procedure must be approached very cautiously, however; it should not be made to sound like an ultimatum.

When children are present, the parents should be requested to have them leave the room while the problem is being discussed to prevent their witnessing the traumatic event.

Giving Advice   The officer should avoid giving advice about divorce procedures. If the subject arises, the spouses should be told that this decision is theirs alone. Scolding or moralizing seldom aids and should be avoided. The officer should be strictly neutral, since his main responsibility is keeping the peace and preventing criminal acts.

Retrieving Property   At times, a separated spouse will return to the home to retrieve personal property. The permission of the occupant should be secured before the premises are entered. Again, the officer's obligation is to preserve the peace and prevent crime. Since property rights might be questionable, he should in no case force an entry to enable a spouse to remove items. Judgments on husband-wife property rights are a complex court responsibility, and so the parties should be referred to their attorneys or to a court.

Landlord-Tenant and Lien Disputes

Frequently the patrol officer is called upon to settle a dispute between a landlord and a tenant or between a person providing services and a customer. The problem may involve a complex civil issue which the patrol officer should not attempt to adjudicate; however, he should be familiar with local baggage and mechanic lien laws and other related statutes in order to take appropriate action when this type of complaint is received or a pertinent criminal act has occurred.

Baggage Liens   Occasionally a landlord will seize property belonging to a tenant because the tenant fails to pay rent. Assuming that no criminal act has been committed, the officer should avoid giving legal advice concerning these matters. He is, however, obliged to keep the peace and may advise the parties of their rights to arrest as private persons if an offense is committed by one against the other. He should refer them to their attorneys for resolution of the controversy. A tenant who cannot afford private legal counsel should be referred to the office of the public defender, a legal aid society, or other free legal service in the community. The officer should not assist the landlord in enforcing the baggage lien nor the tenant in regaining the property seized.

Ordinarily, the law does not give a landlord the right to seize objects which are necessities of life or are needed for carrying on a livelihood. Determining what items fall in these categories is a complex legal issue that should not be attempted in the field by the patrol officer.

Sometimes a landlord who believes a tenant will try to circumvent the baggage lien law will lock out the tenant. If the tenant destroys or damages the landlord's property in attempting to recover his own, the destruction may constitute a criminal offense requiring the officer to take action or to assist the landlord in doing so.

Shutting Off Utilities   The landlord may shut off the tenant's utilities for nonpayment of rent. This action often is unlawful under local laws, but enough proof to support an arrest might be exceedingly difficult to obtain. The officer should accordingly notify the parties of their rights and liabilities under controlling statutes. The tenant should be advised to take his case to the local prosecutor for resolution if the acts continue.

Eviction Orders   When a patrol officer is called upon to assist a marshall, sheriff, or other public official enforcing a legal eviction order, his primary job is to keep the peace. If summoned by the official serving the court order to assist in making an arrest for a refusal to obey the order, the patrol officer is obliged to aid.

Mechanics Liens   Mechanics, builders, and others providing services and building or repair materials ordinarily are entitled to retain possession of the property serviced or repaired until the charges for services and materials are paid. Usually the work is performed under a contract which specifies the costs agreed to by the parties.

The police frequently receive complaints from owners of automobiles, television sets, household appliances, etc., alleging that repairers charged excessively or increased charges over those initially quoted. The owners want their property, but the repairers refuse to release it if the charges are not paid. As in other civil disputes, the officer is obliged to keep the peace. He can advise complainants that they can secure their property by paying the charges and then sue or consult an appropriate agency that investigates consumer frauds. If there appears to be fraud, the officer should make a memorandum report that will provide a basis for a follow-up investigation by detectives or the appropriate consumer affairs agency.

Repossession Disputes

Patrol officers are frequently called upon to settle a dispute when a seller attempts to reclaim property because the buyer has allegedly become delinquent in his payments under a conditional sales contract. Often the buyer did not understand the contract before signing and finds that, although he has possession of the property, he does not have a clear title to it. The title is ordinarily retained by the seller until the property is fully paid for. When the buyer falls behind in payments, the seller repossesses.

The repossessor may be the seller, his employee, a person or business establishment that bought the contract, or a legally recognized collection agency. The laws that apply are usually those of the state where the repossession is made.

Stolen Property Reports   In most jurisdictions, repossessors must notify the police department if a repossession is made. This notification allows the police department to avoid a stolen property report if the possessor tries to declare that the property was stolen. Thus, when someone reports that a vehicle or other property was stolen, the officer should question the party involved to determine whether the article was purchased on a conditional sales contract and if the payments were up-to-date. The answers may give a clue to the whereabouts of the property and, if a record of repossession has been made, obviously no stolen property report need be taken.

Objection to Repossession   Often a repossessor believes that property can be repossessed without the owner's permission wherever it is found. Sometimes he believes that breaking and entering for this purpose is legal. This misunderstanding of the law gives rise to many repossession disputes. Even if the repossessor has a legal right to take the property, he may do so only if this can be accomplished peaceably. Otherwise he must obtain a court order to enforce his right to repossession.

Virtually all states have claim and delivery, or replevin, laws that provide for the repossession of property on a court order. Safeguards are usually provided for the debtor. In the Mitchell case,[3] the United States Supreme Court modified the Fuentes rule[4] by stating that a debtor is no longer entitled to a hearing before a magistrate if other adequate safeguards are provided for the debtor's rights. According to the Court, the Louisiana law involved provided these safeguards by requiring the creditor to support his claim with an affidavit, obtain a writ from a magistrate authorizing seizure of the property, and put up a bond to reimburse the debtor if the creditor loses his case later.

A repossessor who fails to properly establish his right to make a repossession is a trespasser if he enters the buyer's private property without permission to repossess an item. The officer must be guided by the laws pertaining to his particular jurisdiction; however, he has the obligation to take appropriate action to prevent a breach of the peace. The repossessor is not entitled to commit an assault, a disturbance, or any other crime.

Ordinarily the buyer, the buyer's spouse, or another party in legal possession of the property can prevent the repossession by objecting to it before the repossessor has taken control. If a car is left in a commercial parking lot, the attendant is responsible for the property and can object to its being taken by a repossessor, since no right to repossession exists in this case. The right to object does not extend to friends or neighbors who do not have actual possession of the property.

Resolving Repossession Disputes   The officer summoned to the scene of a repossession dispute should determine if the repossessor has a right to take the property. An authorized official who is making the repossession under a court process should have a copy of the court order which he is serving. The order is prima facie evidence that the seizure complies with the law.

A repossessor will usually have proof of his right to seize the property, a copy of the contract, identification from the company holding title, or a description of the property, and an authorization from the

---

[3] *Mitchell v. Grant,* 94 S. Ct. 1895 (1974).

[4] The Fuentes rule provided that property could not be repossessed until the debtor had been given written notice that the property was subject to repossession because he was in arrears in his payments and has had a hearing before a magistrate on the merits of the case. See *Fuentes v. Shevin,* 92 S. Ct. 1983 (1972); *Wyman v. James,* 400 U.S. 309 (1971); *Blair v. Pitchess,* 5 Ca. 3d. 258 (1971); *McCallop v. Carberry,* 1 C. 3d. 903 (1970); *Cline v. Credit Bureau of Santa Clara Valley,* 1 C. 3d. 908 (1970); *Sniadach v. Family Finance Corp.,* 395 U.S. 337 (1969).

seller to repossess it. The repossessor must comply with the provisions of the law, or the possessor of the property has a legal right to object to its seizure. If the person holding the property objects before the repossession is completed, based upon the failure of the contract holder to comply with the law, the repossessor has no right to the property and should be advised to take legal action if the repossession cannot be made peaceably. Ordinarily, a bona fide repossessor knows his legal limitations and will try to avoid trouble even if he has tried trickery or stealth in attempting to gain possession of the property.

Often the buyer has left personal property in a vehicle being repossessed or has added equipment after the purchase and is extremely reluctant to have it taken with the car. Sometimes a mistake has been made relative to payments he alleges were made. The dispute may become even more heated under these circumstances. The best advice the patrol officer can give the parties in such cases is to consult their attorneys. If the repossession is completed before the buyer objects, he has the right to remove any personal property not attached to the vehicle before it is taken. Equipment attached to the car after its purchase may not be removed, but the repossessor should give a receipt to the buyer who may reclaim the equipment after the repossession is complete.

Should either party commit a public offense in the officer's presence, an arrest might be indicated. If a minor offense has been committed before the officer's arrival, the victim should be advised of his rights to make a private person's arrest.

Street Disturbances

Street disturbances often present a more difficult problem than neighborhood disturbances, because the participants usually feel none of the neighborhood pressures that are present when loud parties or noise annoy other persons living nearby. Frequently, profanity or vulgarity in street groups becomes so offensive that the police are called. Often the complainants will refuse to identify themselves, but the police are nonetheless obligated to take action.

Street brawls demand immediate intervention because of their potential danger to persons or property. Usually, two or more officers should be dispatched to the scene of such disturbances—especially when adults are involved. It is not unusual for the participants and onlookers to turn on representatives of the law. Members of the group are more apt to attack a lone officer, rather than two or more, attempting to control such an incident. Other units hearing the call dispatched should move in the general direction of the incident in case they are needed to assist. Rules of their department will generally specify whether they should leave their beats in such cases.

Upon arrival at the scene, the assigned officer or officers should immediately stop the fight. They should inform the participants in a courteous but firm manner that they are disturbing others. A belligerent, officious, or threatening manner should be avoided as it will only generate resentment and hostility. Usually the group will comply with the officer's suggestion to disperse or cease the disturbance. Force might be necessary if they refuse. If many people are involved, such action should be delayed until sufficient units are present to control them.

If the fight ends before the officers arrive, the crowd should be dispersed and order restored. If one of the parties wishes to make a private person's arrest, the officers should render aid as needed. Ordinarily, the officer could make the arrest if a felony had been committed. If the crime was a misdemeanor, he should advise the victim of his authority to make a private person's arrest then provide whatever assistance is needed if the victim desires to do so.

Individuals committing criminal acts in the officer's presence are of course subject to arrest either immediately or later depending upon whether the offense is a felony or misdemeanor. The officer should determine the facts surrounding the incident before taking a person into custody. Arresting a person fighting to defend himself or someone else is not justified.

If there is evidence that the group itself is committing an unlawful disturbance or is assembled for some illegal purpose, the officer may be obliged to notify them that the assemblage is unlawful and that they must disperse. He should do this, however, only when sufficient assistance has arrived to help him enforce a dispersal order. Failure to comply with the order may, after a reasonable time, be sufficient grounds to arrest those refusing to disperse. The officers must, however, be able to later testify that the order was clearly apparent to the person or persons arrested. The techniques of handling major disturbances are discussed in detail in Chapter 13.

Mentally Disturbed Persons

The law has traditionally recognized the need to take mentally ill persons into custody when they are dangerous to themselves or others. Mental disorder alone, however, may not justify the officer in restraining a person, unless he or she is a juvenile in need of treatment not being provided by his parents. The law in most jurisdictions gives the officer considerable latitude in dealing with juveniles in those cases.

Crimes by Mentally Ill Persons   When a mentally ill person commits or attempts to commit a criminal offense, the officer should make an arrest as in any other case. The mental condition could then be considered by the court in disposing of the matter.

The case in which a mentally ill person has committed no overt criminal act is most troublesome to police officers. They are not expected to act as diagnosticians. The courts are responsible for providing the expert psychiatric services for that purpose.

Ordinarily, there are no provisions in the law which give an officer the authority to enter private premises purely to take a mentally ill person into custody. The officer may have authority to do so, however, in making an arrest if a crime had been committed, in serving some court order, or in protecting life or property on an errand of mercy. An officer who encounters a mentally disturbed person in a public place is ordinarily not authorized to take custody of that individual against his will if the person is not a danger to himself or others. Rather, the officer should offer to help the person if necessary. If the person is elderly or lost, he or she will usually accept the offer.

Precautions   Due to emotional instability, a mentally ill person often responds to a situation differently from a normal person. For this reason, the officer should be especially alert for unexpected reactions when dealing with such a person. He should be removed promptly from the presence of a curious crowd or the onlookers should be dispersed to prevent them from unnecessarily exciting or aggravating him.

A mentally ill person may explode into violence without apparent provocation if he thinks his freedom is being endangered. Once he is convinced that he is being helped and will be treated fairly, he will usually become cooperative. Every effort, therefore, should be made to gain his confidence without lying to him about where he is to be taken and how he is to be helped. Usually it is not practical to attempt to appeal to such persons on a logical basis. The officer should therefore maintain a friendly, kind, but firm manner—always on the alert for the unexpected.

Searching the Subject   Whenever mentally ill people are detained, they should be searched and relieved of any objects which could be used as weapons. They may have strong feelings of persecution and, in their belief that others are trying to harm them, may arm themselves for protection. Objects such as scissors, fingernail files, sharpened combs, shoes, or purses may be used by them with disastrous results.

These people should be kept under constant observation while in custody to prevent them from grabbing any object that might be used as a weapon. The officer should be especially alert to prevent his firearm being seized and used against him or in a suicide attempt.

Restraint   Handcuffs should be used to restrain a mentally ill person taken into custody if it appears that he or she may become violent or try to escape. Restraining straps should be used to bind the subject's ankles to avoid injury to himself or the officer. When he is transported to the police station, hospital, or elsewhere, the same precautions should be followed as in the case of a felony suspect because of the unpredictability of the mentally ill. Relatives should not be used to provide this security except under very unusual circumstances; although a relative, friend, or other responsible person known to the subject should be asked to accompany him to the hospital wherever practicable as a stabilizing influence.

Deceptive Cases   There are a number of factors that may mislead the officer into a false conclusion of mental illness. Epileptics, senile people, those with head injuries, high fever, or amnesia may appear to be mentally ill. The officer should be alert for such conditions that require medical attention and ambulance service.

Personal Injury Cases

There are four reasons to investigate and report accidental injuries occurring on public and, at times, private property: to render aid or secure it for the injured person, to collect evidence of the cause of the injury to protect the public or private property owner against unwarranted claims for damages, to discover hazardous conditions in need of correction, and to record the occurrence as a service to those requiring such a record for insurance purposes.

Injury Investigation Procedures   The officer's first responsibility is to render aid to the injured person. If an ambulance has not been summoned, the officer should call one himself if necessary.

The injured person should be interviewed at the scene if his condition permits. Otherwise, he should be interviewed at the hospital as soon as possible. Details of what happened immediately before the accident, how the accident occurred, and what happened immediately after should be obtained from him. This might throw light on any possible neglect which contributed to the injury. Statements made by the victim should be noted and reported in the injury report. These might be vital in civil suits. The officer should make no public statement about the incident. Surely he should never speculate how it occurred.

It is imperative that accidents resulting from faulty public equipment or facilities be investigated completely because of the potential liability. Witnesses should be queried about the accident. Persons who were present but did not see it occur should be identified and their negative statements should be recorded in the injury report so that these may be used to discredit later testimony that they may give describing what happened.

Photographing and Sketching the Injury Site   Photographs should be taken and the scene sketched in the officer's notebook when possible governmental liability exists in connection with the injury. The position of the injured party before and after the accident, the exact location where the injury occurred, the dimensions of the hazardous object and its exact location should be accurately depicted in the sketch. Pertinent physical evidence should be collected and preserved as in any investigation.

Reporting the Injury   The nature of the injury should be obtained from the attending physician and described in the appropriate report. A description of any hazards contributing to the injury, their exact location, witnesses' statements, and descriptions of photographs taken and other physical evidence should also be included. A copy of the report should be forwarded to the responsible governmental unit so that corrective action may be taken to prevent a recurrence of the accident. Physical evidence should then be booked or registered for later use if it is needed in a defense against an unwarranted civil claim for damages.

Death Cases

When a death inquiry is begun, officers must be guided by the laws of their jurisdiction and rules of their department in notifying detectives, their superiors, and the coroner. The first patrol officer at the scene must protect it from alteration or contamination. No one not directly concerned with the investigation should be permitted to enter. The officer must safeguard evidence until the investigators arrive for the follow-up inquiry. If the patrol officer conducts the investigation he must proceed as in other cases. His responsibilities at the scene were detailed in Chapter 7.

It is the coroner's or the medical examiner's duty in most jurisdictions to determine the circumstances, manner, and cause of all violent, sudden, or unusual deaths. He or she is also responsible for the inquiry into deaths in which the deceased has not been recently attended by a physician and those relating to suspected or known criminal abortion, criminal homicide, suicide, or accidents. He ordinarily takes charge of the personal property of the deceased and holds it for proper disposition. He may, however, deliver it to the police if it is needed as evidence in a homicide investigation.

Evidence such as weapons and notes connected with a killing should be retained by the police, with the coroner's permission, until ballistics and other laboratory tests can be made and notes reproduced if necessary. This evidence is extremely important for determining if the death was criminal, accidental, or self-induced.

Deaths from poisoning are usually the most difficult to evaluate until the stomach and vital organs of the deceased have been analyzed in a laboratory; therefore, special efforts must be made to locate any substance suspected of being poison. Vials, drinking glasses, cups, etc. with unknown residue should be carefully preserved for comparative laboratory tests.

Criminal Homicide and Assault Cases   When an injury or death has resulted from a criminal act and the officer knows of suspects, he should broadcast descriptions of the people wanted, their cars, and other pertinent details of the incident to alert other units. If someone is wanted for an interview but is not a suspect, the patrol officer should make this clear in his broadcast.

An officer answering a death call should assume that the death has resulted from a criminal act unless he was given evidence to the contrary when he was assigned. Consequently, when he approaches the scene, he should be alert for vehicles leaving hurriedly, possible fleeing assailants, persons with bloody clothing or injuries, and the like. He should record license numbers, descriptions, etc., for possible later use.

Officers have five major obligations in these cases: to save any victim who is not dead, to apprehend the perpetrator if possible without neglecting other duties, to protect the scene from alteration or contamination, to collect evidence for determining the cause of death and the identity of the perpetrator, and to record their findings.

Entering Premises in Death Cases A lone officer assigned a death call should await the arrival of a cover car before entering a building involved. He may decide not to await for assistance if he has some added details of the case that would justify his entering alone. Otherwise, when the assisting officer arrives, both should enter the premises. Both will then be able to testify to their findings and to statements by potential suspects. In addition, they will be able to protect each other against attack or against a later allegation that property of the injured or deceased person was improperly removed by them. A quick inspection should be made of the premises for the suspect or other persons who might provide information about the victim.

Determining If Death Has Occurred If the evidence remotely suggests that the person is still alive, an ambulance should immediately be summoned. Pending arrival of the ambulance, first aid should be administered if possible. Appropriate first aid would ordinarily involve one or more of the following: stopping bleeding, restoring breathing, or treating shock. If death is not unmistakably clear, the officer should take care to avoid disturbing, destroying, or contaminating evidence while determining if the victim is alive.

The victim's breathing, pulse, and reflex action should immediately be checked. In checking his breathing, he should be turned on his back. By baring his abdomen and noting if movement is present just below the lowest ribs, the slightest breathing can be detected. Even though no movement is observed in this area, the officer should feel for a pulse by placing his fingers at the inside of the victim's wrist on the radial artery toward the thumb. If he cannot feel any pulsation, he should lightly touch the victim's eyeball. Any movement of the eyeball or eyelids indicates the victim is alive.

When the ambulance personnel arrive, the officer should direct his efforts toward removing the victim without disturbing, destroying, or contaminating evidence. When photographs cannot be taken of the scene prior to his removal, the position of his body should be outlined with chalk before he is removed from the premises. Any disturbances of the scene from the time the officer's arrive until the follow-up investigation is started should be carefully noted and pointed out to investigators.

When the ambulance personnel remove the victim for treatment, an officer may decide to accompany them to the hospital. While he is with the victim, he should be alert for statements constituting a dying declaration as described in Chapter 7.

Arrests in Assault and Criminal Homicide Cases   The officer may have information providing reasonable cause to arrest a suspect at the scene of a felonious crime, charging assault with intent to kill, assault with a dangerous weapon, murder, manslaughter, or some other unlawful act contributing to the victim's death. An immediate arrest might be appropriate unless it would prevent giving life-saving first aid to the victim. In this case, the immediate care needed by the victim should take precedence over the arrest. If the victim is unmistakably already dead, the arrest should obviously be made. The prisoner should be immediately handcuffed. He should not be allowed to wash his hands, change clothing, take an alcoholic drink, or do anything that could later be used as a defense or discredit evidence. Any spontaneous utterances, admissions against interest, or acts relating to the case—the res gestae of the killing—should be carefully recorded by the officer in his notebook as soon as possible. Such evidence is usually admissible against the suspect.

The suspect's mental state at the time of the arrest; his lucidity, sobriety, and physical condition; the disarray of his clothing and presence of stains, tears, and debris—all these should be carefully observed and recorded. The clothing should then be taken from the suspect as soon as practicable and preserved for laboratory analysis. The arrestee should be removed from the scene for questioning, follow-up investigation, and booking.

Recording Pertinent Information   If a death is discovered but the cause is unknown, the assigned officer should record in his notebook the time he arrived at the scene, the name and time of arrival of the assisting officer, the names of all other persons then or later at or near the scene, the license numbers of cars there, statements made by witnesses, and a description of the conditions he finds. The positions of doors, windows, shades, drapes, the victim, and his clothing, should be included, as well as the nature of odors present. The descriptions and locations of blood stains, weapons, footprints, cartridges, fingerprints, and other evidence may provide clues leading to the solution of the case.

Preliminary Action at the Death Scene   After the death scene has been properly secured against contamination or alteration and after appropriate photographs have been taken and sketches made, items of evidence should be collected and preserved for laboratory examination as described in Chapter 7.

If the muscles of the body have stiffened in *rigor mortis*, if a purplish discoloration called *post mortem lividity*—caused by settling of the blood in the portions of the body nearest the ground—has set in, if decomposition of the body has started causing putrefying odors, if the body has been decapitated, or if the victim is found hanging and unmistakable signs of death are present, the body should be left as it was found until the on-scene investigation has been made. Murders are sometimes made to look like suicides. Should a reasonable doubt exist that the death was self-inflicted, it should be treated as a potential criminal homicide.

If the room is filled with gas, it should be ventilated and the gas valves shut off. Lights and electrical appliances should not be turned on nor should matches be lit, as either might cause a dangerous explosion and fire. If the victim is bound or has strangled, the bindings should be cut but the knots should be left intact. They may indicate whether the victim tied himself or may lead to the identification of the suspect through a comparison of the knots with those used in other crimes.

Suicide   The ultimate conclusions that a death was a suicide may be exceedingly important to the family for many reasons. Their religion might make such considerations vitally important. Also, the settlement of the deceased person's estate, especially insurance, might be affected by the cause of death. Some life insurance policies are not collectible by the beneficiary in the case of suicide by the policyholder. Others have double indemnity provisions for accidental death. The officer must therefore exercise great care that his conclusions are accurate.

Attempted Suicide   An officer is not often called upon to prevent a person from committing suicide, but when he is he must take some positive action to prevent the act. Someone really intent on self-destruction usually will succeed without advising anyone beforehand of his plans. Sometimes, the person threatening to kill himself or informing someone that he has just made an attempt to do so doesn't actually wish to commit suicide. His statement may really be a cry for help or an attempt to gain sympathy spurred by hopelessness, shame, dishonor, loneliness, marital discord, a lover's quarrel, frustrations, financial difficulties, illness, depression, etc.

Regardless of the motive for a suicide attempt, the police officer must do everything in his power to prevent the act because its interruption may cause the person to have second thoughts. Therefore, unless a better course of action presents itself at the time, the officer should employ delaying tactics. Talking is often successful. When there is a threat of imminent suicide, the officer should encourage the person to talk or talk himself, if necessary. By this method the individual may be convinced that unacceptable conditions can be changed. If he can be brought to the point of seeking help from professional counselors in suicide prevention, the chances for preventing self-destruction will be greatly enhanced.

When the act of attempted suicide constitutes a breach of the peace, such as when a person climbs to the roof of a building and threatens to jump, legal justification may be present to arrest him. He may then be deterred from similar acts by appropriate therapeutic treatment. In some jurisdictions, the officer is authorized by law to take a person into custody when he constitutes a danger to himself. Again, a delay for counseling or treatment can be gained by following the arrest procedure.

Natural Death   Details of a call involving a natural death should be recorded by the responding officer in his notebook. The usual notifications must be made as required in the case of other deaths.

Body Search   The body of the deceased should not be searched by the patrol officer unless he is permitted to do so by law. Usually this is the responsibility of the coroner or medical examiner. A receipt should be obtained from the person to whom personal property not on the body is released.

Removal of the Body   When a person dies in a public place from natural causes and his body is exposed to public view, every effort should be made to move the corpse to the morgue as promptly as possible. Information that might identify him should be obtained from witnesses at the scene. Unidentified bodies can be photographed and fingerprinted at the morgue for identification.

Drunkenness

The patrol officer frequently is required to take persons into custody when they are intoxicated in public places and are unable to care for themselves. Drunkenness is involved in many other types of calls and sometimes is the cause of considerable aggravation and annoyance to others. Often, the intoxicated individual becomes a hazard to himself and others because he wanders onto a busy highway, or may become the victim of a "drunk roll," or theft and assault.

The officer becomes directly involved when persons overindulge and become a police problem requiring protection or control. If he finds it advisable to make an arrest for this offense, he should take precautions to avoid being unexpectedly attacked by the intoxicated person whose behavior is often unpredictable. Usually a firm, friendly, good humored manner will do much to calm him and keep him from becoming belligerent. Moralizing seldom has any effect because the intoxicated person rarely engages in self-analysis. Rough or offensive treatment—even though considerable force may be justified at times to control the individual—rarely accomplishes anything constructive but only serves to aggravate him. Any jailer experienced in receiving persons taken into custody for drunkenness soon learns to detect from the demeanor of the arrestee how he was treated by the arresting officer. Experience has indicated that most "fighting drunks" become so because they have been agitated during the arrest procedures. The field officer could be the key to the tranquility of such persons.

Nuisance Calls

Some calls for service result from circumstances considered nuisances by persons offended. The patrol officer is expected to take appropriate action to terminate the nuisance but usually has few legal tools to rely upon. Children skating or playing ball on the street, barking dogs, dilapidated vehicles parked in a residential area, and similar matters are sources of irritation to many people who are prone to call the police for relief.

The patrol officer usually can resolve these problems by gentle persuasion. A threat—even when it can be carried out—seldom is advisable in such cases. Especially in his relationship with juveniles in these matters, the officer should be friendly, helpful, tactful, and understanding. He should avoid a tough attitude. Much can be gained by taking the time to explain why some actions are disturbing others.

Summary

In the many nonemergency cases an officer is called upon to dispose of, he has virtually no guidelines because the circumstances of each occurrence are different. Therefore, he must improvise. Usually, solutions can be attained by applying established basic principles of police work coupled with sound judgment and common sense.

Disputes involving neighborhood conflicts, family quarrels, landlord-tenant controversies, or disagreements between service people and customers are among the most difficult of all calls and often the most distasteful. They can also be hazardous.

Neighborhood disputes and disturbances can ordinarily be settled if the officer can convince the parties to calmly appraise their differences and settle them amicably. If the problem has arisen over a civil matter, he should advise the disputants to seek legal advice concerning the available remedies.

Family disputes ordinarily can best be resolved by the same general procedures used in other conflicts. The officer is sometimes obliged to arrest one of the parties who has committed a criminal offense to prevent further violence; but he is well advised to avoid arresting one spouse for a minor offense against the other—especially when children are likely to suffer as a consequence—if there are other practicable means of settling the dispute. Sometimes, if the husband or wife is arrested, both spouses will turn on the officer or the victim will refuse later to sign a complaint or testify against the aggressor.

In recent times there has been an increased emphasis on consumer protection against frauds and the arbitrary practices sometimes involved in the repossession or holding of personal property for non-payment of a debt. More and more complaints are being received by the police to settle controversies arising from these acts. Usually these are civil matters and, unless a crime has been committed, the parties should be advised to consult their attorneys for a solution. The officer's primary responsibility is to restore order if necessary and prevent a breach of the peace. Repossessions can be made only if they are peaceable. The buyer is no longer entitled to a notice and hearing before property can be repossessed if adequate safeguards are provided to protect his interests. Should the possessor of property object to the attempt to repossess it, the repossessor has no legal right to take it without a court process.

A mentally disturbed person who poses immediate danger to himself or others may generally be taken into custody. An officer must exercise great caution in dealing with these persons, because they often develop strong feelings of persecution and may explode into violence without provocation. They will usually respond favorably if treated in a friendly, kind, but firm manner.

When an officer is called upon to investigate an injury involving public property, the officer has the responsibility of providing and/or securing medical aid for the injured person if it is needed. The patrol officer is also responsible for protecting the governmental unit for which he works against unwarranted liability claims by investigating the circumstances surrounding the accident and reporting the incident so that any hazardous conditions may be corrected. A complete investigation of the matter should be made so that physical evidence, witnesses' statements, sketches, and photographs may become a part of the record for future reference.

When the officer is assigned a death or assault case, he is responsible for making appropriate reports of his findings. Death may result from a criminal act, a suicide, an accident, or natural causes. If there is any doubt about the cause of death, the matter should be treated as a criminal homicide. If a suspect is present, he should be apprehended. The scene must be protected, the preliminary investigation completed, and the information obtained referred to the follow-up investigators.

Review

Questions

1. Could an officer make a valid arrest of a person who was creating a disturbance by a loud radio if there were no identifiable complainants available? Explain why or why not.
2. What are some of the alternate courses of action an officer might take in resolving a dispute over a fence which had been placed on a neighbor's property without permission?
3. What are the basic responsibilities of an officer in a neighborhood dispute case?
4. Why are family dispute calls so difficult to handle?
5. What should be your role in a family dispute?
6. Why should you avoid giving advice about a divorce?
7. What is a mechanic's lien?
8. What is a baggage lien?
9. What is the officer's primary obligation when called upon to help a deputy sheriff in an eviction process?
10. What is the present law on the repossession of property as decided by the U.S. Supreme Court in the Mitchell case?
11. Who may make legally authorized repossessions?
12. If a repossessor has gained control of an automobile under proper authority but the person from whom it was repossessed demands to remove some equipment he had placed on the car, what should he be allowed to do?
13. Why are mentally disturbed persons often so dangerous?
14. Give three examples of conditions that are often misinterpreted as mental illness.
15. What are the four objectives of an officer assigned to investigate a personal injury that resulted from a faulty public sidewalk?

16. Name the noncriminal types of homicides.
17. Why is it important that the cause of death be accurately evaluated in an apparent suicide case?
18. What is the prime consideration in trying to prevent a person from taking his own life?

Exercises

1. Explain some of the factors that make unknown trouble calls so dangerous.
2. Explain how you would handle a disturbance on your first visit if the call involved a loud party about which neighbors had complained. What would you do on your second or third visit if the complainant had told you he would neither make a private person's arrest nor appear in court against the offenders if they were arrested?
3. Describe what should be done in handling a family dispute call where the husband has slapped the wife repeatedly before your arrival and has threatened her life if she calls the police. There is no felony involved at this point. The wife does not wish to arrest her husband. There are three small children under ten years of age in the house.
4. What should you do if a wife who has left home asks you to help her get some personal property but the husband will not permit you or her to enter the premises?
5. Describe how you would handle a dispute in which a repossessor is trying to repossess a bed and some furniture over the objections of the householder.
6. Explain what you would do if you were assigned a call involving a street fight.
7. If you suspect a person is mentally disturbed and he commits a minor crime in your presence, how do you handle the case?
8. Explain three simple ways you can determine if a person has died.
9. You arrived at the scene of a criminal homicide and arrested a suspect there. Explain what you do to protect your case.
10. Describe how an intoxicated person should be handled if he or she is not belligerent.

10

Crimes in Progress

The combinations of circumstances that can confront an officer at the scene of any call involving a crime in progress are infinite. For this reason, there are no hard-and-fast rules which will cover every contingency that may arise in connection with these incidents. Most of them can be adequately handled by the application of common sense, certain basic principles, and some simple techniques. With slight modifications, these can ordinarily be adapted to handle even the most unusual situation.

Experience has indicated that those officers who have been most successful in apprehending criminals while crimes were being committed have understood and consistently applied effective methods. The application of these proven techniques has kept many criminals from escaping and has increased the safety of officers and others involved and innocent bystanders.

All Units Calls

Police incidents which involve serious crimes in progress or violence and which require the immediate dispatching of units to the scene with other nearby units providing backup assistance are usually known as *all units* calls. The purpose of the initial broadcast is to inform all units of the incident so that they may respond if they are nearby or deploy themselves strategically if they are not reasonably close. One or more units are then assigned the call so that the responsibility for handling it may be fixed. The successful disposition of assignments of this type depends on how effectively the units responding work as a team.

Treat as Actual Emergencies   Many of these calls involve robberies or burglaries. Some are initiated by mechanical or electronic alarm systems; they may turn out to be false alarms, but officers should treat each one as if it were an actual emergency, never as just another "routine" incident. Approximately 10 percent of robbery silent alarms have been found to be valid.[1] The police officer cannot afford to gamble his life on odds of 1 in 10 that such an alarm will signal an actual holdup in progress.

Recording Essential Information   The first information an officer receives about emergencies or calls involving crimes in progress usually comes by way of radio. If the broadcast contains considerable detail, the officer in a one-man unit may find it necessary to stop his vehicle safely out of a traffic lane and record accurately the essential data. In a two-men unit, the passenger officer performs this task while the unit continues toward the scene. A request for clarification should be made if broadcast information is garbled or otherwise unclear. Accurate descriptions of suspects, vehicles used, weapons involved, addresses, and circumstances surrounding the crime are often vital to the safety of personnel responding. Many officers have been injured or even killed because they did not have sufficient information or because they did not evaluate properly what information they had and failed to take precautionary measures to protect themselves and backup units responding.

---

[1] Los Angeles Police Department, "How to Handle 'All-Units' Calls," *Patrol Bureau, Roll Call Training*, Series 3, Lesson 5 (unpublished), April 17, 1963.

Assignment of Call   The radio dispatcher will usually direct several units to a call which should receive the attention of more than one officer. Ordinarily, a call will be assigned to the nearest unit in the vicinity. It may be reassigned, however, if that unit is delayed by other important police work or if another unit reaches the scene first and so notifies the dispatcher. The dispatcher should avoid such reassignment whenever possible, however, because of the confusion it can cause.

The officers to whom the call is given should acknowledge it promptly. If they are performing a routine task such as issuing a traffic citation or handling some minor incident, they should not permit it to delay them in responding. To do so might jeopardize other officers involved. If they receive the assignment as they arrive at the scene, they should acknowledge it before leaving the police vehicle.

Use of Siren   When the call is of an emergency nature, only the officers assigned should use the siren and then only if such use is indicated. Its limitations should be kept in mind, as well as the liability that exists when officers drive under emergency conditions as described in Chapter 3.

If several units approach the scene with sirens operating, the officers may not hear each other and the chances of a collision will be greatly increased. The siren should be stopped and the red light turned off far enough from the scene to avoid warning the suspects that the police are approaching unless there is evidence that the criminal is doing violence to his victim, or the call involves an assault upon another officer. In these cases, sirens and other noise started near the scene may deter the suspect from further violence.

Patrol Strategy—General Procedures

When a crime-in-progress call is broadcast to all units, those available in the area and reasonably close should proceed directly to the scene unless departmental tactics dictate otherwise. Those further away should patrol *toward* the location, depending on the estimated time that has elapsed between the commission of the offense and the broadcast if these times are known. They should station themselves in positions where they would be most likely to be able to intercept a fleeing suspect. Often, regulations will require that these units remain in their own beats. They must then decide at what locations in their assigned areas they might best post themselves. Intersections, major traffic arteries, alleys, parking lots, etc., should be placed under observation if it appears likely that the criminal will use them in his escape from the location of the crime.

Response Procedures   While crime-in-progress calls are thrilling police experiences, they do not justify the officer's driving recklessly in responding. If he is involved in a collision en route, the safety of other officers who are depending on him for assistance may be jeopardized. The saving of a few seconds does not justify the risks involved in driving at breakneck speeds, and these speeds do not permit the officer to observe effectively what is taking place in the vicinity as he approaches. If he drives at a reasonable speed, he may recognize a good suspect by scanning the streets, sidewalks, doorways, and vehicles as he proceeds toward the location of the call.

On the way, officers in two-men units should discuss the location of the call and how to approach it. They should decide what each should do when they arrive. They should agree where to stop, who will cover the doors, etc.

Officers in one-man units should decide generally how they might best handle the call with a follow-up unit. They should try to visualize the premises involved and the surroundings, if they are familiar with them, and how best to cover the area. Time will be saved at the scene if as many decisions as possible are made beforehand. This is the essence of good planning.

Approaching the Scene   As long as speed is not unnecessarily sacrificed, the police unit should usually approach the scene in such a way that it will not come into view of suspects or lookouts until the last possible moment. The officer's familiarity with an area may be of inestimable value in such cases. If he knows the geographical layout of side streets which can be used for the approach, he may achieve the surprise so often desired.

He should be especially alert for suspicious cars on the streets; lookouts on the sidewalks, in doorways, or in vehicles; signals such as the sound of whistling, horns, or racing motors; or persons working on vehicles, urinating, simulating drunkenness, walking dogs, and the like. If suspicious vehicles are observed but the circumstances do not justify stopping them for investigation at that time, their license numbers and other descriptive data should be recorded for later investigation.

The techniques to be followed by the officer when he nears the scene which are described here apply particularly to burglary and prowler calls but may be adapted to others as conditions warrant. Incidents involving car clouters, some types of thefts, malicious mischief, etc., should be approached in much the same manner.

The approach to the immediate scene should be made slowly, noiselessly, and without lights (if it is night) to avoid alerting the suspects to the officer's presence. Tire squeals caused by fast turns or noise caused by driving the police car into a driveway and hastily backing it out, striking low branches with the antenna, or running over loose manhole covers should be avoided.

As the officer nears the scene, he should notify the dispatcher of his arrival. This information should be broadcast so that other officers will know when there are enough units at the scene to handle the matter. They can then deploy strategically in the area, if this is indicated, or resume their normal duties.

Arrival at the Scene   When the officer arrives at the scene, he should select a strategic location to park. He should use the emergency brake to stop rather than the foot brake if the car is not equipped with a cutoff switch to avoid flashing the stop lights. Noise can be reduced if seat belts are disengaged and the buckles tucked in the seat as the car is brought to a stop.

Before the officer opens the car door, he should turn down the radio so that it will not be heard outside. This will permit him to use it later if the need arises without a warming-up period.

The dome light should be turned off if the car is equipped with a switch so that it will not shine when the door is opened. When the officer leaves the car, he should remove the keys and conceal them inside; if they are put into a pocket with other items that might rattle, they should be covered with a handkerchief. Upon leaving the vehicle, the officer should press the door closed without slamming it and proceed with other officers to surround the premises or area involved as quietly as possible, unless (as previously noted) an officer or another victim is being assaulted.

If the incident does not require other units at the scene, the officer assigned the call, or the first officer to arrive if the assigned unit is delayed, should cause this information to be broadcast.

Summoning Assistance   One of the most important differences between one- and two-men patrol units is that the one-man unit must rely largely on the communications system for assistance rather than on a partner. The officer working alone often feels insecure because he does not have another officer immediately available to back him up, but with modern communications, other units can readily be summoned from adjacent areas for this purpose.

In cases where only one unit is assigned a call and the responding officer concludes from the circumstances that one or more follow-up units should also be dispatched because of the danger present, he should notify the dispatcher of the kind and amount of assistance he needs so that the units he needs will be dispatched. He should always summon a backup unit when he is in doubt about the danger present. He should not become blindly involved when he finds himself in a situation in which a wise man would hesitate before acting alone. Courage is a commendable attribute, but without logic and reason, it becomes foolhardiness. An officer should not fear that he will be criticized by his peers for requesting assistance in a hazardous situation and waiting for it instead of rushing in and risking becoming a casualty. A correct assessment of the situation may take a few additional seconds but may save the officer from serious injury or death. After others arrive, the officers can provide protective cover for each other. The same general procedures should be followed when 2 one-man units are assigned a potentially dangerous call.

Disposition of Call by a Single Officer   A lone officer may sometimes decide to handle a potentially dangerous situation himself. He should do so only if, after weighing the circumstances carefully, he concludes that he can proceed alone with reasonable safety. Occasionally he will take a calculated risk and handle such an incident alone if he believes there is imminent danger of violent injury to a victim at the hands of a criminal and such violence can reasonably be prevented by prompt action. If he becomes a casualty because he fails to assess the dangers correctly, he will accomplish little.

Injured Victim   Upon their arrival at the scene, officers should promptly determine if any person has been injured as a result of the incident. If so the victim should be given first aid and an ambulance or medical assistance summoned if needed. It may be necessary for one officer to ride to the hospital with the victim and try to obtain further details of the crime from him if he cannot be interviewed at the scene. If the victim is injured so seriously that he may die, the officer should try to obtain a dying declaration from him without delay concerning the act and person that caused his injury as described in Chapter 7.

Crime Scene Strategy

If a serious crime is in progress in a building, and the suspect is believed to be still there, the first officer at the scene should station himself in a strategic location where he will be most able to prevent an escape and wait for assistance. Once the building is secured, the means to be used to effect an arrest can be decided on. If the suspect has left the scene, officers should take steps to care for injured persons, obtain more information about the incident for relay to other units, and protect evidence from contamination until it can be gathered and preserved.

Follow-up Broadcast After emergency aid has been given to injured persons in cases where the suspect has fled, one of the first officers at the scene should interview the victims or witnesses briefly, while another should protect evidence and control onlookers. When further pertinent details about the incident and the perpetrator have been obtained, this information should be promptly relayed to other units if they are to help apprehend the suspect. If he is believed to still be in the vicinity, this fact should be relayed to other officers in the area who should post themselves or patrol at strategic locations in an attempt to intercept him. A five-minute delay would let a suspect drive leisurely almost 4 miles and would make his apprehension considerably more difficult because such a wide area would have to.be searched.

The who, what, when, where, how—and sometimes the why—of the crime should be broadcast. The number and initial description of suspects (sex, race, ages, i.e., adult or juvenile, clothing, vehicle, equipment carried) is the *who*. The *what* relates to the type of crime and the type of premises involved. The *where* is the location of the occurrence. The *when* is the time of the offense, and the *how* refers to the means used by the suspect to commit the offense and leave the scene. This should include a general description of any weapons, e.g., blue steel two-inch revolver, etc., the direction taken, and the method used in fleeing, i.e., in a car or on foot. If a vehicle was used, it should be described as completely as possible to assist other units in identifying it. As much information as possible should be obtained, such as the color, year, make, body type, license number, and other identifying characteristics of the car such as stickers, emblems, broken windows, dents, etc. This will give other officers enough basic data so that they may concentrate their efforts on good suspects in the area. Other facts should then be gathered rapidly so that supplemental broadcasts may include more detailed descriptions of the suspects, the loot taken, the vehicle, and the crime and correct any errors made in previous broadcasts.

Gathering Evidence   One of the officers assigned the call should immediately take steps to protect the scene so that evidence is not lost or contaminated during the initial inquiry. Sightseers, including officers not concerned in the matter and representatives of the press, should be excluded until pertinent evidence has been collected. Another officer should rapidly obtain the names, addresses, and telephone numbers of witnesses who might leave the scene before they are interviewed. The follow-up investigator will then have enough information to contact such persons later. Witnesses should be interviewed separately so that they will not be influenced by other persons' versions of the incident.

Notifications   When additional help is needed at the scene to collect evidence, complete the preliminary investigation, secure the scene, etc., it should be requested by telephone if land lines are available. The precise type of assistance needed should be indicated so that it may be dispatched promptly.

When weapons have been fired or persons injured during the incident, appropriate notifications should be made to the watch commander or a supervisor at the scene by the assigned officer. He is also usually responsible for all necessary crime and related reports even though detectives have started their investigation. Officers must follow their organizational policies in this respect.

Area Search   Officers looking for the suspects in peripheral areas should estimate the distance they might be able to travel in a given time after the crime occurred. Efforts to apprehend them can then be concentrated. In business areas, the probability that the suspects may have taken a bus, taxi, or streetcar from the scene; gone into a nearby bar, rest room, or restaurant to throw off pursuit; or mingled with crowds in the street, a lobby or waiting room of a public building, a store, a market, or another crowded place should be considered. A thorough search of the area should be made as described in Chapter 6. Particular attention should be given to those locations where a suspect might go to remain inconspicuous.

In less congested residential areas, backyards, storage places, back porches, garages, sheds, trees, incinerators, etc., are sometimes used for hiding. Suspects have even been found trying to conceal themselves under or inside a house after their avenues of escape had been effectively blocked by responding police units.

Building Search   In most cases other than burglaries, officers will be able to ascertain from witnesses and victims whether the suspect has remained in the building. If it appears that he has, enough assistance to secure the premises, prevent his escape, and make an interior search if one is necessary should be summoned. Special equipment such as body armor or gas may be needed as a last recourse to force him out. Often he will voluntarily surrender when he is told that he is surrounded and has no chance to escape. This is desirable because it eliminates the danger and complications that may arise if armament and/or gas are needed to apprehend him. He should therefore be given every opportunity to surrender on his own volition. If he does, he should immediately be restrained and searched for weapons and evidence. The presence of a second suspect should then be considered, and steps should be taken to apprehend him.

Frequently, however, in calls involving burglaries, the suspect will refuse to respond to instructions to come out, he will have left the premises before the police arrive, or the call may be a false alarm. In either case, a physical search of the interior may be indicated. Dogs have been used effectively to locate suspects who might escape detection in a search by humans.

The search should be systematic and thorough. Precautionary measures will vary according to the arrangement of the premises. Each place where a suspect might escape should be guarded by an officer. The number of personnel needed to make a proper search will depend upon the size and characteristics of the building. The U.S. Army system of building searches,[2] which may easily be modified to meet the needs of the moment, provides an excellent guide in such operations and offers appropriate safeguards for searchers as follows: A searching team composed of at least two officers is supported by a cover team to protect and aid the searchers when the danger to them appears to be great. The searching team

[2] United States Department of the Army, *Civil Disturbances and Disasters Field Manual FM 19-15*, Headquarters, Department of the Army, Washington, D.C., March 1968, pp. 7–16, 7–18; see also Jude T. Walsh, "Search of Buildings," *Law and Order*, vol. 20, no. 4, April 1972, pp. 20–24.

should move forward to the building under the protection of the cover team, which occupies positions from which it can best observe. Once the searching team enters the building, the cover team members secure the avenues of escape and provide whatever assistance they can from their stations outside the premises. The searching team should be kept as small as practicable to avoid injuring each other by dangerous crossfire should a gun battle ensue. Each officer should carry his weapon in his hand uncocked. He should take advantage of cover available and should fire only when legally justified.

If many rooms are involved, the team should search one room at a time. The first officer should enter rapidly through the door in a crouched position, back quickly against the nearest wall, and cover the second officer, who should enter in the same way. They should then carefully search the room. All places of concealment must be examined. Burglars have been found hiding under beds, in closets, lying on upper closet shelves behind clothing, in wardrobe cabinets, in attics, braced near the ceilings in closets, behind and in furniture, rolled up in rugs, in refrigerators, in chimneys, etc.

Wherever practicable, in multistory buildings, the search should proceed from the top of the premises downward. If the suspect is forced to the top, he may become more dangerous when cornered or escape over adjoining roofs. If he is forced downward, he may be captured with relative safety by the cover officers. As each portion of the building is searched, it should be secured or kept under observation while the searching officers move to the next room or portion of the building.

When a building is darkened at the time a search begins, searching officers should avoid silhouetting themselves when entering. They should pause and listen for sounds, quickly examine the interior with the flashlight held to the side away from the body, allow their eyes to become accustomed to the darkness, locate the main electrical switches, and flood the building with light. A criminal hiding inside has an advantage over the officer when he has the cover of darkness to conceal his movements. He can see the officer, who must rely on his flashlight, but cannot be seen readily when the beam of light is not focused directly upon him. Lights should be left on after rooms are searched to restrict the movement of the suspect.

When a suspect is located, he should be kept covered until he is carefully handcuffed and searched. He should then be handed over to the cover team while the searching team looks for a partner or partners who might still be hiding on the premises. Not until the building has been completely searched can officers be assured that this task is completed.

Preliminary Investigation   The preliminary investigation, involving the collection and preservation of evidence that might later be needed in the prosecution, identification and interview of witnesses, and, at times, the interrogation of suspects, should then be initiated.

The premises should be secured by officers before leaving if the proprietor or a responsible employee is not present or cannot be located to do this. A note should be left in a conspicuous place requesting the proprietor to promptly contact the person handling the follow-up investigation for the purpose of identifying property which might be recovered and furnishing other information that might be needed in the prosecution.

Hostages

There are times when an officer is faced with an exceedingly difficult decision involving perhaps the very life of a victim who has been taken hostage by a dangerous criminal—often a psychopath on whom a logical appeal will have no effect.

Dealing with the Suspect   The criminal who seizes a hostage will expect something in return for the victim's release. Usually he will demand that officers withdraw or provide him with a means of escaping. It is a general rule followed by many law enforcement officers that the police should not make "deals" with the criminal in this type of situation. It cannot be said that an absolute rule such as this is the answer since no hard-and-fast rule can be applied to every case. Each case will have to be judged on its own merit. There are, however, some basic factors to be considered by the officer in deciding whether he should acquiesce to the criminal's demands or refuse outright to do so. Should he do the latter, he may unnecessarily jeopardize the life of the victim. Should he accede to the demands and trade the suspect's freedom for the life of the victim, there are bound to be some who contend that the suspect was "bluffing" or that, by giving in to his demands, the police will only encourage others to try the same.

Obviously, attempts to rush the suspect may end with two people being killed—the officer *and* the hostage. A dead hero is of no use to anyone, especially if he sacrifices his life and accomplishes nothing.

Request Special Equipment   As soon as it is determined that the suspect holding a hostage will not release him, the officer should request special equipment such as gas, armored clothing, and a bullhorn. These may be of value later and should be available when needed.

Making a Logical Appeal   If the criminal appears to be rational, a logical appeal to him to surrender because he is surrounded or assurrance that he will be treated fairly if he surrenders and won't be hurt may cause him to have second thoughts about carrying out his threats to harm the hostage. Sometimes a member of his family or a close friend may help convince him to give up.

On the other hand, the psychotic, the psychopath, the paranoiac, or a person afflicted with a severe neurosis or other mental trouble may not react to this type of approach. These are the mentally disturbed individuals whose behavior cannot be predicted. If they feel that everyone is trying to harm them, a logical approach may accomplish little.

Even an illogical appeal to the person may be of value in some cases. An attempt should be made to find out what has caused the grievance. Whether it is imagined or real, it may cause him to kill the hostage and then himself. To him, the grievance is important although it may sound trivial to another person. He should be assured that everything possible will be done to help him.

If the officer is convinced that the person with whom he is dealing is really willing to kill and that he has no fear of the consequences, it must be assumed that he is exceedingly dangerous. A calm, patient appearance must be exhibited in all communications with him. Every attempt should be made to stall for time. He should be encouraged to talk. When he talks, time is gained, and an opportunity may arise sooner or later to overpower him with reasonable safety. The hostage may push or kick him, throw something at him, or run. The officer should be ready to take advantage of any opportunity to gain the initiative. When it presents itself, he should take advantage of it—swiftly and conclusively. If he fails to do so, he may unnecessarily cause the injury or death of the hostage, himself, or the suspect.

A clergyman, friends, or members of the suspect's family may be helpful in dealing with such persons—either the normal or the emotionally troubled ones—but should not be exposed to the danger of being taken hostage themselves and further aggravating the situation. This may be avoided by having them use a bullhorn or telephone to talk with the suspect.

Wounded Suspects

On occasion, during the commission of a crime, a suspect will be wounded in a gun battle with police. The mere fact that he has suffered gunshot wounds does not make him less dangerous. Often he becomes even more dangerous when he has been wounded.

Many criminals believe that society owes them something, or they believe that they are being persecuted by those who bear any symbol of power. They attempt to justify their criminal acts with these misconceived notions. They soon become embittered by the circumstances that they mistakenly believe have forced them into the commission of criminal acts. They resent the authority the law enforcement officer represents and will do anything to get revenge by taking to death with them as many police officers as possible.

Searching Wounded Suspects   For these reasons, after wounding a suspect, officers should remain behind cover until they have reloaded their weapons before approaching him. Two officers should work together in the search. One should cover him at all times until he is searched and securely handcuffed with his hands behind his back. If he is lying on his face, this should be done before he is turned over. His person, the area under his body, and the immediate area within his reach should be carefully searched. Extreme care should be taken during this period to prevent him from seizing and using his firearm even if it appears that he has been fatally wounded.

Small weapons can easily be overlooked if the search is not carefully made. Even if one weapon has been recovered, it should never be assumed that the suspect has been disarmed. Holdout weapons have been found even after what was supposed to have been a careful search. The band around the waist, the lower legs, and the groin area—which is sometimes subconsciously avoided in a search—should be examined carefully as these places are often overlooked in a search and are favorite areas for the concealment of holdout weapons.

When the suspect is placed in an ambulance, an officer should accompany him to the place of treatment and confinement. He is a prisoner, and every effort must be made to prevent his escape and to protect the ambulance driver, nurses, doctors, and other persons attending him. This responsibility is present until he is securely confined.

Interrogation of Wounded Suspect   Before the suspect is asked any questions, he must be advised of his rights under the Miranda decision as described in Chapter 6 if his responses are to be admissible against him in court.

Positive Approach   A positive interrogation approach should be used. Although the techniques of interrogation are so voluminous that they cannot be given in detail in a book of this nature, a few simple rules are in order at this point. A direct approach has been found to be productive, sometimes unexpectedly, when the suspect is relatively inexperienced in crime and has not previously spent time in prison. When asked how many other jobs he has pulled, many suspects will respond and give considerable detail that will help to clear other crimes.

Deathbed Confession   If the nature of the wound is such that it is likely to cause his death, he should be made aware of this fact. It should be suggested that he will feel better if he makes a clean breast about what he did before he dies. This realization of impending death may cause him to do so and name his partner or reveal facts about other crimes in which he was involved. A statement such as, "It will be better for you to tell us . . . ," implies a threat or promise and may cause the response to be excluded in court because it was not voluntarily made.

Often a false sense of loyalty will make the suspect refuse to identify his partner. However, when it is suggested to him that the partner was to blame for his predicament, he will often have second thoughts about protecting the partner, especially when it is pointed out that he is the person about to die, not the partner.

At times, an appeal to his emotions may elicit a responsive answer. If he is married, an offer to notify his wife of his condition may help to make him cooperate. He may then reveal information regarding the disposition of stolen property or details which may help to clear other crimes.

Patience is the first requirement for a good interrogator. Even though one approach does not work, others may. Continuous refusals to respond to questions should not visibly anger the officer.

There are times when no approach is effective in obtaining answers to questions, but patience and persistence have resulted in many full confessions. The practice described in the admonition, "Never conclude an interrogation at the time when you feel discouraged and ready to give up, but continue for a little while longer—if only for ten or fifteen minutes,"[3] has produced highly successful results.

Robbery-in-Progress Calls

Perhaps one of the most hazardous of all police patrol operations is the response to a robbery-in-progress call. The officer involved knows he may be dealing with armed suspects, so he must choose a course of action that will enable him to protect himself and other officers, the victim or innocent bystanders, and possibly hostages, and at the same time will be effective in apprehending the suspects.

He must realize that his first obligation is to protect innocent persons. If a decision has to be made between holding his fire and allowing the suspects to escape, or firing and risking the lives of innocent persons, his choice should be clear.

Approach to a Holdup Call The response to a call of this nature should be made with utmost caution. Little is gained if an officer becomes injured in a traffic accident on his way to the scene. The mere fact that the call involves a major crime does not justify hazardous driving practices. A few seconds lost in driving with reasonable caution are seconds well spent in the long run.

The usual precautions, which have been discussed previously, should be taken when approaching the scene. While on the way, the officer should plan the course of action he will take when he arrives. No specific techniques are applicable to all calls of this nature, but they have common features. The police unit should not be stopped directly in front of doors or windows of the premises where the incident is taking place. This might expose the officer to gunfire from suspects inside. If it is necessary for the officer to double-park the police car, he should do so. Keys should be removed and hidden in an easily retrievable place in the vehicle when the officer leaves it to keep the suspects from using the vehicle to escape should they gain the advantage.

---

[3] Fred E. Inbau and John E. Reid, *Criminal Interrogation and Confessions*, The Williams & Wilkins Company, Baltimore, 1967, pp. 113–114.

Assess the Circumstances   Officers should evaluate the circumstances present and not walk blindly into the premises involved. They should consider exits the suspects might possibly use, the means of flight, how many criminals are probably involved, how many victims might be taken as hostages, etc. Officers themselves have been taken hostage, disarmed, and had their own weapons used against them in the past because they entered a building without assessing the facts first. Ordinarily, it would be foolhardy for a single officer to try to capture several bandits committing a robbery inside a large market. It would be far better to wait, call for assistance, and give responding units enough basic information so that they will not drive blindly into the area. The officer should then arm himself with his shotgun and try to locate the suspect's vehicle and disable it. When doing so, care should be exercised to avoid being shot by a lookout or a driver waiting in the car. The officer should then wait at a vantage point under protective cover for the suspects to leave the premises and come into the open where they are most vulnerable to capture.

Deployment at the Scene   When assisting units arrive, officers should keep separated and station themselves strategically under cover to avoid each other's crossfire should a gun battle follow. When taking their positions, they should make use of whatever cover is available, such as sheds, parked cars, trash bins, etc. The strategy of flanking a suspect and placing him in a crossfire has been proven in warfare and can be used to good effect by the police. Each officer should have previously given much thought to the prospect of having to kill another person. If this course of action is necessary as a last resort to save an innocent person's life, in self-defense, or to apprehend the resisting felons, it should be taken without hesitation.

Because of the utter confusion that exists in some calls of this nature caused by the flashing lights, the police vehicles approaching the scene, and the interchange of directions and warnings, officers should be careful not to shoot innocent persons running from the scene who are mistaken for bandits. Often, in their fright and panic, innocent persons will not hear calls to halt. Officers will have to treat each such case individually. It is better to not shoot a fleeing bandit than to shoot an innocent person.

As previously described, special weapons such as gas, body armor, floodlights during the night, bullhorns, etc., and, if they are available, specially trained personnel should be called for if the suspects are contained in a building. A warning of hazardous conditions present should be broadcast so that they can be considered by other officers approaching the scene. It may be necessary to seal off the area to motorists and pedestrians if gunfire is likely to jeopardize their safety. Building roofs or upper-story windows may provide excellent observation posts and afford cover for an officer posted to observe the area and help keep others informed of the acts of suspects.

Detectives or other plainclothes officers should attach their badges conspicuously to their outside clothing and should pair up with uniformed officers to avoid being mistaken for the suspects; however, they should not remain so close together that they will make good targets for the bandits.

Bystanders should be asked to leave the scene to avoid injury if gunfire is anticipated. A portable bullhorn can be effectively used to control onlookers in these situations.

When the area is secure against escape of the felons, an effort should be made to convince them to surrender—that resistance is useless. Should they do so, the risks involved in removing them can be avoided. Should they refuse to give up, plans to capture them with the least risk to the officers and property involved can be formulated carefully.

Prowler Calls

Calls from excited persons reporting that a prowler has been heard or seen on the premises are among the calls most commonly received by the police. They are also among the most frustrating to officers since the percentage of such calls resulting in arrests is small.

Prowler calls are not invariably dangerous. They do not ordinarily pose a grave threat to the occupants of the premises. The greatest hazard lies in the fact that the average patrol officer soon comes to view them as routine and tends to become lax in handling them. Sooner or later he will encounter a prowler who is exceedingly dangerous, so caution must always be exercised in dealing with this type of incident. Often a suspect who was first reported as a prowler turns out to be a thief, a burglar, or a burglar-rapist who is among the most dangerous of criminals—especially where his victim is concerned.

Those officers who have had the most success in apprehending prowlers invariably have refined their techniques by combining patience with thoroughness. They consider every such call valid and treat it accordingly. As a consequence, their success rate in capturing potential burglars or otherwise disposing of incidents that are so traumatic for householders is equaled only by the excellent public relations value of their efforts. Few experiences are more disconcerting to the average person—especially a person alone—than those involving the peeping tom at a bedroom or bathroom window or a person prowling around a house, especially during the night. True, many of these calls are figments of the imagination and involve nothing more than a bush rubbing against the window, a cat or dog in the shrubbery, or the like; yet, the fear caused in the mind of the victim is often just as real as that caused by a burglar trying to pry open a window. Consequently, such incidents should be viewed in that light by the officer responding.

Response to Prowler Calls   The general techniques which should be followed in responding to these kinds of calls were described earlier in this chapter. A brief review is in order at this point: A good knowledge of the area is of special value in this type of incident as it will enable the officer to approach at right angles to the street where the address is located. If he turns at the last intersection nearest the scene, he will largely avoid signaling his approach to the prowler.

When it becomes necessary to check house numbers for the address, those on the opposite side of the street should be illuminated by flashlight. Curb numbers should be checked, if they are present, as the light is less conspicuous than when it is flashed over the front of houses. Numbers of houses in the same relative positions in other blocks may give clues to the location of the call.

Upon nearing the scene, the officer should coast noiselessly to a stop one or two houses from the place of the call. He should avoid overshooting the address, as this may warn the prowler of his arrival. If he should stop beyond the place he is looking for, he should not back his vehicle, as the backup lights will likewise announce his arrival.

Some officers in two-men units have found an alternative procedure effective in apprehending prowlers. One officer quietly drops his partner off at the rear of the location where the prowler was reported. He then approaches noisily from the front and flushes the prowler into his partner's arms. He should be careful to avoid endangering his partner by crossfire should a gunfight occur.

Two or more one-man units communicating directly with each other can sometimes deploy effectively in a similar manner. If they do not have car-to-car radio equipment, the first officer at the scene can notify the dispatcher of his location and request that other units be advised so that they may position themselves most strategically upon arrival.

If any vehicle is seen hurriedly leaving the scene, it should be stopped and checked. Appropriate notifications should be made to the dispatcher in this event.

Search of the Scene   The officer should move quickly but silently into the shadows upon his arrival, avoiding pavement and gravel whenever possible to reduce the sound of footsteps. He should then stop, listen, and watch for suspicious activities. The unexplained presence of an individual in the area should be questioned immediately.

When no suspicious activities are observed, the officer should position himself near the front corner of the concerned building where he may observe the front and side until another unit arrives to assist in the search. The second officer to arrive should take a position at the opposite front corner. By signals, one officer should proceed to search his side of the premises, the backyard area, and outbuildings. If the suspect is flushed from the premises, he is likely to run away from the approaching officer into the arms of the other officer. It should be strongly emphasized that in areas where attacks on law enforcement personnel have been prevalent, the officers should not separate and risk running into an ambush. Rather, one should follow in a position where he can cover the other while he makes the search.

The search should be conducted slowly and cautiously. The officer should walk in the shadows to avoid silhouetting himself unnecessarily. The flashlight should be used only when necessary. It should be held to the side opposite the gun hand and away from the body to avoid giving a suspect a lighted target. An oblique light played on the grass—especially when it is wet with dew—may reveal footprints indicating the prowler's path of exit or hiding place.

Low fences, wires, and clotheslines should be noted to avoid injury should a backyard foot pursuit occur. Barbecue pits, refuse containers, garbage disposal areas, etc., should be carefully examined. Shrubbery and trees, including the upper branches, outbuildings, roofs, and other potential hiding places should be searched as described in Chapter 6.

Places of access into the building should be examined for pry marks or other evidence of entry or attempted entry. When the officer has thoroughly searched the side and backyards of the premises, he should signal the officer at the front corner of the premises, then assume a position at the rear corner of the building. He should remain quietly concealed in that location, watching and listening while the other officer interviews the complainant.

Any available description of a suspect should be broadcast to other units after the householder has been reassured that appropriate action is being taken. He should be asked to remain indoors if a further search is indicated.

Follow-up Search   The follow-up search should be conducted by at least two officers who have agreed on the system to be followed and signals of recognition. The entire outside premises should again be searched systematically to make sure that the prowler did not escape detection in the first search. Simultaneously, other officers should search the neighborhood by vehicle or on foot if the geography of the area so indicates. The tactics to be used should be decided on so that each officer may systematically cover a specific area. They should consider that many prowlers and burglars avoid streets and alleys in their flight from the scene, but cross hedges and fences in backyards for several blocks—always paralleling the streets being searched. They then cross the street and leave the area some distance from the scene.

The spotlight should be used extensively in all locations that may provide a hiding place. Many suspects have been apprehended when they panicked because of the light and tried to flee.

Checking Suspicious Persons   Persons observed under suspicious circumstances, running, hiding, standing in dark areas, or acting furtively should be investigated. What appears to be an innocent petting party in a vehicle in the vicinity may be a lookout for a burglar or thief and might indicate that an inquiry should be made into the reason for the presence of the occupants.

An examination of the hands, face, feet, or clothing of the suspect may reveal that he has been moving through shrubbery. Heavy breathing and perspiration or a rapid heartbeat may indicate that he has been running. If he is wearing tennis shoes or sneakers, or carrying a can opener, screwdriver, knife, or any other implements that can be used to get into a building, he should be viewed with suspicion. Burglars have often posed as drunks to help them explain their presence when detected in an unusual place or under unusual circumstances. Even a person walking a dog or one with a dog chain but no dog should be investigated. When they are observed in an alley or other unusual place, they may try to mislead the police by claiming they are looking for their dog.

Questioning Suspects   Should the officer decide to question a person observed in the area under suspicious circumstances, he should frisk the suspect for offensive weapons if there is the slightest reason to believe that he is armed. Careful questioning of such persons may show that they have a bona fide reason for being in the area, that they live nearby, that they are familiar with the neighborhood, that their attitude does not arouse suspicion, etc. Although such factors do not always indicate guilt or innocence, they often give the officer enough clues to help him make a decision as to the course of action he should take. He should bear in mind that burglars and other criminals usually will have a very plausible explanation for being in an unusual place at an unusual time. To avoid apprehension should they be stopped and questioned, they prepare elaborate explanations which are designed to allay the suspicions of the police.

Stakeouts for Prowlers   Persons in or under parked vehicles—especially trucks or campers—in a residential area should be asked for the reason for their presence. Vehicles in the immediate area of the call should be checked for recent use. A warm radiator and a registration address some distance away may indicate that a stakeout is in order. If so, the dispatcher should be so informed so that other units can be alerted to avoid the area. The stakeout position should be far enough from the suspect's vehicle not to arouse his suspicion, yet close enough to provide a clear view of any person returning to it and enable the officer to take appropriate action to detain him before he has the opportunity to drive away. The officer might decide that the best position to stand and observe would be behind bushes, trees, or some other cover which would permit him to see without being observed. Since his hat is the most conspicuous part of his uniform, it should be removed during the stakeout so that any silhouette he makes will blend better with his background.

Contacting Victim   When the search of the area has been completed, the officer assigned the call should return to the scene to notify the complainant of the outcome and recommend action if the problem recurs. The complainant should be advised not to turn on outside lights if he hears the prowler again, but to quietly telephone the police, stay inside, and await their arrival. He should also be informed that other units will be alerted so that they may maintain a close watch of the area.

Leaving the Scene   Upon leaving the complainant, the officer should make his departure from the immediate area obvious, then quietly reverse his course and return to a strategic location where he

can wait and observe. Many prowlers and burglars have been apprehended upon leaving their hiding places and walking into the street
after they thought the police had left the area. If one officer of a
two-men unit is left at the scene to observe while the other drives
away, two doors of the police car should be closed to give the impression that both officers have entered the vehicle and driven away.
Burglars and prowlers are usually alerted to the presence of one
officer at the scene when they hear only one door of a police vehicle
manned by two officers close.

Burglary in Progress

When the presence of a burglar is made known to the police, the
effectiveness with which they handle the incident is directly proportional to the coordination of effort between the person receiving the
call, the officers assigned to it, and other units blocking the escape
of the perpetrators.

Dispatching Procedures   When information is received that a
burglar is attacking a building, the person receiving the call should
ask the informant to remain on the telephone. Meanwhile, at least
two police units should be dispatched to the scene. Additional information may then be obtained from the informant and broadcast to
responding units. A brief description should be obtained of the
premises, the place where entry is being or has been made, the
number of suspects, places where they are likely to exit, escape
routes near the premises, what persons may legitimately be on the
premises, such as night watchmen, late workers, and custodial personnel, employee vehicles parked in the immediate vicinity, and the
location of the burglar's vehicles and its description if these facts are
known.

These data, broadcast to responding units, will be most helpful to
officers planning how they should handle that particular call. As
additional information becomes available it can also be broadcast.

Initiation of Calls   Many of these calls come from private persons who observe the burglar or see things that indicate he is present
in a particular location. Others are initiated by agencies which install
and maintain silent alarms. These are usually designed to be activated by the movement of a person inside the premises in which the
alarm is installed, by some interference with a light beam, by the

presence of body heat, or by the tripping of some trigger mechanism. Other alarms are wired directly to the police communications center. Field units are notified electronically by precut tape recordings or by the police dispatcher if the alarm mechanism is disturbed.

The most common alarm systems are those in which a bell is activated when a wire or tape trigger mechanism attached to doors and windows is disturbed. These are often triggered by rain, wind, or animals and are the source of many false alarms; however, each should be treated as if it signaled the actual presence of a burglar.

The silent alarms give the burglar no warning that they have been activated by his presence. Consequently, the police are often able to apprehend him at the scene or trap him within the building.

Identifying the Place of Entry When an officer is notified that a burglary is taking place, he should respond in much the same manner as in the case of a prowler call. Upon his arrival, he should check carefully all possible places of entry for evidence that a suspect is actually inside the building. Points where buildings are most frequently entered are windows and doors. These are usually easily accessible to burglars and can ordinarily be readily opened or "jimmied" with a knife, screwdriver, pry bar, or the like. Other points where burglars gain access to buildings are roofs, skylights, walls, and tunnels under the floor. The officer examining a building to discover the place of entry should check to determine if windows or doors have been pried; panes of windows or doors broken, loosened, or removed so that they could be opened; or walls disturbed. Boxes piled against walls, ladders leaning against a building, or adjacent roofs, fences, trees, and the like are often used by burglars to gain access to the roof, where they enter through skylights, ducts, vents, or the roof itself.

Often the officer cannot get into the building to check the interior and is unable to locate the proprietor. When a careful check reveals that the building is securely closed and there is no evidence it has been entered, the officer ordinarily should notify the alarm company, record the circumstances of the call, and depart. If the call originated from a silent alarm, the officer should wait for a representative of the alarm company, who will usually open the building for inspection if that course of action is indicated. When this occurs, the officer assigned the call, a follow-up unit, other officers as needed, and the alarm company representative should carefully search the interior. The techniques of the building search should follow the procedures outlined earlier in this chapter.

Summary

Most crime-in-progress calls can be handled adequately by applying certain basic principles combined with common sense. With slight modifications, the basic techniques applicable to most of these incidents can be modified to meet the needs of even the most unusual situations.

The effectiveness with which calls of this nature are handled depends to a large degree upon how the responding units work together as a team, both at the scene and in the surrounding area. The unit assigned the call should drive cautiously in approaching the area, evaluate the situation upon arrival, summon assistance if it is needed, render first aid when indicated, then obtain information and relay it by radio to other units in the area so that they can deploy themselves strategically at locations where they are likely to intercept the suspect if he has fled the area.

At the scene, the assigned officer and a backup unit—if one has been dispatched—should interview victims and witnesses and take steps to preserve evidence which may have been left by the suspect.

When the suspect is believed to have remained in the vicinity of the crime, a thorough, systematic search should be made of the area. In high-risk areas, officers should cover each other during the search rather than search separately. Special attention should be given to those places where the suspect might go to remain inconspicuous or hide.

At times, it will be necessary to search a building to determine if a burglar is hidden inside. Such a search should be conducted by at least two officers who can provide cover for each other. A cover team to protect them and apprehend the suspect if he is flushed from the building should also assist when enough units are available.

If a suspect is contained in a building, he should be encouraged to surrender. This can avoid needless risk to the police. If he refuses to give up, plans must be made to remove him.

At times, a suspect will seize a person and hold him as a hostage, expecting something in return for the hostage's release. No hard-and-fast rules can be made for all such cases. Each will have to be decided on its own merits after careful consideration is given to all circumstances surrounding the incident. The emotional and mental condition of the suspect and his motives in holding a hostage should be evaluated as carefully as possible by the officer in determining what action to take. Every attempt should be made to gain time in which to convince the suspect that this is the wrong course for him to follow. If family members or friends are available, they may help in this respect, but they should not expose themselves so that they too become hostages. When an opportunity presents itself, the officer should take the initiative by quick, conclusive action.

Calls involving unknown trouble are exceedingly hazardous and should be approached cautiously. The information on which they are based is usually incomplete, garbled, or distorted. The patrol officer must therefore be prepared to act swiftly to protect himself should he encounter violence.

On occasion, he may become involved in a gun battle in which the suspect is wounded. Such suspects should be considered extremely dangerous and should be approached cautiously by the officer, whose weapon should be loaded and ready to fire if necessary. After the suspect is carefully searched and securely handcuffed, he should be interrogated about the offense and other related crimes. A Miranda warning should be given him before he is questioned if his statements are to be used against him in a criminal proceeding.

Review

Questions

1. Why should a dispatcher avoid reassigning a crime-in-progress call? When might reassigning such a call be justified?
2. What factors should patrol units consider in deciding whether to go directly to the scene of an "all units call" or deploy elsewhere?
3. What are some of the best locations at which an officer could position himself to intercept a suspect escaping from a crime scene in a rural area? In a densely populated residential area? In an industrial area?
4. What plans should officers in a two-men unit make on their way to the scene of a prowler call? Robbery-in-progress call? Burglary-in-progress call?
5. Generally, when should a patrol officer summon assistance at the scene of a crime-in-progress call?
6. What data should the follow-up broadcast contain?
7. Why should witnesses to a crime be interviewed separately?
8. Why should unknown trouble calls be approached with extraordinary caution?
9. What should an officer do when he wounds a suspect in a gun battle?
10. Why should robbery suspects be approached with special caution?
11. Why should multistory buildings be searched from the top down?

Exercises

1. Assume a robbery suspect has disarmed and is holding a fellow police officer and the proprietor hostage in a market. The suspect

is contained in the building and is unable to escape but threatens to kill the hostages within thirty minutes if a vehicle is not provided and he is not given an opportunity to escape. Explain what course of action should be taken in handling such an incident.

2. Describe the techniques a patrol officer should use in approaching the immediate scene of a prowler call at night. A burglary-in-progress call. A robbery-in-progress call.

3. Explain how a search should be made for the suspect in an area within a block or two from the scene of a burglary shortly after its occurrence when the suspect is believed to be in the vicinity.

4. Describe how a small two-story building with a basement and numerous rooms should be searched by four officers for a suspect believed to be inside. How should two officers search the building?

11

Attacks against the Police— Survival Techniques

Many devices and techniques used by vicious killers in assaults against the police are of recent origin; others are as old as recorded history. But officers are often unprepared emotionally to take effective defensive measures against such attacks and unfamiliar with the basic techniques of countering the commonly used weapons and tactics. The patrol officer needs to learn all he can about what is termed "urban guerrilla action" in order to protect himself from its violence.

Defense techniques often involve the officer's mental attitude and his previous conditioning to take action swiftly and decisively when attacked. He should not wait until his life is in imminent danger before deciding what to do in a perilous situation but should condition himself emotionally and physically for protecting himself, fellow officers, and innocent victims. He should practice a few basic techniques which he can apply if he suddenly finds himself trapped in an ambush, assaulted with a fire bomb, involved in a gun battle, or disarmed by a criminal.

Attacks from Ambush

J. Edgar Hoover[1] has described ambushes on law enforcement officers as cowardly assaults committed on victims who have no opportunity to defend themselves. His description sums up the hazards faced by officers lured into an ambush and shot—often in the back.

Most ambush slayings do not involve police negligence, but patrol officers must be always on the alert to this terrorism. The first lesson in survival for the officer is learning that no call can be considered routine. This fact is evident by the increasing frequency with which officers have been slain from ambush in responding to calls and while on regular patrol.[2]

The ordinary criminal is obviously responsible for the vast majority of the assaults against law enforcement officers. He may shoot if trapped or to avoid capture, but he seldom goes out deliberately looking for police to kill. It has been the rise in revolutionary-ideological violence in the past several years that has contributed so markedly to the increase in these incidents. This violence is linked to the concept of guerrilla warfare in urban areas, emphasizing violent acts against the Establishment of which the police are the first target.

The terrorists can usually find adequate concealment in a crowd—many of whom may support them and be willing to help them avoid detection. For this reason, their activities are difficult to counter except with an almost prohibitive expenditure of police time and personnel.

Often for urban guerrillas, no weapons or tactics are barred. Their object is to destroy the police by ridicule, harassment, physical injury, or death. They disappear when the initiative is taken from them, harass if their enemy defends, and attack whenever he becomes vulnerable or if he withdraws. The police, by knowing what tactics are likely to be used, can often turn these to their own advantage.

The revolutionary feels it a moral duty to strike at the police wherever and whenever the opportunity presents itself. "This revolutionary-guerrilla mood," said J. Edgar Hoover, "makes for a trigger-happy, violence-prone mentality of offensive violence which increases

---

[1] J. Edgar Hoover, "Message from the Director," *F.B.I. Law Enforcement Bulletin*, vol. 41, no. 4, April 1972, n.p.
[2] Ibid.

the danger to the officer."[3] A goal of the revolutionary is to ambush or snipe at police officers.[4] These terror tactics make it imperative that officers remain constantly alert to counter the one element without which an ambush will usually fail—surprise.

The Nature of an Ambush Ambush tactics have remained substantially unchanged through the ages. The ambush is a surprise attack—a hit-and-run encounter—not affected greatly by the development and refinement of modern weaponry. It takes place at close quarters and does not involve the capture and holding of ground. It is a widely used technique of guerrillas operating from cover, and its most important characteristic is the element of surprise. It thrives on confusion and disorganization. Ambushers usually block streets with automobiles, fire, trees, etc., to close escape routes. Secondary ambushes are often established along thoroughfares which must be taken in withdrawing from the danger zone.

The terrorists choose the time and place for attack—often luring police officers singly, in pairs, or in small groups to the chosen area by placing false calls for help or involving them in a pursuit and leading them into a trap or other ruses. With an intimate knowledge of the area and great mobility, the guerrillas can strike and run. The primary target is usually the police officer; the secondary goal is often capturing weapons, equipment, and supplies.

Ambush Sites and Weapons Ambushes are usually planned for locations where and at times when the ambushers can attack from cover then fade into the darkness or their surroundings without detection. Alleyways, rooftops, sewers, cellars, attics, and other pathways available in most cities are common ambush sites.

Favored locations to bushwack the police are areas where they can be immobilized by the geographical arrangement of streets, buildings, walls, hedges, bridges, storm drains, etc., and places where little cover is present or where the element of surprise can easily be achieved. Attacks might come suddenly from cover, along routes frequently used by officers to go to and from the station, on dead-end streets, in alleys and cul de sacs which can be easily blocked by the ambushers, at routine coffee or meal stops, in locations that can be booby-trapped or where snipers can be concealed, in unprotected

[3] J. Edgar Hoover, "Law Enforcement Faces the Revolutionary-Guerrilla Criminal," *F.B.I. Law Enforcement Bulletin*, vol. 39, no. 12, December 1970, pp. 20–28.
[4] ————, "The Police Officer: The Primary Target of the Urban Guerrilla," *F.B.I. Law Enforcement Bulletin*, vol. 41, no. 2, February 1972, pp. 21–22.

areas such as parking lots, and after a false alarm call or other incident or meeting.

Firearms of all types, including automatic and sawed-off weapons, fire bombs, fragmentary grenades, pipe bombs, booby traps, and a host of others are used to kill and maim the unsuspecting police officer. Those which cannot be rather easily obtained through normal market channels can be constructed with little difficulty.

Defensive Measures   Officers can best protect themselves against ambush by being constantly alert for clues that a trap has been set for them when they answer a call or patrol in isolated areas, avoiding driving their beat in a set pattern which those bent on ambush can readily learn by watching them, avoiding exposed places where they can be easily ambushed, avoiding congregating with other officers at the scene of police incidents, using scouts when groups of officers move from place to place, learning to recognize the clues that suggest the presence of an ambush, and becoming familiar with the actions they can take to minimize its effect should they be trapped in one.

Ambush Clues   Should they note while on patrol an unusual absence of children playing or other pedestrians, traffic or noise in an area, or that people on the streets are hurrying away when the police car appears, or that houses and business establishments which are usually lighted are darkened, they should proceed with great caution. If a combination of these conditions exists in the vicinity of a call, they should drive by the address without stopping and call for backup units if it is necessary for them to leave their vehicle. The suspected location should be kept under observation from a safe distance for further clues which might verify their suspicions.

When the backup units arrive and the officers leave their vehicles, they should remain together to provide each other cover although not so close as to make themselves vulnerable as targets. A distance between them of 5 to 10 yards is usually sufficient to protect them from an effective range shotgun blast. They should not allow themselves to be trapped in narrow pedestrian passageways or other areas devoid of cover and should not risk passing together through gates or pathways in bushes since these are favorite locations used by ambushers to place trip wires connected to booby traps. When officers find it necessary to traverse such routes, one should walk to the rear and to the side. He should wait for his partner to proceed to a cover position before using the same route. As the partner moves, the backup officer covers him. While he moves forward, he is covered by his partner. This same procedure should be followed in passing through doorways.

It is fundamental that neither officer stands in front of a door when they knock to announce their presence at the scene of a call. Booby traps are sometimes designed to kill a person in front of a door or a suspect inside may fire through it at the officers.

Counter Ambush Tactics—From a Vehicle   As with most police operations, there are no two ambush situations exactly alike; consequently, there can be no standard procedure of defensive action suitable for all such incidents. The ambushers have the advantage of planning the time and place of the assault. They also have the element of surprise on their side and can strike and move if the police do not act swiftly to assume the initiative. While this is not always easy to accomplish, officers can gain the advantage if they can determine the strength and positions of the ambushers then quickly react by taking offensive action instead of trying to escape along a route covered by sniper fire.

The most hazardous area in which the officer can remain is the zone controlled by, and under fire of, the ambushers—a portion of the street, a sidewalk, an area between buildings, or any location void of cover. This is the unprotected position in which they wish to hold him.

If he is fired upon while in his vehicle, he should drive immediately into a driveway if there is one, over a curb, or onto the sidewalk in the direction of the fire to avoid getting trapped in the primary danger zone. The ambushers will have a clear zone of fire at the vehicle if it is driven away from them down the street. This type of flight may also cause the officer to run into a secondary ambush because, usually, that is the course of action he is expected to take in his panic.

His first and main concern is to get out of the immediate danger zone and, at the same time, avoid a secondary ambush. By turning in the direction of fire and remaining on the same side of the street as the ambushers, he will force them to change positions to fire again. In the meantime, it may be possible to outflank them. While he takes advantage of the cover afforded him by his vehicle, he should, if possible, quickly notify the dispatcher of the ambush and the location with a warning that the street or area is under fire and should be avoided by other units. He should return the fire as soon as possible to distract the attackers. He should abandon his vehicle and seek better cover in any house or building available, behind a wall or tree, etc. The vehicle is not a good source of shelter at this time because it will normally be under gunfire and will be in an untenable position. If necessary, the officer should break through a window or door or take any action necessary to gain a safer position inside a building where he can await help. If a telephone is available there, it can be used to give the dispatcher whatever information is indicated.

Counter Ambush Tactics—On Foot   When an officer moves from place to place on foot, especially when he has the slightest suspicion that he may be vulnerable to a surprise attack, he should make a mental note of the cover available to him should such attack occur. If he finds himself under fire when on foot, the speed of his reactions will usually determine whether he survives. The first sensation of the untrained, unconditioned person when the attack comes by surprise is sheer panic. Panic often displaces common sense. One's immediate reaction is to flee. That urge is counted upon by the attackers, who are likely to position other ambushers so that the retreat route becomes a clear field of fire under their control and a death trap for the officer. He should therefore do the unexpected— attack. By immediately firing back at the ambushers, his chances of distracting them while he moves quickly to cover are immensely improved. He should not empty his weapon in returning the fire and run the risk of his attackers charging him when he has an unloaded gun. Rather, he should reload before firing the last round or two. He should seek a curb, a position behind an automobile with a wheel between him and the ambushers, a tree, a building, a wall—any place out of the danger zone which will provide immediate protection. He may then have time to reload and seek better cover or fire at an attacker and charge in an attempt to overrun his position, capture him and use him as a hostage or use his weapons, if necessary, against other attackers. The officer's chances of avoiding injury if he takes such evasive action are considerably better than if he simply lies flat in the danger zone and submits to the ambushers' fire.

Fire Bomb Attacks

The number of incendiary fires has increased alarmingly during recent years. Many of these do not directly affect the patrol officer, because fire departments ordinarily have primary responsibility for their control; however, a large percentage of such incidents are initially reported to fire departments by patrol officers. In many cases, fire bomb attacks are unsuccessful. The fire is quickly extinguished without causing damage or it goes out quickly. The incident therefore is reported to the police department as a crime. The fire department first learns of the occurrence when it receives a copy of the police report.[5]

Molotov Cocktails   The use of fire bombs against the police is becoming more and more common. These are popularly called Molotov cocktails through use by the Russians during World War II. They are also known as frangible incendiary grenades.

In many cases, the patrol officer and his vehicle are made the targets of Molotov cocktail attacks. These are used more frequently by militants than are explosive devices because they are easy to construct and are capable of extensive property damage. The components are cheap and easily obtainable and are virtually impossible to trace.

Fire bombs are safer to handle than bombs made of explosive substances. Fortunately, they are less dangerous to the police officer also. Their very simplicity often causes them to fail to ignate. When they do ignite, the fire can often be easily controlled before causing serious injury or property damage because of the warning given by the ignition itself.

Construction of Fire Bombs   The Molotov cocktail is usually constructed of a glass container, gasoline (sometimes mixed with oil), a cloth wick, and a bottle cap. Other substances are sometimes mixed with the gasoline to thicken or gell it. This will enable the mixture to adhere to the target, increase its burning time, or limit its spread. A napalm-like paste is sometimes made by mixing alcohol and soap into the gasoline or by adding lye, egg whites, animal blood, or crushed styrofoam to the filler, thus allowing the mixture to cling and burn longer than gasoline alone.[6] The breaking of the bottle

[5] Much of the data in this section was based on information obtained by Captain Robert Dove, security officer, Los Angeles Fire Department, from tests conducted in conjunction with the Los Angeles Police Department; see also the California Council on Criminal Justice, *Bulletin*, vol. 4, issue 6, Sacramento, August 2, 1971, wherein it was reported that there were 1,128 bomb incidents in California alone from March 1970 to February 1971. Approximately two-thirds of these incidents involved incendiary devices and one-third were explosives. Most of the bombs were homemade from easily obtainable materials.
[6] National Bomb Data Center, *Recognition of Explosive and Incendiary Devices: Part I—Hand and Rifle Grenades—03-1*, International Association of Chiefs of Police, Washington, D.C., n.d., pp. 114–129.

upon impact with the target frees the gasoline mixture which is ignited by the flaming wick. The resulting fire burns violently and generates intense heat.

Sometimes, the wick is impregnated with chemicals which cause ignition when the bottle breaks upon impact and the gasoline comes in contact with the impregnation. The use of a burning wick is thus not necessary, and the danger to the person lighting it is eliminated. Because of this chemical ignition, fire bombs with chemical wicks are more reliable than those requiring a flaming wick and more dangerous to the officer, since they may explode into flame in his hands if the bottle breaks or the gasoline is allowed to contact the chemically saturated wick. When officers seize fire bombs of this type, they should be alerted to the nature of the device if a wick is wrapped *around the bottle.*[7]

Fire bombs are also constructed with an encased fuse and explosive charge of black powder attached to the bottle. Upon explosion of the black powder, the flash ignites the gasoline mixture. They are also made with plastic bottles filled with gasoline. Ignition is accomplished by ordinary highway flares attached to the bottle. When the flares are lighted, the heat melts the plastic causing fire. Fire bombs sometimes are made of common household plastic bags filled with gasoline which is ignited by the explosion of an ordinary firecracker with a long wick or string.

When a witness describes a discharge of a shotgun and an immediate fire, the officer should suspect an attack by a fire bomb of this type. He should then look for small bits of paper from the firecracker instead of shot from a shotgun shell. Commercial napalm used in burning crops is easily obtainable and its use by arsonists is increasing.

Methods of Delivery of Fire Bombs to the Target   Fire bombs are not always thrown against the target. Often they are carried to it and ignited there. Every conceivable means of packaging and delivery has been employed by bombers bent on destroying property. Packages, luggage, shopping bags, shoe boxes are some of the common types of concealment. They have even been implanted under or in potted plants.[8]

[7] Robert R. Lenz, *Explosives and Bomb Disposal Guide*, Charles C Thomas, Publisher, Springfield, Ill., 1965, pp. 89–90.
[8] Dove, *loc. cit.*; see also National Bomb Data Center, *Recognition of Explosives and Incendiary Devices*, pp. 114–129.

Use against Police Although the police have become the victims of numerous fire bomb attacks by militants during riots and other civil disorders, experience has shown that an officer need not be injured under normal circumstances if he keeps calm and reacts to such attacks properly.

Tests conducted by the Los Angeles City Fire Department on the effect of fire bombs used against vehicles revealed several noteworthy facts.[9] It was found that, if windows were closed tightly when a police vehicle was struck by a fire bomb and the fire was confined to the *outside* of the car, the temperature inside the car ranged from 90° at the floor to 135° at the steering wheel and from 154 to 160° near the roof after the fire had burned for about five minutes. Flames inside the vehicle could cause the temperature to rise to 1500° Fahrenheit. Windshields will resist the fire. The flames on the outside of the car burn out in less than one minute, and a car can ordinarily be moved to safety in this time. In these tests, the gas tank did not explode after seven minutes of exposure to the flames, nor did the tires ignite.

Defenses against Fire The tests suggest that the occupants of a police car should immediately close all windows tightly to keep the flames outside if it is attacked with fire bombs. The car should be kept moving so that it will not become the static target of other missiles or sniper fire. The officer should drive through the fire and out of the danger area to a safe place if possible before stopping.

Fire Barricades Fire barricades are sometimes used as a means of stopping the police vehicle so that the occupants can be attacked when they leave their vehicles. Should this happen, the officer should drive through the barricade. If it becomes necessary to stop, the motor should be kept running at high speed.

Remaining in the Vehicle The officer should not leave the protection of his vehicle if doing so would expose him to attack, unless flames inside make such action imperative. When he is forced to abandon it, he should move quickly to cover, holding his breath when he passes through the flames to prevent damage to his lungs. He should try to avoid any burning gasoline around the outside. The intense heat can quickly cause severe burns about the feet and ankles. Should his trouser legs become ignited, he should *immediately* smother the fire by wrapping a jacket, shirt, etc., tightly around the

[9] Ibid.

burning area if an extinguisher is not available. Obviously, he should seek cover first if he is under fire by snipers.

Extinguishers   Small fires inside the car can often be smothered by a coat, shirt, hat, etc., or by use of an extinguisher if prompt action is taken. Dry chemical extinguishers containing bicarbonate of soda under pressure are effective in gasoline fires. The discharge should be started well away from the flame to prevent spreading it with the pressure. The chemical should be fanned across the flames in quick side-to-side motions. When the fire is extinguished, the spray should be stopped. A reflash will require that the action be repeated.

The carbon dioxide extinguishers are most effective against electrical fires but are useful for gasoline fires also. They are limited in their usefulness, however, by their relatively short range of discharge. These should be sprayed *slowly* from side to side with the spray aimed at the base of the flame.

Officers should extinguish any small fires whenever practicable not only to protect themselves from the flames but to demonstrate how easily they can be controlled. The psychological effect upon the fire bombers tends to discourage further attacks with these objects.

Collecting Evidence in Fire Bomb Cases   All evidence which might lead to the apprehension and prosecution of perpetrators of fire bombings should be gathered meticulously. In some cases, the bomb or arson squad should be summoned to perform this work because of the nature of the attack, the type of victim, etc. As in the collection and preservation of evidence in other cases, the officer should avoid contaminating or destroying any item or trace which might be useful in the investigation. Residue, oil or gas marks, marks or debris left by flares, pieces of the glass container, any materials that would indicate that several bottles were used together, wax or candle remains, timing devices, fuse parts, gasoline cans, or charred remnants of other materials which might indicate the type of product used for ignition of the device should be preserved for analysis. Odors of petroleum products or other flammable liquids should be noted and recorded for future court use. The names and addresses of witnesses or persons showing unusual interest in fire-fighting activities should be secured for the follow-up investigation if they cannot be interviewed at the time.

Motive for the Attack   As with any case of arson, property may be attacked for reasons other than those which arise from civil disorders. Arson is often perpetrated to cover other crimes or to defraud insurance companies. Many motives may be involved—even revenge by disgruntled employees.

The officer should look for a logical reason for a fire which might reveal the identity of the arsonist. Any evidence of motive should be recorded in police reports for reference in the follow-up investigation and whatever court proceedings may follow.

Defensive Use of Firearms

Occasionally, as a last resort, an officer is forced to use his gun to protect his life or that of someone else when he is confronted by an armed criminal or a psychopathic individual with a lethal weapon. The law, universally applicable in cases where the use of deadly force is necessary to defend life, clearly justifies such an act irrespective of whether it involves a juvenile or an adult. The legal and moral aspects of using deadly force against a fleeing or resisting offender have been discussed previously.

Gun Fights Speedy reaction is necessary when the officer's life is in imminent danger and he has no option but to kill or be killed. Each officer must evaluate the circumstances of the particular incident he faces in accordance with the legal and moral issues involved in the taking of a life. Obviously, no hard-and-fast rules can be established to cover all situations but a few basic defensive techniques can be applied with good effect.

When the need for shooting becomes apparent and the officer is on foot, he should employ some simple tactics that he has practiced so often beforehand that they have become conditioned reflexes. Reducing the size of the target he presents to the assailant is one of the most basic and effective of these tactics. The novice combat soldier knows the importance of hitting the ground when under enemy fire; yet, many police officers have not fully applied this basic tenet of defensive action when fired upon.

The full body provides a relatively large target which can be greatly reduced by turning sideways or dropping to one knee or to a prone position. It is far better to tear a uniform or bump a knee than to risk providing a full, body-size target to the attacker. While hitting the ground is not always practicable, any evasive action or movement such as diving for cover, running in a zig-zag course toward the assailant, or moving swiftly and suddenly from one cover to another, makes a target more difficult to hit.

When return fire is practicable in a short-range gun battle under 10 yards, the officer should fire rapidly at the suspect or suspects—double action if he is armed with a revolver. The first several rounds may distract the suspect and give the officer an opportunity to assume a less exposed position. He should then fire the next several rounds carefully, deliberately, and with deadly effect. Except under unusual circumstances, he should avoid emptying his gun but should try to reload it before using the last round or two. These should be kept in reserve in the event his assailant rushes him before he has an opportunity to reload. Likewise, if he is attacked by two suspects, he should fire at both of them rather than concentrating his fire at only one. By doing so he will distract them so that neither will have a clear, unimpeded opportunity to fire at him.

He should select the widest part of the attacker's body, the torso, as his target. At ranges up to 25 yards, he should follow the same tactics as in the case of a short-range gun battle. He should fire immediately and rapidly at the suspects to distract them, dive for cover or drop to a prone position to reduce the target if he is not able to gain cover, return the fire at the suspects with careful deliberation, and reload before emptying his gun. If he has not disposed of his assailants by this time, he should consider moving suddenly and swiftly to avoid providing a fixed unprotected target.

Use of Firearms against Vehicles   Although modern ammunition has considerable penetrating capacity, tests reveal that the kind often carried by police officers is generally ineffective against the plate glass and metal bodies of automobiles under field conditions.[10]

Several significant conclusions were drawn from these tests. Irrespective of the legal justification for shooting in any particular incident, these findings should influence the decision of the officer whether to shoot at moving vehicles with the ever-present risk of a ricocheting bullet injuring or killing innocent bystanders. Seldom will the 158 or 200 grain bullet penetrate the metal body of a vehicle. Even a higher velocity bullet striking an automobile at almost right angles must penetrate inner liners, seat cushions, braces, window attachments, etc., before it can have effect upon the occupants. The slanted windows of modern cars usually cause bullets—even those with extremely high velocity—to ricochet.

---

[10] Data from tests conducted by the Los Angeles Police Department under simulated field conditions in 1958 with 158 and 200 grain, 38-caliber bullets (unpublished); Los Angeles Police Department, "Ammunition Limitations—Shooting at Cars and Plate Glass," *Patrol Bureau, Roll Call Training*, Series 3, Lesson 14, (unpublished), April 1963.

Moving vehicles are most difficult to hit from another moving vehicle, especially if the officer firing is also driving. Usually his efforts will be futile. Passenger officers in two-men units are able to fire and reload more effectively but they also experience difficulty making their shots count. It is even more difficult to hit the gasoline tank. Even when this happens, only a portion of the fuel will drain and operation of the vehicle will not be substantially impaired. If the bullet rips a large hole in the lowermost portion of the tank, the car can still be driven for several miles before losing all its fuel. Some modern tires and tubes treated with puncture sealants will not deflate nor otherwise be affected by bullet holes, even if the officer is lucky or expert enough to hit them with his gunfire.

If the shooter does not wear protective glasses, the hot, unburned particles of powder may be blown into his eyes causing considerable damage. If he leans out the window to fire his shotgun, he may be thrown from the car if it lurches sharply.[11]

A revolver can be reloaded but only with considerable difficulty and risk by a lone officer in the police unit. Driving under pursuit conditions is difficult under ideal conditions without the added hazard of reloading a firearm. Should the suspects finally abandon their car, an officer with an unloaded weapon is at a grave disadvantage if he is confronted by them and they are armed. In exceptional cases, should he be fired at by occupants of a vehicle, he might be justified in returning their fire to interfere with their aim.

Gunfire at Plate Glass Windows   Ordinarily, 158 and 200 grain bullets, and many heavier ones, will glance off plate glass. Penetration will occur occasionally if the glass is struck at almost right angles, but the bullet loses most of its effective velocity. If the officer is being fired upon from inside a building, he would be justified in returning the fire to distract the suspects; however, under such circumstances, other more effective means such as gas or heavier arms would usually be available in offensive action against them.

Survival Techniques—The Decision to Resist or Surrender

There are circumstances in police work where an officer is placed in grave jeopardy by an unexpected encounter with a dangerous, armed criminal who can relieve the officer of his sidearm, kill him,

[11] Massad F. Ayoob, "Vehicular Aspects of Police Gunfight Situations," *Law and Order*, vol. 20, no. 10, October 1972, pp. 34–43.

hold him hostage, or release him. At times, the officer may believe that he has no option but to give up. He might reason that he may later have an opportunity to overpower the criminal under conditions more favorable than those in which he finds himself at the moment. He should realize, however, that surrender is no guarantee of his safety or of that of others who may be involved. Many officers have been executed by their captors in such incidents and have never had an opportunity to resist effectively. Others have managed to overpower their captors at a more opportune time, while others have been released unharmed.

Whatever individual decision is made, it must not be made lightly. It should be based on general plans the officer has decided upon for himself or with his partner beforehand to cope with this type of incident. Should he decide to submit and surrender his sidearm, he should do so only with the full realization that a later opportunity to overpower his captor may or may not present itself. These considerations must be balanced against the fact that the criminal obviously does not wish to murder the officer at the moment or at that particular place or he would have done so. Furthermore, if the criminal is attacked, he may fire but miss or his gun might misfire and it may be possible to overpower him. Even if these things do not happen and the officer is struck, bullet wounds are not always fatal. These factors must be contemplated. The officer has certain advantages if he has made a plan, if he is mentally prepared for what is happening and what is about to happen if he attacks, if he has confidence in himself and his brother officers who might be involved, and if he is able to choose the time and place to act.

Establishing a Plan   When officers are assigned to two-men units, they should establish a simple code to signal the moment when both should spring into action if they are confronted by such an incident. They should plan what each should do if the decision is made to resist.

The risks are indeed grave, but when the odds are prohibitive the officer may decide that his greatest chance lies in resistance. Should he make this decision as a last resort, his action should be instantaneous. Should he fail, he might die. He should remember that his assailant probably will have no compunctions against killing a representative of the law.

There are many sophisticated defensive maneuvers that can be used effectively in this type of incident, but they require a great deal of practice and conditioning. Few officers have the necessary skill to disarm an assailant with the speed required before he pulls the trigger, but every officer can use surprise. Sometimes, when it is coupled with a ruse or a blow, the officer gains the advantage.

Defensive Action The emergency action described here is suggested under these circumstances.[12] A loud yell may startle the assailant and give the officer a split second advantage as he goes into action. This may also bring help. Something should be thrown at the criminal, if possible, such as a flashlight, clipboard, citation book, hat, or dirt in his eyes. He should be hit with anything available. If the assailant orders that the belt or other items be taken off, they can be used as weapons against him. A pencil jabbed into the eye or jugular vein is effective. A kick or knee in the groin or a jab in the eyes, a blow with the edge of the hand to the throat or upward under the nose, or a blow in the pit of the stomach with the elbows or knee may have disabling effects.

The old ruse of telling a nonexistent officer not to shoot may cause the criminal to turn his head or distract him for an instant and give the officer an opportunity to attack. Other acts that may increase the officer's chance to survive include dropping to the ground to give another officer an opportunity to shoot or dropping to the ground and rolling against the suspect's legs and at the same time pulling sharply on his ankles to upset him.

By stepping forward and pivoting to the left, if facing a right-handed assailant, it may be possible to grab a revolver by the cylinder and hold it. This will prevent the weapon being fired more than once even if it is cocked. It cannot be recocked if the cylinder is kept from turning. In most cases, a person holding a weapon in the right hand will pull it to his left when he fires it—especially if the trigger is jerked. Thus the officer, by pivoting to his left, may avoid being struck even if the gun is fired before he can grab it. If the weapon is a military-type 45 caliber automatic, it will not fire if the barrel is jammed back even though it is cocked.

If the officer is carrying a backup gun, he may find an opening before or during his counterattack to use it. He must take advantage of all opportunities that present themselves in this type of critical situation.

[12] Los Angeles Police Department, "Officers' Survival—Suggestions for Emergency Actions," *Patrol Bureau, Roll Call Training*, (unpublished), March 15, 1963; Dean H. Grennell and Mason Williams, *Law Enforcement Handgun Digest*, Follett Publishing Company, Chicago, 1972, pp. 169–171.

Summary

With the increase in urban guerrilla action, law enforcement personnel should learn all they can about means of countering its violence and the weapons used in attacks against the police. The patrol officer is especially vulnerable to ambush from vicious killers who will lure him into a trap. The site chosen for an ambush is usually one in which the victim can be immobilized without cover and attacked with gunfire, incendiary weapons, fragmentary grenades, and other lethal devices. Surprise is relied upon in the attack. Officers should bear in mind that they may be able to use against the guerrilla his own tenets of disappearing or retreating if attacked, harassing the enemy when he defends, and attacking him when he retreats.

The prime defense of the police against ambush is constant watchfulness for evidence of an impending attack in exposed places. An unusual absence of foot and vehicle traffic or noise in the vicinity of a call or darkened houses or business places which are usually lighted may be indicators of an ambush.

Should an officer fall into a trap while in his vehicle, he should immediately take offensive action by turning into the direction of the fire and driving into a driveway or over a curb to escape the danger zone which is controlled by the ambushers. He should immediately call for help by radio if that is feasible, then quickly seek cover better than his vehicle—firing at his attackers while doing so to distract their aim. If necessary he should break a window or door of a building if cover is available inside. Details of the attack can be relayed to his dispatcher by land line if a telephone is available in the building.

If attacked while on foot, the officer should immediately return the fire of the attackers to distract them, then advance upon them and seek cover in the direction of their fire. By advancing instead of retreating, he will force his attackers to change their position for their second shot and will avoid a secondary ambush often established along an escape route.

If attacked with a Molotov cocktail while he is in his vehicle, he should not abandon the car if the fire has not penetrated the interior but should quickly close all windows tightly, continue moving to avoid becoming a static target to snipers, and drive out of the danger zone —through fire barricades if necessary. If he stays within his vehicle, the heat from the fire outside can be tolerated with safety. If he abandons the car, he may become a target for other missiles or sniper fire or a casualty from the fire around the car.

Every officer should prepare himself for the possibility of becoming involved in a gunfight with a criminal or psychopath. The speed of the officer's reaction may save his life. His first reaction should be to reduce the size of the target he presents to his assailant by turning sideways, dropping to one knee or to a prone position, or taking other evasive action, drawing his weapon and firing for effect. His first swift fire is calculated to upset the aim of his attackers. The next rounds should be fired with more deliberation.

Gunfire directed at vehicles usually has limited effects because of the difficulty in striking a sensitive area or penetrating the body. The dangers to innocent bystanders from ricochets may outweigh the questionable results achievable.

One of the gravest decisions an officer might ever be called upon to make is whether to surrender or resist an armed criminal who gains the initiative over him. Three options are available—to surrender his weapon and await a better opportunity to overpower the criminal, to surrender his weapon in the hope that he will be released unharmed, or to resist because he believes he will be murdered in any event. Should he decide to take the latter course, his action should be swift and without hesitation. The odds of his survival will depend upon the surprise with which he springs into action and the mental and physical conditioning he has undergone in preparing himself for such a happening.

Review

Questions

1. What is considered the danger zone in an ambush?
2. What is a secondary ambush? Where is it most likely to be established?
3. What are the objectives of urban guerrilla action? What are the general tactics used?
4. Describe the nature of an ambush.
5. What are the usual weapons used by ambushers?
6. What are the favorite sites for ambushes against the police?
7. Describe some of the clues that an officer should look for as indicators of an ambush.
8. Describe the basic types of Molotov cocktails.
9. Why are oil and other substances often added to gasoline in Molotov cocktails?
10. Why is gunfire from a sidearm unlikely to be effective against moving automobiles?
11. To which side do most persons jerk a pistol or revolver when they pull the trigger? Why is this important for the law enforcement officer to know?

Exercises

1. Assume you have received a call which you believe is a ruse to lead you into an ambush. Describe what action you would take.
2. Assume you are ambushed midblock in an alley in a residential district. It appears that there are two suspects. They open fire with sidearms while you are still in your police vehicle. You are working alone. Describe what you should do. What would you do if you were the passenger officer in a two-men unit?
3. What would you do if the attack described in Exercise 2 occurred in a business area while you were alone in a police vehicle? Describe what you would do if you were on foot.
4. If you were attacked with a fire bomb while you were in your vehicle, what course of action would you take?
5. What should you do if the alley in which you are driving is barricaded with fire to keep you from escaping?
6. What are some of the hazards you would encounter if you left your vehicle when it was burning on the outside from a fire bomb?
7. Describe what types of evidence you would look for at the scene of a fire bomb attack against property.
8. Describe the defensive action you would take if you were confronted by an armed criminal who had opened fire upon you at close range.
9. What are some of the things an officer should do if he becomes involved in a gun fight with one suspect? With more than one suspect?
10. Assume you are unexpectedly confronted by an armed bandit at the scene of a robbery. He has you covered with a small caliber revolver at close range (two yards) and orders you to drop your weapon. He tells you he is going to kill you. Describe what you do. Would your course of action be different if he told you that you would be used as a hostage? Why?
11. What plans should officers make with their partners to cope with situations such as those described in Exercise 10?

12

Special Problems of Patrol

Most of the patrol officer's time is spent performing more or less routine tasks. Occasionally, however, he is confronted with a problem that requires special procedures. Often these will tax his ingenuity because he rarely has an opportunity to develop through experience a plan of action suitable for each incident. Applying existing basic precepts to the problem—modifying them as the circumstances dictate—usually will resolve the issue adequately.

Most of these special problems do not directly involve the officer in criminal matters, which are essentially negative in nature. Rather, they give him a splendid opportunity to provide a positive form of service, assistance, and protection to the public.

Missing Persons

The formal procedures for handling lost or missing children and adults—including those who have disappeared intentionally or unintentionally for a variety of reasons and those troubled by senility or mental incompetence—are ordinarily determined by departmental rules. The patrol officer is usually first on the scene and is the key to locating the missing person promptly in most of these cases. His success will be directly related to how effectively he collects the facts, evaluates them, and follows the clues they suggest.

Lost Children

One of the most important of all calls—at least from a parent's viewpoint—is that involving a missing child. Usually, distraught parents will call the police only after they have made some preliminary efforts to locate the child. When these fail, the parents become more and more concerned and finally, after a critical lapse of time, they call for help as a last resort.

The age of the child has a direct bearing upon the seriousness of the incident. The younger the child, the less capable he is of providing for his own safety.

The officer responding to the call must make a decision about the need for a widespread search or give his superiors information that will help them to do so. This decision must be based upon the child's age and sex, whether he has previously run away, the places he normally plays, the circumstances of his disappearance, the area involved, the attractive hazards located nearby, how long he has been missing, the circumstances under which he was last seen, his mental and physical conditions, his fear of punishment, whether he was recently scolded or punished, and any other facts which might be useful in assessing the type of action that should be taken by the police. If the child has disappeared before, the parents often can provide valuable information as to where he might have gone based on their past experiences. Often they will have checked these places, but the officer should never rely upon a search made by parents, friends, or neighbors. Parents especially will usually look only in the most obvious places. The child's playmates usually can provide the best clues as to his possible whereabouts.

Search of Immediate Area   In many cases, the child is found during the initial investigation made by the first officer at the scene. After he has interviewed parents, playmates, and other persons who might provide information as to what happened, the officer should search the immediate area from which the child disappeared.

Areas inside the house and outside in the immediate vicinity should be thoroughly and systematically inspected even if the parents protest that they have already done this and that time is being wasted by going over the same area again. Many lost children have been found inside their homes or in their yards even though the parents claimed they had made a careful search of those areas. Closets, under beds, unmade beds, garages, sheds, caves, gullies, tree houses, and every conceivable hiding place or places in the immediate area where the child might have wandered should be examined. Containers such as trunks, large tool cases, refrigerators, freezers, boxes, septic tanks, cisterns, etc., should be checked thoroughly even though the door or cover is closed by a hasp or self-activating lock. There have been cases where a playmate has locked a child in such a place—not realizing that he may suffocate—and then panicked and, because of fear, not told anyone what he had done. At times a parent should accompany the officer in the initial search if this is not prohibited by department rules. This will sometimes save time in identifying a child believed to be the one sought.

Organizing a Search   After the officer has searched the immediate area from which the child disappeared and—having considered all the evidence available—concluded that a crime was not involved in the disappearance, he may decide that an extended search is indicated. He should then request aid and make the appropriate notifications to his superiors and other police units that might be involved. If a crime is suggested by the evidence, the officer should notify the officers normally responsible for the investigation of such offenses and be guided by their advice.

The dispatcher should be notified of the child's description, clothing, interests, habits, and play areas, and other information, such as hazards to which the child might be exposed, that should be broadcast to alert other police units that the child is missing. Parents should be instructed to notify the police immediately if the child returns or if other evidence relating to the disappearance is found. Other police units involved in the matter can then be kept informed of progress in the case.

Usually, a supervisory officer will organize a search by a group of officers; however, responsibility for directing the group may be placed upon the officer to whom the call was initially assigned. A command post should be established at the center of operations where progress may be reported by radio. A radio car is usually very adequate for this purpose.

Officers available for the search should be assigned specific areas and given specific instructions for searching depending upon the individual case. Each area assigned should be plotted on a map to avoid duplication of search patterns. Neighbors, boy scouts, and other organizations may volunteer their services in the search. When they do, they should be assigned particular areas in which to concentrate their efforts. They should be placed under the charge of an officer so that they may systematically and methodically cover the widest area most effectively.

House-to-House Search   Search party members should be organized into teams, each preferably of four persons. They should be instructed to start the search at the end of a block nearest the scene and work outward with two searchers on each side of the street. The team should proceed from house to house—two to each side of the street—examining carefully the side yards, alleys, vacant lots, garages, outbuildings, and every conceivable hiding place or hazard in the area.

The most attractive hazards, such as swimming pools, caves, excavations, sumps, storm drains, ditches, wells, gullies, tree houses, construction projects, lumber piles, unsealed box cars, sheds, garages, wooded or brushy areas, etc., should first receive attention. These have many times hidden the body of a child who fell into them or entered and was unable to extricate himself. Residents and their children should be contacted in each dwelling for any information on the lost child's whereabouts. When the dwellings fronting the street on that block have been searched, the four members of the team should meet and compare whatever clues they have uncovered. The search should be continued onto the next block. Meanwhile, at least one unit should be assigned to check playgrounds, parks, public swimming centers, roller rinks, etc., and to follow up other leads the lost child's playmates may have provided.

The extent of the search will be the subject of a command decision. Ordinarily, it will be continued until the child is found.

Open Area Searches   When a child has disappeared in a sparsely settled, brushy, wooded, or mountainous area, helicopters, other aircraft, or dogs trained in tracking may be called into service even though considerable time has elapsed since the child was last seen. If dogs are not available, other persons should be asked to help search. They should be organized into search lines several yards apart to search segments of rough terrain. Lines should be kept intact on a relatively straight line by the search party leader. Periodic halts will allow all searchers to proceed at the same speed and will assure that every conceivable place that may conceal a person is covered. After each area has been searched carefully, it should be plotted on a map. The searchers should then be moved to another area.

The possibility that the child may have been the victim of foul play or kidnapping should not be overlooked. If evidence indicates that the disappearance resulted from a crime, a full investigation should be immediately initiated. Parents should be asked not to make any arrangements with any person for the child's return without first consulting the police.

Found Children

Frequently, a small child who does not know his name, his home address, or his telephone number is found wandering in a business district, a large market place, a parking lot, or a residential area. The police are called and the child is turned over to the patrol officer to locate the parents. The officer should record the details of the incident in his notebook for future reference if needed. He should then contact his dispatcher to determine if an inquiry has been received at the station about the child.

Ordinarily, before calling the police, the parent of a child missing in a business district or at a bus station or the like will search there for him. The officer should therefore remain for a reasonable period at the place where the child was found to give the parents an opportunity to locate him. If this does not occur, the child should be taken to the station. In almost every case, the parent will call there when they fail to find him.

In a residential area, the officer should cruise the immediate area where the child was found looking for his home. Other children should be asked about the identity of the lost child. They can often provide a clue that will enable the police to identify him and his place of residence. If, after a reasonable search, the child's home is not found, he should be taken to the station as in the case of children found in other places.

Unfit Homes

The principle of parens patriae, or the responsibility that the state has as a governmental agency to protect the welfare of children, has been universally followed throughout the nation by lawmakers. In fulfilling this responsibility, they have framed a great body of law designed to protect children from hazards over which they have no control. The obligation to enforce these rules generally is delegated to the police and has become an integral part of the patrol officer's duties. Therefore when he is called to a residence to handle a family dispute, a runaway child, or other type of case, the officer often encounters evidence of child neglect or mistreatment or conditions that are likely to endanger the welfare of the children residing there. He must therefore become familiar with the laws of his jurisdiction and the rules of his agency that specify what courses of action he should follow. He may find that a child has run away from home because it is an unfit place to live. Ordinarily, in unfit home cases it is not necessary to prove that the children have actually been harmed, but it is imperative that there be proof that they are likely to be endangered by the conditions in which they live.

Juvenile investigators should be notified if they are available to handle this type of case. If not, the officer should be guided by the rules applicable to the investigation of other cases.

Evidence of Child Neglect   Symptoms of malnutrition in the children or lack of edible food for them; evidence of improperly cared for injuries and their cause; uncleanliness of the home beyond mere untidyness as reflected by filthy conditions and the presence of vermin; numerous empty liquor containers or spoiled food; unclean or insufficient bedclothes on the children's beds; unsuitable or filthy clothing; hazards such as unvented heaters; evidence of very young children exposed to fire hazards, locked in rooms, or unattended for long periods of time; and any other condition showing that their health and welfare are in danger should be carefully noted and described in an appropriate report along with statements of parents and witnesses that reflect the home as an unfit place for the children. Whenever possible, witnesses should provide testimony concerning the parents' conduct that has contributed to the conditions, the continuing nature of the problem, and the necessity for neighbors to feed the hungry children and otherwise care for them.

Photographs of the unfit home should be taken to portray the physical conditions of the premises. These will add materially to the proof of the case.

Arrest of Parents   When there is enough evidence to arrest the parent or parents and the officer decides to follow that course of action, he must make arrangements for the care of the children. Details of the incident, the disposition of the children, a description of the evidence, and statements of witnesses and concerned parties should be shown in the arrest reports.

Missing Adults

A request for assistance in locating a missing adult should be processed according to the needs of each situation. Often, there are no unusual circumstances involved in the case. The missing person is a husband, wife, or grown child who has caused concern because he or she was unexpectedly delayed and failed to notify the person asking for help. This concern is very real to the worried caller, who should be treated with understanding and reassuring confidence.

The officer might quickly locate the person by checking to determine if he is in a hospital as the result of an accident or is in police custody. Ordinarily, an investigation would not be indicated unless the person had been missing for an inordinate period or under unusual circumstances. A threat to commit suicide, circumstances which might indicate foul play, senility, or mental defect would generally constitute grounds for an investigation. By calling nearby police agencies, the coroner's office, and emergency receiving hospitals, the officer may be able to locate the missing person without a full-scale, follow-up investigation.

When the missing person is senile or mentally incompetent, a search of the area into which he might have wandered may be indicated. It should be conducted much like a search for a lost child except that it should be concentrated upon places where the missing person customarily spends time, such as theaters, the homes of friends or relatives, parks, and nearby shopping centers.

A broadcast of the description of the missing person and his automobile, if he drives one, should be relayed through the dispatcher so that other units may be on the lookout for him. When he is found, the broadcast should be promptly canceled.

Occasionally, the police will be told that a person has not been seen for an unusual period of time and a neighbor, friend, or relative has become concerned. There may be many explanations but the individual bringing the information to the attention of the police has become alarmed after some efforts to locate the missing person have failed. The person may have disappeared as the result of a criminal act, illness, or accident, or may merely have taken a vacation without notifying the informant. In any event, the matter can usually be resolved by the patrol officer with a brief inquiry. Much good will can be generated by his efforts.

The individual reporting the matter should be interviewed to determine the circumstances surrounding the disappearance and the reason for alarm. The age, sex, and health of the missing person; the existence of marital problems or threats to commit suicide; his habits; the names, addresses, and telephone numbers of friends, close relatives, and the employer should be ascertained, along with any other data that may be needed if a full follow-up investigation is indicated.

The officer should then try to determine the whereabouts of the missing person. He should first inquire at place of residence. If there is no response, he should check the garage for the family vehicle and look through windows for evidence of foul play, illness, or accident. Should circumstances indicate that the missing person may be inside and in need of help, the officer should enter the premises. The reporting person should be asked to accompany him when he does and remain with him while he examines the interior.

If the preliminary investigation reveals no evidence that the person is there and does not suggest that a crime has occurred, the officer should try to contact either the missing person's spouse at his or her place of employment, or relatives, or friends in the neighborhood for information that may throw light on the matter. When the person is employed, usually the matter can be clarified by a telephone call to the employer, since few persons will take time off work without informing their employer.

Once the reason for the missing person's absence has been determined, the officer should notify the person who reported the matter to eliminate further concern. Should the circumstances reveal evidence that a missing person follow-up investigation should be initiated, the officer should prepare the appropriate reports describing the action he took and the information obtained during his inquiry.

Disaster Control—General Procedures

There are many types of occurrence that can cause widespread destruction of property, injury, and loss of life. Some of these result from acts of nature, such as floods, fires, tornadoes, and earthquakes. They cannot be prevented but their aftereffects must be controlled.

Other types of disasters result directly or indirectly from the acts of man. Explosions in manufacturing or storage establishments resulting from ruptured gas or chemical containers or from industrial processes, or the release of dangerous fumes or explosive gases from broken conveyance lines can threaten the safety of persons in a wide area. Control measures to prevent further damage from side effects of the occurrence must be swiftly implemented just as in the case of an aircraft crash or a train wreck.

Field Intelligence   With few exceptions, the patrol officer will be the first representative of the police to arrive at the scene of a sudden and unexpected incident of disaster proportions. The speed and effectiveness with which appropriate control measures can be put into operation will depend on the information he collects and makes available to his superiors and other agencies concerned.

The first thing the officer should do is assess rapidly the incident to determine tentatively its nature and scope. He should inform his headquarters of the amount and kind of damage, the number of persons injured and the general nature of their injuries, the amount of medical aid—including ambulances and medical personnel—needed at the scene, and the number of persons dead. He should estimate the amount of equipment necessary if special equipment is needed and rescue specialists have not yet become involved and the number of persons required for vehicle and pedestrian control at the scene and at the perimeter to keep out curious onlookers. He should request assistance to keep rescue routes to and from the area open and to aid at the scene. He should see that public utilities agencies are notified when their property is involved.

As further details become available, the officer should communicate these data to his headquarters so that plans can be promptly revised as indicated. Such communications should be by land line if telephones are available close by. Radio channels can then be kept open for more urgent messages. Logs of police activities at the scene should be kept for future reference.

Invariably, when a catastrophic incident occurs, the patrol officer will be promptly relieved by superiors of his responsibilities for directing police operations. His activities in collecting and providing information during the initial, critical several minutes and the effectiveness with which he initiates controls to keep the immediate area free of persons who will only complicate police procedures will largely determine how effective subsequent measures will be.

Disaster Evacuation Procedures   Determining whether or not to evacuate persons in the area into which the disaster might spread or in the area already affected by it should be the responsibility of the highest ranking personnel available because of the liabilities a governmental agency would suffer from an ill-advised decision. However, when there is imminent peril to persons in the area and quick action is necessary to save them, the officer should not hesitate to initiate evacuation procedures.

Panic can be averted or largely reduced by the demeanor and attitudes of the police. The individual officer can contribute most to the control of such incidents if, by showing confidence, he can calm those who might panic and encourage them to engage in self-help.

Aircraft Accidents

Occasionally, an aircraft crashing in a residential community, on a public highway, or in some populated area will require disaster control procedures because of the magnitude of the problem. It may involve a craft carrying only a pilot and crashing in an isolated area with little damage other than that to the plane, or it may involve a large commercial jetliner causing great property damage and loss of life. The patrol officer usually will be the first agent of government at the scene to initiate rescue and control procedures.

Primary Police Duties   The primary duties of police units in connection with such accidents involving death, injury, and property damage is to render first aid if practicable when ambulance service is not available, to protect the scene from unauthorized removal or disturbance of aircraft cargo or parts, to prevent looting of bodies or baggage, and to make appropriate notifications of the occurrence. Secondary duties of the police include immediate rescue, traffic control at the scene and perimeter, and assisting rescue or fire control units.

As in the case of other accidents, an officer should not try to move seriously injured persons who cannot walk unless they are in danger of further injury from fire, explosion, or chemicals released from the plane. Their removal from the scene should be the responsibility of ambulance crews.

Rescue Precautions   Well-meaning spectators and control personnel at the scene should be kept away from the cockpits of military aircraft unless they are familiar with ejection mechanisms. Almost all such craft are equipped with oxygen and ejectable canopies, seats, and tip tanks. All jet aircraft are equipped with ejectable seats, as are many others. These seats are ejected by an explosive charge activated by a mechanical firing pin or a gas charge. The charge is fired by pulling a seat handle, an arm rest, or a ring located either above the pilot's seat or between his legs. The releases are normally painted conspicuously yellow or yellow and black. They should not be moved, pulled, or otherwise disturbed nor should any other protrusions on the seat itself be manipulated. An accidental release of the ejection charges might cause serious injury or death to the occupants of the plane and the rescuer.[1]

Notification When the immediate aid needed by injured persons has been given, the officer assigned the call should give his dispatcher the details of the accident for notification to concerned agencies. The initial broadcast should include a request for ambulance service to handle injured persons, the circumstances of the accident, the time and place of occurrence, a description of the aircraft including the type and class of craft and number, the owner's name, the pilot's name and address if available, the extent of damage to the craft and other property, the number of passengers, the number injured or killed, the injuries or deaths to others, and whether United States mail was in the cargo.

If a military aircraft was involved, the type of aircraft and other details concerning its cargo, explosives, and armament should be included, as well as data which will help rescue units reach the scene. In this respect, exact locations, landmarks, and available locations that will accommodate helicopters are important. This information will enable the dispatcher to promptly notify the postal authorities, if United States mail was involved, the Civil Aeronautics Board, the Civil Aeronautics Administration, or the military authorities, who will make appropriate investigations.

Isolating the Scene In the absence of a supervisory officer at the scene, the patrol officer assigned the call must take steps to minimize the number of spectators. A traffic perimeter should be decided upon to divert motor vehicle and pedestrian traffic away from the scene and to enable emergency equipment and personnel to enter and leave the area. Other officers can then be directed to specific posts in the traffic perimeter by the dispatcher. Appropriate instructions should be relayed to them from the officer in charge at the scene.

---

[1] Los Angeles Police Department, *Training Manual of the Accident Investigation Division*, 1971, pp. 186–187.

Photographs of Aircraft   The officer investigating the incident should take photographs of the accident for use in the investigation. Military aircraft should not be photographed[2] unless this is requested by authorized military personnel. Authorized reporters should not be prevented from taking pictures since military authorities are responsible for control of such photographs; however, spectators should be discouraged from photographing any military aircraft. Those observed doing so should be identified and reported to military authorities.

Reporting   Data necessary for the death, injury, or traffic accident report—or a memorandum report if the foregoing are not required—should be collected. Witnesses' names, addresses, telephone numbers, and statements should be included. In the investigation, the officer should attempt to determine if a violation of the law was involved in the accident and collect evidence for prosecution of the offender.

Removal of Aircraft from Highway   If the aircraft has crashed on a public roadway where it might jeopardize the safety of motorists, the officer should cause the appropriate agencies to be notified so that the aircraft may be removed promptly. When military craft are involved, military personnel should supervise the removal.

Explosives and Infernal Devices

Modern police operations bring with them modern methods of harassing the agents of law. The patrol officer is vulnerable to injury from homemade bombs or explosive devices in even the most routine call. The technical aspects of such instruments of destruction are complex and voluminous and cannot feasibly be incorporated in a text of this nature. Some general safety rules are included here so that the patrol officer may at least become aware of the hazards of handling potentially dangerous explosives and explosive devices and of booby traps.

Danger from Explosives in Containers   Three dangers arise from the ignition of explosives in containers—projectiles resulting from fragmentation of the container and the expulsion of fragments in the container, blast or concussion that occurs on ignition, and

[2] *United States Code*, Title 18, Section 791.

incendiary action. Fragments inside containers such as nuts, bolts, nails, scrap metal, metal chips, and other projectiles which are thrown by the explosive blast can have devastating effects. They have the destructive capacity of a fragmentation grenade. The blast itself poses a threat because of the tremendous speed at which the shock waves travel, especially when the explosion occurs inside an enclosed building. The vacuum or suction effect that follows the blast wave often causes almost as much damage as the initial compression wave. Incendiary action, consisting of a flash of flame and heat, may ignite other explosive or flammable substances.

Handling Explosives

The officer responding to a call involving an explosive substance or explosive device should call an expert if he has the slightest doubt about his ability to handle the materials involved properly. Most explosive devices are simple homemade bombs consisting of an explosive material and a trigger.

Bombs may be of any size or shape from a short, capped pipe to a shoebox or suitcase. Almost any object *may* contain a hidden bomb. Its trigger may be made from very simple or very sophisticated materials. Common clothespins, mousetraps, mercury or other electrical switches, thermostats, clocks, electronic devices, pressure, release of pressure, chemicals, and trip or pull wires are a few of the types of triggers which may set off an explosive charge. The slightest movement of a bomb rigged to an electrical switch may cause a lethal blast. It is therefore imperative that the officer assume the very worst if he has the slightest suspicion that a container of any type is rigged with a trigger and an explosive.

The trigger mechanism is ordinarily the most dangerous part of a bomb. Therefore, any package an officer suspects of containing an explosive and a trigger should be left to experts. An inexperienced officer risks his life and those of others if he touches, moves, carries, or transports this kind of device. Explosives without triggers are, with the exception of nitroglycerin, relatively safe to handle if common-sense procedures are followed.

Black powder is one of the most popular of the explosives used to construct homemade bombs[3] because the necessary ingredients can

---

[3] Joseph F. Stoffel, *Explosives and Homemade Bombs*, Charles C Thomas, Publisher, Springfield, Ill., 1970, p. 11.

be obtained easily. It may be manufactured in shiny black or brown granular or pellet form. It is used primarily in mines and is frequently stolen from mine stocks for illegitimate civilian purposes.

Black powder is extremely sensitive to sparks, static electricity, heat, flame, or friction.[4] Obviously, then, if the officer *must* transport a container of black powder or a homemade bomb constructed with it, he should be very careful. He should not smoke anywhere near it. If he has to touch it, he should ground his body to a pipe immediately before handling it to eliminate static electricity. He should avoid handling it with a metal tool, but should use a non-sparking material. If it must be transported, the back seat away from any radio components is probably the safest location.[5]

Smokeless powder is easy to obtain in bulk from stores handling ammunition reloading components or from shotgun ammunition. It is therefore frequently encountered by law enforcement officers. It is manufactured in black, amber, or brownish flakes or grains for loading ammunition and is easily recognized. It is considerably less sensitive than black powder and can be transported reasonably safely in a sealed container. Precautions should be taken against heat or flame.

If it is in a sealed container with a triggering device, it may be easily exploded by applying percussion to the primer, just as when the firing pin of a firearm strikes the primer and explodes powder in a cartridge. Therefore, great care should be exercised in handling an explosive device constructed in this fashion.

Nitroglycerin is an extremely powerful and dangerous explosive occasionally encountered by an officer investigating the burglary of a safe. It may, however, be used for other purposes. It is a yellowish, brownish, or milky liquid if impure but may be a clear liquid if pure. Because of its extreme sensitivity to heat, shock, and friction, it should *never* be touched or handled by an officer. At times, it may explode spontaneously. Stoffel[6] recommends that an expert use chemicals to dispose of it where it is found.

Dynamite is commonly packaged in stick or cartridge form, usually in manila paper treated with wax. It is ordinarily easily recognized because the manufacturer's containers are well marked. It is easy to obtain from mining, farm, or construction operations and is therefore often used in the construction of explosive devices.

---

[4] Robert R. Lenz, *Explosives and Bomb Disposal Guide*, Charles C Thomas, Publisher, Springfield, Ill., 1970, p. 36.
[5] Stoffel, *Explosives and Homemade Bombs*, pp. 11–12.
[6] Stoffel, *Explosives and Homemade Bombs*, p. 14.

If it is found or turned over to an officer and is unfused, it may be transported if necessary by sealing loose sticks in a cardboard box and transporting it in the back seat of the car with common-sense safety precautions taken against heat and fire. It cannot be over-stressed that *fused or triggered explosive devices* may operate as booby traps and be exploded by inexpert handling.

T.N.T. or *trinitrotoluene* is used almost exclusively in military am-munition but sometimes finds its way into civilian use through theft. It is seldom encountered by the police officer and when found or turned over to him is not particularly dangerous if it is not fused and is handled with common sense. Smoking and fire precautions should be observed, however. It should be handed over to the military.

Plastic explosive is a pure white, dirty white, or brownish putty-like substance seldom encountered outside the military. If it does not contain a detonator, it should be handled with the same care as T.N.T.

Military munitions of all types have often been collected as souve-nirs and brought to this country. Such objects frequently come to the attention of law enforcement personnel. These items may be ex-tremely dangerous regardless of age, and no attempt should ever be made to disassemble them.

Except for small-arms ammunition with which he is familiar, an officer should not handle military munitions. Rather, he should call upon the military to dispose of it. Until military personnel take charge of the object, he should keep all persons away from it.

Fixed ammunition under 50 caliber, fireworks, railroad flares and fuses, and tear gas canisters and projectiles can be transported safely if common-sense precautions are taken. Unnecessary handling of these items should be avoided.

Usually departmental regulations will specify how explosives should be processed. When there is any doubt about their disposition, the officer should consult an expert.

Bomb Threats

As explosive devices become more sophisticated and easier to con-struct and as militancy against the establishment becomes more widespread, the patrol officer will be called upon more and more to take action of some sort in bomb threat calls. Often the caller will only wish to destroy property. He may indicate when the bomb is to be exploded so that persons in the vicinity can be evacuated. More often, however, the caller will warn of the impending explosion without indicating when it will happen or the location of the explosive device.

Bomb Threat Notifications   The patrol officer, usually being the first representative of the police present at the scene, should immediately survey the scene and notify his headquarters by telephone of the circumstances. The dispatcher should alert other agencies which might be involved if circumstances so indicate. Planned courses of action, which every department should have developed to cover such contingencies, should then be put into effect.

Evacuation Responsibility   When a threat is made against a business establishment, industrial concern, school, or other public building, it is the responsibility of the person in charge of the building concerned to decide whether to evacuate occupants to a safe location. Usually this responsibility falls upon the principal or president of a school or the person in charge of other public or private buildings. They will, however, almost invariably seek the advice of the police representative at the scene. The problem should be discussed privately with the person in charge to avoid rumors and alarm. It is far wiser for the officer to be overly conservative and advise an evacuation which later proves unnecessary than to advise against evacuation when it should have taken place. There is always an element of doubt in such cases until a complete and thorough search has been made. However, the officer's first consideration obviously must be for the safety of persons who might be injured if the bomb exploded.

In schools—especially at the lower levels, which have not been centers of conflict and dissent—many bomb threats are made by students who want a recess or a holiday from school. Some schools treat every such call as bona fide until a search can be made, then require students to make up the time lost. This ordinarily discourages further false reports.

Whether to evacuate schools and other public buildings is a difficult decision for public officials because of the disruptive influence such action has on operations and the liability always present. The decision to evacuate will depend upon many factors such as the possible motives for destroying a building and its occupants, recent disorders or threats involving that particular facility or similar ones, the nature of the facility and the type of operations in which it engages, impending labor difficulties, disgruntled employees, etc. Common sense at this time is imperative.

Bomb Threat Evacuation Procedures If evacuation is indicated, all persons except authorized control personnel should be moved out of the immediate area. How far they should be moved will depend upon numerous factors, among which are the existence and types of shelters which might act as shields in the area, the nature of the area surrounding the building, the type of building threatened, etc. The usual fire drill procedures should be avoided, since they ordinarily involve shutting off lights and closing doors and windows. Turning off lights may trigger a device rigged to the switch. The closing of windows and doors will cause unnecessary property damage from the blast effect if an explosion occurs.

Persons in surrounding buildings should be notified of the potential danger if possible. Doors and windows in these buildings should be opened to reduce the concussion effect should a bomb explode. Occupants should be instructed to remain in the side of the building furthest from the place where an explosion might occur to avoid injury from flying glass and other debris.

The person in charge should be warned of the possibility of thefts if the building is cleared. It should be suggested that he post guards to keep unauthorized persons out of the building while the search is taking place.

If the person making the threat has indicated a specific time at which the bomb is to explode, personnel searching the premises should allow themselves a reasonable time to clear the area. They should not return until at least five minutes after the specified time of detonation. Traffic must be diverted if it is exposed to blast danger. Gas and other utilities that might aggravate an explosion should be shut off.

Bomb Search Whenever there is reasonable cause to believe that a bomb or explosive device has been hidden in a building, a search is justified. A telephone or other threat provides such reasonable cause. The courts have held that the search may extend considerably further in this type of case than in ordinary searches, and a warrant is not required because of the urgency of the search.[7]

When an explosive device is hidden in a building easily accessible to many persons, it can easily be so well hidden that it is almost impossible to find without a very thorough search. In such a case, the danger to searching personnel is increased.

Once it has been decided that a search of the premises should be made, the search should be conducted as quickly and thoroughly as

---

[7] *People v. Superior Court*, C.A. 1, 1 Civ. 27716 (1970).

possible under the circumstances of the particular case. A minimum number of searchers should be used. A basic search plan should be made, taking into consideration the probable amount of time available and the area to be searched.

Officers will find that a mirror, a flashlight, or a good penlight will help them search under furniture and in crevices. A combination screwdriver set will be useful in removing or unscrewing wall plates or receptacle covers.

A person familiar with the building—especially custodial personnel—should accompany each searching officer to point out objects foreign to the area. These persons should be instructed not to touch anything to avoid triggering a bomb. Keeping in mind that the mere opening of a drawer may trip a trigger and cause an explosion, searching personnel should inspect closets, storage or records compartments, in and about furniture or equipment, in ventilation shafts, behind inspection plates or doors, in trash or waste containers, under stairwells, in fire boxes, and in every place where a bomb could be concealed with relative ease. Lunch racks, brief cases, objects that appear to have been left behind, or things that appear to be out of the ordinary because of either their location or their nature should be suspected of concealing a bomb. Once a bomb is located, the damage it can cause can easily be minimized.

If no bomb is found, the officer should so advise the person in charge of the facility. *He should not, however, state or imply that the building is safe.*

Protection to Building   Should a bomb be discovered, experienced bomb disposal personnel equipped with protective devices should be summoned to remove or disarm it. The radio should not be used to call, as the radio waves might trigger the explosive charge.

Hand-carrying the bomb without protection may be essential in very unusual cases, but it should be avoided if possible. Before doing so, unless the bomb clearly poses no danger to him, the officer should weigh the feasibility of moving it remotely with cords or other protective encasements, blowing it in place, or sandbagging it until it can be removed safely. Sandbags properly placed will deflect the blast and reduce the danger from fragmentation.

Booby Traps

Soldiers are trained to watch for booby traps at all times when entering abandoned facilities, bunkers, or other places recently occupied by the enemy. Since more and more of these devices are being used by militants to destroy their greatest enemies—the police—officers should likewise be alert for such hazards.

Trip devices and triggering mechanisms attached to fragmentation bombs can be simply constructed and easily installed to kill or maim unsuspecting officers. The triggers may be electronically activated by radio waves, temperature changes, movement, electricity, light beams, etc., or activated mechanically by trip wires, pressure, release of pressure, switches, etc.

The officer entering a building or other facility presently or recently occupied by such militants must be extremely careful to avoid triggering a booby trap. If possible, he should obtain the assistance of an expert before entering, but he must usually enter without such assistance or advice. In doing so, doors or windows should be opened very carefully with a baton or long stick. If the officer enters a door immediately after a suspect has entered, the likelihood of the suspect's having had time to set the trigger of an explosive device should be considered.

Fragmentation devices are lethal when they explode. Consequently the officer must shield himself as best he can by standing to the side of a door or below a window when opening it. An open door or window does not guarantee that that passageway is free of a trap. A light beam across the opening may trigger a bomb when the ray is broken.

Items which appear to be evidence may be left lying around intentionally to prompt an officer to pick them up. In doing so, he may trigger a booby trap. Even the most innocent clothespin, mousetrap, or boxtop may trigger an explosive charge. Therefore, if *visual* examination reveals a possible trap, the item should be touched only by an expert who is trained to disarm it. All other personnel should be removed from the immediate area until it is safe to return.

Fires

Officers of every police department are called upon from time to time to aid firemen in a variety of places. Buildings are burned accidentally or on purpose; brushy areas, vacant lots, or open fields covered with weeds or grass are ignited by incendiaries, by children playing with matches or fire, or by careless smokers, campers, motorists, etc.

Often the patrol officer arrives before the fire fighting personnel. His primary concern is to control motorists or pedestrians who interfere with firemen. Anti-looting patrol at times becomes part of his primary responsibility. He may even engage in rescue operations and render medical aid under some circumstances.

Summoning Fire Control Personnel and Equipment   Whenever the patrol officer observes or learns of a fire, he should notify his dispatcher. He should never assume that some other person has notified the fire department.

The initial information transmitted should be as complete as possible. It should include the type and size of fire, a description of the area, the property involved, the type of area and structures which are immediately endangered, the direction of any wind, its velocity, its potential effect on the fire, unusual circumstances present, and the actual or likely effect the fire may have on public utilities. If the fire or sightseers have obstructed some of the routes into the fire zone, he should so notify his dispatcher and should recommend alternative streets that provide access for emergency equipment.

If there is no immediate need to evacuate persons from the surrounding area and a supervisor is not present to assume command, the officer should evaluate the perimeter and recommend what additional police personnel should be deployed. He should specify where they should be stationed and what equipment, such as barricades, rope, etc., they may need to screen vehicular and pedestrian traffic into the area and keep emergency routes clear.

He should also assess what additional police personnel might be needed at the fire site to control traffic. If he is to assume control of police operations at the scene, he should consult with the person in charge of fire operations to determine what police assistance is needed. A command post should then be established near the fire department command post. The radio car is usually satisfactory for that purpose and will provide an adequate communications medium with headquarters in most situations. Should continuous communications be necessary regarding the progress of the fire, land lines should be used if they are available to avoid unnecessary interference with radio transmissions related to other police matters.

Fire Evacuations   When the fire is of such magnitude that it is likely to imperil occupants of nearby buildings, residents of recreational camps in brushy or woody canyon areas, or those in densely built residential communities, he should take steps to notify them of the impending danger. His major efforts should be directed toward that end. The siren, horn, and loud speaker or bullhorn—if the police car is so equipped—should be used for this purpose although, especially at night, in isolated areas where persons may not hear the warnings from the street, or when they don't acknowledge that they heard, the officer may find it necessary to notify them in person. Aged persons, those with impaired hearing, and those who sleep soundly may not hear a routine warning given from a moving vehicle. When too wide an area is involved for one patrol officer, additional help may be required to make these notifications.

The decision to evacuate an area should be carefully weighed, as in any other evacuation case. Consideration must be given to the liability that may exist either when persons rely on a warning, abandon their property unnecessarily, and suffer damages as a result or when injuries or deaths result from a failure on the part of the police to give a reasonable warning when it is possible to do so. Officers should therefore familiarize themselves with the pertinent laws of their particular jurisdiction so that their judgments do not result in civil liability to them or their agencies.

The officer fulfills his primary responsibility of protecting lives when he warns endangered persons about a spreading fire and helps them to leave the area safely. If their property is not directly involved and if they desire to stay on it in an attempt to save it from the spreading fire, it would be ill-advised to force them to leave if they refuse to do so. Exceptional cases where the person does not have control of his mental or physical faculties may dictate another course of action. Aged, young, crippled, or sick persons may require special assistance to enable them to avoid being trapped by a fire.

Depending upon the type of area endangered, occupants of buildings should be advised to take whatever preventive measures possible to protect their property if they are threatened by a spreading fire. They should close all doors, windows, and venetian blinds in all buildings. If the fire is confined to stairways in a multistory apartment or other building, the door to the roof should be opened to keep the fire from spreading laterally to adjacent rooms.

Brush Fires   If a brush fire is threatening an area and if time permits, residents should be advised to remove inflammable curtains, garden furniture, and combustibles—especially those near gas or butane tanks—from around buildings. Combustibles that may be ignited by the heat should be moved to a safe place.

Residents should be told to connect hoses and leave them in an easily seen location. Available ladders should be placed where they can be seen and used by fire fighters to gain access to the roof to quench burning embers that may light there. Vents should be sealed if practicable to prevent drafts and lessen the danger of ignition. Lights should be left burning to discourage looters.

Anti-looting Operations   Frequently, where large areas are affected by fire, sightseers and thieves will penetrate to the inner area before the outer perimeter is closed. Some will be mere spectators who clutter the streets and impede fire-fighting operations. Others will go into an area where persons have been forced to abandon their property with the specific intent of stealing objects that are not safeguarded.

Officers assigned to anti-looting patrol must be alert for those who take advantage of a fire disaster to steal. Persons in the area should be required to identify themselves and should be checked for possession of apparently stolen property. If they have no legitimate business there and live elsewhere, they should be instructed to leave if legal authority exists for doing so. If not, a record should be made of the contact so that they may later be identified if necessary.

Identifying Suspects   Circumstances in some cases may justify the arrest of unauthorized persons in the fire area. They may be thieves, burglars, or arsonists and may be prime suspects for the arson investigators to question if it is determined that the fire was of incendiary origin.

Persons in or near the fire zone carrying wooden matches or having in their possession a spring-type clothespin or paper matches affixed to a cigarette or any such device which is often used by arsonists should be the subject of an intense inquiry. Investigators responsible for the follow-up investigation should be notified of any such device found on a suspect.

Personal Safety Precautions in Fires

When an officer carries an evacuation warning to residents of a community threatened by a brush fire, he faces a number of hazardous conditions himself. Experience indicates that following the safety procedures recommended by the United States Forestry Service and the Los Angeles Fire Department[8] substantially lowers the

---

[8] Los Angeles Police Department, "Police Action at a Brush Fire," *Patrol Bureau Memorandum No. 23* (unpublished), July 18, 1963, pp. 18–19.

risk of injury or death from the fire. Should the officer become trapped on foot in a brush fire because of a shift in the wind or some miscalculation on his part, he should avoid the immediate impulse to try to outrun the blaze. To do so may be disastrous. Rather, he should take refuge in the nearest residence or join firemen, if possible, and be guided by their actions. Should he seek shelter in a house, he should close all doors and windows, draw drapes, and proceed to the center of the building. If the fire penetrates the house, the closed doors will slow its progress from room to room. Before the house becomes untenable, the major part of the fire on the outside will usually have moved past and survival outside will be possible.

High ground above the fire should be avoided because of the danger from smoke and heat drafts. These can cause death from heat or suffocation due to the lack of oxygen.

When the officer finds it necessary to drive through the fire, he should close all the windows and vents of his car to exclude heat and smoke from the interior, turn on his headlights, and proceed slowly to safety. He should avoid leaving the protection of his car, but, should he have to do so to make a notification, he should not shut off the motor as the heat may affect the starting mechanism so that it cannot be restarted.

Should he find it necessary to park his vehicle, he should move it off the roadway where it might impede the movement of emergency equipment or be struck by a driver whose vision is restricted by the smoke. The safest and most practicable way to avoid such hazards is to back the vehicle into a driveway so that it can be moved quickly back onto the street with maximum visibility.

If the officer is trapped by the fire and it is not practicable to drive through it, he should try to park behind a building or other available cover on the far side of the fire, keep all windows and vents closed, keep his motor running, and wait until the fire passes. The interior of the car will withstand great heat and will not ordinarily become untenable if fire does not penetrate.

Summary

Standard operating procedures will normally have to be only slightly modified to handle the many special problems the police are called upon to deal with. Most of these do not involve criminal matters but offer a splendid opportunity to provide service, assistance, or protection to the public.

One of the most important of all calls from a public service standpoint is a request for help from a parent whose child has vanished. The officer should collect all pertinent facts which may give him a clue to the child's whereabouts. Usually, the missing child will be found in the immediate neighborhood, or even within his own home in an unmade bed, under it, in a closet, in the garage, or in some other place where he has hidden, fallen asleep, or wandered to play.

When the child cannot be located in the initial search and a criminal act is not suspected, an organized house-to-house search of an extended area may be indicated. If such a search is initiated, it should be conducted in a systematic, methodical manner to make sure that all places where the child might conceivably be are examined.

In woody, brushy, or mountainous areas, dogs trained in such searches may be used to locate a child who has wandered away from his parents or become lost. These areas pose special search problems because of the need to cover every bush and patch of foliage that may conceal a child.

When a child is found wandering unattended in a parking lot, a shopping center, or a residential area and does not know his name, address, or telephone number, the officer should not immediately leave the vicinity to search for the child's parents, but should remain there for a reasonable period. Usually the parents will begin a search when they discover the child is missing. If after a reasonable period they have not made themselves known, the lost child should be taken to the police station, where the parents almost invariably will call.

The procedures for handling a missing adult call will vary slightly from those followed in locating a missing child. In many cases, adults who have been reported missing have merely failed to inform their families that they would be delayed. Elderly, senile, or mentally incompetent persons occasionally wander away and cause concern to those responsible for them. They often are found visiting friends or neighbors or in a nearby park or theater.

Calls to receiving hospitals and nearby police departments sometimes reveal that the missing person has been involved in an accident or is in police custody. Often a call to his place of employment will provide information that will relieve the anxiety of those concerned.

The patrol officer's primary role in a disaster caused by an earthquake, conflagration, train wreck, plane crash, explosion, or the like involves the implementation of control measures designed to protect life and property from the aftereffects of the occurrence. He must collect and transmit field intelligence to headquarters regarding the nature, extent, and effect of the happening so that disaster control measures can be put into operation.

Standard procedures usually include the control of pedestrians and vehicular traffic at the immediate scene and at the outer perimeter.

Emergency routes into and out of the area must be kept open. Spectators and unauthorized persons must be excluded so that they will not impede disaster control operations. Evacuation should be implemented only when there is imminent peril to persons in an affected area. Interior patrols should be maintained to prevent looting of evacuated areas. Rescue, medical relief, and fire-fighting activities are normally the responsibility of specialists.

When the patrol officer is called upon to handle a call involving a box, package, or object thought to contain an explosive device, he should assume the very worst. If there is the slightest suspicion that it has a triggering mechanism, he should not open a suspected box or package or touch, move, tilt, or lift any other suspected object. An expert should be summoned to remove or deactivate it.

Occasionally a warning that a bomb has been planted in an industrial plant, school, or other structure will be received. While the officer is not responsible for the decision to evacuate a building, his advice is often solicited. He should carefully assess the probabilities of a bomb having actually been concealed before giving such advice. He should be ultraconservative in his appraisal of the matter. It would be far wiser to advise the person in charge to evacuate the premises when later events prove it was unnecessary than to advise against evacuation when developments indicate it should have taken place.

Review

Questions

1. Why should you not rely upon parents' assurances that they have searched the immediate area surrounding their home when their four-year-old child has been missing for five hours?
2. What are some of the most obvious places to look for a missing child around his home?
3. Why should you look into a large chest when you are searching for a lost child even though the hasp is closed from the outside?
4. What are some of the factors that would probably justify an immediate search for a missing aged woman in an urban area?
5. What are the primary duties of police units at the scene of a large aircraft accident?
6. What colors are canopy and seat ejection levers in military aircraft?
7. How are the explosive charges for ejection equipment fired on military aircraft? Where are the releases usually located?
8. What are the three dangers from explosives in containers?

9. What are some common devices used to trigger homemade bombs?
10. What is the most dangerous component of a bomb?
11. How should black powder be handled?
12. Describe nitroglycerin. What would you do if you found a small vial of this substance at the scene of a safe burglary?
13. What precautions should be observed in handling T.N.T.?
14. Who is responsible for deciding whether or not a building should be evacuated if a bomb threat has been received?
15. What is a booby trap?
16. What are some of the most common methods of triggering booby traps?
17. Why should a person avoid high ground above an intense fire?

Exercises

1. In order to evaluate the case, what information should you get from a parent whose six-year-old son has been missing from home for twelve hours?
2. Explain how you would organize a house-to-house search for a missing five-year-old girl.
3. Explain how a search for a small child should be conducted in a brushy, mountainous area.
4. Describe how you would handle a found three-year-old child in a large shopping district parking lot; in a residential area.
5. How do searches for aged or senile persons differ from those involving small children?
6. Explain what you would do if a person called you and asked for help in finding out what happened to her friend and neighbor, a forty-year-old widow, who has not been seen around for several days.
7. Explain how you would develop a case against a parent in a child neglect case involving an unfit home.
8. Enumerate the standard police operating procedures in disaster control operations.
9. Describe some of the hazards that the officer should be aware of at the scene of a military aircraft crash.
10. If you were assigned a call to a small industrial building covering about one-quarter of a square block and containing manufacturing area and office space occupied by fifty persons and were told by the manager that he had just received a telephone call that a bomb was concealed in the plant and would be exploded in one-half hour, what action would you take?
11. Explain how an evacuation of the building in item 10 should be carried out.

12. Explain how a search for a bomb in a large building should be conducted.
13. Explain how you would enter a building fifteen minutes after it had been vacated by militants because of the arrival of police.
14. What should you tell householders to do to protect their property if they are forced to leave their homes because of an approaching brush fire?
15. Explain what you should do if you are trapped on foot by a brush fire.

13

Unusual Incident Control

The increasing frequency with which the police are expected to take affirmative action to control legal groups of people or those who band together illegally to disrupt the orderly processes of government makes it imperative that every officer understand his role in dealing with such problems. These incidents may be sit-ins, parades, marches, or peaceable assemblies with relatively few minor disturbances or they may involve massive civil disorder. Even when limited to a few persons, they may be symptomatic of other smoldering and potentially dangerous social conflicts. Frequently, thousands of persons may be involved requiring a major effort of government to control. Often, disputes between labor and management over economic issues are the source of these conflicts. The police must intervene when it becomes necessary to protect the innocent members of society from becoming victimized by such events.

Those who assemble peaceably without encroaching upon the rights of others are constitutionally within their rights. When they

317

go beyond the reasonable restrictions imposed on them and transgress the rights of others, the justification for assembling and speaking freely may disappear.

Whatever form these conflicts take, the police have the duty to preserve the peace, to protect the rights of all persons, to arrest those who commit crimes, and to prevent and suppress fights. This role does not include the suppression or restraint of any lawful activity. Momboisse[1] stated, "the police have neither the authority nor the responsibility to adjudicate or solve the social and legal problems which inspire demonstrations and acts of civil disobedience."

Organized unlawful activity is a different matter. Those who disregard laws they believe to be unfair must be made to understand that the consequences of their acts will be unattractive. Interfering with the orderly conduct of business, blocking traffic on roads or sidewalks, or occupying public buildings is not a constitutional right.

The tactics utilized by law enforcement agencies to control large gatherings—orderly or disorderly—usually are developed for group action by a considerable number of police personnel. Officers should be trained to act in concert in contemplation of the increasing number of conflicts with which they must deal. The objective here is to familiarize the patrol officer with those facets of the problem that apply to him and to let him know how he can best handle them when individual action must be taken.

Special Events

While proper planning for policing athletic contests, parades, festivals, and the like is the responsibility of commanders, the effectiveness of the overall strategy depends upon the manner in which individual officers perform their duties. The patrol officer's performance is especially significant, because the patrol force ordinarily provides most of the control personnel for such events.

Athletic Contests   The factions that are almost invariably present at athletic events are frequently the source of small fights. These should be broken up immediately to keep them from spreading to larger groups. Drinking may contribute to such conflicts. Usually the person drinking and annoying others should be asked to leave if he

---

[1] Raymond M. Momboisse, *Riots, Revolts and Insurrections*, Charles C Thomas, Publisher, Springfield, Ill., 1967, p. 308.

is likely to precipitate a fight. If he refuses to leave and an arrest becomes necessary for drunkenness in public, disturbing the peace, fighting, assault, etc., additional officers should be summoned to assist. The offender then should be removed swiftly and quietly.

Usually an arrest should be avoided if the problem can be otherwise resolved. The officer should not assume an authoritarian, officious manner in dealing with such problems. It seldom is as effective as a friendly but firm attitude and may provoke unnecessary violence.

Political Meetings

Political meetings can be especially volatile, because they are likely to attract agitators from opposing parties. Ordinarily, control of major political meetings involves large scale police operations; yet the individual officer can contribute immensely to maintaining peace by refusing to overreact to attempts to force a confrontation on him. The ultimate goal of some agitators at the Chicago Democratic National Convention of 1968[2] was to topple what they considered the corrupt establishment by impeding orderly processes of government and to expose authorities to ridicule and embarrassment. They used any incident that could be construed as police overreaction as a justification for their conduct. Each officer should therefore recognize this strategy. The techniques of causing overreaction of control personnel are described later in this chapter.

Parades

An officer assigned to parade duty should be particularly attentive to his personal appearance. He will be closely observed by hundreds or even thousands of spectators, and, as he exemplifies the image of law enforcement in the community, his appearance and demeanor should be faultless.

As such details often extend over a considerable period, he should eat before reporting for duty and avoid spicy foods which may make his breath offensive.

If the officer is assigned to the parade formation areas he should prevent unauthorized persons or vehicles from entering the parade after it has started, and they should not be permitted to enter parade

---

[2] City of Chicago, *The Strategy of Confrontation—Chicago and the National Democratic Convention—1968*, The Gunthorp-Warren Printing Co., Chicago, 1968, p. 49.

lines elsewhere along the route. This will help in controlling the cadence of the parade.

When the officer assigned to the parade line arrives at his post, he should try to seat children on the curbs in front of the spectators. This technique has been found effective in discouraging those in the rear from pushing forward, because parents generally will resist surges that may endanger their children.

Wherever possible, he should face the crowd to be in a favorable position to foresee problems as they develop. His job is to maintain order and protect the onlookers—not to watch the parade. He should, however, face it to salute the flag when it first passes. He should repeat the salute each time the flag passes only if his attention is not required elsewhere.

When spectators overcrowd certain places of observation, he should thin the group or change its position by directing his request to individuals instead of the group as a whole. When directing instructions or suggestions to the spectators, he should do so in a loud, clear voice without any suggestion of officiousness. Lack of tact will not make an unruly crowd cooperative.

Spectators should not be permitted to stray out of the specified spectator area into the parade zone. Because of the limited visibility of drivers of decorated parade vehicles, children are sometimes injured when they run in front of horses or vehicles to pick up candy, flowers, or small playthings. This practice should be discouraged at the planning stage, but when it occurs the officer should be alert that the youngsters do not run into the street and become casualties.

Routes should be kept open at the rear of the spectator lines to permit persons on foot to enter and leave the area. Selected intersections should also be kept free of spectators to permit the passage of emergency equipment if necessary. When the parade ends and congestion becomes severe, officers assigned to direct traffic should follow the techniques described in Chapter 8, using plans developed beforehand for the event.

Sightseeing Crowds   Many incidents draw curious sightseers who annoy governmental units attempting to control the effects of the occurrence. The attraction should be removed as soon as practicable to avoid any problem. Spectators may steal from injured or dead persons, hinder rescue and control operations, and generally become a nuisance.

A crowd of curious onlookers will gather rapidly at the scene of any heavy concentration of police, a traffic accident, arrest, fight, fire, or similar incident. Such crowds fortunately are usually orderly. Under normal conditions they are not a significant problem to law enforcement except for the congestion and confusion they cause moving from one place to another.

These groups are usually transient, with spectators gathering, staying until their curiosity is satisfied, and leaving—to be replaced by others who go through the same process. However, when this transient development stops—when they arrive but do not leave—the phenomenon should alert the officer that trouble may be developing or that control measures are ineffective. The stimulation that brought them to the scene either has not been removed or has grown so attractive that the crowd will continue to increase and become a bigger problem than the original incident.

The danger always exists that the situation will be exploited by persons desiring a confrontation with the police. When a crowd develops into a mob—an unreasoning, violent group with no respect for law—it becomes of great concern to the police.

Civil Disorder

The riot that occurred in the Watts section of Los Angeles in 1965 is an example of how a crowd formed at the scene of an ordinary arrest and turned swiftly into a riotous mob as the result of a minor conflict between officers and the arrestee. The riot involved perhaps ten thousand persons who took to the streets in marauding bands for six days. Damage of over 40 million dollars resulted in addition to the untold misery and hardships suffered by an entire community.[3] Although the riot may eventually have been precipitated by some other incident, the fact that it occurred in connection with a minor police action stresses the need for officers to be sensitive to latent hostility that might flare into violence at any time.

Field Intelligence Sound planning depends largely on the intelligence gathered from all field forces. It is thus imperative that all officers performing their normal duties report the existence of volatile rumors promptly. These may then be properly evaluated and utilized as a basis for decisions regarding control measures in case mob violence occurs.

[3] State of California, "Violence in the City—an End or a Beginning," *A Report by the Governor's Commission on the Los Angeles Riots*, Sacramento, California State Printing Office, December 2, 1965, pp. 1–9.

Beat officers have many sources of information available to them. They should be alert for any evidence of unrest in the community. Acts of ·hostility toward government agencies, especially the police, an increase in the number of rumors, and evidence that conflicts are developing and grievances are increasing are clues that demand attention. Field personnel should be alert for information which might reveal the objectives of a group planning a demonstration, the strategy to be followed, any plans for embarrassing the control personnel, weapons and tactics to be used, etc., and should convey it to their superiors promptly. Seemingly unrelated bits of information may provide a rather extensive picture of an incipient disorder. Such information is vital in evaluating the seriousness of tension and grievances in a community that may give rise to social conflicts. Handbills espousing demonstrations, changes in behavioral patterns of persons in a neighborhood, many strangers in groups, etc., are examples of information which should be passed on. This information, even though not supported by substantive evidence, should be conveyed promptly to superior officers for evaluation, collation, and operational use.

The Department of the Army[1] lists twenty-one critical items of information required for sound planning and operations for civil disorder control:

1. Objectives of riotous elements.
2. Times and locations of disturbances.
3. Causes of disturbances.
4. Identity of individuals, groups, or organizations who will create the disturbances.
5. Estimated number of people who will be involved.
6. Probable assembly areas for crowds.
7. Presence and location of known leaders and agitators.
8. Organization and activities planned by the leaders.
9. Prominent people, newspapers, radio or television stations, and friends and sympathizers who are in ,positions to actively support leaders of the disturbance.
10. Source, types, and location of arms, equipment, and supplies available to the leaders.
11. The riotous element's intended use of sewers, storm drains and other underground systems.
12. Identification of new techniques and equipment not previously used by riotous elements in civil disturbances.

---

[1] United States Department of the Army, *Civil Disturbances and Disasters Field Manual FM 19-15*, Headquarters, Washington, D.C., March 1968, pp. 5–3, 5–4.

13. Attitude of general populace toward dissenting groups, civil authorities, and federal intervention.
14. Possible threat to public property.
15. Identification of Department of the Army personnel (military or civilian) who are or may become involved.
16. Estrangement of officials/law enforcement from the local populace and loss of faith in local government.
17. Elements that are unresponsive to higher authority.
18. Adequacy and competence of leaders.
19. Attitude/cooperation of public information media.
20. Sources of financial and material support to riotous elements.
21. Communications and control methods employed by riotous elements.

Studies of many disorders have indicated that the existence of good field intelligence, the accurate assessment of the initial incident and the type of control needed, the speed with which sufficient personnel respond, and the decisive use of force determine whether a disturbance remains a relatively minor police problem or develops into a serious disorder.[5]

Motives of Rioters Those committing acts of civil disobedience generally do so to protest a policy or practice of government or to test the constitutionality of a law. An arrest can be the basis for a constitutionality test; a confrontation with the police can focus public opinion on a *cause*. Militants anticipate being arrested and usually plan to have the arrests occur in public surrounded by their peers and under the spotlight of the news media. It is in this environment that acts by the police and other representatives of government can be made to appear unreasonable—if not downright brutal—and can be selectively exploited to discredit law and order and to gain sympathy.

Control Techniques—General Officers assigned to civil disorder control should do their utmost to prevent incidents which may grow into riots. In periods and areas of high social tensions, persons should be discouraged from assembling into crowds that may erupt into violence. This is an exceedingly delicate matter but should be achieved by persuasion wherever possible, even if force is sanctioned

---

[5] Arnold Sagalyn, *The Riot Commission: Recommendations for Law and Order in Confrontation—Violence and the Police*, C. R. Hormachea and Marion Hormachea (ed.), Holbrook Press, Inc., Boston, 1971, p. 160.

by laws such as those relating to obstructing entrances and exits to buildings and impeding traffic on sidewalks or streets. Everyone should be treated fairly and impartially in every such encounter.

If the temperament of the crowd is hostile to control efforts, control personnel should try to avoid provoking attack. For example, if the objective is to disperse a crowd rather than to make arrests, their is no point in forcing the group into a position from which there is no escape route. This would likely provoke an attack, as would the undue use of force. Officers should avoid making threats, giving ultimatums that may be difficult to carry out, or bluffing. If action is required they should take it quickly and decisively. When force is used to disperse a crowd that refuses to obey warnings to disperse or to apprehend persons committing illegal acts, it should be limited to what is necessary to accomplish police objectives. If an arrest is involved the person or persons arrested should be quickly removed from the scene. Great force is never condoned to overcome minor resistance. The courts have generally permitted the use of only that force which can be equated with the amount of resistance.

Major Disturbances   An officer assigned a call wherein a group has assembled for an unlawful purpose should stop at a strategic location away from the immediate scene and evaluate the situation. It would be foolhardy and unnecessarily dangerous for one or two officers to commit themselves in an attempt to disperse a large, hostile group.

The dispatcher should be notified from that position of the nature of the incident, the number of people involved, and whether they are armed. Additional police assistance that might be needed to handle the matter should be specified and a meeting location or staging area indicated. When assisting units arrive, police vehicles should be parked where they are least exposed to harm and an officer left to guard them. The officers should then disperse the group without delay.

If members of the assemblage are fighting or engaging in other unlawful acts, the officers should advance in a close group with their batons carried in the port arms position ready for action. This show of force often causes a dispersal without the necessity for arrests. If the laws of a particular jurisdiction require a dispersal order, it should be made clearly to refute any claim that the announcement was not heard. Ordinarily, an officer is posted at the furthermost border of the crowd to signal that the order was clearly audible. He can testify to this fact should a prosecution later take place.

After a reasonable time has elapsed, officers should quickly move in to break up the group, leaving an avenue of escape. When arrests appear necessary, efforts should be generally concentrated upon the leaders of the group. Force should be used only to overcome force or resistance. Excessive force often will only cause antagonism and lead to further violence. Sometimes, when the leaders or the objects of an attack are removed, the group loses its will to carry on the disturbance and disperses of its own accord. Once a crowd has been dispersed, small groups should be prevented from reforming. They should be dispersed rapidly without being harangued or threatened.

Demonstrations in Commercial Establishments

The right to use and enjoy private property is a cherished right under our form of government. Merchants have a right to conduct their business free from attempts by those who believe the freedom to speak and assemble is unlimited. While the responsible exercise of these rights must be protected, persons cannot injure property or interfere with the right of others to conduct business. For example, if a number of persons enter a restaurant, occupy all the seats without ordering, or order only a cup of coffee, remain throughout the breakfast, lunch, or dinner hours, and eventually force the owner to close his doors, they may not be in violation of any statute if they act in a quiet, peaceful manner. In such a case, the officer receiving a complaint from the proprietor may have no authority to act. If, however, the protestors establish a picket line, distribute literature espousing their cause, sing, chant, etc., in a way which shows an intent to interfere with operations of the business rather than patronize it in the *usual business manner*, their acts may constitute a violation of the law.

Every officer should familiarize himself with the trespass statutes of his jurisdiction and those relating to the intentional obstruction of business in order to be aware of his authority to act should he be called upon to do so. Blocking entrances, interfering with traffic, disturbances of the peace, etc., are the usual violations associated with these incidents.

Protestors have demonstrated at one time or another in every conceivable type of business. Banks, department stores, markets, restaurants, bakeries, and other establishments have all suffered from some of the highly sophisticated techniques employed. Blocking passageways, aisles, and counters of markets, occupying all tellers in a bank in counting small coins, and removing large amounts of perishable foodstuffs from market shelves and leaving them to spoil in baskets without making a purchase are examples of attempts to interfere with, obstruct, or injure lawful business. Usually these acts are prohibited by statute.

When statutory authority exists for the arrest of such individuals, ordinarily a private person's arrest is proper since the victim is the proprietor in whose presence the offense or offenses were committed. Officers should abide by the victim's decision to arrest or not to do so. The officer is thus left in the neutral position of merely assisting in the arrest and receiving the prisoner from the private person.

Handbill Distribution

Handbill distributors often are a real nuisance to merchants. Their actions are similar to those of demonstrators in some respects, since they often utilize the property of others to advance their convictions. When such property has been opened to the public, the mere passing of handbills is ordinarily not illegal. The officer should therefore advise proprietors of business establishments that they should consult their attorneys before taking arrest action.

Demonstrations in Public Places

The right to assemble peaceably as a form of petition to government for the redress of wrongs—imagined or real—is guaranteed by the U.S. Constitution. It does not guarantee a right to assemble for an illegal or violent purpose, nor does it guarantee any right to be free from any reasonable restriction. Persons assembling for peaceful demonstrations are entitled to protection from those who would deny them that right solely because of a difference in their beliefs.

Prearranged demonstrations have specific objectives. They are organized and have leaders who often are cooperative and can control the members. They usually are orderly, lawful events. In the preliminary planning stages, usually agreements are made between demonstration leaders and the police for control of the participants; but there are times when an assemblage that starts out as an orderly group turns into a violent mob, touched off by agitators or by isolated incidents used as an excuse for violence by militants who are quick to place the blame upon the police. Frequently, small bands of zealots use large demonstrations as a screen for their criminal acts.

Agitation   Often an inactive mob can be urged into violent action by a skillful agitator. This is usually accomplished through intensive propaganda. Rumors are spread; facts are distorted; and natural prejudices, grievances, and desires are aggravated by the agitators. Their basic technique is supported by a forceful harangue by a fiery speaker—probably the most effective method of raising the pitch of the mob to violence. The crowd is sometimes brought to this point by the appearance of an initiating object or individual.

Accomplishing one violent act, such as resisting arrest, spitting upon an officer, interfering with officers trying to perform their duties, may touch off other acts. An emotion-provoking rumor, regardless of its accuracy, can incite an otherwise orderly gathering to riotous action.

Officer Response to Provocation   Riotous acts can be exceedingly destructive not only to property damaged or destroyed by looting or burning, but to the persons and morale of officers assigned to control duty. The ingenuity of the militants in their efforts to accomplish this should never be underestimated. Many of their tactics are devised to demoralize officers and to cause overreactions so that pictures, often edited, can place them in the worst possible light in the eyes of the public. Such pictures are usually exploited in charges of police brutality.

Each officer must expect and learn to ignore offensive conduct and the verbal abuse heaped upon him in the form of insults, vile remarks, taunts, jeers, and ridicule of him and his family. These tactics are purposeful. Officers should not retort in kind, throw objects back, or allow themselves to become so emotionally involved that they are unable to perform their duties properly. Their smart appearance and discipline impress the public and facilitate the accomplishment of police objectives. Their behavior will have a strong effect upon the crowd.

Weapons should not be displayed unnecessarily. Guns, batons, saps, mace dispensers, gas grenades, etc., may only incite antagonism and violence if shown in a provocative way. Bodily contact with participants will only expose the officer to unnecessary danger and may cause resistance that will inflame a crowd to riotous action.

Attacks by Demonstrators against Police   Personal attacks by members of the mob against the police may take the form of beatings with fists, feet, or clubs or assaults with thrown objects such as bottles, rocks, razor blades embedded in wood, potatoes or apples, human excrement in sacks which break upon contact, bombs, cans of urine, paint, golf balls with sharpened nails protruding, live black widow spiders, dart guns, staples taped together, red pepper, and oven cleaner.[6] These objects may be thrown from windows, roofs, overpasses, etc. On slopes, vehicles, fired carts, barrels, flammable liquids, and other dangerous items can be directed against police personnel, or self-propelled vehicles can be driven against control forces or roadblocks on level ground.

Fire and demolition weapons of all types are commonly used against control personnel to impede their advance or control efforts. Even animals with explosive charges attached to their bodies have been used by rioters against police or troops. The charges may be exploded by fuse or remote control. Dikes and dams have even been breached by explosives, and areas have been flooded to hinder disturbance control efforts.[7]

Sniping or massed fire is sometimes directed against control personnel. Firearms of all types from handmade ones to sophisticated automatic weapons have been used against the police in civil disorders. Officers should therefore be alert for such attacks from windows, roofs, or from the ranks of the rioters.

Arrests   Ordinarily, making mass arrests is ill advised at the scene of demonstrations because of the difficulties of identifying offenders for later prosecution and the burden placed upon the police agency in processing the arrestees. When an officer is attacked, however, other officers should go to his assistance and arrest and remove the assailant quickly.

It is not always wise to arrest leaders in a demonstration that has become illegal. Sometimes it is better to take others who are the real agitators into custody if it appears that the leaders will be useful in helping the police exercise control of the crowd. Occasionally, such agitators need not be arrested at the site of the disturbance. They can be followed and taken into custody when they leave the group. The arrest can then be made with considerably less danger.

Labor Disturbances

Settlement of the economic disputes that occur between management and labor is not one of the responsibilities of law enforcement.

---

[6] City of Chicago, The Strategy of Confrontation, p. 56.
[7] United States Department of the Army, *Civil Disturbances and Disasters*, pp. 3–7.

An obligation exists, however, whenever strife between labor and management jeopardizes life or property, causes a breach of the peace, or deprives any person of his civil rights.

The type of law enforcement at the scene of a strike has a marked psychological effect upon participants—from both management and labor. If the police exhibit an impartial, unbiased attitude; if they manifest by their actions that they fully understand their role; and if they reflect confidence and assurance derived from appropriate training, it is unlikely that they will constantly be required to prove themselves capable of handling the situation.

Feelings run high at the scene of a strike. Heated and often violent conflicts between strikers and fellow employees are soon forgotten after the matter is settled. But the police are not forgotten. The strong feelings their conduct may have caused will remain. Officers should therefore exercise the greatest discretion in their relationships with participants. They must keep in mind that a strike is a form of protest. It is a legitimate exercise of the right of free speech, which must be protected as long as it remains lawful; but the interests of nonparticipants must be protected also.

Characteristics of Labor Disputes Labor disputes have many characteristics that are similar to those of civil disturbances and should be treated in much the same manner. A strike is a form of demonstration. Generally, it is directed at a particular service, firm, or product and has a material objective. Usually labor demands a better contract. Participants in other kinds of demonstrations usually want to focus attention on some social issue.

Feelings run high in both situations. The police officer working a tension-laden strike is apt to be baited by derision and insult in much the same manner as when he is assigned to control civil disorder. In both assignments, he must exercise the highest degree of self-control so that he does not become emotionally involved in the issues. He must not allow himself to be provoked into an overreaction which may be exploited against the police. Both types of demonstrations may become violent. Control measures involve similar techniques and procedures.

Labor-Management Agreements When an officer learns of a strike that has not been brought to his department's attention, or when he is called to the scene of a newly established picket line, he should notify his headquarters of the details of the occurrence. He should provide information about the type of business involved, the number of pickets, the type of dispute, the names of a representative of the union and management. In many cases, police agencies do not assign personnel other than the patrol officer on that beat to control duty, because most such disputes do not pose a special police problem. It is not unusual for a patrol officer to have several small strikes in effect at the same time on his beat. He is usually expected to periodically check the scene of each to insure that the strike is being conducted peaceably and lawfully.

Because the first few hours of a strike are the most critical, he should arrange a meeting with a representative of management and the picket captain to establish the ground rules with which the strikers and management are expected to comply. Both should clearly understand the responsibility of the police as neutrals in the matter. Usually the picket captain and management representative will welcome such a meeting.

If the number of pickets is limited by court order, the parties should be fully aware of the necessity of adhering to the order. The officers should be familiar with the fire ordinances and other laws pertaining to blocking sidewalks, streets, and entryways and exits to buildings, so that he may explain these to the parties. He should also explain the statutory provisions relating to maliciously damaging property by such acts as puncturing tires, disabling vehicles, hitting them with picket signs, or interfering with other employees as they enter driveways or leave parking lots. Likewise, those acts by management that might be unlawful or which might precipitate violence should be discussed and agreements reached to eliminate such incidents. Harassment of pickets by taunting, threatening, or attempting to provoke an incident should be discouraged at the onset.

Officers' Demeanor at Strikes   Officers assigned to strike duty should maintain strictly impartial relationships with all participants in a labor dispute. Unnecessary conversations or discussions with involved parties about the merits of the issues may make the officer's job considerably more difficult and subject him to accusations of bias. Fraternization either with representatives of management or with those of labor are likely to be construed as a showing of partiality. Likewise, taking gratuities such as coffee and doughnuts or using management telephones, rest rooms, parking lots, etc., will only strengthen the feeling of some that the officer favors one side over the other. Accusations that officers are acting as strike breakers may arise from the slightest show of partiality—even by just eating with union or management personnel. The officer must give only one impression—that his job is to maintain law and order and to protect the rights of the public and all parties in the matter.

Firearms, special weapons, and batons should remain in their carriers and should not be displayed unnecessarily. To do so is only likely to provoke trouble.

Strike Scene Inspections When the beat patrol officer is assigned to make periodic inspections of a strike scene, usually he can do so by observing from a distance. At other times, he should have a friendly chat with the picket captain to maintain the best possible relations and to lessen tensions that might be brought about by his presence. If delivery services are involved indirectly in the strike, attention should be given to routes used by delivery vehicles to prevent coercion of the drivers by strikers.

Strike Scene Tactics Pickets may urge patrons to withdraw their patronage from a particular firm, but they may not physically coerce them into doing so. Usually such coercion is the first step toward violence. It is at this initial stage that the beat officer should consider the need for assigning control personnel to the strike. He should convey his observations promptly to superiors.

When picket lines unlawfully block exits and entrances to business establishments and pickets attempt to prevent persons or vehicles from entering or leaving, the line must be broken by coordinated police efforts. Clear orders should be given to let pickets know what they are expected to do. Officers should then, as a group, effect an opening in the line for pedestrian or vehicular traffic to enter or leave. As soon as this is accomplished, the pickets should be allowed to resume their line of march. When the picket line is broken for the passage of vehicles, however, officers should not use the traditional hand signals employed in traffic direction. They can thus avoid giving the impression that they are encouraging or forcing persons who are undecided to enter the premises.

When disrupting a picket line to provide a passageway through it, officers should face the pickets. In this position they may best observe what is taking place and anticipate resistance. This is also the best position for preventing anyone from taking their firearms, batons, or other equipment.

The use of force in stopping, detouring, or interrupting picket lines, or otherwise dealing with the parties should be temperate.

Harsh or officious treatment or the use of unnecessary force will only cause those afflicted to retaliate and incite others to do the same.

Arrests at the Strike Scene   If an officer is assaulted, other officers quickly should come to his aid. The assailant should be immediately removed from the scene as quietly as possible after the arrest. Should some minor offense, such as drinking in public, be committed by a picket, the picket captain should make arrangements to remove him promptly from the scene. Incipient troublemakers can usually be dealt with for minor offenses more effectively by their peers than by the police.

Strikers who place themselves in exits to premises and refuse to allow those on the inside to leave are in effect imprisoning people. This may constitute false imprisonment or a violation of fire ordinances and may necessitate arrests to remove the demonstrators. Should they go limp to resist passively the efforts to remove them, it may be necessary to carry them from doorways on stretchers. Such passive resistance may be a resistance to arrest that might form the basis for a separate, successful prosecution. Officers should acquaint themselves with the laws of their jurisdiction applicable to such incidents.

Occasionally, arrests are required because of the malicious damaging of property. Objects such as can openers or bolts concealed in the palm are sometimes used to gouge the sides of vehicles or break windows of nonstrikers' cars when they pass into a struck plant. Evidence should be collected by the officer witnessing the incident as in the case of other crimes.

Officers should be on the alert for anyone slashing tires, cutting ignition wires, placing tacks in driveways, pouring sugar in gas tanks, or using pellet guns, sling shots, and other instruments to damage property and injure nonstrikers. In fact, all the techniques used by the most violent militants in other civil disorders to damage property or to coerce or assault persons, including police personnel, have been used by strikers in labor disputes.

Summary

Police measures to control crowds become increasingly important with the trend toward urbanization. The frequency with which the police must assign large numbers of personnel to control lawfully or unlawfully assembled groups places an extremely heavy burden upon law enforcement and makes it imperative that agencies involved develop and perfect plans for coping with such incidents.

All persons have a constitutional right to assemble peaceably. When they do, they pose no particular problem to the police; but, when their acts become licentious and encroach upon the rights of others, the justification for the assembly may disappear.

Crowd control measures for special events such as parades, athletic events, political rallies, or meetings are devised to prevent disorder and to reduce congestion by facilitating the movement of large groups of people from one place to another with a minimum of conflict. Most of the groups involved in such events are orderly and require little control. Minor fighting usually can be easily controlled by prompt action by the police.

It is when large groups of persons become inflamed that mob violence may spread throughout a community. Underlying such incidents of mass civil disorder are usually some strong social conflicts. The individual officer should be sensitive to the evidences that tension is developing in a community. When volatile rumors about police brutality or harassment come to an officer's attention, he should be alert for other symptoms of civil unrest. He should convey to his superiors whatever field intelligence he is able to collect so that appropriate plans may be made for coping with any resulting disorders. Studies have revealed that the initial action taken to control and contain riotous acts in large part determines how severe and widespread the incidents become. Planning can be only as good as the intelligence it is based upon.

Every officer should be aware of the ultimate goal of agitators who attempt to inflame a crowd into mob violence. It is to bring about a confrontation with the police or to force arrests that can be used as a basis for challenging the constitutionality of the police authority used to restrain such activities. The militants try to force individual officers to overreact to taunts, jeers, and physical attack. Such reactions are then exploited as police brutality to embarrass the agents of government. Officers must therefore exercise the greatest degree of restraint to avoid overreacting. They must use only that force necessary to legally accomplish police objectives.

A strike or a protest against the practices of a business enterprise may be conducted as a constitutionally protected activity, so long as the strikers or protestors do not unlawfully deprive others of their rights to conduct a business. Acts such as blocking doorways to the premises and preventing persons from entering or leaving by physically coercing them, by damaging their property, or by intentionally obstructing business in other unlawful ways are commonplace. The officer assigned to control such situations must maintain strict impartiality. He is obliged to take action when it is needed. He should avoid arrests for minor offenses that can be best handled informally by a picket captain or a demonstration leader.

Review

Questions

1. Generally, when does the constitutional protection to assemble cease to exist?
2. What are the fundamental duties of the police in controlling civil disorder?
3. What are some of the special events officers are called upon to police?
4. What are the main problems encountered by the police at athletic events? How should these be handled?
5. What are the usual major objectives of agitators at political meetings?
6. What is an officer's main responsibility at a post along a parade route?
7. What are the main problems usually associated with sightseer crowds?
8. What are some of the potentially dangerous aspects of sightseer crowds at the scene of a police incident involving an arrest of a suspect who is a member of a minority race in a community with a preponderance of residents of the same race?
9. What are some of the nonphysical methods used by militants to provoke police officers at the scene of a civil disorder?
10. What are some of the weapons used by militants to assault the police?
11. What are some of the typical unlawful acts committed by strikers against management, employees, or patrons entering or leaving a struck plant?
12. What should officers do if a minor offense such as drunkenness of a picket occurs at a strike scene?
13. What general rules should officers follow relative to making arrests at a strike which, with few exceptions, has been nonviolent?

Exercises

1. Explain how you should prepare for duty at a parade expected to last at least six hours.

2. Assume you have been assigned to a post at the formation area of a large parade. Explain what you do when you first arrive at your post and after the parade has started.

3. Describe what you do when you first arrive at an assigned post along the parade route where many spectators have gathered. How should you conduct yourself during the parade? What should you do as the parade breaks up? Assume that you have not received any orders that might conflict with ordinary police practices in handling such events.

4. Explain the usual phenomenon of the transient development of a sightseer crowd at the scene of some police incident.

5. Discuss what happens when the transient development described in Exercise 4 stops. Discuss the usual causes for this. How can it be prevented?

6. Describe the symptoms a patrol officer may perceive on his beat that might indicate mass civil disorder is developing.

7. Describe the types of information which should be passed on by patrol officers when they learn that a mass demonstration with racial overtones is being planned and it appears that agitators will attempt to force a violent confrontation with the police.

8. What are the four main criteria which determine whether an unusual disturbance remains a relatively minor police problem or develops into a serious disorder?

9. Discuss the general control techniques officers acting as individuals should apply at the very outset of a civil disorder before large, riotous groups become involved.

10. Describe what should be done by a single patrol officer and a backup unit assigned to a call involving a street fight with six to ten participants and about twenty onlookers.

11. Describe how a patrol officer should handle a peaceable demonstration involving a protest against a business enterprise if he is called to the scene by a distraught manager. Describe how the incident should be handled if the protestors occupy all the seats in a restaurant, order only coffee, and leave only when others come in to do the same in relays. The manager complains that they have been doing this for several days and are about to drive him out of business, but he admits there have been no disorders.

12. Describe what an officer's demeanor should be at the scene of a strike.

13. Describe how an officer might unconsciously give the impression of bias against one side or the other at a strike assignment.

14. How should a patrol officer inspect a strike scene if he is the only officer assigned to check it as part of his beat duties?

Selected References

Ayoob, Massad F.: "Vehicular Aspects of Police Gunfight Situations," *Law and Order*, vol. 20, no. 10, October 1972.

Baker, J. Stannard: *Traffic Accident Investigator's Manual for Police*, The Traffic Institute, Northwestern University, Evanston, Ill., 1970.

California Council on Criminal Justice: *Bulletin*, vol. 4, issue 6, Sacramento, August 1971.

California Highway Patrol: *Enforcement Tactics*, H.P.G.70.6, Sacramento, 1969.

————: "Shooting Incident, Newhall Area," *Information Bulletin*, Sacramento, July 1, 1970.

California State Department of Education: *Police Report Writing*, Sacramento, 1964.

California, State of: "Violence in the City—An End or a Beginning," *A Report by the Governor's Commission on the Los Angeles Riots*, State Printing Office, Sacramento, December 2, 1965.

Center for the Environment of Man, Inc.: *A Study of the Problem of Hot Pursuit by the Police—Final Report*, Hartford, Conn., July 1970.

Chicago, City of: *The Strategy of Confrontation—Chicago and the National Democratic Convention—1968*, The Gunthorp Warren Printing Company, Chicago, 1968.

Culliford, Bryan J.: *The Examination and Typing of Bloodstains in the Crime Laboratory*, National Institute of Law Enforcement and Criminal Justice, Washington, D.C., 1971.

Dewey, Richard and W. J. Humber: *An Introduction to Social Psychology*, The Macmillan Company, New York, 1966.

Ditzel, Paul: "The Risks of Rescue," *Westways Magazine of the Southern California Automobile Club*, March 1969.

Federal Bureau of Investigation: "Spikeblock," *F.B.I. Law Enforcement Bulletin*, vol. 41, no. 20, February 1972.

————: *Uniform Crime Reports*, U.S. Government Printing Office, Washington, D.C., 1971.

Flesch, Rudolph: *The ABC of Style: A Guide to Plain English*, Harper and Row, Publishers, Incorporated, New York, 1964.

Gourley, G. Douglas and Allen P. Bristow: *Patrol Administration*, Charles C Thomas, Publisher, Springfield, Ill., 1961.

Grennell, Dean H. and Mason Williams: *Law Enforcement Handgun Digest*, Follett Publishing Company, Chicago, 1972.

Harrison, T. R., Raymond D. Adams, Ivan L. Bennett, Jr., William H. Resnick, George W. Thorn and M. M. Wintrobe, eds.: *Principles of Internal Medicine*, McGraw-Hill Book Company, Inc., New York, 1958.

Hoover, J. Edgar: "Law Enforcement Faces the Revolutionary-Guerrilla Criminal," *F.B.I. Law Enforcement Bulletin*, vol. 39, no. 12, December 1970.

————: "Message from the Director," *F.B.I. Law Enforcement Bulletin*, vol. 41, no. 4, April 1972.

————: "The Police Officer: Primary Target of the Urban Guerrilla," *F.B.I. Law Enforcement Bulletin*, vol. 41, no. 2, February 1972.

Hotis, John B.: "The Warrantless Search of Motor Vehicles," *F.B.I. Law Enforcement Bulletin*, vol. 40, no. 1, March 1971.

Iannone, N. F.: *Supervision of Police Personnel*, Prentice-Hall, Inc., Englewood Cliffs, N.J., 1970.

Inbau, Fred E. and John E. Reid: *Criminal Interrogation and Confessions,* The Williams and Wilkins Company, Baltimore, 1967.

Insurance Institute for Highway Safety: "Debris Hazard Control and Cleanup," *Highway Safety Program Standard 16,* Washington, D.C., November 2, 1968.

International Association of Chiefs of Police: *Manpower Allocation and Distribution,* Washington, D.C., 1966.

International City Managers' Association: *Municipal Police Administration,* 5th ed., Chicago, 1969.

James, William: *Principles of Psychology,* Holt, Rinehart and Winston, Inc., New York, 1908.

Krech, David and Richard S. Crutchfield: *Elements of Psychology,* Alfred A. Knopf, Inc., New York, 1958.

Lenz, Robert R.: *Explosives and Bomb Disposal Guide,* Charles C Thomas, Publisher, Springfield, Ill., 1965.

Los Angeles Police Department: "Ammunition Limitations—Shooting at Cars and Plate Glass," *Patrol Bureau, Roll Call Training,* series 3, lesson 14, (unpublished), April, 1963.

———: *Daily Training Bulletin,* Charles C Thomas, Publisher, Springfield, Ill., 1958.

———: "Drivers Under the Influence," *Training Bulletin,* part IV, vol. II, issue 13, 1970.

———: "How to Handle 'All-Units' Calls," *Patrol Bureau, Roll Call Training,* series 3, lesson 5, (unpublished), April 17, 1963.

———: "How to Operate a Motor Vehicle under Emergency Conditions," *Daily Training Bulletin,* vol. 1, Bulletin 54, 1949.

———: "Officers Survival—Suggestions for Emergency Actions," *Patrol Bureau, Roll Call Training,* (unpublished), March 15, 1963.

———: *Physiological and Psychological Effects of a Pursuit Situation Upon a Police Officer,* March 1970.

———: "Police Action at a Brush Fire," *Patrol Bureau Memorandum No. 23,* (unpublished), July 18, 1963.

———: *Training Bulletin,* vol. III, issue 23, May 3, 1971.

———: *Training Manual of the Accident Investigation Division,* 1971.

Minnesota Department of Public Safety: *The Alcohol-Impaired Driver and Highway Crashes,* St. Paul, 1970.

Momboisse, Raymond M.: *Riots, Revolts and Insurrections,* Charles C Thomas, Publisher, Springfield, Ill., 1967.

Mortimer, R. G., M. W. Kenlan, L. D. Filkins, and J. G. Lower: "Identifying a Major Hazard on the Highways—The Problem Drinking Driver," *Police,* vol. 16, no. 8, April 1972.

Munn, Norman L.: *Psychology,* Houghton Mifflin Company, Boston, 1956.

National Bomb Data Center: *Recognition of Explosive and Incendiary Devices: Part I—Hand and Rifle Grenades—03-1,* International Association of Chiefs of Police, Washington, D.C., n.d.

National Institute of Law Enforcement and Criminal Justice: *Training Police as Specialists in Family Crisis Intervention,* U.S. Department of Justice, Washington, D.C., 1970.

Nelson, Alfred T. and Howard E. Smith: *Car Clouting,* Charles C Thomas, Publisher, Springfield, Ill., 1958.

Northwestern University: *Background for Traffic Law Enforcement*, Pub. no. 2022, Traffic Institute, Evanston, Ill., 1959.

————: *Charts and Tables for Stopping Distances of Motor Vehicles*, Traffic Institute, Evanston, Ill., n.d.

————: *Taking Enforcement Action, Publication No. 2017*, Traffic Institute, Evanston, Ill., 1959.

O'Connor, George W. and Charles G. Vanderbosch: *The Patrol Operation*, International Association of Chiefs of Police, Washington, D.C., 1967.

Rsanoff, Aaron J.: *Manual of Psychiatry and Mental Hygiene*, 7th ed., John Wiley and Sons, Inc., New York, 1938.

Sagalyn, Arnold: *The Riot Commission: Recommendations for Law and Order in Confrontation—Violence and the Police*, eds. C. R. Hormachea and Marion Hormachea, Holbrook Press, Inc., Boston, 1971.

Samen, Charles C.: "Major Crime Scene Investigation—Sketching the Scene," *Law and Order*, vol. 19, no. 10, October 1971.

Sassone, Rich: "New York's Mounted Police," *Law and Order*, vol. 20, no. 11, November 1972.

Siepola, E. M.: "A Study of Some Effects of Preparatory Set," *Psychology Monograph*, vol. 46, no. 210, n.d.

Soderman, Harry and John J. O'Connell: *Modern Criminal Investigation*, 5th ed., Funk and Wagnalls Company, New York, 1962.

Stoffel, Joseph F.: *Explosives and Homemade Bombs*, Charles C Thomas, Publisher, Springfield, Ill., 1962.

Svensson, Arne and Otto Wendell: *Techniques of Crime Scene Investigation*, 2d ed., American Elsevier Publishing Company, Inc., New York, 1965.

U.S. Department of the Army: *Civil Disturbances and Disasters Field Manual FM 19-15*, Headquarters, Washington, D.C., March 1968.

U.S. Department of Transportation: *Alcohol Safety Countermeasures Program*, National Highway Safety Bureau, Washington, D.C., 1970.

U.S. House of Representatives: *Report No. 1700*, 89th Congress, 2nd Session, July 15, 1966.

Van Dersal, William R.: *The Successful Supervisor in Government and Business*, Harper and Row, Publishers, Incorporated, New York, 1962.

Volpe, John A.: "Drunken Driving," *The Police Yearbook*, International Association of Chiefs of Police, Washington, D.C., 1971.

Walsh, Jude T.: "Search of Buildings," *Law and Order*, vol. 20, no. 4, April 1972.

Warnock, Madeline: "Editing for Better Understanding," *Proceedings of the 1962 Institute in Technical and Industrial Communications*, ed. Herman A. Weisman, Institute in Technical and Industrial Communications, Fort Collins, Col., 1962.

Weston, Paul B. and Kenneth M. Wells: *Criminal Investigation; Basic Perspectives*, Prentice-Hall, Inc., Englewood Cliffs, N.J., 1970.

Wilson, O. W.: *Police Administration*, 2d ed., McGraw-Hill Book Company, New York, 1963.

Younger, Evelle J.: *Admissibility of Out-of-Court Confessions—Law Enforcement Legal Summaries, No. 3*, California Office of State Printing, Sacramento, January, 1972.

————: "Stop and Frisk," *Law Enforcement Legal Information Bulletin*, Los Angeles County District Attorney, vol. IV, no. 6, June 1968.

Index